P. C. Sense

A free Enquiry into the Origin of the Fourth Gospel

P. C. Sense

A free Enquiry into the Origin of the Fourth Gospel

ISBN/EAN: 9783337277215

Printed in Europe, USA, Canada, Australia, Japan

Cover: Foto ©Lupo / pixelio.de

More available books at **www.hansebooks.com**

A FREE ENQUIRY INTO THE ORIGIN
OF THE FOURTH GOSPEL

A FREE ENQUIRY INTO THE ORIGIN OF THE FOURTH GOSPEL

BY

P. C. SENSE, M.A.

"*SEARCH THE SCRIPTURES*"

WILLIAMS AND NORGATE
14 HENRIETTA STREET, COVENT GARDEN, LONDON
20 SOUTH FREDERICK STREET, EDINBURGH
AND 7 BROAD STREET, OXFORD

1899

PREFACE.

MANY people are deterred from the perusal of works bearing on the authenticity of the Gospels by the feeling that they are wanting in the erudition which they deem necessary for the proper understanding of the subject. I make no pretension to the possession of erudition. The chief characteristic of this work may be said to be that it is one in the perusal of which common sense is necessary, but erudition not necessary. As erudition is not necessary for the perusal of the English version of the Gospels, it is equally unnecessary for the perusal of this work, which treats of one Gospel chiefly, and incidentally of the other three. All that is really needed by the reader is the exercise of common sense.

In this work is set forth the discovery of the real author of the Fourth Gospel, which has hitherto been erroneously attributed to the Apostle John. That discovery followed upon the discovery of the substitution of the little word 'water' for 'dove' in John xix. 34. Theologians, I believe, are now agreed that the Synoptic Gospels are not original writings, but were based on writings that preceded them: but what those antecedent writings were could not be ascertained. I trust I have definitely indicated in Chapter IV. the sources from which the Synoptic writers derived their information.

Ecclesiastical Christianity, proceeding from such peculiar sources as those that my investigations have revealed, cannot be regarded as likely to continue to be the religion of civilised peoples. I believe and hope that a Moral System of Christianity will succeed the Religious System that has existed for eighteen centuries. If such a reformation should follow in the unknown future, the sceptre of morality can still be retained in the hand of Jesus. It is possible for all mankind to agree on a moral system, but history has proved that unanimity on a religious system is impossible on earth.

25th May 1899.

TABLE OF CONTENTS.

CHAPTER I.

Cerinthus and his Doctrines. The Prologue of the Fourth Gospel. The Miraculous Conception unknown in the First Century. Descent of the Dove from Heaven, ... 1

CHAPTER II.

The Declaration of the Unknown Father. The Apostle John not the Author of the Fourth Gospel or of the First Epistle of John, ... 35

CHAPTER III.

Polycarp's Martyrdom. The Ascent or Return Flight of the Dove to Heaven. Cerinthus the Author of the Fourth Gospel. Lucian's great joke, ... 46

CHAPTER IV.

The Original Materials and Origin of the Synoptic Gospels. Christianity, a Moral System in the First Century, corrupted into a Religious System in the Second Century. Means of the Change. Jewish and Gnostic or Greek Corruptions. Paraclete, ... 62

CHAPTER V.

The First Epistle of John and the Revelations, . . 111

CHAPTER VI.

An Attempt to Restore the Original Writing of Cerinthus, . 125

CHAPTER VII.

The Restored Writing of Cerinthus, the Original of the "Gospel according to John," 209

CHAPTER VIII.

Interpolations made in the Revised Fourth Gospel of the Second Century, subsequent to its Publication. Moral Condition of Christian Society in the Second and Third Centuries. The Knavery and Roguery of Bishops Zephyrinus and Callistus, Popes of Rome, ... 229

CHAPTER IX.

The Dishonourable Conduct of Bishop Irenæus, . . 329

CHAPTER X.

The Origin of the Doctrine of the Trinity in Unity, . . . 339

CHAPTER XI.

Concluding Remarks. Decadence of Ecclesiastical Christianity. Substitution of a Moral System, ... 349

INDEX, ... 454
INDEX OF TEXTS, ... 456

ON THE ORIGIN OF THE FOURTH GOSPEL.

CHAPTER I.

CERINTHUS AND HIS DOCTRINES. THE PROLOGUE OF THE FOURTH GOSPEL. THE MIRACULOUS CONCEPTION UNKNOWN IN THE FIRST CENTURY. DESCENT OF THE DOVE FROM HEAVEN.

I PROPOSE to give in the following pages the results of my investigation of the subject of the authorship of the Fourth Gospel. Some ten years ago I was much struck by the coincidence between the story of the dove of Cerinthus as related by Irenæus, and the dove of the Gospels which descended on Jesus in Jordan at His baptism. Steadfastly keeping this remarkable coincidence in mind, and following up small trifling clues, discerned obscurely after long intervals of time, and availing myself of the great help to be had from the writings of learned divines, I have now come to the definite conclusion, for very definite reasons, that Cerinthus, the Gnostic Christian of the first century, was the author of the Fourth Gospel. I may recall to the recollection of the learned that this is not the first time that the Fourth Gospel has been attributed to Cerinthus.

For the benefit of those of my readers who are not conversant with early Christian history, but whose sensible and unprejudiced judgment I desire to invite to the consideration of this subject, I extract the following short account of Cerinthus from the *Encyclopædia Britannica.* "Cerinthus was the founder of one of the earliest sects of the Christians. He was brought up in Egypt, but removed to Asia Minor where he propagated his doctrines. He flourished, according to Eusebius, in the time of Trajan (98–117 A.D.). . . . . We know nothing of the death of Cerinthus." We know no more of the personal history of Cerinthus than is stated in the above short account. The religious opinions of Cerinthus are stated by Irenæus in his great work, *Against Heresies,* Book I. xxvi. 1, as follows :—Cerinthus, a man in Asia, taught that the world was not made by the primary God, but by a certain power far separated and remote from that Potentiality which is over all, and which power was even ignorant of Him, who is, above all, God. He represented Jesus, not as born from a virgin (for that seemed impossible to him), but that he was the son of Joseph and Mary, similarly as other men are sons of their parents, and that he excelled men in justice, prudence, and wisdom. And that after the baptism Christ descended upon him, in the form of a dove, from that Potentiality which is above all; and that then he announced the unknown father and perfected his virtues ; but that at the end Christ flew away from Jesus, and that Jesus suffered and rose again ; but that Christ remained impassable, being a spirit."

The above passage from Irenæus contains all that is known authentically of the doctrines of Cerinthus. With his views regarding the primary and secondary gods, or principalities and potentialities, we are not concerned. Cerinthus illustrated and expanded his views regarding Jesus in the Fourth Gospel, which, after my careful study of the subject for several years, I believe to have been written by him. He represents Jesus throughout the Fourth Gospel as man, the son of human parents : at the beginning of his ministry he received the Spirit, or Æon, Christ, as Irenæus says, an emanation from God the Father, in the form of a dove ; he declared the unknown Father ; at the crucifixion the Æon or Spirit left him in the form of a dove.

The Fourth Gospel begins with a striking epigrammatic prologue, which, on examination, shows clear indications of having been tampered with. The first two verses are, without any apparent reason, merely repetitions of the same statement. "In the beginning was the Word, and the Word was with God" are statements which are essentially the same as "The same was in the beginning with God." One is at first sight puzzled to ascertain why two successive verses should be employed to repeat the same statement. We are so little accustomed to question the propriety of anything in the Scriptures that we placidly accept what we find in it, without reflection, confident (or perhaps indifferent) that the text conveys some meaning although not evident to us. It was only after a research of a few years that I have been able to set aside the traditional meaning put on the first verse, and to come to the conclusion that the initial words of the first verse of the Fourth Gospel do not mean the beginning of the world, but the beginning of the Gospel. The words 'in the beginning,' 'from the beginning,' 'at the beginning,' are very often used in the New Testament and in other Christian writings of the first and second centuries, and they invariably mean the beginning of the Gospel, unless the context clearly indicates the alternative meaning. The words 'in the beginning' in the first verse of the first chapter of the Fourth Gospel mean exactly the same, chronologically, as the words 'from the beginning' and 'at the beginning' put into the mouth of Jesus in chapters xv. 27 and xvi. 4 ; as the words 'the beginning of the Gospel' in the first verse of the first chapter of Mark ; 'from the beginning' in the second verse of the first chapter of Luke, and in the great majority of passages in which these words are used. The earliest transcript of this passage in Christian literature is in the writings of Theophilus, Bishop of Antioch about A.D. 168. It is noteworthy that in Theophilus' quotation of the passage the second verse is omitted, and in place of the second verse is an intercalary statement of the author explaining the sense of the initial words. The quotation occurs in the Letter to Autolycus, ii. 22, and has been translated by Bishop Lightfoot as follows :—" Whence the Holy Scriptures and all inspired men teach, one of whom, John, says: 'In the beginning (ἐν ἀρχῇ) was the Word, and the Word was with God'; showing that at the first (ἐν πρώτοις) God was alone, and the Word in Him. Then he says, 'and the Word was God; all things were made by Him, and without Him was not anything made.'" Theophilus, for a dogmatic reason that he mentions, makes it plain that he desired the words 'in the beginning' to be understood to mean from the beginning of the world, but felt it necessary to stop in the middle of the quotation and to change the expression to another (ἐν πρώτοις).[1] Irenæus, who wrote some years subsequently to Theophilus, also quotes the same passage (*Ad Her.*, III. xi. 1), but in his quotation the second verse occurs, clearly indicating that the second verse was felt to be necessary to remove ambiguity and to convey the desired meaning, and was hence supplied in the interval.

Another writer of the second century, contemporary with Irenæus, but perhaps writing earlier, also refers to the first verse of the Fourth Gospel. Bishop Lightfoot conjectures that the writer was Pantænus, the Apostle of the Indies, but Bunsen attributes the writing to Marcion. The passage occurs in the eleventh chapter of the Epistle to Diognetus. "For which cause he sent forth the Word, that he might appear unto the world, who, being dishonoured by the people, and preached by the apostles, was believed in by the Gentiles. This Word, who was from the beginning, who appeared as new and yet was proved to be old, and is engendered always young in the hearts of saints, etc." (Lightfoot). I understand the writer to mean the beginning of the Gospel, not of the world, when the Word was sent forth and appeared as new.

It is obvious to me from these two early writers that the original and colloquial meaning of the words 'in the beginning' in the first verse was in the beginning of the Gospel, but in order to throw back the chronology of the Word to

[1] It will be interesting information to the modern Christian to know that Theophilus was of opinion that in the beginning of the world the Word was implanted in God's own bowels, ἐνδιάθετον ἐν τοῖς ἰδίοις σπλάγχνοις, ii. 10, and always in the heart, or may be stomach, of God, ἐν καρδία θεοῦ, ii. 22. Theophilus was the head of the Christian Church in the second half of the second century, if he be the same bishop spoken of by Eusebius in *Eccl. Hist.*, v. 23.

Eternity the second verse was added. If the words 'in the beginning' had always the same meaning in both first and second verses, then the second verse is here surplusage and unnecessary. It is obvious from the evidence that the second verse did not exist in the Gospel used by Theophilus (*Ad Autol.*, ii. 22), while it did exist in the later Gospel used by Irenæus (III. xi. 1). If the meaning be not as I state it, there can be no reason for the interpretation and existence of the second verse.

The words 'in the beginning' in the first verse fix the chronology of the Word in the Fourth Gospel, and there was a very great temptation and inducement in the second century to nullify this chronology in the interests of the rival doctrine of the incarnation which arose in the second century, which was opposed to the doctrine presented by the Fourth Gospel. The first verse fixes the chronology of the three sections of the Prologue. In the beginning of the Gospel was the Word: in the beginning of the Gospel was a man sent from God, whose name was John: in the beginning of the Gospel the Word was made flesh. The incarnation of the Word according to the Fourth Gospel took place about thirty-one years after the incarnation inculcated by the rival doctrine of the second century, which latter incarnation occurred at the conception of Jesus by the Virgin Mary. Hence arose the great temptation and strong necessity to annihilate the chronology of the Fourth Gospel. It was accordingly done by the simple expedient of interpolating the second verse, and of making no distinction in the phrases 'in the beginning' in the first and second verses, which effected the desired object in a peaceable and harmless manner. I understand the words 'in the beginning' in the first verse to mean the beginning of the Gospel, but in the interpolated second verse to mean the beginning of the world.

In the next verse also there is clear evidence of tampering, a few words being abstracted from the fourth verse and added on to the third verse. It is remarkable that by this proceeding no change of sense is produced in the third verse; but the effect on the fourth verse was lamentable, as the latter was rendered obscure, if not absolutely unintelligible. It seems clear to me that this new allocation of the words in the two verses was effected by design, and was not due to the errors of copyists. The earliest transcript of the passage is in Irenæus (c. A.D. 182), who quotes it thus: "*In principio erat Verbum, et Verbum erat apud Deum, et Deus erat Verbum; hoc erat in principio apud Deum. Omnia per ipsum facta sunt, et sine ipso factum est nihil. Quod factum est, in ipso vita erat, et vita erat lux hominum, et lux in tenebris lucet, et tenebræ eam non comprehenderunt*" (*Ad Hercs.*, III. xi. 1, Stieren's Edition). These words are exactly reproduced in the Vulgate, with the exception that a few words are withdrawn from the beginning of the fourth verse and added to the conclusion of the third verse, thus: "*Omnia per ipsum facta sunt: et sine ipso factum est nihil, quod factum est. In ipso erat vita, et vita erat lux hominum.*" The received Greek text, from which our version has been made, has the same change of words, as shown above in the Vulgate. All theologians, I believe, concur in favour of the reading given above by Irenæus. Bishop Westcott, in his remarks on these verses in the *Speaker's Commentary*, says: "The original words admit two very distinct divisions. The last clause of verse 3 may be taken either (1) with the words which precede, as Authorised Version, or (2) with the words which follow. It would be difficult to find a more complete consent of ancient authorities in favour of any reading than that which supports the second punctuation: *Without Him was not anything made. That which had been made in Him was life.*

The import of the change is not perceptible until the fourth verse is considered. As it is rendered in our Authorised and Revised versions, this verse is to me unintelligible. The ascription of life to a God is unnecessary, for what is a God without life: but how the life of the Word is the light of men is most obscure. Bishop Westcott, in his *Commentary on the Fourth Gospel*, labours hard to extract a meaning from the passage; but he can hardly be congratulated on success when he has been constrained to remark regarding his own explanation that "human language is necessarily inadequate to express distinctly such a conception as has been faintly indicated."

With Irenæus's reading, however, the meaning becomes clear and definite and not at all metaphysical. It can hardly be questioned that the original Greek for the words '*in ipso*,' employed by Irenæus, was ἐν αὐτῳ, as in our received text, and that the proper rendering is *per ipsum* or by him: the preposition having here an instrumental meaning *by* or *by means of*, and no other meaning of the preposition can be intelligibly used in the passage. I accordingly translate the fourth verse thus, following the lead of Bishop Westcott's rendering: "That which hath been made by him was life, and the life was the light of men." Such a passage was intelligible to Christians of the second century, but sounds strange to us from our want of familiarity with the epithets employed and the idea embodied in the words. In the Fourth Gospel the epithet 'life' is repeatedly employed to indicate Jesus: chapters v. 26; vi. 35, 48; viii. 12; xi. 25; xiv. 6, etc. Irenæus applies the expression 'the life of the Word' to Jesus in the Letter to Florinus (see Stieren's Edition, p. 823). The writer of the First Epistle of John also applies the epithets 'the word of Life' and 'life' to Jesus, chapters i. and ii. Clement of Alexandria exclaims: "He who denies the Saviour denies life; for the light was life" (Stromateis, iv. 7). The fourth verse appears to me to have been the formula of an ancient Christian dogma of the second century, now extinct, but which was inculcated by an apocryphal writing, the Protevangelium, or Gospel of James, which has survived to our days. According to this writing, the active agent in the procreation of Jesus was not the Holy Ghost but the Word. Justin Martyr may have seen and accepted this part of the Gospel of James, for he boldly maintains with great emphasis in his *First Apology*, xxxiii., that it was the Word "that came upon the virgin and overshadowed her, caused her to conceive not by intercourse but by power."[1] In chapter lxvi. Justin repeats this statement that Jesus was made flesh by the Word of God. Irenæus also may be fairly suspected of

---

[1] This and all subsequent translations from the Fathers are quoted from the Ante-Nicene Christian Library, published by T. & T. Clark, Edinburgh, except when otherwise stated. I must here express my deep obligation to these excellent translations of the Fathers.

having been infected by the dogma, for he speaks of the "Word united to its own workmanship." ("*Verbum unitum suo plasmati.*" *Ad Her.*, III. xviii. 1.) This ancient dogma, that the Word produced Jesus, was consistent with the statement of the third verse that the Word made all things: but unfortunately it did not accord with the rival dogma that also originated in the first half of the second century, which assigned the active agency in the procreation of Jesus to the Holy Ghost. Considerable latitude of belief, within wide limits, was apparently permissible when the dogmas of the Christian religion were in course of formation. Hence it happened that a much revered Christian saint and martyr was permitted publicly to avow a dogma which was superseded by the dogma of the immaculate conception of the Virgin Mary by the Holy Ghost. To this divergence of dogma may be justly attributed the change effected in the text. It is perfectly clear what the original Greek text was in the second century: at what epoch the change was effected is unknown, but I perceive the first trace of it in the Latin translation of Irenæus, which was probably made in the course of the third century, by the change from the words 'by him' to 'in him.' The operators of changes in the Scriptures were not particular in their manner of procedure: but craft was pre-eminent in their action. They did not hesitate to destroy or muddle the sense of a passage, when they were from any reason unable bodily to change it. In the fourth verse they succeeded in destroying the sense in a most ingenious manner, being unable otherwise to deal with an epigrammatic passage which was widely known in the second half of the second century and subsequently. The first five verses of the Prologue form a section by themselves: they contain theological statements regarding the action of the Word, the production of Jesus, and the mission of the latter as the light of men. This section will come up again for discussion further on.

The next group of verses, which also form a natural section, verses 6-12, relate to the testimony of John. The meaning of these verses is clear throughout, with the single exception of one clause, which introduces confusion of thought, and breaks the continuity of the sense, viz., the clause in verse 10, "and the world was made by him." In the first section of the original Prologue the theological statement is clear that the world, or all things, were made by the Word, and that the life or Jesus was made by Him, and that Jesus was the light of men. In the second section of the Prologue, these clear ideas are thrown into confusion by the clause in verse 10, which implies that not the Word, but Jesus, or the life and light, made the world. The clause would have been quite appropriate and in accord with the context if it had been put in the first section of the Prologue; but it is surely out of place and inconsistent with the context in the second group of verses. It has the look of a gloss, or parenthetical clause, that introduces a great theological statement out of keeping with the context, and not supported by a single word in the rest of the Fourth Gospel. Dr Westcott says that the clause adds to the pathos of the passage; but it does so in the same sense in which the feebleness of women and children adds to the pathos of a calamity befalling them: a sense incompatible with the conception of the almighty power of divinity. Bishop Walsham How of Wakefield says, in his commentary, that the sentiment evoked is 'sorrowful astonishment.' This strange clause spoils the symmetry of the passage, is out of keeping with the meaning, and in my judgment it has the character of an interpolation. Although I have not succeeded in finding another reading, I think it justifiable, on grounds of reason and common sense, to regard this clause with great suspicion and even to delete it. The perusal of the writings of Irenæus gives good ground for the conclusion that this clause was needed for the exigencies of controversy in the strange discussions regarding the theological opinions of the Gnostics (see Irenæus, III. xi. 1 and 2); and the demand naturally gave rise to the supply. This remark will not appear strange to those who are familiar with the practices of early Christians, especially of the second century, in manipulating the manuscripts of sacred books to suit their special views or purposes. Except for the needs of controversy in the second century, this clause, so far as I know, has been put to no use, and has not been a subject of practical belief. The body of Christians do not believe that the historical Jesus, "This Jesus, the son of Joseph, whose father and mother we know," made the world. The creator of the world in the Christian mind is a metaphysical conception of Jesus, as the Word, the God-man, the Son of God, the Second Person of the Trinity, God the Son, and so on. Dr Westcott, in his comment on verse 10, says: "It is impossible to refer these words simply to the historical presence of the Word in Jesus as witnessed to by the Baptist. The whole scope and connection of the passage requires a wider sense." I cannot avoid thinking that the learned commentator was influenced in forming this opinion solely by the presence of the very clause which I believe to be interpolated. From my point of view, I understand this section of the Prologue to refer to the historical Jesus, the light of men, to whom John is alleged to have borne witness, and not to the metaphysical word of Christian thought. Regarded from this point of view, the clause, 'and the world was made by him,' is incongruous to its context, and cannot be forced to fit in with it. On the supposition that Cerinthus was the author of the Fourth Gospel, it must be admitted that his view was as I represent.

Perhaps those who may not be influenced by grounds of reason and common sense on this subject, may be convinced by the fact that, if not the same clause, the idea contained in it has been expunged in the Revised Version from the received text in another part of the New Testament, viz., Ephesians iii. 9. In the Authorised Version this text reads as follows: "And to make all *men* see what *is* the fellowship of the mystery, which from the beginning of the world hath been hid in God, who created all things by Jesus Christ." The words 'by Jesus Christ,' which render the final clause of this verse equivalent to 'the world was made by him,' in the tenth verse of the Prologue of the Fourth Gospel, are expunged in the Revised Version. The deep cunning of the Christian forger and the facilities with which he transacted his trade are conspicuous here. So far as my knowledge goes, these are the only two passages in the New Testament in which the historical Jesus is represented to have created the world; of these two passages one has been expunged and the other ought to be. In all other passages the metaphysical Word, or Son of God, etc., is the creator of the world.

The next two verses of the Prologue, 13 and 14, form a distinct section, and include, in my judgment, a distinct subject. In the received text, verse 13 is read as a continuation of the previous verse 12: but there does not seem to be an easy and natural connection in the sense. In verse 12 those who receive the light obtain the privilege of becoming the sons of God: it is clear that they become sons in a religious or moral sense, and not at all in a physiological sense. What, then, can be the meaning of the statement that they "were born, not of blood, nor of the will of the flesh, nor of the will of man, but of God"? This subsidiary statement is utterly irrelevant, inappropriate, and purposeless. To clear up the sense of this passage, I am in a position to quote the first transcript of it in Christian literature, which is found in the writings of Irenæus. In this early quotation of the passage, the subject of verse 13 is not 'the sons of God' in verse 12, but it is 'the Word' in verse 14. A change of punctuation has effected a change in the sense, as pointed out by Bishop Westcott, in connection with verses 3 and 4. Irenæus cites the passage thus: "Not by the will of the flesh, nor by the will of man, but by the will of God, was the Word made flesh" (Bk. III. xvi. 2). The first negation, 'not of bloods,' which is found in the received text, is omitted by Irenæus. The omission, however, is not to be blindly accepted. My opinion is that it is a suspicious omission, and that this negation must be replaced in the text, the authority for doing so being adequate. The reason which probably weighed with Irenæus for dropping this negation will be stated further on. This passage, as quoted and understood by Irenæus, with the omission supplied, will give an easy and natural sense to the two verses of the third section of the Prologue.

I believe that I can indicate the stages of the gradual abstraction of verse 13 from verse 14, and of its attachment to verse 12. It is clear to me that in the original text the subject of verse 13 was the 'Word' in verse 14, and that verse 13 had no connection whatever with verse 12. The earliest trace of this passage that I have been able to find in Christian literature is in the *Trypho* of Justin Martyr, ch.

lxiii., where, speaking of Jesus, Justin remarks: "His blood did not spring from the seed of man, but from the will of God" (ἀλλ' ἐκ θελήματος θεοῦ). The next reference to the passage in succession of time is that of Irenæus quoted above, which, in the Latin translation, was as follows: "*Non enim ex voluntate carnis, neque ex voluntate viri, sed ex voluntate Dei, Verbum caro factum est.*" It should be remarked that in these two, the earliest references to this passage, there is no mention of birth or of being born, but of creation or being made. It is regrettable that Clement of Alexandria is silent on verse 13. The next writer in order of time is Tertullian: and he quotes verse 13 in this fashion: "*Non ex sanguine, nec ex carnis voluntate, nec ex viri, sed ex Deo natus est*" (*De carne Christe*, xviii., and again in xxiv.). (He was born not from blood, nor from the will of flesh, nor of man, but from God.) The idea of birth and the words, *natus est*, are here introduced, which are not found in Irenæus's earlier quotation. Tertullian complains that the passage had been tampered with, and that 'they maintain' that the verb should be in the plural '*nati sunt*, were born,' " as if designating those who were before mentioned [in verse 12] as 'believing in his name.'"[1] Though Tertullian indicates the heresiarchs, Marcion and Valentinus more particularly, as the tamperers, it is impossible that the change in the canonical text could have been effected without the participation of the orthodox leaders. The last change, which was the addition of a relative pronoun to connect verse 13 to verse 12, and a full stop at the end of verse 13, was established in our received Greek text. A very clear and definite object was attained by the final change of the text, as will be seen further on.

The Prologue of the Fourth Gospel, restored to its original form as far as is now possible after the lapse of nearly eighteen centuries, would read as below. Just and reasonable grounds, I trust, have been given for the slight but important restorations that have been made. The Prologue, which contains difficult and unintelligible passages, which, in the judgment

---

[1] There is confusion about the words '*natus*' and '*nati*' in various editions of this Latin Father.

of a learned bishop and commentator, cannot be explained adequately by human language, when restored to its original form, becomes a simple, clear, and connected theological statement, which is intelligible to all, or can be made so, by explanation within the compass of human language. If the reader would keep the Greek text before his eyes, he will be the better able to appreciate the justice of the restorations made.

Received Text.	Restored Text.
1. In the beginning was the Word, and the Word was with God, and the Word was God.	1. In the beginning [*of the Gospel*] was the Word, and the Word was with God, and the Word was God.
2. The same was in the beginning with God.	(2. The same was in the beginning [*of the world*] with God.)
3. All things were made by him, and without him was not anything made that was made.	3. All things were made by him, and without him was not anything made.
4. In him was life, and the life was the light of men.	4. What was made by him was life (or Jesus), and the life (or Jesus) was the light of men;
5. And the light shineth in darkness, and the darkness comprehended it not.	5. A light which shineth in darkness, and which was not comprehended.
6. ¶ There was a man sent from God, whose name was John.	6. ¶ There was a man sent from God, whose name was John.
7. The same came for a witness, to bear witness of the light, that all men through him might believe.	7. The same came for witness, that he might bear witness of the light, that all might believe through him.
8. He was not that light, but *was sent* to bear witness of that light.	8. He was not that light, but *came* that he might bear witness of the light.

9. That was the true light, which lighteth every man that cometh into the world.	9. He was the true light, who lighteth every man that cometh into the world.
10. He was in the world, and the world was made by him, and the world knew him not.	10. He was in the world, and the world knew him not.
11. He came unto his own, and his own received him not.	11. He came unto his own, and his own received him not.
12. But as many as received him, to them gave he power to become the sons of God, *even* to them that believe on his Name:	12. But as many as received him, to them gave he the right to become sons of God, *even* to them that believe on his Name.
13. Which were born, not of blood, nor of the will of the flesh, nor of the will of man, but of God.	13. ¶ Not of bloods, nor of the will of the flesh, nor of the will of man, but of God,
14. And the Word was made flesh, and dwelt among us (and we beheld his glory, the glory as of the only begotten of the Father), full of grace and truth.	14. Was the Word made flesh, and tented among us, and we beheld his glory, the glory as of the only begotten of the Father, full of grace and truth.

The sentence 'the Word was made flesh' in the fourteenth verse of the first chapter of the Fourth Gospel is usually understood to indicate the birth of Jesus from the Virgin Mary through the overshadowing of the Holy Ghost. Dr Westcott admits (comment on ch. i. 14 of the Fourth Gospel in the *Speaker's Commentary*) that the theological fact of the miraculous conception is not stated by the Evangelist, but adds that it is necessarily implied. It is natural that he should think so from his point of view. But it is permissible to me, who see the hand of Cerinthus in the composition of the Fourth Gospel, to draw attention to the fact of the non-statement, and to declare that the implication is not necessary, but occurs only in the modern Christian mind with its preconceptions. In the first section of the restored Prologue occurs the theological statement that the Word made Jesus. As already said, Justin and even Irenæus corroborate this statement. There is nothing in the Fourth Gospel which implies the miraculous conception. Irenæus, on whom I rely greatly in this investigation, states his opinion that Cerinthus did not believe in it. There is no trace of the doctrine of the immaculate conception to be found in the Fourth Gospel.

Irenæus states that Cerinthus represented Jesus not as born from a virgin, for that seemed impossible to him, but that he was the son of Joseph and Mary. I find nothing in the Fourth Gospel which contradicts this account of the view of Cerinthus regarding the person of Jesus: on the contrary, I find passages which give it substantial support. In the account of the call of Philip and Nathaniel, the former is made to speak of the Master as "Jesus of Nazareth, son of Joseph" (i. 45). Again, in one of his discourses, Jesus spoke of himself as the bread come down from heaven. Thereupon it is stated in vi. 41 and 42, the Jews murmured and said: "Is not this Jesus, the son of Joseph, whose father and mother we know?"; and the evangelist who, in other passages, makes explanations and corrections in parentheses, allows these passages to remain without a word of correction. Compare these verses with Mark vi. 3. I am disposed to think that Cerinthus, assuming him to be the writer of the Fourth Gospel, was not fully acquainted with the evangelical biography, for in ch. vi. 41 and 42 he makes no parenthetical correction of the mistake of the people regarding the descent and native place of Jesus, and in fact gives prominence to the error that Jesus came out of Galilee, and not, as the Scripture said regarding Christ, of the seed of David and from the village of Bethlehem, where David was. There are great divergences in the Fourth Gospel from the general narrative of the Synoptics, and one reasonable explanation of this undoubted fact is the ignorance of Cerinthus of the fully-developed Gospel story as it progressed in the second century. I will venture to maintain that Irenæus, writing about a century after Cerinthus, in making the statement above referred to, was simply expressing his own opinion of Cerinthus's doctrines and not the opinion of Cerinthus himself, for the latter had no idea of the virginity of the mother of Jesus, and could have given no thought to that subject. I can find no evidence that the important theological fact of the immaculate conception was known and promulgated in the first century, when Cerinthus flourished. It was well known and widely disseminated in the second century, especially in the second half of it. As already said, there is no trace of it in the Fourth Gospel, which, under correction, must be taken as written in the first century, whether regarded as a work of the Apostle John or of the Gnostic Christian Cerinthus, or other unknown person. Nor have I succeeded in finding any trace of this important theological truth in the authentic Christian writings of the first century which have come down to us. I have carefully and earnestly searched without success for any indications of the vital doctrine of the miraculous conception in the following authentic Christian writings of the first century and early part of the second century:—

1. Paul's Epistle to the Romans.
2. „ First Epistle to the Corinthians.
3. „ Second „ „
4. „ Epistle to the Galatians.
5. So-called Paul's Epistle to the Philippians.
6. „ „ Ephesians.
7. „ „ Colossians.
8. „ First Epistle to the Thessalonians.
9. „ Second „ „
10. „ First Epistle to Timothy.
11. „ Second „ „
12. „ Epistle to Philemon.
13. „ „ Titus.
14. „ „ Hebrews.
15. James's General Epistle.
16. First Epistle of Peter.
17. So-called Second Epistle of Peter.
18. Jude's General Epistle.
19. John's Revelations.
20. The Didache, or Teaching of the Apostles.

21. Clement of Rome's First Epistle to the Corinthians.
22. So-called First Epistle of John.
23.   „   Second   „   „
24.   „   Third   „   „
25. The Shepherd of Hermas.
26. Polycarp's Epistle to the Philippians.

I have excluded from the above list all writings subsequent to A.D. 125, and hence the Epistle of Barnabas, A.D. 132 or perhaps later, and the so-called Second Epistle of Clement, A.D. 140, find no place in it. I have also excluded the Letters of Ignatius, because they are unreliable, and it is not now possible to separate the numerous and extensive interpolations and falsifications from the original text. These are the only writings of the early part of the second century that I have excluded. Bishop Lightfoot says that seven letters of Ignatius were written at that period. One epistle of Ignatius, condemned as spurious, is addressed to the "Christ bearing Mary," whom he asks "for information." In the Epistle to the Ephesians (edited by Bishop Lightfoot) he speaks of the "blood of God," and employs very plain expressions on the subject of the immaculate conception, such as "out of Mary and out of God" (ἐκ Μαρίας καὶ ἐκ Θεοῦ, see Bishop Westcott's translation of the Greek preposition in note on John i. 32, in the *Speaker's Commentary*); "For our Lord, Jesus the Christ, was conceived in the womb of Mary of the seed of David and *of the seed* of the Holy Ghost" (ἐκ σπέρματος μὲν Δαυεὶδ πνεύματος δὲ ἁγίου); and in the Epistle to the Smyrneans, "Son of God, by the divine will and power, truly born of a virgin." Let any person who cares to do so endeavour to amplify the middle one of these three quotations in the terms of anatomy and physiology. Ignatius does not say whence he obtained the details of his information, but there can be no doubt that he did not obtain them from the Gospels: and perhaps no Christian, outside the sphere of the coarse and ignorant ecclesiastics of the second and fourth centuries, ever uttered so gross a view of the miraculous conception.

The above solid body of early Christian literature, comprising as it does the writings of Apostles of the Lord, of great preachers and expounders of the Gospel, many of them men of education and learning, bishops of the Christian Church, and Greek philosophers or learned Greeks, ought surely to have contained, at the very least, some slight allusion to the pre-eminent theological fact of the miraculous conception if that fact had been known to the authors, or if known had been considered *véridique*. It is simply astonishing that no allusion whatever to this great theological truth is found in the whole body of authentic early Christian literature of the first century: no single sentence from which may be inferred that this great theological truth was in the minds of the writers, and was known to or believed by them. The nearest approach to this important theological truth that I have been able to find are expressions that the Son of God came into the world 'made of a woman,' or was 'manifested or revealed in the flesh,' 'came in the flesh,' or similar words: and though a great deal is said regarding virgins, there is no allusion to the Virgin Mary. Even the Pauline expression, 'made or born of a woman,' may be correctly translated 'born of a wife,' the Greek word used by Paul being similar to the corresponding French word which means woman or wife.[1] It appears plain to me that Paul intended to convey the meaning that Jesus was born in legitimate Jewish wedlock, from the clause that he immediately added, 'made under the law' (Gal. iv. 4). According to the present orthodox doctrine, Jesus was not born under the law but contrary to the law, being illegitimate, because not born in wedlock under the law. I am constrained to conclude that the miraculous conception of theologians was not implied in the Fourth Gospel and was unknown to the Christians of the first century. In the Shepherd of Hermas is to be found a theory of the Incarnation which I regard as a modification of the doctrine as displayed in the Fourth Gospel:

[1] On this point I may refer to the circumstance that Paul makes a distinction between 'woman' and 'virgin.' A woman is not a virgin according to Paul, and *vice versâ*. See 1 Cor. vii. 1, 2, 3, 4, 10, 11, 13, 14, 16, 27 for woman, and 25, 28, 34, 36 for virgin. It was the invariable custom of Christians in the early centuries to discriminate between women and virgins even when the latter were antique or 'old maids' as we call them. Virgins formed a distinct class of early Christian society.

a theory which takes no account at all of the miraculous conception. It is given as the interpretation of a parable. "The Holy Pre-existent Spirit, which created the whole creation, God made to dwell in flesh that He desired. This flesh, therefore, in which the Holy Spirit dwelt, was subject unto the Spirit, walking honourably in holiness and purity, without in any way defiling the Spirit. When it had lived honourably in chastity, and had laboured with the Spirit, and had co-operated with it in everything, behaving itself boldly and bravely, He chose it as a partner with the Holy Spirit; for the career of this flesh pleased [the Lord], seeing that, as possessing the Holy Spirit, it was not defiled upon the earth" (Bishop Lightfoot's Translation of the Shepherd of Hermas, S. 5, vi.). The investigation of this subject is within the power of every person who will take the trouble to read the New Testament from the Fourth Gospel to Revelations, and also Bishop Lightfoot's *Apostolic Fathers*, the abridged edition, a valuable work procurable for sixteen shillings. A knowledge of Greek, though useful, is not indispensable for the purpose, as Bishop Lightfoot's work contains the translations of the original writings.

The first appearance in authentic Christian literature of the theological statement of the virgin birth is in the *Apology* of Aristides, which was presented to the Emperor Hadrian in A.D. 125 or later. A Syriac translation of the Greek original of this *Apology* was discovered a few years ago by Professor Rendel Harris of Cambridge, in the convent of St Catherine on Mount Sinai *(Contemporary Review* for July 1891). Aristides says: "The Christians reckon the beginning of their religion from Jesus Christ, who is named the Son of God Most High; and it is said that God came down from Heaven, and from a Hebrew virgin took and clad Himself with flesh, and in a daughter of man there dwelt the Son of God. This is taught from that Gospel, which a little while ago was spoken amongst them as being preached; wherein if ye also will read, ye will comprehend the power that is upon it." At this epoch, *i.e.*, the first half of the second century, a mushroom growth of writings, many of which were subsequently named Gospels, appeared, one probably from each sect or division of Christians or pseudo-Christians ; a large fragment of one only has come down to our days ; the majority, and these of much interest, being lost in all but a few trifling fragments. It is a moral certainty that the story of the virgin birth originated in these popular tales or story-books that appeared in the first half of the second century. To this epoch Tischendorf has assigned the more ancient of the surviving so-called Apocryphal Gospels. Mr B. Harris Cowper, editor of the *Apocryphal Gospels*, says (p. lxix. of the Introduction): "Justin Martyr speaks of Jesus doing carpenter's work (*Trypho*, 88) in almost the same words as pseudo-Thomas speaks of Joseph (1 Thomas, xiii.). Irenæus, also, when speaking of Marcus, the founder of the Marcosians, mentions the mysteries he found in the alphabet (Bk. I. 10–17). Special reference is made by Irenæus to 'an unspeakable multitude of apocryphal and spurious writings,' which these heretics forged, and from one of them he contrasts the story about Jesus and the man who went to teach him letters, much as we have it in some copies of Thomas," *i.e.*, the Gospel of Thomas, or Gospel of the infancy of Jesus. Irenæus further states (Bk. I. xxxi. 1) that a sect that entertained peculiar notions regarding Cain and Judas produced a fictitious history, which they called the 'Gospel of Judas.' The names of about a score of these Gospels, and small fragments of a few of them, have come down to us ; but the immense majority of them with their names have disappeared. Lately an interesting fragment of the Gospel of Peter has been exhumed from a grave in Egypt. It is this exuberant evangelical literature of the first half of the second century, much of it no doubt having been passed on to the second half of the century and to subsequent centuries, that the editors of the Fourth Gospel, who added ch. xxi., had in mind in their final verse : " And there are also many other things which Jesus did, the which if they should be written every one, I suppose that even the world itself could not contain the books that should be written." The late Bishop Lightfoot, in his historical essays on *Christian Life in the Second and Third Centuries*, speaks "of the vast volume of Christian literature in the second century, which, with a few meagre exceptions, has altogether perished." The later writers in the New Testament, who are referred to the early part of the second century in my list of early Christian literature, and some of these may date even subsequent to A.D. 125, make allusions to these evangelical histories or tales. The writer of the First Epistle to Timothy says, i. 4: "Neither give heed to fables and endless genealogies, which minister questions rather than godly edifying which is in faith"; and again, iv. 7: "But refuse profane and old wives' fables, and exercise thyself rather in godliness"; and again, vi. 20: "O Timothy, keep that which is committed to thy trust, avoiding profane and vain babblings, and oppositions of science falsely so called." Some learned men consider the word translated in this passage 'oppositions' to be the *Antitheses*, a genuine work so named of Marcion, the great Gnostic Christian of the first half of the second century.[1] The writer of the Second Epistle to Timothy says, ii. 16: "But shun profane and vain babblings: for they will increase unto more ungodliness"; and again, iv. 4: "and they shall turn away their ears from the truth, and shall be turned unto fables." The writer of the letter to Titus also says, probably with reference to the same class of evangelical litterateurs under discussion, i. 14: "not giving heed to Jewish fables, and commandments of men that turn from the truth." The writer of the Second Epistle of Peter says, i. 16: "We have not followed cunningly devised fables, when we made known unto you the power and coming of our Lord Jesus Christ, but were eye-witnesses of His Majesty," an unblushing statement made by a Christian writing in the second century; but I quote this writer to obtain his testimony, on this point perhaps reliable, to the prevalence in his time of popular evangelical

[1] I believe that theologians make a mistake in referring all the allusions to the popular Christian literature of these times, which I have collected together, to the Gnostic literature alone. In doing so they follow Irenæus (see the Preface to his work *Against Heresies*), who had his own reasons for so limiting these allusions. The Jewish popular gospels or story books were subjects of offence to early Christian writers of the better sort. Genealogies were not Greek Gnostic productions, but the work of Jewish Christians. Two of these genealogies are preserved in the Gospels according to Matthew and Luke.

stories. I believe the evangelical *cocoëthes* of this epoch was
not limited to sectaries, but was shared by members of the
parent Church or society of Christians. The writer of the
Epistle to the Ephesians speaks of evangelists (ch. iv. 11)
as saints possessing a special grace or gift. I dissent from
the meaning imposed upon the well-known word 'evangelist'
of preacher or missionary, and not writer of a narrative, subsequently called a gospel. There were numerous preachers
and missionaries in the first century, to none of whom was
the word evangelist applied by contemporary writers. The
gift of gospel-writing was not conspicuous in the first century,
and it has no place in Paul's catalogue of gifts (1 Cor. xii. 28).
It certainly became so in the second century, and it would
indeed have been strange if the members of the parent
Church, or the saints, had escaped the contagion. But it was
certainly not so. Philip (in the first century) is called 'the
evangelist' in Acts xxi. 8, who was not preacher or missionary,
but a deacon, as is specially mentioned in the passage quoted.
The preacher and missionary was the Apostle Philip, who is
spoken of in Acts viii. 5-14 as a missionary to Samaria, where
he was joined by the Apostles Peter and John, and afterwards
to the south (verses 26-40). I understand by the word
'evangelist,' applied to Philip the deacon, that he wrote a
gospel. Timothy was also engaged in the work of gospel-
writing in addition to preaching (2 Tim. iv. 5). In Luke i. 1
there is ample evidence that a goodly number of the saints
had employed themselves in the congenial occupation of
gospel-writing: "Inasmuch as many have taken in hand to
set forth in order a declaration of these things which are
most surely believed among us," etc. There is a dogmatic
motive for ignoring the existence of many evangelists,[1]

---

[1] In connection with the interpretation of the word evangelist as
missionary and not gospel writer, the mind naturally reverts to Dean
Swift's *Tale of a Tub*, in which three sons resort to a theological method of
getting over the difficulty occasioned by the prohibition in their father's
will, in which he charged and commanded his three sons to wear no sort of
silver fringe upon or about their coats. "The brother so often mentioned
for his erudition, who was well skilled in criticisms, had found in a certain
author, which he said should be nameless, that the same word, which in the

viz., to corroborate the great historical misrepresentations deliberately written by an influential ecclesiastic, supported by the silliest of reasons—that of Irenæus, in Bk. III. xi. 8 : "It is not possible that the Gospels can be either more or fewer in number than they are. For since there are four zones of the world in which we live, and four principal winds," etc. These evangelical histories or tales that were in circulation amongst Christian people in the first half of the second century were elaborated under skilled revision in the second half of the century, care being taken to preserve the short notes of the discourses of Jesus made by Matthew the Apostle, and perhaps also of the teaching of Peter by Mark, as stated by Papias (Eusebius' *Eccl. Hist.*, Bk. III. 39), these contributions from Matthew and Mark, and probably a few others, being the only authentic portions of the histories, and brought out as the Gospels according to Matthew, Mark, and Luke. The history of the Gospel according to John will be developed in the course of this treatise. The first intimation we have of the existence of the four Gospels as we have them in the present day is in the writings of Theophilus and Irenæus, both writers of the second half of the second century. If the preceding statements be correct, and I have no reason for doubting their accuracy, I am justified in concluding that Cerinthus, writing at the close of the first century, had no knowledge of the miraculous conception, and that the incarnation of the Word spoken of in the Prologue of the Fourth Gospel was not of the nature of the incarnation recounted in the Gospels according to Matthew and Luke.

The doctrine of the miraculous conception was without doubt a new departure of the second century, for there is no

will is called fringe, does also signify a broomstick, and doubtless ought to have the same interpretation in this paragraph."

After I had written this passage in the text, I met with Professor Ramsay's important work, *St Paul as Traveller and Roman Citizen*. The learned Professor states that Philip the Evangelist was the authority for part of the Acts, viz., chapters vi. to viii. 39 (ch. xvi. sect. 5). I have also found in *Pistis Sophia*, a Gnostic Gospel probably of the second half of the second century, very distinct testimony to the Gospel writing of Philip the Evangelist (see pages 69-73 of the edition (1896) issued by the Theosophical Publishing Society). Paul, Peter and others were great preachers of the Gospel, but they were never called evangelists.

trace of it in the Christian writings of the first century. The genealogies appended to the Gospels according to Matthew and Luke were in all probability made out and had got into general circulation before the new doctrine had been started. Genealogies are referred to and condemned in Titus iii. 9 in the early part of the second century. A natural explanation would thus be obtained of the fact that these genealogies are Joseph's, who was probably known and acknowledged in the first century to be the father of our Lord, but not in the second after perhaps the first quarter. In the Second Gospel and in the Gospel used by Marcion, considered by some, with good reason, to be the original of the third Gospel, the introductory chapters regarding the miraculous birth, etc., of Jesus did not exist. I suspect the source of the new doctrine was a prophecy which came under the cognisance of imaginative Christians in the early part of the second century. Justin, A.D. 150, is the first Christian writer who refers to the prophecy of Isaiah vii. 14 in his *First Apology*, ch. xxxiii.; but the discovery of it had probably been made before his time, as Aristides, A.D. 125, refers to the *on dits* regarding the birth of Jesus. The early Christians had more faith in prophecy than in miracle. Justin Martyr is full of prophecies, and rooted them out of the Old Testament in such abundance that a good many of them have been since abandoned as surplusage, whereas he was shy of miracles. The fact of the existence of such a prophecy as that of Isaiah, "Behold a virgin shall conceive and bear a son, and shall call his name Immanuel," stimulated the Jewish Christian imagination; and the fulfilment of the prophecy in the person of the mother of Jesus was brought about. The Christian intellect was specially active at this period, a great literary epoch, as the outcome of the swarm of writings testifies: "An unspeakable number of apocryphal and spurious writings," as Irenæus says (Bk. I. xx. 1). I cannot avoid the conclusion that the calumnies regarding the legitimacy of the birth of Jesus originated at this period, such as the scandals collected by Celsus, which the strange story of a Hebrew girl impregnated by a ghost was very likely to give cause to. The imputation that Jesus was born of fornication is very prominently mentioned in the *Acta Pilati*, now known as the

Gospel of Nicodemus, which Tischendorf believed was a production of the middle of the second century, and known to Justin Martyr. There was nothing of this nature that occurred, or is suspected of having occurred, in the first century. Nor is there wanting some evidence of passive resistance to the new doctrine on the part of orthodox congregations or churches. In the interesting find of a Syriac palimpsest of the Gospels, deciphered and translated by the indomitable perseverance and energy of Mrs Lewis and her sister, Mrs Gibson, of Cambridge, the text of the canonical Gospel according to Matthew is dexterously manipulated so as to retain the new doctrine of the virgin birth, and yet not to discard the paternity of Joseph. Whatever may be the precise date assigned to Mrs Lewis's Gospels by experts, I am inclined to believe that they are of earlier date than any other extant codex of the Gospels. In the Protevangelium, or Gospel of James, which Tischendorf dates from the middle of the second century, and which was perhaps known to Justin[1] (*Trypho*, ch. lxxviii.), the new doctrine is very fully developed, but a singular modification is introduced, which certainly implies priority of time to the Fourth Gospel, and is a clear proof of the influence of that part of the Prologue which attributes the production of Jesus to the Word, and it thus gives support to my rendering of the fourth verse. The passage runs thus: " And behold the angel of the Lord stood before her, saying, Fear not, Mary, for thou hast found favour before the Lord of all, and thou shall conceive from his Word. And when she heard she disputed in herself, saying, Shall I conceive from the Lord, the living God, and bear as every woman beareth? And the angel of the Lord said, Not so, Mary; for the power of the Lord will overshadow thee; wherefore also that holy thing which is born of thee shall be called the son of the Most High" (Cowper's *Apocryphal Gospels*, Gospel of James, ch. xi.). In the above account not the Holy Ghost, but the Word, is the active agency. Justin has a passage to a similar effect. This blessed father had sometimes a blundering way of putting his argument; but I am dealing with his argu-

---

[1] Justin mentions that Jesus was born in a cave, which is stated in the Gospel of James, but not in the Synoptic Gospels.

ment such as it is, and not with its appropriateness. After quoting the address of the Angel, " Behold thou shall conceive of the Holy Ghost," etc., he proceeds to argue : " It is wrong, therefore, to understand the Spirit and power of God, as anything else than the Word, who is also the firstborn of God, as the foresaid prophet Moses declared ; and it was this which, when it came upon the Virgin and overshadowed her, caused her to conceive, not by intercourse, but by power" (*First Apology*, ch. xxxiii.). These two passages, found in Christian writers of the early half of the second century, look like an attempt to reconcile the earlier Christology of the Fourth Gospel with the new doctrine of the miraculous conception.

If, then, the author of the Fourth Gospel had no knowledge of the miraculous conception, in what manner did he exemplify his own statement that the Word was made flesh? To me it appears clear that Irenæus has succeeded in averting the attention of Christendom from the form of incarnation of the Word taught in the Fourth Gospel. In his account of the doctrine of Cerinthus he does not use any expression that would clearly indicate incarnation ; and in Bk. III. xi. 3 of his work he says, that "according to the opinion of no one of the heretics was the Word of God made flesh." But, notwithstanding this explicit statement, the careful reader will have no difficulty in perceiving that in the same passage (III. xi. 3) he wholly contradicts himself; and that after all his volubility on this subject, the real truth (which Irenæus knew very well) was that the Gnostic Christians, or, rather, many of them, Cerinthus included, were reluctant, from their exalted sense of the sanctity and sublimity of the Divine Nature, to inculcate the conversion of the Word into human or bestial flesh. The Fourth Gospel announces the incarnation of the Word in Jesus through the testimony of John in ch. i. 32. "And John bare record, saying : I saw the Spirit descending from heaven like a dove, and it abode upon him." It will now be obvious that verses 13 and 14 of the restored Prologue are strictly applicable to the form of incarnation of the Word in the Fourth Gospel, and not at all applicable to that described in the First and Third Gospels. " Not of bloods, nor of the will of the flesh, nor of the will of man, but of God was the Word made flesh and tented amongst us." The Word was made flesh in a manner worthy of the Divine Nature directly by the creative will of God (*i.e.*, the incarnate dove was created in heaven), and not on earth by means of material physiological fluids and of human sexual organism. Now will be apparent why Irenæus omitted the first negation, 'not of bloods,' in his transcript of verse 13 of the Prologue (Bk. III. xvi. 2). The Divine Will is represented in the Fourth Gospel to be that the Word created incarnate in the form of a dove descended from heaven, and lodged or took up its abode in the person of Jesus, the chosen vessel of God.[1] The Fourth Gospel puts forward a man named John as the witness of the reception of the incarnate Word by Jesus in the beginning of the Gospel.

This pretty conceit of Cerinthus of the Spirit descending from heaven in the form of a dove, and abiding in Jesus, is the most ancient of Christian myths. I have not been able to trace it to an earlier source than the Fourth Gospel and Cerinthus. It does not appear to have come very early under general Christian cognisance, for I do not remember any allusion to it in the New Testament writings, excluding the Synoptic Gospels, nor in the writings of the Apostolic Fathers. The first authentic notice of it occurs in the writings of Justin Martyr (about 150 A.D.), who says that he derived it from the writings "of the Apostles of this very Christ of ours." Thus the inference is justifiable that it had been before Justin's time appropriated by the authors of the numerous writings that sprung up in the first half of the second century. From the time of Cerinthus to that of Justin, perhaps some forty or fifty years, the myth had grown and undergone changes, some new details were added, while some old ones were omitted, and the myth was brought within the sphere of prophecy! But there were still remaining sufficiently distinct, though much distorted marks of its original purport, namely, the columbine incarnation of the

---

[1] In the Epistle of Barnabas Jesus is called the 'vessel of the Spirit,' τὸ σκεῦος τοῦ πνεύματος; "because he was in his own person about to offer the vessel of the Spirit a sacrifice for our sins" (ch. vii.).

Word at the beginning of the Gospel. A very strong leaning, however, is perceptible to a changing of the original intent and purport of the myth. Justin's version of the dove story of Cerinthus is found in the *Dialogue with Trypho*, ch. lxxxviii. "When, then, Jesus had come to the River Jordan, where John was baptising, and when Jesus descended into the water, a fire burned in the Jordan; and when he came out of the water, the Apostles of this very Christ of ours have written that the Holy Spirit like a dove flew upon him. Now we know that he did not come to the river because he was in need of baptism, or of the descent of the Spirit in the form of a dove; . . . . it was necessary when John was baptising to give men proof that they may know who is Christ. For when John remained by the Jordan, and preached the baptism of repentance, wearing only a leathern girdle and a vesture made of camel's hair, eating nothing but locusts and wild honey, men thought him to be Christ; but he cried to them, 'I am not the Christ, but the voice of one crying; for he that is stronger than I shall come whose shoes I am not worthy to bear.' And when Jesus came to the Jordan, he was believed to be the son of Joseph the carpenter; and he seemed uncomely, as the Scriptures declared; and he was considered a carpenter (for he used to do carpentry when he was amongst men, making ploughs and yokes; thereby teaching the duty of righteousness and an active life); the Holy Ghost, for man's sake, as I have already stated, flew on him in the form of a dove, and a voice came from heaven at the same time, which had been said by David, speaking as if in the person [of Christ] what was to be said to him by the Father: 'Thou art my son: this day have I begotten thee'; saying that his generation would take place for men at the time when their knowledge of him would begin."

In this version the Spirit of the Fourth Gospel becomes the Holy Ghost, and the prime purport of the myth is thus at once changed. But the utterance of the voice partially brings back the lost meaning of the original but now perverted myth: "Thou art my son: this day have I begotten thee." These words in the original passage in Psalms ii. 7 cannot be understood in a literal sense; nor can they be so understood here: they can only be taken to express that on this day God had caused Jesus to enter upon the dignity and functions involved in the title 'my son.' Justin's explanation, however, that it means his birth or generation taking place for men at the time when they would acquire the knowledge of him, is too far-fetched and gross to be regarded merely as a blunder: it gives me the impression that he meant to turn off the mind of his readers from the Cerinthian doctrine of the columbine incarnation of the Word in Jesus that was alleged to have taken place at that time. Justin's explanation of the voice indicates the progress already made in the conversion of the purport of the myth from *incarnation* to *generation*, while the chronology is in accord with the original purport of the myth, but antagonistic to the changed purport.

In Justin's version the Spirit of Cerinthus is without ceremony changed into the Holy Ghost; and without scruple or hesitation the dove story, or part of it, is brought within the domain of prophecy. Justin, who had a great weakness for prophecy, regarded the dove story of Cerinthus as the fulfilment of Isaiah xi. 1–3. "There shall come forth a shoot out of the stock of Jesse, and a branch out of its roots shall bear fruit: and the spirit of the Lord shall rest upon him, the spirit of wisdom and understanding, the spirit of counsel and might, the spirit of knowledge and of the fear of the Lord." He represents the Jew, Trypho (ch. lxxxvii.), as "most discreetly and most prudently" inquiring how Christ, a pre-existent God, become incarnate, was "filled with the powers of the Holy Ghost, which the Scripture by Isaiah enumerates as if he were in lack of them?" Justin represents himself as replying: "Truly, there does seem to be a difficulty; but listen to what I say, that you may perceive the reason of this also. The Scripture says that these enumerated powers of the Spirit have come on him, not because he stood in need of them, but because they would rest in him, *i.e.*, would find their accomplishment in him, so that there would be no more prophets in your nation after the ancient custom: and this fact you plainly perceive. For after him no prophet has arisen among you." Justin is silent regarding the dove; he let it alone: he could not find a prophecy to put upon it, and he made no attempt to explain it away.

Other versions of the dove story appear in the Synoptic Gospels, which must be regarded as writings of the second half of the second century. The nuclei or first beginnings of the Gospels according to Matthew and Mark may, as stated by Papias (Eusebius' *Eccl. Hist.*, Bk. III. 39), have been written in the first century: but the original writings of Matthew and Mark, probably very brief, have been so overlaid by additions, and otherwise altered, that it is not possible to come to a consensus regarding what portion is original and what portions are alterations and additions, though reasonable conjectures may be made as to original and changes and accretions. The third Synoptic Gospel professes to be merely a compilation: and the statement in Luke i. 2, that the things which the compiler had put together were delivered " by eye-witnesses and ministers of the Word," is of the same value as the statement of Justin Martyr, that he quoted the writings of Apostles. The Synoptic Gospels must necessarily be taken as writings of the second century, in the second half of which they were in all probability trimmed and put into definite shape under skilled editorship, were named, became generally known and accepted, and were quoted as distinct publications. In the first two synoptics there is a partial reversion to the original myth, as the 'Spirit of God' and 'Spirit' are represented as assuming the form of a dove, and not the 'Holy Ghost' as in the third synoptic. But the original purport of the myth was neutralised or concealed by an alteration in the words of the voice as given by Justin from a quotation of the Psalms (ii. 7), " Thou art my son, this day have I begotten thee," to a paraphrase of Isaiah (xlii. 1), " Thou art my beloved son, in whom I am well pleased." The spring from David to Isaiah, though effective in practically obliterating the original purport of the myth, failed, however to extinguish the vitality of the dove. The dove remained intact.

The explanation given by Justin Martyr of the descent of the Spirit did not satisfy the minds of the early Christians, for we find Irenæus, a few decades later, discussing the same subject from a different point of view. Unlike Justin, he felt no obligation to explain the words of the voice, which were now of a neutral character.[1] Irenæus, like all the others, leaves the dove alone. His explanation of the import of the descent of the Spirit is in important points different from Justin's. Justin's free and easy conversion of the Spirit in the dove story into the Holy Ghost, and from that to powers and gifts of the Spirit, had lost its ground; and the reason why these gifts were necessary to Jesus, who is not merely the Light of men, the enlightener and teacher of the Fourth Gospel, but also the Creator of the World and true God, had shifted ground. Justin's blundering explanation that the object of the spiritual gifts to Jesus was their resting or accomplishment or extinction, so that the race of prophets would end, did not find favour with Irenæus. This great theologian, like Justin, relied on prophecy to explain the dove story; but unlike Justin, but with exactly the same freedom from ceremony, he added an additional element—ointment or anointing oil—which he derived from prophecy also. While Justin converted the dove into the Holy Ghost, Irenæus converted the ointment or anointing oil aforesaid into the Holy Ghost. But most remarkable of all, and this is a cardinal point, the Spirit who was transformed into a dove, not being now the Holy Ghost, is represented to be the Father Spirit (*Pater Spiritus*), who applied the ointment or performed the anointing with oil. There is no doubt in the case of Irenæus that he was well acquainted with the dove story of Cerinthus, and with the Fourth Gospel; whereas in the case of Justin we are unable to gauge the extent of his acquaintance with the Fourth Gospel, or whether he had any considerable knowledge of Cerinthus and his doctrine. There is also no doubt that Irenæus was aware of the statement in the Gospel according to Luke (ch. iii. 22), and in Justin and in other writings accessible to him, that the Spirit in the dove story was

---

[1] It is remarkable that although Irenæus quotes the voice from heaven saying, "Thou art my beloved Son, in whom I am well pleased," as stated in Matthew iii. 17, Mark i. 11, and Luke iii. 22, Clement of Alexandria, his contemporary, quotes the voice at the baptism as saying, "Thou art my beloved Son, to-day have I begotten Thee" (*Pæd.*, i. 6).

regarded as the Holy Ghost. Notwithstanding this knowledge in his mind, Irenæus deliberately states that the Spirit is *Pater Spiritus*, a term unique in early Christian literature, but by which there can be no doubt that Irenæus meant God the Father. This extreme statement is made in the following two passages in his work *Against Heresies* :—

"And then, referring to the baptism, Matthew says, 'The heavens were opened to him and he saw the Spirit of God, as a dove, coming upon him; and behold, a voice from heaven, saying, 'This is my beloved Son, in whom I am well pleased.'" For Christ did not at that time descend upon Jesus, neither was Christ one and Jesus another: but the Word of God—who is the Saviour of all, and the ruler of heaven and earth, who is Jesus (as we have already shown), who did also assume flesh, and was anointed by the Father Spirit (*unctus est a Patre Spiritu*)[1] was made Jesus Christ, as Esaias also says: 'There shall come forth a rod from the root of Jesse, and a flower shall rise from his root; and the Spirit of God shall rest upon him: the Spirit of wisdom and understanding, the Spirit of counsel and might, the Spirit of knowledge and piety,' etc. .... And again Esaias himself, signifying beforehand his unction and the reason why he was anointed, says: 'The Spirit of God is upon me, because He hath anointed me: He hath sent me to preach the Gospel to the lowly, to heal the broken in heart, to proclaim liberty to the captives and sight to the blind; to announce the acceptable year of the Lord, and the day of retribution, to comfort all that mourn.' For inasmuch as the Word of God was man from the root of Jesse, and son of Abraham, in this respect did the Spirit of God rest upon Him, and anoint Him to preach the Gospel unto the lowly (Bk. III. xi. 3)."

"For in the name of Christ is implied he who anoints, he himself who is anointed, and the unction with which he was anointed. And the Father anointed, but the Son was anointed with the Spirit, who is the unction; as the Word declares by Isaiah, "The Spirit of the Lord is upon me, because he hath

---

[1] In the translation of Irenæus, in the Ante-Nicene Christian Library, this clause is rendered "and was anointed by the Spirit from the Father," which is a modification of the original text.

anointed me, signifying both the anointing Father, the anointed Son, and the unction, which is the Spirit" (Bk. III. xviii. 3).[1]

It should be noted in the above remarkable transformation of the dove story of Cerinthus, that Jesus was simple Jesus before the dove incident, but Jesus Christ after ; and that the great theologian further distinctly differentiates the man from the God in the personality of Jesus. Irenæus was merciless and unsparing in his denunciations against the Gnostic Christians, because they split up the Son of God, separating Him into parts, *i.e.*, into Jesus and Christ. Is not his own view of Jesus of the same nature ? " *Sententia homicidialis, comminuens autem et per multa dividens Filium Dei*," comminuting the Son of God, and dividing Him into many parts (*Ad Her.*, III. xvi. 8).

It must be observed, in justice to Cerinthus, the author of the myth of the dove, that he is in no way responsible for these extraordinary developments which second-century theologians inflicted upon his pretty creation.

The Cerinthian, and generally Gnostic, doctrine that God, or His emanation, the Spirit, descended from the pleroma or Gnostic heaven, and occupied the body of Jesus, and influenced His teaching and conduct, is still alive among theologians. The latest modification of it is to be found in the writings of Dr James Martineau, the nestor of English theologians. *Les idées ne meurent pas.*[2] The passage is a long one, but I beg the learned writer's permission to copy it in full, so that all possibility of misapprehension be avoided. " I know not whether others can draw a sharp line of separation between the human spirit and the Divine, and can clearly say where their own soul ends and God's communion begins : but for myself, with closest thought, I confess my darkness ; and can only say that somehow He certainly stirs among our higher affections, and mingles with the action of our proper nature. If, in Christ, this divine margin was not simply broader than elsewhere, but spread till it covered the whole soul, and brought the

---

[1] Irenæus' view is expressed in Acts x. 38. It is the view adopted by the Church ; see Pearson on the Creed, Art. ii.

[2] Ideas never die.

human into moral coalescence with the Divine, then was God not merely *represented* by a foreign and resembling being; but *personally there*, giving expression to His spiritual nature, as in the visible universe to His causal power.

"Such is the thought which inspires the marvellous Gospel of my text. ['He was in the world, and the world was made by him, and the world knew him not. He came unto his own, and his own received him not. But as many as received him, to them gave he power to become the sons of God.' John i. 10-12.] He, whose intellect overarches us in the vault of stars, whose beauty rests on the surface of the earth and sea, embodied his affections and his will in the person of the Son of Man. By the same Divine Mind, whose gentlest glories centred in that lowly form, was the world made in which he was; yet the world knew him not; and though he came only to his own, his own received him not" (*Hours of Thought on Sacred Things*, vol. II. xiv.; *Christ the Divine Word*, i. p. 205). It is almost a pity to spoil the beautiful language and thought of this passage by suggesting that an honest introspection of one's soul may lead to a difficulty in discovering the line of demarcation between our lowest affections and the devil, and that Satan worshippers, a sect that existed in history and may still exist for aught I know, may draw awkward conclusions. Dr Martineau's doctrine is Gnosticism, and differs from the ordinary doctrine of the incarnation in being Hellenic thought, while the latter is Jewish. Such views are inconsistent with the real facts of the life and character of Jesus, as displayed in the Gospels, when the latter are denuded of their supernatural and metaphysical embellishments. To an ordinary mind of common sense, the thoughts and conduct of Jesus were purely human, comparable to the thoughts and conduct of other men, about whom there is no suggestion of divinity.

CHAPTER II.

THE DECLARATION OF THE UNKNOWN FATHER. THE APOSTLE JOHN NOT THE AUTHOR OF THE FOURTH GOSPEL OR OF THE FIRST EPISTLE OF JOHN.

IT has, I trust, been clearly shown in the preceding chapter that the Fourth Gospel (i. 32) contains the first link of the doctrine of Cerinthus as declared by Irenæus (I. xxvi. 1), namely, that the æon Christ, or the Spirit, descended upon Jesus in the form of a dove. The Fourth Gospel, however, does not say that this occurrence took place at the baptism of Jesus. A little reflection will suffice to convince the reader that the addition of the statement regarding baptism was due to Irenæus, writing late in the second century, introducing his preconceptions into a historical account, just as he had previously introduced his preconception of the virgin birth. Cerinthus had no notion of the virgin birth, nor of the baptism of the Lord; regarding both notions he is absolutely silent. There is no allusion to the baptism of Jesus in the authentic Christian writings of the first century; there is none in the Fourth Gospel, and I am uncertain whether the great heretics of the first half of the second century accepted the baptism of the Lord. Cerinthus and Marcion certainly did not. The Third Gospel represents the baptism of Jesus as occurring subsequent to the imprisonment of John the Baptist, so that the latter was not the baptiser (iii. 19-22); and thus the account of Matthew and Mark is discredited by that of Luke and by the silence of the Fourth Gospel.

The next link in the doctrine of Cerinthus, as declared by Irenæus, is the following: that, having received the dove, Jesus announced the unknown Father. This announcement of the unknown Father is made very early in the Fourth Gospel: "No man hath seen God at any time; the only begotten Son which is in the bosom of the Father, He hath declared *Him*" (i. 18). This is a sentiment opposed to the Hebrew Scriptures, in which personal communion with God is related of many men—Adam, Moses, Elijah, and others. Later on, speaking of the Father, Jesus, in addressing the Jews, says: "Ye have neither heard His voice at any time, nor seen His shape" (v. 37), obviously meaning that the Father was unknown to them, and that the statements to the contrary in their Scriptures were untrue. Towards the close of his ministry, he anticipated persecutions to his disciples, which he attributes, as a result, to ignorance of the Father: "these things will they do unto you, because they have not known the Father" (xvi. 3).

The declaration of the unknown Father is made repeatedly and forcibly throughout the Fourth Gospel. In iv. 24 it is said: "God *is* a spirit: and they that worship Him must worship Him in spirit and in truth;" in iii. 16, 17: "God so loved the world, that He gave His only begotten Son, that whoso believeth in Him should not perish, but have everlasting life. For God sent not His Son into the world to condemn the world; but that the world through Him might be saved." "Jesus cried and said, he that believeth on me, believeth not on me, but on Him that sent me. . . . . For I have not spoken of myself; but the Father which sent me, he gave me a commandment what I should say, and what I should speak. And I know that his commandment is life everlasting: whatsoever I speak, therefore, even as the Father said unto me, so I speak" (xii. 41, 49, 50). "The word which ye hear is not Mine, but the Father's which sent Me" (xiv. 24). "All things that I have heard of the Father I have made known unto you" (xv. 15). "And this is life eternal, that they might know Thee, the only true God, and Jesus Christ, whom thou hast sent. . . . . I have glorified Thee on the earth. . . . . I have manifested Thy name. . . . . I have given unto them the words which Thou gavest me. . . . . I have declared unto them Thy name and will declare it" (xvii. 3, 4, 6, 8, 26).

Theologians have with great care and accuracy pointed

out the similarity in thought, and even expression, of numerous passages in the Fourth Gospel and in the writing called the First Epistle of John. Regarding such similarity there can be no doubt. But the inference drawn therefrom by theologians is not absolutely justifiable. Such similarity does not necessarily imply identity of authorship: it may imply, and in this special instance does imply, the relation of master and pupil or of guide or teacher and disciple. Of two unknown authors bearing such a relation to each other, chronology or priority of existence will naturally decide which of the two was master and guide and which was follower or disciple. The writer of the Epistle declares himself to be a contemporary and associate of the Lord (i. 1, 2), and there is no reason to question his veracity, except perhaps the doubts raised by the corruptions that have been deceitfully introduced into his text. The writer of the Gospel (postulating that xxi. verses 24 and 25, are no part of the Gospel, as Bishop Westcott admits when he remarks "that they were probably added by the Ephesian elders")[1] does not claim to be an eye-witness, but the claim has been manufactured for him by theologians, beginning with Valentinus of the second century, and ending with Bishop Westcott of the nineteenth. The latter founds this claim not on direct but on circumstantial evidence, of a nature which no barrister would venture to lay before a jury, without serious damage to his case as well as to his professional reputation. By arguments and statements corresponding to those employed by the learned bishop, Carlyle may be demonstrated to have been an eye-witness of the scenes which he has graphically described in the French Revolution, to have been himself a Frenchman, a Frenchman of Paris, and to have conversed in pure Parisian; or that Freeman was an eye-witness of the Norman Conquest, which he describes with more minuteness of detail and precision of circumstances than can be found in the narrative of the Fourth

[1] I should express Bishop Westcott's proposition in the same way, but with a different allocation of the word probably: "they were added probably by the Ephesian elders." There is no doubt about the addition, but the perpetrators are not known, but only suspected. This is a very important admission by a great theologian, that probably Ephesian elders added to the Gospel.

Gospel. In this treatise direct evidence will be produced to prove that Cerinthus was the author of the Fourth Gospel, and if that fact be successfully demonstrated, it will necessarily follow that the author was not a Jew, not a Jew of Palestine, not an eye-witness, not an Apostle, and not the author of the First Epistle of John, though he undoubtedly uses the thoughts and religious ideas of the disciple of the Lord, who wrote the Epistle, in his own romantic composition.

The similarity of thought and expressions between the so-called First Epistle of John and the Fourth Gospel has been remarked by an ancient ecclesiastical writer, of high position in the Church, and of great intelligence. Dionysius, who held the important post of Bishop of Alexandria, a great seat of learning, in the time of Eusebius, end of the third and beginning of the fourth century, is the earliest writer who has prominently and sensibly brought the similarity to notice. Writing of the asserted identity of authorship of these two works and of the Apocalypse, all three being attributed to the Apostle John (Eusebius, *Eccl. Hist.*, vii. 25), Dionysius admits the identity of authorship of the first two, but excludes the latter writing. "The Gospel and Epistle," he says, "mutually agree, in their thoughts and words, and also in their composition, and they commence in the same way. . . . . He (*i.e.*, their author) keeps to the point, and does not stray from his subjects. . . . . The attentive reader will find in both a great deal of life, a great deal of light, turning away from darkness, holding the truth, grace, joy, the flesh and blood of the Lord, the judgment, forgiveness of sins, the love of God to us, the command to us of love to one another, that it is necessary to keep all the commandments; the condemnation of the world, of antichrist, the promise of the Holy Spirit, God's adoption of sons, the thorough faith demanded of us, and everywhere the Father and the Son; and altogether through all there is set forth the characteristics to perceive one and the same complexion of the Gospel and of the Epistle. . . . . For they are written not only without blundering as to the Greek language, but most learnedly in the diction, in the arguments, and in the structure of the style. It will require much to discover any barbarous word or solecism, or any odd peculiarity of expression in them. For, as it seemed, he (*i.e.*, the author) had the one and the other gift (λογον), that of knowledge and that of language, the Lord having granted both to him." (See also Cruzé's translation in Bohn's Library.)

The belief of theologians in the identity of authorship of these two writings is of old standing, and it will need a miracle to persuade them of their error. But I address here men and women possessed of common sense, which I am desirous they should bring to bear upon this subject. Dionysius, Bishop of Alexandria, a thoroughly competent critic, whose mother tongue was Greek, here expresses his opinion of the perfect knowledge and command of the Greek language displayed by the author of the Fourth Gospel and of the Epistle of John. Does it appear probable after such an opinion that the author of these writings was the Apostle John, a Galilean fisherman, whose earnings probably amounted to sixpence a day,[1] whose mother tongue was Hebrew, or rather Aramaic, but who perhaps had acquired a colloquial knowledge of Greek in his wanderings in foreign countries subsequent to the crucifixion, who had never received an education beyond what he acquired in boyhood from the village rabbi, and who is never known to have undergone literary instruction in after life, who had no Christian literature to study and thereby to educate himself? Under these circumstances it is not possible to conceive that an ignorant Galilean peasant could have risen to the effort of writing two treatises in Greek, the purity of which in expression and style has called forth the admiration of the learned Alexandrian prelate. Bishop Dionysius does not attempt to explain that the Galilean Apostle acquired this proficiency in a foreign language by methods ordinarily pursued by men. He attributes it not even to the force of human genius, that wonderful quality which has enabled men, under the most adverse circumstances, to achieve greatness. The utter inability to explain the phenomenon has compelled the bishop to attri-

[1] Tacitus states in his *Annals* that the pay of a Roman soldier amounted, in our money, to 8½ pence a day. A Galilean fisherman's earnings would naturally be less.

bute it to miracle, a grant of the gift of knowledge and of language from the Lord! John Bunyan is a close approach to the fictitious apostolic author of the Johannine writings, inasmuch as he also was an uneducated man in the lower ranks of society, who wrote a work that is esteemed as classical. But the author of the *Pilgrim's Progress* had undergone for long years a process of self-education by the perusal and study of translations of the magnificent Hebrew literature contained in the Bible, and of Christian literature of a high stamp. Bunyan further wrote his great work, not in a difficult foreign language, but in his mother tongue, and it is understood that the original composition had been corrected in its orthography and grammar in its passage through the press. Though much of Bunyan's achievement must be attributed to natural ability and genius, a process of self-instruction and self-education was undergone before he acquired the capacity to accomplish his great work. But in the case of the apostolic pseudo-author, there were no visible means by which he could have attained to his proficiency in the Greek language. The appeal to miracle is a theological pretence which cannot be accepted outside the sphere of superstitious credulity.

The fact, however, is that the Apostle John was not the author of the Fourth Gospel. All the knowledge that we possess of him is against such a proposition. We know him from evangelical history as a Galilean fisherman, the son and brother of fishermen, a disciple of the Lord, ignorant and uneducated, following a poor avocation, but after the crucifixion holding a high position in the early Church; and, from ecclesiastical history or tradition, as a man relentlessly persecuted, banished to a remote island in the Ægean Archipelago, and finally settling and ending his days at Ephesus, where he was buried. We do not hear of him as the author of the Johannine writings till towards the close of the second century, after which many details of his authorship are related in the subsequent centuries. So scanty is the information regarding him, that Eusebius, the first ecclesiastical historian of any importance, thought it worth while to record a curious story of John, the disciple of the Lord, meeting Cerinthus in a bath-house at Ephesus, and rushing from it, exclaiming, "Let us flee, lest the bath fall in, as long as Cerinthus, that enemy of the truth, is within" (Eusebius, *Eccl. Hist.*, iii. 28, and Irenæus, *Ad Heræs.*, III. iii. 4). This anecdote, while it reflects on the intelligence and Christian forbearance of the Apostle, certainly gives us the assurance that John differed from his brother James on the question of personal cleanliness, and that he and Cerinthus were contemporaries. But we have no anecdote regarding John's assiduity in the study of the Greek language. Irenæus, the pupil of Polycarp, and hearer of his discourses regarding his 'familiar intercourse' with John, is most disappointing in the meagreness of his recollections of anecdotes regarding John. Following the facts, scanty as they are, there can be no reasonable objection made to Cerinthus being the author of the Gospel in respect of his proficiency in Greek, which was his mother tongue. He was a Greek of Alexandria, skilled in the learning of the Ægyptians, and the founder of a sect of Gnostic Christians, for whose use he may reasonably be presumed to have written his work. We know that the early Christian sects possessed each a gospel peculiar to itself or in common with other sects; thus the early Hebrew Christians employed the Gospel to the Hebrews (Eusebius, *Eccl. Hist.*, iii. 25 and 27; Jerome, *Adv. Pel.*, i.), the Cainites had a special Gospel of Judas (Irenæus, I. xxxi. 1), Marcion had a Gospel for the Marcionites (Irenæus, I. xxxvii. 2), the Ophites and Naasseni (or Christian snake-worshippers) adopted the Gospel according to the Ægyptians, that according to Thomas, and the Fourth Gospel, which latter was also appropriated by the Valentinians (*Hippolytus*, Ante-Nicene Christian Library, v. 2, vol. i. pp. 130, 133, etc.). The later Valentinians, besides accepting several other gospels, constructed a special gospel for themselves, which they named "The Gospel of Truth" (Irenæus, III. xi. 2). The presumption that Cerinthus wrote a special work, afterwards called a gospel, is strongly supported by the fact that a sect existed in the second century, covertly alluded to by Irenæus as rejecting both the Fourth Gospel and Paraclete (Irenæus, III. xi. 9), but more fully discussed by Epiphanius (*Hær.*, li.), and called by him the Alogi, who ascribed the Fourth Gospel to Cerinthus, and for that reason rejected it as the work of a heretic. It is remarkable that no Christian writer of the second and third centuries has made any open allusion to this sect. Irenæus has omitted to state for what reason the party referred to by him rejected the Fourth Gospel. That the sect arose in the second century may be inferred from Irenæus's notice, and it was still in existence in the fourth century when Epiphanius wrote. It does seem strange that Clement, Hippolytus, Tertullian, Origen, and Eusebius altogether ignore the sect; while Epiphanius writes an extended account of it in the fourth century. There is a doubt in my mind whether the silence of writers of the third century was not due to design. The same reticence was presumably observed in the schools and churches. There is not a word in the great work of Irenæus, *Against Heresies*, to indicate that any mortal attributed the authorship of the Fourth Gospel to Cerinthus: yet he undoubtedly knew of a sect of heretics who maintained that fact. His allusion to the sect is so covert that at the present day there are learned men who do not comprehend it, and surmise that the sect referred to by him may have been the Montanists. Bishop Lightfoot's keen perception of the meaning of facts, when there are any, has guided him to the right understanding of the allusion (Lightfoot's Essays on *Supernatural Religion*, p. 215 and footnote 2). It was obviously deemed unwise by Irenæus to vulgarise the fact that there existed people, at the close of the second century, who ascribed the Fourth Gospel to Cerinthus. The *môt d'ordre* tacitly given by Irenæus was obeyed by the great writers who followed him in the next century. The men who practically settled the elements or first principles of ecclesiastical Christianity persistently avoided or refused to face the fact of a rival author of the greatest of the Gospels. They did not feel themselves able to combat the proofs which were doubtless available in that age, and were naturally unwilling to direct attention to them. After a century of teaching in the schools and preaching in the churches that John was the author of the Fourth Gospel, the statement had taken deep root in the minds of the Christian communities; and hence in subsequent centuries to the present day ecclesiastical writers were able fearlessly to allude to the Alogi simply as monstrosities or fools, who ascribed the authorship of the Fourth Gospel to a Greek philosopher of the first century, instead of to the well-known Galilean fisherman and Apostle. In my remarks on the silence of Christian writers of the second and third centuries on the subject of the Cerinthian authorship of the Fourth Gospel, I have depended on my perusal of the surviving works of the writers of this epoch. It would be unsafe on such a question to conjecture that a refutation of the Cerinthian authorship was made in the works of the period now lost. We have two comprehensive works by Irenæus and Hippolytus specially and solely devoted to the refutation of heresies: and in neither of them have I succeeded in discovering a refutation of the Alogi, whose main reason for rejecting the Fourth Gospel was that it was the composition of Cerinthus: nor is there any allusion in their extensive works to the sect beyond the covert reference in Irenæus already mentioned. Bishop Lightfoot says that a lost work of Hippolytus, entitled *In Defence of the Gospel and Apocalypse of John*, was apparently directed against the Alogi (Essays on *Supernatural Religion*, p. 215, footnote). This work is only known from its name appearing on the cathedra or episcopal chair of the statue of Hippolytus discovered in an ancient cemetery of Rome in 1551, and now standing in the Vatican Library. Bishop Lightfoot has not stated on what grounds[1] he justifies his statement of the contents of a lost and unknown work, which is not alluded to by any writer of the period or

---

[1] It is possible that Bishop Lightfoot's reason is contained in the remark, "It may be suspected that Epiphanius is largely indebted to this work for his refutation of them." The learned prelate had a fad that these ancient Fathers were so overmastered by piety and zeal that they copied freely from each other without acknowledgment. He wants us to believe that the fifth book of Irenæus was a copy from Papias: his object being to throw back the chronology of the Fourth Gospel. It may be generally admitted that theologians copy from each other, as lawyers, physicians, historians, and all others do: but it will never do to prove a point, especially in chronology, to say that a later writer copied wholesale from an earlier writer unless proof be forthcoming. Bishop Lightfoot gives no proof that Epiphanius was indebted to Hippolytus' lost work: his suspicion is merely his fad. A man cannot be imprisoned or hanged on suspicion founded on fad.

since: while the fact that Hippolytus is absolutely silent about the Alogi in his great work, is a good reason for the inference that he similarly avoided the subject in a smaller treatise. If, however, Bishop Lightfoot be correct in his conjecture, the vigorous and just remark of Bunsen on a certain class of early ecclesiastical literature would be applicable to the lost work: "A good specimen of that monstrous sort of lying literature, where truth is trodden under foot, in order to enthrone old fictions and impostures, aggravated and multiplied" (*Hippolytus and his Age*, Letter v.). I do not, however, believe that Hippolytus' work would have deserved so severe a censure.

Nor was the Galilean fisherman the author of the epistle ascribed to him. It is quite probable, if not certain, that Jesus had some educated followers derived from a higher class of society than fishermen and publicans. Nicodemus and Joseph of Arimathea, the former a ruler of the Jews and the latter a rich man, are examples. In ch. xii. 20–22 of the Fourth Gospel is a statement that certain Greeks sought an interview with Jesus. One can well imagine men of culture being attracted by the moral teaching of Jesus, without taking an active part in propagating it, and becoming apostles and preachers. Justin, a Greek philosopher of the second century, confesses that the moral teaching of Jesus was the source of his conversion, and in his great *Apology* it is the moral teaching of Jesus that he holds forth to the admiration of the emperors and the Romans. Most of the founders of the sects associated later with Christianity, and who greatly contributed to its corruption, were men of Greek culture and bore Greek names. It is more consonant with probability to ascribe the Greek epistle to a cultivated Greek follower and disciple of the Lord than to an ignorant and illiterate Hebrew fisherman hailing from Galilee.

The only English theologian, that I know of, who does not accept the popular belief that the Fourth Gospel was the work of the Apostle John is Dr Martineau, the nestor and *doyen* of English theologians. The same learned theologian withholds his assent to the popular belief that the Gospel and so-called First Epistle of John are by the same author.

Though Dr Martineau has formed his opinions on different grounds from those which have guided my judgment, our conclusions on these subjects are practically identical. My readers are referred to Dr Martineau's criticisms, written in majestic English, in his great work, *The Seat of Authority in Religion*, pp. 208-217, and pp. 509-512, second edition.

CHAPTER III.

POLYCARP'S MARTYRDOM. THE ASCENT OR RETURN FLIGHT OF THE DOVE TO HEAVEN. CERINTHUS, THE AUTHOR OF THE FOURTH GOSPEL. LUCIAN'S GREAT JOKE.

I HAVE now arrived at the final clause of my text from Irenæus, viz., "At the end Christ flew away from Jesus, and Jesus suffered." I have little doubt that many of my readers who have followed me thus far, with more or less agreement with me amongst those who are not of prejudiced minds, will now consider that I have at last reached the end of my tether, for how could such a strange text as this be exemplified in the Fourth Gospel. But this will shortly become apparent. When I first remarked, some ten years ago, the singular coincidence between the descent of the dove of Cerinthus and the dove story of the Gospels, I did not for a moment believe that it was possible to discover in the Gospels any incident corresponding with the return flight of the dove of Cerinthus, in the sad story of the crucifixion. The first glimpse of such a coincidence came upon me with surprise. I obtained it from the writings of an erudite bishop of the Church of England, a man of genius, whom I regard, under correction, as the greatest of his order whom this century has produced. But my surprise at the sight of the dove of Cerinthus at the crucifixion, as related in the Fourth Gospel, was almost eclipsed by my wonder that such a view had escaped the keen perception of the late Bishop Lightfoot of Durham, by whose clear insight my weaker vision had been most materially helped. Without the aid that I obtained from

Bishop Lightfoot's writings, I should never have seen the ascending dove of Cerinthus in the Fourth Gospel, for the necessary erudition and acumen were beyond my unassisted capacity.

I have now more especially to refer to the singular moral aberration of the early Christians, very marked in the second century, in surreptitiously altering, clipping, and adding to the writings of others without ceremony, in issuing false writings as genuine with great names attached, and doing other acts which come under the modern designation of forgery. I am distinctly of opinion that such acts were immoral, and therefore unchristian, and discountenanced by the great master and founder of Christianity. They were known by the perpetrators to be acts of dishonesty, and hence secrecy regarding them was observed. I have no desire to excuse or to consider such acts as not reprehensible because they were said to have been actuated by motives of piety; piety that leads to the commission of such acts is false and hypocritical. I regard all such persons—whether bishops, presbyters or others —as rogues who have committed acts of falsification of documents, or who have been accessory to or aware of such acts, before or after the fact, and have not exposed the fraud, but have accepted and declared the altered writings to be genuine, knowing them to be false. I have already shown how the Prologue of the Fourth Gospel had been altered so as to render it simply unintelligible—this being also a device of the forger; and how the dove story of Cerinthus had its purport gradually transmuted. It is now my task to show how the return flight of the dove of Cerinthus had been abolished in the Fourth Gospel. The means were simple to a degree. The returning dove was changed into water. To employ a commercial expression, it was liquidated.

In the second century flourished an eminent saint and martyr, Polycarp, Bishop of Smyrna, who was born about A.D. 69 or 70, and was martyred in A.D. 155 or 156. Irenæus was personally acquainted with Polycarp, and is supposed, so says Bishop Lightfoot, to have been a pupil of Polycarp sometime between A.D. 135–150. There exists an authentic account of Polycarp's martyrdom, and Bishop Lightfoot most satisfactorily demonstrates, from certain incidents and peculiarities found in this account, that the Fourth Gospel was in existence in the early half of the second century, a fact which had been called in question. As Bishop Lightfoot's remarks upon the account of Polycarp's martyrdom have a very important bearing on my subject, besides possessing their own inherent interest, I should advise the reader to peruse the original in the Essays on the work entitled *Supernatural Religion*, ch. vii. p. 220.

The account of Polycarp's martyrdom is contained in a letter, written immediately after the occurrence, from the Church at Smyrna to the Church in Philomelium, a village in Phrygia, and to the neighbouring Churches. In this letter the brethren of Smyrna point out the coincidence between the circumstances attending the death of their martyred bishop and the Passion of our Lord. "Nearly all the incidents," they say, "came to pass that the Lord from above might show to us a martyrdom according to the Gospel. For he remained that he might be betrayed, as did also the Lord." "This account," says Bishop Lightfoot, "is thus the earliest instance of a favourite type of hagiology, which sees the sufferings of Christ visibly reflected and imaged in detail in the servants of Christ, and of which ancient and mediæval biography furnishes numerous examples." The parallelism between the incidents preceding the martyrdom of Polycarp and those of the crucifixion is pointed out. The name of the convicting magistrate is Herod in both cases. The time of the martyrdom is the Passover, or 'the great Sabbath' as it is here called. Polycarp's place of refuge was ascertained by information obtained by torture from a young slave, who is compared to Judas: and hence Polycarp, like our Lord, was "betrayed by them of his own household." Polycarp, when arrested, was conveyed on an ass to the city, and hence a parallel to Christ's triumphal entry into Jerusalem. His capturers came on horseback and in arms, 'as against a robber.' And so forth.

Most of the incidents have their parallels recorded in the Synoptic Gospels alone or in common with the Fourth Gospel: but there are a few which have their counterparts in the latter alone, and were clearly derived from the Fourth

Gospel and no other. The voice from heaven saying, "Be strong, and play the man, Polycarp," corresponds, says Bishop Lightfoot, to the voice, recorded in John xii. 28, addressing our Lord from heaven. Again, though at the time the intention obviously was to throw Polycarp to the wild beasts, yet, in consequence of a vision, he predicts that he shall be burnt alive. A fortuitous circumstance frustrates the first intention and brings about the fulfilment of the prophecy as to the manner of his death. This was a parallel to Christ signifying by what death He should die (John xii. 32 and 33), although crucifixion, not being a Jewish mode of punishment, seemed at first most unlikely. The most obvious parallelism of all was in the singular incident which happened when the executioner thrust a sword into the body of Polycarp, when the flames failed to consume him: "there came forth a dove and a quantity of blood." This is an obvious parallel to the incident recorded in John xix. 34, when one of the soldiers pierced the body of Jesus, "and forthwith came thereout blood and water."

Nowhere has the great bishop displayed his consummate genius for historical investigation more admirably than in the above passage. These arguments place beyond dispute the parallelism between the dove incident in the account of the martyrdom of Polycarp and the return flight of the dove of Cerinthus in the original Fourth Gospel. It is in vain that the learned prelate endeavours to throw discredit upon the dove incident, by appending a note in which he says: "It is unnecessary for my purpose to inquire whether the words περιστερὰ καὶ [a dove and] should be altered into περὶ στύρακα [about the spear-head], according to Bishop Wordsworth's ingenious emendation, or omitted altogether, as in the text of Eusebius." Nobody should be at a loss to account for the omission in the text of Eusebius: he intentionally omitted it, in accordance with his avowed purpose to exclude everything that did not aggrandise the credit of the Church. Other readings, quite as ingenious as that suggested by the learned Bishop of Salisbury, viz., ἐπ' ἀριστερᾶ, on the left side; περὶ στερνὰ, about the chest; περὶ στερέων, about the middle ribs, offered by great scholars, have been disregarded by the long-headed men who have edited the writings of the Apostolic Fathers. Nor has Bishop Lightfoot himself considered the suggested amendment worthy of being introduced into the text in his own edition of the Apostolic Fathers. I take this passage of the account of the martyrdom of Polycarp, written about A.D. 156, to be the imitation of an original passage of the Fourth Gospel, and thus to give an indication of what the latter was. The account further gives us the early name of the Fourth Gospel, viz., the Gospel of Christ, the martyrdom being said to be according to or "of the pattern of the Gospel of Christ," κατὰ τὸ εὐαγγέλιον Χριστοῦ (ch. xix.). A difficulty now becomes obvious, for the story of the crucifixion in the Fourth Gospel shows the death of Jesus to have taken place before the departure of the dove from His body, which circumstance would be against the account of Irenæus, who says that Jesus suffered after the flight of the dove. The idea was, that so long as the divinity, *i.e.*, the Spirit or Word, in the form of a dove, remained in the body of Jesus, the latter was impassable, *i.e.*, not liable to suffering and death. The clue to the removal of this difficulty is supplied by the Vatican and Sinaitic versions of the New Testament, in which, after Matthew xxvii. 49, is introduced the following verse: "And another took a spear and pierced His side, and there came out water and blood" (see Revised Version on margin of this passage). This introduced verse follows immediately after the giving of the sponge soaked in vinegar, and thus is pointed out the original position of the statement regarding the piercing of the spear. Another indication given by this introduced verse in Matthew is the original position of the word *water* with regard to *blood*, and consequently of the words περιστερὰ καὶ, or *a dove and*, in the Greek text. I would finally call attention to the Greek word ἐξῆλθε, or *came out*, which is used both in the Fourth Gospel (ch. xix. 34) and in the account of the martyrdom of Polycarp (ch. xvi.), and indicates that the objects which escaped from the wound were not both liquids, in which case a verb signifying *to flow* would have been naturally employed, but that one of them was a solid and the other liquid, so that the use of a verb indicating the conjoint issue of bodies of opposite physical qualities was necessitated. From the above considerations, I restore the account of the crucifixion in the Fourth Gospel to its original form as follows: and I would finally call attention to the circumstance that the earlier reading, thus recovered, displays a more natural sequence of incident and remark than the received text.

FOURTH GOSPEL, ch. xix.

28. After this, Jesus knowing that all things were now accomplished, that the scripture might be fulfilled, saith, I thirst.

29. Now there was set a vessel full of vinegar: and they filled a sponge with vinegar, and put it upon hyssop, and put it to his mouth.

30 (34). But one of the soldiers with a spear pierced his side, and forthwith came thereout a dove and blood.

31 (35). And he that saw it bare record, and his record is true; and he knoweth that he saith true, that ye might believe.

32 (30). When Jesus therefore had received the vinegar, he said, It is finished: and he bowed his head, and gave up the ghost.

33 (31). The Jews therefore, because it was the preparation, that the bodies should not remain upon the cross on the sabbath day (for that sabbath day was an high day), besought Pilate that their legs might be broken, and that they might be taken away.

34 (32). Then came the soldiers, and brake the legs of the first, and of the other which was crucified with him.

35 (33). But when they came to Jesus, and saw that he was dead already, they brake not his legs.

36. For these things were done that the scriptures should be fulfilled, A bone of him shall not be broken.

37. And again another scripture saith, They shall look on him whom they pierced.

The amount of change from the prior text that had been effected in the received text is really remarkably little. It was a singular peculiarity of these erratic early Christians that with all their unceremonious alterations of the text of sacred writings to suit their own views, they, on the whole, limited the extent of modification to what was absolutely necessary and no more. In the number for August 1895 of the *Contemporary Review*, Professor Rendel Harris has shown how the early Palestinian and Syrian Churches without ceremony or scruple changed the diet of John the Baptist from 'locusts and wild honey,' as stated in the Canonical Gospels, to 'pancakes[1] and wild honey,' 'milk and honey,' and 'roots and honey,' to suit their own views regarding the proper dietary for a holy man. The letters of Ignatius and the Third Gospel, whether in the case of the latter writing, the Canonical text or the Gospel of Marcion be reckoned the original Gospel, are examples of more complicated modifications; but even in these lengthy forgeries the extent of the alterations are supposed to have been strictly regulated by the necessities of the object in view of the forgers. Throughout this investigation, which has extended over some ten years, I have been struck by the remarkably great results that have been effected by small changes, trifling verbal additions or omissions. The Fourth Gospel has been linked to the writing known as the First Epistle of John by the substitution of the small word ἄλλον, *another*, for the definite article τὸν, prefixed to Paraclete, in ch. xiv. 16; and upon this slight connection has been founded the declaration that the Fourth Gospel and the Epistle are productions of the same writer — of course other reasons being speedily forthcoming for the greater expansion of the connection. There are other passages in the Fourth Gospel which need examination, but these will be investigated further on, on the basis that the original author of the Gospel was Cerinthus. Sufficient proofs have, I trust, been brought forward to satisfy people of common sense that the credit of the authorship of the Fourth Gospel is due to Cerinthus, the Gnostic Christian of the first century. If the steps of my investigation and the conclusions to be drawn from them be found on scrutiny by others to be accurate and justifiable, the Fourth Gospel will be perhaps the only Gnostic writing of the first

---

[1] Such 'pancakes' were perhaps of the same nature as Scotch bannocks, Australian dampers, and Indian chapatties; plain wheaten or rye cakes broiled on a girdle over a charcoal fire or in hot ashes.

century that has survived to our time. The Fourth Gospel, concluding it to have been written by Cerinthus, not merely shows the intellectual quality and reverent disposition of Cerinthus, but it reflects light on the great Gnostics of the second century, Basilides and Valentinus, and on the majestic figure of Marcion, men who have been grossly abused by Christian writers of the second and subsequent centuries.

In the classic literature of the second century, I believe we obtain a glimpse of the Fourth Gospel in a travesty of the dove story in Lucian's account of Peregrinus, who voluntarily burnt himself to death at the Olympian games. What is most interesting in this essay of Lucian's is his frequent references to Christians. His account of them appears to me to be friendly and kindly; and although he holds them up to ridicule, the fun is good-natured. The perusal of Lucian has been of deep interest to me, as I have been much struck by the evidences of his personal knowledge of the Christians, and his familiarity with their amiable weaknesses, which afforded him subject for mirth. I find it difficult to persuade myself that he was unacquainted with the original Fourth Gospel. There is a peculiar expression employed in the Fourth Gospel, which in my judgment is singularly appropriate to the context in which it appears, but which has not found favour with the translators of our Authorised and Revised versions, who have, doubtless for reasons that seemed good to them, not translated it literally. I had never met with the expression in this context in any other writing, ancient or modern, until, to my utter surprise, I found it in Lucian's account of Peregrinus Proteus. In the pathetic address of Jesus to His disciples on His approaching parting from them occurs the following passage, which I translate literally from the Greek (John xiv. 18): "I will not leave you orphans:[1] I will come to you." In the Authorised Version the paraphrase used is 'comfortless,' and in the Revised Version 'desolate.' But Lucian uses the very word *orphans* employed in the Fourth Gospel, and the circumstances under which the expression is employed are parallel,

[1] The Vulgate and the German and French versions retain the word *orphans*.

viz., the approaching departure of Jesus and Peregrinus from this world. The passage is, of course, satirical. "Human life," says Lucian (ch. vi.), "has witnessed two great masterpieces, Jupiter Olympius and Proteus, the modeller and workman of the one being Phidias, of the other Nature. But now will this ornament of the world go away from men to the gods, leaving us orphans." There are two or three other passages in this essay which appear to me to be allusions to the death of Jesus, but they are too unpleasant to be pointed out. The following, however, may be noticed as a touch probably derived from the Fourth Gospel (iv. 46–53): "And, by Jove, it is not impossible that some amongst these numerous fools will be found saying that they were cured by him of the quartan fever" (ch. xxviii.). Peregrinus, or rather Proteus, for the latter name was preferred, is represented by Lucian to have been a vain but clever man, who did all sorts of things from the love of glory, and who finally resolved to convert himself into charcoal at the most numerous assembly in Greece, the Olympian games. He began life as a cynic philosopher, but he combined philosophy with adultery and other crimes, and finally with parricide, for which he had to fly his native land, and to take to wandering from country to country.

"About this time, associating with their priests and scribes in Palestine, he became acquainted with the admirable philosophy or wisdom of the Christians. What happened then? In a short time, becoming prophet, theasarch, and ruler of the synagogue, and himself singly everything, he proved them to be mere children: he expounded and commented on their books, and even wrote many himself. And they regarded him as divine, had him as lawgiver, and inscribed him president.[1] In fact, they still worship that great man who was fixed to a stake in Palestine, because he introduced these novel mysteries into life. Being then on this account apprehended, Proteus was cast into prison. But this very misfortune procured for him not a little consideration for the rest of his life, and the prestige and the popularity

---

[1] The term 'president' is used by Justin Martyr (*First Apology*, lxv.) to indicate the individual who officiated at the Eucharist, which in the second century was administered by laymen as well as by the clergy.

of which he was so fond. When, then, he was in confinement, the Christians, making the matter a common calamity, moved everything, trying to rescue him. But when this was not possible, every other attention was rendered to him, not perfunctorily but with zeal. Immediately after dawn there were to be seen old women, a few widows and orphan girls waiting about the prison; and the men who were in office even slept with him inside, having corrupted the jailers; moreover, food of various sorts was brought in for him, and their sacred words were read, and the most excellent Peregrinus (for he was still called this) was named the new Socrates.

"Nay, more, from the cities of Asia came some Christians, equipped at the common expense, rendering help, offering counsel, and consoling the man. For they display an activity that is something prodigious when any such public matter is in question. In short, they spared nothing. Much money, in fact, came in to Peregrinus at that time on pretence of his chains, and he made not a little provision. For these poor folk have persuaded themselves that they will be altogether immortal, and will live for all time. For which reason they even despise death, and many willingly give themselves up. Moreover, their first legislator persuaded them that they should be all brothers of one another; when, having once gone over, they renounce the Hellenic gods, they worship that sophist of theirs who had been fixed to the stake, and live according to the laws of that one. They despise all property equally, and regard it as common, accepting such views without any strict proof. If, therefore, a cheat or sharp-witted man should come amongst them, being able to use their goods, he in a short time became very rich, laughing at these simple people.

"But meanwhile Peregrinus was released by the then Governor of Syria, a man who wished well to philosophy, and who, knowing his vanity, and that he would accept death so that he might have renown on that account, dismissed him, not regarding him worthy of punishment. . . . . Then he set out a second time wandering, having some Christians as a sufficient source of supply, by whom, attended as a bodyguard, he had enough of everything. And thus he was maintained for some time: then having transgressed in some way even against them (for he was seen, as I believe, eating one of those things forbidden to them), they no longer associating with him, he fell into poverty."

Then after many adventures comes the final act of self-cremation at the Olympic games, of which Lucian declares himself to have been an eye-witness. And this is how he described it to noodles :—

"If, then, I saw an educated man like you, I related the naked facts of what was done: but to simpletons and those who gape with open mouths for the marvellous, I related something tragic of my own invention; such as, when the pyre was lighted, and Proteus rising cast himself in, a great earthquake having first taken place, with a bellowing from the earth, a vulture having flown up from the midst of the flames, went away to heaven, saying in a loud human voice, 'I have left earth, I go to Olympus.' They were then amazed, and trembling they bowed in obeisance, and inquired saying, did the vulture go off to the east or to the west? and I answered them whatever came into my head. Going thence to the great assembly, I encountered a grey-headed man, and by Jupiter, with his beard and his general venerableness, he was well worthy of belief from his appearance, recounting other things regarding Proteus, and that after the burning, he saw him in a white robe a little while ago, and had only just left him walking about serenely, crowned with wild olive, in the Porch of Seven Echoes; then to all this he tacked on the vulture, actually swearing that he had himself seen it flying up from the pyre; which I myself a little while before had let off to fly, laughing at the mob of simpletons and noodles." The reference to the resurrection is unmistakable. The declaration of the venerable preacher, that he saw the vulture, is an obvious travesty of John xix. 35: "And he that saw it bare record, and his record is true; and he knoweth that he saith true"; a statement which means that there was an actual witness of the flight of the dove, which was merely an invention of Cerinthus. The Porch of Seven Echoes was perhaps suggested by John x. 23: "And Jesus walked in the temple in Solomon's Porch."

The main point of interest in connection with the Fourth Gospel in the preceding account is the vulture; and the question is, What was the original of the vulture? Mr William Tuke, the learned translator of Lucian (1820), thinks the vulture was an imitation of the funereal eagle of the Roman emperors. He says, "In conformity to the description handed down to us by Herodian of the apotheosis of the Roman emperors, it formed a part of the solemnity to let an eagle fly up from out of the flaming pile of wood in which the corpse of the new deity was burnt, to intimate that this bird of Jupiter soared aloft, conveying with him the immortal part of the deceased to the seat of the gods. Lucian, therefore (for the purpose of diverting himself at once with Peregrine and with the weak souls with whom he conversed), causes a vulture to fly up from Peregrine's faggot-stack, and perhaps little dreamt that the Christians a couple of years afterwards would cause a dove to fly up from the flames of St Polycarp." Bishop Lightfoot, on the other hand, considers the account of the martyrdom of Polycarp to be of earlier date than Lucian's account of the cremation of Peregrinus Proteus. Speaking of the former, he says, "unless several points of resemblance are accidental, Lucian in his account of Peregrinus Proteus (*c*. A.D. 165) must have been acquainted with the document." These two learned writers disagree in their chronology; Mr Tuke dates the cremation of Peregrinus in A.D. 168. It is to be regretted that Bishop Lightfoot has not mentioned the points of resemblance which struck him in the accounts of the martyrdom of Polycarp and of the cremation of Peregrinus Proteus. It is clear, however, that the one great point of resemblance in which the accounts agree to differ, if I may be allowed to express myself thus, viz., the incident of the dove in the one account and of the vulture in the other, was not one of these resemblances which the bishop alludes to: for he believes the dove incident in the account of Polycarp's martyrdom to be an interpolation by a Christian forger of the fifth century. Turn which way you like in early Christian literature, the Christian forger, perhaps a bishop, a priest or monk, has to be kept in mind and guarded against. Bishop Lightfoot says, "this miracle [of the dove] appears only in the Pionian copies, not in Eusebius," and he declares it to be an interpolation. But unfortunately for this argument, Eusebius, a bishop of the Christian Church, was quite as capable of committing the forgery of omission, and in fact he makes no secret of this weakness but fully confesses to it, as the unknown scribe (a priest or monk) of the Pionian copies was of committing the forgery of interpolation. In this dilemma, the adjudication must be left to the judgment of the long-headed men who edit the literature of the past, and they have decided against Eusebius. Eusebius was aware of Lucian's joke regarding the flight of the vulture from the pyre of Peregrinus Proteus, a quondam Christian saint, and knew very well that it would not be to the credit of the Church to reproduce the story of the flight of the dove from the body of Polycarp. I regret to say that I must here charge Eusebius with another omission, intentionally committed with a definite object, viz., of parts of chaps. i. and xix. of the account of the martyrdom of St Polycarp, in which are the plain statements that the martyrdom was "conformable to the Gospel," and "was after the pattern of the Gospel of Christ," as Bishop Lightfoot translates the Greek. This omission was naturally necessitated by the more serious omission of the flight of the dove: for the two statements go together and explain each other. For without the dove incident, the Church of Philomelium, to which was addressed the letter of the Smyrnæans in which the martyrdom is described, or any other Church, ancient or modern, could not have understood how the martyrdom was after the pattern of the Fourth Gospel, *i.e.*, the Gospel of Christ, under which name the original Fourth Gospel was known in their times. For it could hardly be expected that these obscure and ignorant Christians, or even their more educated and enlightened successors of later times, could have possessed the acute mental perception of a Lightfoot, except their minds were assisted by the appearance of the dove. I regret to say that the account as given both by Eusebius and the Pionian copy does not justify Bishop Lightfoot's remark regarding the dove that emerged from the body of Polycarp, viz., " by the abruptness of its appearance an interpolation is suggested."

On the contrary, the narrator skilfully arranges the incidents of the martyrdom so as naturally to lead up to the appearance of the dove. He says, according to Bishop Lightfoot's translation, "the firemen lighted the fire. And a mighty flame flashing forth, we to whom it was given to see, saw a marvel, yea and we were preserved that we might relate to the rest what happened. The fire, making the appearance of a vault, like the sail of a vessel filled by the wind, made a wall round about the body of the martyr; and it was there in the midst, not like flesh burning, but like [a loaf in the oven or like] gold and silver refined in a furnace. For we perceived such a fragrant smell, as if it were the wafted odour of frankincense or some other precious spice." Could such a marvel as this come of itself without an efficient cause? What was the cause? The sequel explains. "So at length the lawless men, seeing that his body could not be consumed by the fire, ordered an executioner to go up to him and stab him with a dagger. And when he had done this, there came forth [a dove and] a quantity of blood, so that it extinguished the fire; and all the multitude marvelled that there should be so great a difference between the unbelievers and the elect." The body was subsequently burnt by the centurion without the least difficulty. The explanation of the marvel was perfect and complete, and such as the Christians of the second century would regard as marvellously natural and appropriate. The body of Polycarp could not be burned by the flames, however mighty they may be, so long as the divinity in the form of a dove was within the body of the blessed saint. The whole of this passage is quoted by Eusebius, with the exception of the words which Bishop Lightfoot has placed in brackets. Is there anything illiberal or disingenuous or unfair under the circumstances to say that Eusebius omitted these two passages in accordance with his avowed intention and purpose to omit everything in his history which was not to the credit or honour of the Church? It was assuredly not to the honour of the Church to compare a revered Christian saint, bishop and martyr, on such a sublime occasion, to a loaf baking in an oven, nor was it to the credit of the Church to reproduce a story which at once recalled to the mind Lucian's joke of the vulture flying away from the funeral pyre of the quondam Christian saint, Peregrinus, which had set all civilised Pagandom and educated Christendom laughing for a hundred years past. It was perfectly natural for a man of the fibre of Eusebius to have done as he undoubtedly did, to have suppressed what would bring ridicule on his religion and Church, thereby wilfully falsifying a public document. On the other hand, it is futile to charge the scribe of the Pionian copy of the account of Polycarp's martyrdom with the invention of an incident surprising and unexpected no doubt, but this was the very essence of the miracle, which was manifestly arranged to follow after the marvellous narrative of mighty flames respectfully abstaining from carbonising the body of the blessed saint as an explication of the marvel. Did the Pionian scribe, who was doubtless a Christian priest or monk, also invent the amusing comparison of the blessed saint, still living and exhaling perfumery, to a loaf cooking in an oven? Bishop Lightfoot has expressed no opinion upon this latter point. In the second century there were undoubtedly great numbers of simple Christian people who accepted these strange stories as sacred or religious truths; but I hesitate to believe that the bishops of the nineteenth century have many followers who regard such stories as anything else than humorous and mirth-moving narratives.

My conclusion is that Lucian's story of the vulture is a travesty of the flight of the dove to heaven in the original Fourth Gospel. The narrator of the martyrdom of Polycarp describes it as "an example of martyrdom which is conformable to the Gospel" (ch. i.), and "that it was after the pattern of the Gospel of Christ" (ch. xix.). Bishop Lightfoot has proved with a precision and force that has convinced me that the Gospel alluded to by the narrator is the Fourth Gospel: and, if the Fourth Gospel, it must have been the original Fourth Gospel, which contained the story of the return flight of the dove, an imitation of which was reproduced in the martyrdom of Polycarp. The next reasonable and justifiable inference is that the original Fourth Gospel was read in the Churches of Smyrna and Philomelium, and if in these places then likewise in others, in Philadelphia, Tralles, Sardis, Laodicea, Ephesus, Thyatira, Magnesia, Colossæ, Pergamum, and other places in that part of Asia Minor, and was preached by itinerating apostles and prophets. Bearing in mind the zeal of the early Christians, it is not a great stretch of inference to conclude that the Fourth Gospel had spread beyond these limits to the rest of Asia Minor, even to Cappadocia, Pontus and Paphlagonia, and to Syria, and that it was read in the churches of these regions and preached about the country in the second half of the second century, about seventy years after Cerinthus had written it, and during the lifetime of Lucian, a Syrian who had travelled in Asia Minor. Lucian had a better knowledge of Christians than any Pagan writer who preceded him: he speaks of them as being very numerous in Pontus (*Alexander, or the False Prophet*, ch. xxv.). It is not improbable under the circumstances that he may have heard the original Fourth Gospel, called in those days the Gospel of Christ, read out in the Christian churches, which were freely open to the Pagans, or from the itinerant preachers or even from his Christian friends. The words 'leaving you orphans,' which Lucian employs, occurs, so far as I know, in no ancient composition that has survived to our times, except the Fourth Gospel and Lucian's Essay, *De Morte Peregrini*, and the Fourth Gospel is the work of greater antiquity of these two. I think it more probable that Lucian had an acquaintance with the original Fourth Gospel or the Gospel of Christ, a great and important work, rather than, as Bishop Lightfoot thinks, with an epistle addressed to an obscure body of Christians in a remote inland village of Asia Minor: though he may have seen or heard both, or the latter only. But in any case, in my opinion, the vulture of Lucian was the imitation of the dove of Cerinthus. The whole subject of the death of Peregrinus, translated literally, in order to place those who are unacquainted with Greek on an equality with those who read Greek, is now before the reader, and he is free to exercise his common sense in judging whether Lucian had in mind the dove of Cerinthus when he perpetrated the greatest joke of antiquity that has come down to our times.

CHAPTER IV.

THE ORIGINAL MATERIALS AND ORIGIN OF THE SYNOPTIC GOSPELS. CHRISTIANITY A MORAL SYSTEM IN THE FIRST CENTURY, CORRUPTED INTO A RELIGIOUS SYSTEM IN THE SECOND CENTURY. MEANS OF THE CHANGE. JEWISH AND GNOSTIC OR GREEK CORRUPTIONS. PARACLETE.

THOUGH the main body of the Fourth Gospel was the composition of Cerinthus, he was not the sole author of the complete work that has come down to our times. There are clear evidences of contributions to it by other hands. It was not possible that a work of its importance could have passed through the sectarian conflicts of the second century without considerable alterations and additions being made by the sects into whose hands it fell from time to time. I have not been able to find any evidence that the Fourth Gospel was officially adopted by the Parent Church in the first half of the second century and generally read in all the churches in all parts of the Roman Empire. The Gospel of Christ of Cerinthus had the same career as the Gospel of Peter, as the Gospel to the Hebrews, the Gospel of the Ægyptians and others: limited at first to a special sect for whose benefit it was originally written, its currency gradually extended to other sects and even to isolated orthodox churches or groups of such churches, as the asperity of sectarian variances gradually abated or wore off. A sect or an orthodox congregation found a writing employed by a rival sect which contained much that was congenial to it: it unceremoniously took it, removed such matter as was grievously objectionable and appended such additions as would make the adopted gospel more agreeable to its members. It is only by an hypothesis of this nature, in the dearth of definite facts, that we are able to account for the circumstance that divergent sects are found to have used certain gospels and religious writings in common. There is no other way of explaining the singular fact that the Parent Church in the second half of the second century took possession of gospels written for and current amongst sects that were in rivalry with it. The act being of a nature that was common and general, and widely practised in the Christian communities of various sorts, appears to have drawn no special attention; and with the single exception of the protest made by some Christians, undoubtedly orthodox, against the adoption of the Fourth Gospel by the Parent Church, there is no notice amongst Christian writings of the period of any opposition made to such appropriation of sectarian gospels.

It has not been hitherto ascertained what special writings were regarded by the Parent Church as authoritative on the subject of the biography and teaching of the Founder, in the first century and the greater portion of the second century to a decade or two from its close. Justin Martyr, who wrote as late as A.D. 150, gives us information which is obscure. He was on the whole well-informed on the biography and teaching of Jesus: but there were some points in the history of Jesus with which he was unacquainted (or perhaps it would be just to say, he does not speak of), and there are some other points which are in excess of our own knowledge and not to be found in the orthodox and authoritative Christian literature which we possess, and there are some points on which his information does not correspond with ours. The familiar names of Matthew, Mark, Luke, and John are not mentioned by him in association with the writings from which he derived his information. He refers in one passage (*First Apology*, lxvi.) to "the apostles, in the memoirs composed by them, which are called Gospels," in others (ch. lxvii., and *Trypho*, cvi.) "the memoirs of the Apostles," and of their followers, in a third (*Trypho*, cvi.) to the "memoirs of him," and it is uncertain from the context whether the memoirs of Peter or the memoirs of Jesus are meant. These memoirs, recollections, or *memorabilia* (ἀπομνημονεύματα, *commentaria*) are stated by Justin to be the sources of his information. Whether a writing of this name, *Memoirs of the Apostles*, existed as an official publication of the Parent Church in the first half of the second century is unknown; but we can find no trace of it in other writings, and no writing of that name has come down to our times. The probability, if not certainty, is that Justin used the expression 'memoirs' to indicate the numerous writings and story-books regarding Jesus, his birth, sayings and doings, which we certainly know were current in the first half of the second century. Had there existed in his days authoritative and accredited writings of the Gospel story bearing the names of Matthew, Mark, Luke, and John, we should have expected that he would have mentioned them. The surprising fact must, however, be realised that these familiar names are conspicuous in Justin's comprehensive writings by their absence. In his Apology to the Roman Emperors the mention of the names of Apostles and early disciples would have given force and value to his quotations from their writings, just as did the mention of the names of Moses and Isaiah (*First Apology*, lxiii., lix., liv., etc.), Ezekiel (lii.), Jeremiah (li.), Zephaniah (by mistake for Zechariah xxxv.), and Micah (xxxvi.). Not only are the familiar names of the evangelists of later times absent from the memorial to the Roman Emperors (who were as little acquainted with Christian writers as with Hebrew prophets), but their absence is equally conspicuous, and if possible even more remarkable, in the interminable dialogue with Trypho the Jew, who was acquainted with the Christian literature of the period (*Trypho*, x.). Justin mentions the Apocalypse and its author John (*Trypho*, lxxxi.), a fact from which it may be inferred that he had no antipathy to the mention of the names of Christian writers, and that he was not in fear of offending the alleged delicate modesty of the early Christian scribes by trumpeting forth their names, or of breaking the custom of not mentioning names said to be observed by Christian apologists. Justin mentions an ancient story-book called *Acta Pilati; or the Acts of Pilate*, to which he refers the Roman Emperors in his *Apology* (i. 48) as an authority for information on the healing miracles of Jesus, wrought in fulfilment of prophecy. This writing, since called also the Gospel of Nicodemus, has survived to our times, and the depositions of witnesses before Pilate on the subject of their cure by Jesus are found in it (see Ante-Nicene Christian Library, *The Apocryphal Gospels*, p. 133; Tischendorf's *Evangelia Apocrypha*, p. 225 ff.). Justin refers the emperors to the *Memoirs* and to the *Acta Pilati*, without distinction, as writings of equal authority and credibility. We know the merits of the *Acta Pilati*, and are justified in regarding the *Memoirs of the Apostles* as of the same quality. Justin's beliefs and doctrines, as he declared them in his Memorial to the Roman Emperors, were based upon the *Acta Pilati* and the *Memoirs of the Apostles*. Though I find no mention made by him of the evangelists Matthew, Mark, Luke, and John, or of their writings, it is clear that he was acquainted with much of the information regarding the evangelical story of Jesus which is to be found in the Canonical Gospels. The main deficiencies of his information, if I may so regard what he has omitted to speak of, are the miracles of Jesus, apart from those of healing, the parables, with the exception of the sower (*Trypho*, cxxv.), and the story of Judas. Justin was also silent or ignorant regarding the ascension of Jesus on a cloud, and the descent of the Holy Ghost at Pentecost, and other stories related in the Acts.

I think I am justified in concluding from the works of Justin, that in his day the writings recognised by the Parent Church were those that Justin utilised. We are acquainted with the *Acts of Pilate*, a work still surviving; but the identity of the *Memoirs of the Apostles* quoted by him has not yet been ascertained. As the numerous texts cited by Justin from these *Memoirs* correspond in great measure with passages in the Synoptic Gospels, and their variances with these are not greater than the variances of the Synoptics between themselves, I think it is justifiable to conclude broadly that the same materials were used by Justin and the Synoptic writers, *i.e.*, Justin and the Synoptic writers used in common documents which were recognised and sanctioned by the Church. As Justin had no temptation or reason to modify the language of the documents he used, such as the Synoptic writers had while writing a continuous narrative and arranging the position of discourses and sayings of Jesus when chronology or the sequence of events was in sad confusion, I consider that Justin's quotations are exact transcripts from the original documents, while the Synoptic writings were necessarily not exact transcripts in all passages.

The history of the documents used in common by Justin, the Synoptic writers, and by other Christian writers of the period, documents which obviously were accepted and approved by the Church, is a subject of the utmost importance, exceeding that of the history of the Synoptic Gospels. Regarding the latter, a clue to their origin is to be found in the result of my investigation into the origin of the Fourth Gospel. This, the most prized Gospel of the four, we found to have been a wholesale appropriation of the writing composed by Cerinthus, for the use, obviously, of his own sect. I have not yet fully investigated the Synoptic Gospels, and hence my views regarding them are still in the formative stage. But so far as I have gone, I perceive the great probability of a similar origin to the Synoptic Gospels. The Third Gospel, that according to Luke, has a remarkable similarity to the Gospel used by Marcion for his sect. We know as an absolute fact that Marcion flourished in the first half of the second century, but we have no knowledge of Luke or of his Gospel as existing at this period. Irenæus and Tertullian accuse Marcion of pirating the Gospel of Luke, and of mutilating it to suit his own purposes. But they give no evidence that Luke or his Gospel was contemporary with or anterior to Marcion ; their works contain much assertion and more vituperation and invective, which do not bring historical conviction to my mind. The origin of the Gospels of Matthew and Mark is more obscure. In apostolic times, the Christians, who were Jews, like Jesus and Paul, retained the ritual and discipline of the Jewish law; in fact, continued to be of the Jewish religion. In course of time, as Christianity extended and Gentile converts increased, the proportion of Jewish Christians was naturally reduced, and they were regarded as a sect. These Christian Jews participated in the second century in the corruptions introduced into the system of Jesus. We find Irenæus (I. xxvi. 2) speaking of them, immediately after his account of Cerinthus, under the name of Ebionæi, as heretics whose opinions were similar to those of Cerinthus and Carpocrates, that they observed the Jewish law, and used the Gospel according to Matthew only. Hippolytus (*Ref.*, x. 18) also states that they regarded Christ in a similar manner with Cerinthus, but he does not endorse Irenæus' statement that they used the Gospel of Matthew. Eusebius (*Eccl. Hist.*, iii. 27) speaks of the sect in a similar fragmentary manner. According to him, they were two branches of the sect: one (obviously the earlier sect) denied the miraculous birth of Jesus; the other accepted it. The latter used the Gospel according to the Hebrews only. Later on, the Ebionæi or Ebionites or Nazarenes are said, by Jerome, to have used the Gospel of Matthew. These facts are rather scanty on which to base the obscure origin of these two Gospels; and I can only make a reasonable conjecture. The Jewish characteristics of these Gospels give grounds for the conclusion that they were of Jewish origin. The earlier Ebionite sect received the dove of Cerinthus, but rejected the miraculous birth, both facts being impressed on their unknown Gospel; the later sect admitted both the dove and the miraculous birth, and used the Gospel of the Hebrews. When these Gospels were appropriated by the Parent Church, they were christened the Gospels of Matthew and Mark. The Gospel of the earlier sect (the new Gospel of Mark) was the older of the two. These four Gospels, namely the Cerinthian, Marcionite, and the two Ebionite Gospels, were presumably chosen from the mass of sectarian gospels accumulated in the second half of the second century, on account of relative superiority of diction, and a certain freedom from ultra-fantastic statements. We have little or no knowledge regarding the rejected Gospels, except of one, the Gospel of Peter, a large fragment of which was recently discovered. Judging from this fragment, the Gospel of Peter may be justly described as a screaming religious farce; and notwithstanding its great antiquity, its rejection by the Church can be only approved. The rest of the rejected Gospels were presumably of the same quality, and were rightly deemed unfit to be introduced into the religious repertory of a Church progressing in intelligence.

I have alluded to the corruptions of the Church; but the Church is now so thoroughly corrupt that it is necessary to say what the word in this connection indicates. I take it as a fact manifest in the early Christian writings that Jesus introduced no new religion. He was himself a Jew, was born, lived, and died a Jew, so far as we know anything of his career. His Jewish followers, eleven of the twelve Apostles,[1] Paul and others remained Jews, and we have no evidence that they renounced Judaism.[2] The Ebionites or Christian Jews remained Jews and observed the law for centuries. I regard these indisputable facts as inconsistent with a new religion, assumed to have been introduced by the founder of Christianity. Jesus showed no active disposition to effect a change in the prevailing religions of the time, nor his disciples in the first century. Jesus postulated a belief in God and no more on the side of religion; but he demanded a personal moral regulation of the thoughts, feelings, and conduct of individual men and women by themselves. His system was indifferent to religion, except the belief in God, though it was consistent with every known religion. A disciple of Jesus, or a genuine Christian, may be a Jew, Pagan, Mahomedan, Buddhist, Mormon, or anything else. Justin was conscious of this great fact, for he says: "Whatever things were rightly said among all men are the property of us Christians;" "the teachings of Plato are not different from those of Christ, but they are not in all respects similar, as neither are those of the others, stoics, and poets, and

[1] Simon the Canaanite, one of the twelve, was a Pagan; but we have no evidence of his conversion to Judaism or of his abandonment of Paganism.

[2] The pious Eusebius admiringly quotes Hegesippus, 'an ancient and apostolic man,' who valiantly states that James, the brother of the Lord, and first Bishop of Jerusalem, officiated in the Temple of Jerusalem as a priest and high priest, while acting as the head of the Christian Church at Jerusalem. "To him only it was permitted to enter the holies" (Eusebius, *Eccl. Hist.*, ii. 23). As Joseph the carpenter and his sons were of the tribe of Judah and not of Levi, from which alone were derived the Jewish priests and high priests, this historical statement is a sample of the use of the long bow.

historians;" Christ "was partially known even by Socrates" (*First Apology*, xxxiii., Ante-Nicene Christian Library). Clement of Alexandria proposes Pagan philosophers as models of morality for the imitation of Christians[1] (see page 318). Provided the system of morality announced by Jesus was followed, the religious beliefs of the man, beyond the belief in God, were a matter of indifference; the obvious, though perhaps erroneous, expectation being that the extraneous beliefs will follow and become consistent with the morality.[2] The system of morality announced by Jesus contained in its elements nothing new: these elements were announced before him by men holding the multifarious religious systems prevailing in his time and for centuries before, by Hebrew prophets, Greek and Roman philosophers, Persian, Indian, and Chinese sages. The gratitude of mankind is due to Jesus for inculcating *the personal practice of morality by individuals, each by himself and herself*: and it is unjust to hold him responsible for the knavery and roguery of *soi-disant* followers, perpetrated long after his death.

The system of Jesus being a system of morality postulating a belief in God, every addition that was made to it after His disappearance from public life which tended directly or indirectly to convert it into a religious system was a corruption. I can only deal here with the corruptions that have a direct connection with my subject. These corruptions may be

[1] The brilliant phalanx of smart curates should remember the opinions of these great fathers. I have heard one, and he is not a solitary example, speak of agnostics in the pulpit, in a tone not of compassion but of contempt, as lost ignoramuses. College dons would do well to utilise a few odd moments to instruct theological students regarding Darwin, Spencer, Huxley, and other agnostics, who lived lives which are models of pure living, and who were certainly not ignoramuses.

[2] A teacher of morality can be as indifferent to the religion professed by his pupils as a teacher of chemistry, astronomy, law, medicine, or the natural sciences. It is a matter of unconcern to a teacher of physiology if some of his pupils profess a religion in which their god or gods came into being from virgins impregnated by ghosts, through the ear or any other mode: he teaches the function of generation and reproduction all the same, and leaves the knowledge he imparts to have its natural effect. The teacher of morality is, or ought to be, on the same footing as the teacher of physiology. I can find no evidence that Jesus taught religion along with morality.

roughly divided into two classes—supernatural and metaphysical—the former proceeding almost solely from the Jewish disciples and the latter from the Greek disciples. The unexpected reappearance of Jesus after the crucifixion produced a belief that he rose from the dead, a belief that can only have arisen originally amongst people of extreme ignorance, such as Jesus' earliest disciples, or most of them, are represented in Christian writings to have been. Amongst people of moderate intelligence the natural inference would have been that Jesus had recovered from injuries that had proved insufficient to cause death.[1] The erroneous belief, however, spread, and doubtless was instrumental in bringing in more followers to accept the moral system which Jesus had inculcated. The belief in the resurrection was the first corruption of Christianity, as it endowed the person or body of Jesus its founder with the supernatural attribute of spontaneous resuscitation after death. It is manifest that this corruption was the outcome of pure ignorance; but it is an undoubted fact in the history of the human race, that a belief, however started, whether due to ignorance or to fraud, if it be held by a number of people, however ignorant, is apt to infect the minds of people of a higher grade of intelligence and to be accepted by them. The fact is certain that Paul, an educated Jew, shared the belief, when he met with Jesus not long after the crucifixion. But it is also clear that the belief was not universal amongst the followers of Jesus, and was not, for the first two centuries at least, considered by the Christian community of the importance that was given to it subsequently (see page 205). Paul deduced, apparently as a corollary from his belief in the resurrection, that Jesus would never again die, but would remain immortal on earth. This secondary belief he had the good sense to abandon, or perhaps substantially to modify it into 'knowing him no more' in the flesh on be-

---

[1] Tertullian says, *De Carne Christi*: "*Crucifixus est Dei Filius: non pudet, quia pudendum est. Et mortuus est Dei Filius: prorsus credibile est, quia ineptum est. Et sepultus resurrexit, certum est, quia impossibile est.*" The Son of God was crucified: one should not be ashamed of it because it is a thing to be ashamed of. And the Son of God died: it is above all things credible, because it is absurd. And He was buried and rose again; this is certain, because it is impossible.

coming aware of a substantial reason for the abandonment
or change (see page 202). Crucifixion was an ignominious
mode of punishment, especially repulsive and horrible to
the Jewish mind. It will be admitted that the Jewish disciples must have bitterly felt the undeserved infamy that had
befallen the memory of their beloved master, who, though
still living, was socially dead. It required an ingenious mind,
of higher than the common order, to contrive a means of
covering the stigma of a shameful death. Hence, I think,
the device adopted was the offspring of the education and
talent of Paul, and not of the generally ignorant mind of the
Christian society. To Paul, I think, must be attributed the
ingenious conversion of the ignominious death of Jesus on
the Cross to what the Jewish as well as the Greek mind
would revere as a noble sacrifice to God in expiation and
redemption of sin. To Paul must be attributed the initial
institution of the conversion and degradation of the moral
system inculcated by Jesus into a religious system, which in
the second century was aggravated by fraud, greed of money,
of influence, and of power into a religion which, for many
centuries, has covered the civilised portions of the earth with
mental darkness and with the tears and blood of mankind,
which suffocated the moral teaching of Jesus while it utilised
it for the aggrandisement of its hierarchy in wealth and
power. Ecclesiastical Christianity has been the most successful financial and commercial enterprise in history. Even
now in the days of its decadence, hemmed in, as it is, and
restricted on all sides by the forces of civilisation, it has
no peer in financial prosperity, and hence is a formidable
opponent to the might of modern legislatures. But though
Paul originated the ideas which subsequently evolved the
materials from which a religion was constructed, he himself
preached no new religion. His efforts were directed to the
inculcation of the morality taught by Jesus; and he was
desirous of persuading the Jews to accept the belief that he
himself had in the resurrection, without disturbing their belief
and practice of pure Judaism; and he was a strenuous opponent of the conversion of the Gentiles to Judaism as a preliminary condition for their admission into the Christian society.

I am unable to convince myself that the Christian association or ἐκκλησία deified Jesus in the first century. I can find no statement, expunging interpolations and glosses of the second century, in Paul's writings or in the writings of others in the first century, that could justify the inference. The supernatural idea of the body or person of Jesus had probably penetrated the Christian mind; a body that had spontaneously revived from death, and believed possibly by some, besides for a season by Paul himself, to be incapable of dying again. But beyond that, I find no further advance in the first century. The utmost extent of Paul's supernatural belief may have been that Jesus was an angel of God,[1] as Gal. iv. 14 may be interpreted to mean: the Jews having a belief that angels were a divine race of beings, human in form and attributes, the messengers of God, immortal, but not objects of adoration. There was, however, some belief that was struggling to establish itself towards the close (seventh or eighth decade) of the first century, the exact nature of which I find myself unable to discern. The existence of it can only be inferred from the writing called the First Epistle of John, of which the main object appears to have been to condemn the struggling belief, which must negatively be described to have been that Jesus Christ did not come in the flesh (1 John iv. 3). How it was proposed that he did come is not stated, and I am unable to penetrate the dense darkness that pervades this period of Christian history.

Such history as we possess of the doings of the original Apostles of Jesus gives no information that they taught a new religion. The profession of a new religion implies the abandonment of the previous religion held; but I can gather no

---

[1] It is singular that the Mormons, who were organised into a Church in 1830, regarded their founder as an angel in 1881, or perhaps earlier. In a work by W. G. Marshall, M.A., named *Through America, or Nine Months in the United States*, 1881, is a report of an excellent sermon delivered by the Mormon elder Cummings on Rev. xiv. 6 and 7. The preacher expounding the verse said: "We claim that this angel that John saw, ninety-six years after the commencement of the Christian era, was Joseph Smith." I am unaware that Joseph Smith has yet been deified. Bishop Westcott alludes to the angel of the Revelations in connection with Joseph Smith, but I cannot recall the passage.

evidence that the religion of individuals was abandoned when they were received into the Christian society. The Acts of the Apostles is a chronicle containing things probable and credible, things improbable and incredible, things positively false and which could be proved to be so, and things which are anachronisms, that is, offices, customs and usages of the second century are spoken of as in existence in the first century in apostolic times. I believe the Acts of the Apostles was written in the second century, and was in great part a falsification, partly intentional and partly unconscious, of early Christian history. But unreliable as this chronicle is in general, it gives no information indicating that a new religion was inculcated by the original Apostles. One remarkable circumstance, perfectly probable and credible, frequently mentioned in the Acts, is that the Apostles preached in the synagogues of the Jews (ix. 20; xiii. 5, 14; xiv. 1; xvii. 2, 10; xviii. 4, 19, 26; xix. 8; xxiv. 12). Is it likely that a turbulent, aggressive and intolerant people like the Jews of the first century would have permitted a new religion to be preached in their own synagogues? Human nature was pretty much the same in the first century as it is in the nineteenth. Would the Jews allow such a proceeding in the present day in their synagogues? Would the Dissenters allow Mormons or Mahomedans to preach their strange religion in their meeting-houses? Would the churches of the Anglican and Roman religions be placed at the disposal of missionaries of a new religion? The subjects that the Apostles preached in the synagogues were 'the Word of the Lord,' 'the Way of God,' 'the Word of God,' that 'Jesus was Christ,' that 'Christ was the Son of God,' and 'Jesus and the resurrection.' The Jews objected to the statement regarding the resurrection of Jesus, and mobbed the Apostles. Festus described the accusation made by the Jews against Paul, when he referred the subject to King Agrippa, as "certain questions against him of their own superstition, and of one Jesus, which was dead, whom Paul affirmed to be alive" (Acts xxv. 19). In the private interview of Paul with Felix, who was desirous of knowing the "uttermost of the matter" (xxiv. 22), Paul "reasoned of righteousness, temperance, and judgment to come" (v. 25). In these statements I am unable to perceive the doctrines of a new religion, but merely an interpretation of the Mosaic Law and the prophets, according to the view taken by the Apostles of the mission of Jesus. I perceive no trace of the attribution of divinity to Jesus, not a tittle regarding His incarnation and birth from a virgin, which with the resurrection and ascension on a cloud form the religious basis of ecclesiastical Christianity, and constitutes its claim to be a religion. To accept the teaching of the Apostles, the Jews were not called upon by them to renounce Judaism: the teaching was not inconsistent with the religion of the Jews. In the same manner I find statements in the Acts that the Apostles preached not only to the Jews in the synagogues, but also to the general public, who were Pagans. Pagans were accepted as disciples by the Apostles, and they formed with Jewish disciples a mixed association, both being called 'Christians' (Acts xi. 26). In the Christian society at Antioch the Pagans outnumbered the Jews: yet, notwithstanding their numerical majority and the attention that numbers usually obtain, I find no statement that the Pagans were required to abandon Paganism. Their only qualification was to accept the belief in Jesus, and his resurrection, and the Word of the Gospel, exactly the same qualification as was required of the Jewish Christians. The religion professed by the applicant for admission into the Christian association was no hindrance to his reception, and there is no statement that he was called upon to renounce it. We know as a definite fact that the Jews retained their religion, and I am hence justified in concluding that the Pagans also retained theirs. In the Christian association or ecclesia at Jerusalem, the Pharisees, who were members, who are known to be an aggressive and fanatical party amongst the Jews, objected to the Pagans and demanded that they should be circumcised and made to adopt Judaism (Acts xv. 5). A dispute on the subject arose, and the question was considered by the Apostles. In the discussion which followed, Peter is represented as saying that God had chosen that " the Gentiles should by my mouth hear the Word of the Gospel and believe," and had " put no difference between us and them, purifying their hearts by faith." James' opinion is declared to have been "that we trouble them not, which from among the Gentiles are turned to God." The unanimous decision arrived at was that 'no greater burden' be put upon the Pagans than the following 'necessary things': abstinence from meats offered to idols and from blood, from things strangled, and fornication. This decision was favourably received by the Pagans, and "they rejoiced for the consolation" (Acts xv. 4-31). It would be a great strain on credulity to regard these four 'necessary things' as equivalent to an abandonment of the Pagan religion: the Pharisees could not have regarded Christianity or the Christian ecclesia, of which Pagans were members, as a distinct religion of itself; and the reasonable conclusion is that the Pagan members of the ecclesia or society retained their own religion.

In Paul's hands, early Christianity approximated more to a religion. He introduced religious innovations, which I regard as corruptions of the moral system of Jesus. Paul condemned idolatry and the usages of Paganism. These, though very undesirable, were not incompatible with good morals, and their exclusion was not essential.[1] Paul's views were impressed on the societies or ecclesiæ which he established amongst Pagan communities in Galatia. But these societies or ecclesiæ were manifestly not satisfied with, and did not consider, Paul's Christianity, which they accepted, as a religion. After Paul's departure, they reverted to idolatry and Pagan usages, although still adhering to Christianity (Gal. iv. 8-9), and continuing in the membership of the Christian society. Some Pagan members were desirous of adopting Judaism, which Paul objected to as unnecessary (Gal. iv. 21). These facts will be remarked in the passages quoted from Paul's Epistle to the Galatians. He speaks with contempt of idolatry and Pagan customs, as "beggarly elements, whereunto ye desire again to be in bondage." He is very wrathful with the proposal to adopt Judaism, expresses

---

[1] The reader should bear in mind that Virgil, Lucretius, Cicero, Seneca, Socrates, Plato, Epictetus, Theophrastus, Cornelia, Zenobia, the Catos, Brutus, Julius Cæsar, Marcus Aurelius, and many others were Pagans, whose morality will bear comparison with that of Christian writers, poets, philosophers, and generals.

sentiments on the subject which can only be attributed to senseless rage (Gal. v. 2, 4), and in his anger he even sinks to obscenity (Gal. v. 12 is not literally or even correctly translated in the Authorised Version and Revised Version). His recourse to sophistry is well displayed throughout this epistle, but it is very difficult to understand. Paul admitted that circumcision or uncircumcision was indifferent, or "availeth anything" (ch. v. 6): how then could the adoption of Judaism, which was a matter of indifference, lead to the conclusions that "Christ will profit you nothing," "ye are fallen away from grace," "ye should not obey the truth" (verses 2, 4, 7), which evangelical forms of expression, translated into colloquial language, mean that the morality taught by Jesus would be useless or be departed from, if Judaism be adopted, Judaism, further, being the religion which Jesus Himself professed. Paul, however, makes up for these failings by his enumeration of the immoralities to be avoided by the Christian societies at the conclusion of ch. v. 13-21 : amongst these, his religious predilections induced him to insert idolatry, witchcraft, and heresies. And he further adds the virtues to be practised. All these exhortations are not in the epigrammatic form which later writers adopt in teaching the morality of Jesus. From which circumstance I conclude that in Paul's days there was no written Gospel from which to quote, such as the work which Matthew (according to Papias) put forth, containing the λόγια or moral precepts of Jesus. In the Christian writings of the first century, the inculcation of morality was the paramount object of the writers ; but in two writers, Paul and the author of the Epistle to the Hebrews, there is a marked proclivity to introduce theological conceptions, which I regard as corruptions.

The Epistle of James, which I regard as an early writing of the first century, is addressed wholly to Jews who had accepted the moral system of Jesus. It is entirely moral, with a few Jewish conceptions of a religious nature interspersed. It is impossible to deduce from this epistle that Christianity, as James understood it, was a new religion, distinct from Judaism and other religions. James' Christians of the Jewish faith frequented the synagogue : ii. 2, the word is erroneously translated in the Authorised Version 'assembly.' There is not a trace in this epistle of any of the conceptions of ecclesiastical Christianity, such as the divinity, resurrection, and ascension of Jesus on a cloud, the virgin birth, or any other. He refers to Paul's doctrine of justification by faith, only to oppose it in a very commonsense way (ii. 14-26).

The Epistle to the Hebrews is a writing of the first century, dating sometime in the last three or four decades.[1] It was addressed by a Christian Jew to Christian Jews (Heb. iii. 1), *i.e.*, all men of the Hebrew faith, who had joined the Christian society. It does not seem to me probable that they were professing simultaneously two religions. The writer specially differentiates Christianity in some passages, and he does not speak of it as a religion. In iii. 1, iv. 14, x. 23, the Greek word employed to indicate Christianity and not Judaism implies that Christianity was not regarded by the writer as a separate religion. The word ὁμολογία does not mean religion; it is translated in the Authorised Version 'profession,' and in the Revised Version 'confession.' In Greek Lexicons it is explained as agreement, an agreement made, compact; in war, terms of surrender or treaty; an assent, admission, confession; accord, convention, unanimity, and so on, but not religion. The Greek words for religion are ἡ Θεοῦ θεραπεία, θρησκεία, θεοσέβεια, and perhaps a few others may bear the meaning from the context, but never ὁμολογία. This word, I think, has in these passages the sense of the commercial expression, 'terms or articles of association,' and may be translated in the Canonical text as 'convention' instead of 'profession' and 'confession,' which words have a religious meaning.[2] There is no doubt that the writer of the epistle considered the Christian association or ecclesia to be of a religious character, like our Bible Society, but not

[1] I think it would be reasonable to take the later rather than the earlier decades, so as to allow time for the development of the more advanced theological views expressed by the writer since Paul's time.

[2] The word ὁμολογία must have given a few unhappy moments to the translators. The Authorised Version translators obviously tried to make it out a religion, and in ch. x. 23 they forced the Greek into a 'profession of faith.' The Revised Version translators more correctly render the Greek expressions used, 'confession of hope.'

a religion in itself. I am unable to discover in the epistle any advance upon Paul's notion that Jesus was an angel (Gal. iv. 14). The superstition regarding angels prevailed in those days; they were thought to be divine beings, in the form of men, immortal, but not deities to be worshipped.[1] The writer compares him with the angels, rather than makes him an angel. He was made a little lower than the angels, he says in ch. ii. 9, as he suffered death, which angels could not: "we see Jesus, who was made a little lower than the angels, for [on account of] the suffering of death (διὰ τὸ πάθημα τοῦ θανάτου), crowned with glory and honour." After suffering death, He "sat down on the right hand of the Majesty on high"; there is no account taken of his resurrection after the death on the Cross in the epistle[2] (see p. 204), and then he became 'better than the angels,' as he obtained a better name, namely, that of Son (ii. 4, 5, 13). After these definite statements, I do not see how other statements in the first chapter, in which he is deified (verse 8), made an object of worship to angels (verse 6), and represented as the maker of worlds (verses 2 and 3), can be accepted as genuine. Such statements were alien to the spirit of Christianity in the first century, and must be set down as interpolations of the second century. There is documentary proof that verse 3 and the following verses have been largely interpolated. This and the following verses are quoted in the First Epistle of Clement, and the contrast between the original passage and the interpolated verses is very marked:—

FIRST EPISTLE OF CLEMENT, ch. xxxvi.	EPISTLE TO THE HEBREWS, i. 3-13.
Who being the brightness of His Majesty is so much greater than angels, as He	Who being the brightness of his *glory, and the express image of his person, and up-*

[1] The peculiar superstition regarding angels appears in Heb. xiii. 2: hospitality to strangers is enjoined, because "some have entertained angels unawares."

[2] This writer did not accept the alleged fact that Jesus rose from the dead after the crucifixion (see p. 204). His belief appears to have been that Jesus died at the crucifixion, and went straight up to the right hand of God; while ordinary mortals go to Sheol or Hades after death.

hath inherited a more excellent name.

For so it is written; Who maketh his angels spirits, and his ministers a flame of fire; but of his Son the Master said thus; Thou art my son, I this day have begotten thee. *Ask of me and I will give thee the Gentiles for thine inheritance, and the ends of the earth for thy possession.* And again He saith unto him: Sit thou on my right hand, until I make thine enemies a footstool for thy feet. (Bishop Lightfoot's translation.)

holding all things by the word of his power, when he had by himself purged our sins, sat down on the right hand of the Majesty on high; being made so much better than the angels, as he hath by inheritance obtained a more excellent name than they.

For unto which of the angels said he at any time, Thou art my son, this day have I begotten thee? *And again, I will be to him a Father, and he shall be to me a son? And again, when he bringeth in the first begotten into the world, he saith, And let all the angels worship him.* And of the angels he saith, Who maketh his angels spirits, and his ministers a flame of fire. *But unto the Son he saith, Thy throne, O God, is for ever and ever: a sceptre of righteousness is the sceptre of thy Kingdom* (also verses 9, 10, 11, 12). But to which of the angels said he at any time, Sit on my right hand, until I make thine enemies thy footstool?

It will be seen from the verses which I have printed in italics from the Authorised Version how largely the original passage had been touched up, recast, and interpolated with words and quotations which bestow divinity on Jesus. The attribution of godhead to Jesus would, in the first century, have been regarded as simple blasphemy by Jewish Christians. There cannot be a doubt that these interpolations were introduced into the original Epistle to the Hebrews in the second century: and my suspicion falls upon Clement of Alexandria as the culprit.[1] The passages in the original epistle which I have printed in italics form some of those very few instances of omission or deletion from the originals of the sacred writings which are very difficult to discover.

The writer of the Epistle to the Hebrews, while keeping pace with Paul with regard to the person of Jesus, made, I think, a considerable stride towards advancing Christianity into the position of a religion. He is usually regarded as a profound theologian: if profundity be the same as obscurity, his right to it cannot be disputed. He is as difficult to understand as Browning. His data bear no resemblance to those which have influence over the minds of investigators of history or natural science. They are texts from the Hebrew Scriptures, which doubtless were regarded by Christians of the Hebrew faith as of binding authority, and chimeras founded upon them. Paul also made use of the Hebrew prophecies, but he associated them with genuine, or apparently genuine, facts, which they were assumed to have predicted. The Christian Jews of the second century, likewise, had recourse to prophecies, but they associated them with facts which they fabricated in fulfilment of them. The writer to the Hebrews displays in great perfection a quality peculiar to theologians—the absence of ceremony. He unceremoniously calls upon the Christian Jews to consider Jesus the High Priest of the Christian fraternity (iii. 1), on the strength of the Scriptural statement: "Thou art a priest for ever, after the order of Melchisedec" (Psalms cx. 4). The Jewish High Priest obtained entrance into the Holy of Holies, "not without blood which he offered for himself and for the errors of the people" (ix. 7), but Jesus "by his own blood entered at once

---

[1] Two other interpolations were also, I think, perpetrated by this eminent Christian, viz., the clause in Heb. v. 2, "and of laying on of hands," and in xiii. 20, "that brought again from the dead" to the end of the verse. The laying on of hands was a second century practice. The officials of the Christian societies were elected by the lifting up of hands in the first century (see *Didache*, ch. xv.). "Vote by raising the hand ($\chi\epsilon\iota\rho o\tau o\nu\eta\sigma a\tau\epsilon$) bishops and deacons for yourselves." Regarding the second interpolation, see page 204.

into the holy place, having obtained eternal redemption for us" (verse 12). The Levitical priesthood of the order of Aaron must necessarily be imperfect, since there was a need for a priest of the order of Melchisedec; and the priesthood being changed, there arises a necessity for "a change also of the Law" (vii. 11 and 12). "There was verily a disannulling of the commandment" regarding the Law, issued previous to the appointment of the priest of the order of Melchisedec (verses 16-18). Under the Law, there were many priests, by reason of death, but this man Jesus, because He lives for ever, hath an unchangeable and perpetual priesthood (verses 23, 24). Under the Law, there was need of daily sacrifices for the sins of the priest and of the people; but Jesus, when He offered up Himself, sacrificed once for all (verse 27). The first covenant of the law being faulty, has fallen into decay and waxed old, and was ready to vanish away (viii. 13), and to make place for the new covenant promised in Jeremiah xxxi. 31. "This is the covenant that I will make with the house of Israel after those days, saith the Lord; I will put my laws into their mind, and write them in their hearts," etc. (verses 8-13). Jesus was the mediator of the new covenant (xii. 3). This is the substance of the elaborate web of sophistry which the writer of the Epistle to the Hebrews constructed to convert the moral system of Jesus into a plausible religious system to take the place of Judaism, which he declared effete. Paul did not display animosity to Judaism, the religion which he himself professed, but he considered it not a necessary condition for the reception of the moral system of Jesus. I am unable to perceive in the Epistle to the Hebrews any inkling of the essentials of ecclesiastical Christianity, the incarnation or birth from a virgin, the resurrection and ascension of Jesus on a cloud. The very fact that the writer was urgent on the recognition of Jesus as a High Priest militates against the idea of the deification of Jesus, the office of the priest not being to stand as a god, but to act as a minister or servant to a god.

The writing called the Epistle of Clement to the Corinthians is of the same approximate date as the Epistle to the Hebrews, but written subsequently. We have no knowledge of its author, and its attribution to "Clement of Rome" is hypothetical. It is a letter of remonstrance from the society or ecclesia at Rome to that at Corinth on the subject of the dismissal of presbyters by the latter society. There is no obscurity in the writing such as is observed in the previous epistle. The tone throughout is Jewish and Pauline. In this writing also I can perceive no trace of the conceptions of ecclesiastical. Christianity, except of the resurrection of Jesus from the dead (ch. xxiv.), which was taught by Paul. There is not an inkling of the divinity of Jesus, of the virgin birth or of the ascension to heaven in a cloud. The society or ecclesia at Rome had evidently accepted the recommendation of the writer of the Epistle to the Hebrews to regard Jesus as High Priest, for He is spoken of as "our High Priest and Guardian Jesus Christ" (ch. lxiv. and elsewhere); but this circumstance made no difference in the relation between Judaism, the religion professed, and Christianity, or the moral system of Jesus, which was practised. It appears to me that the writing in some passages places Judaism and Christianity in antithesis: for instance, in ch. iii. is the statement of the man who "walketh neither in the ordinances ($\tau o \hat{i} s\ \nu o \mu i \mu o \iota s$) of His commandments, nor liveth according to that which becometh Christ." Again in ch. lxii. it is said, "concerning those things which befit our religion ($\theta \rho \eta \sigma \kappa \epsilon i a$), and those things which are most useful for a virtuous life." In these two passages there is a distinction made between the religion Judaism, and the moral system or conduct of life of Jesus. Again in ch. xiii. a passage from the Old Testament is quoted: "Let not the wise man glory in his wisdom," etc. (Jer. ix. 23, 24), and the $\lambda o \gamma i a$ of Jesus: "Have mercy, that you may receive mercy; forgive, that it may be forgiven you. As ye do, so shall it be done unto you. As ye judge, so shall ye be judged. As ye show kindness, so shall kindness be showed unto you. With what measure ye mete, it shall be measured withal to you." The former is called commandment or order ($\dot{\epsilon} \nu \tau o \lambda \hat{\eta}$), the latter precepts ($\pi a \rho a \gamma \gamma \dot{\epsilon} \lambda \mu a \sigma \iota \nu$), a distinction being thereby drawn between the commandment of God and the precepts of a man.

I ought perhaps to allude to two passages in this writing which theologians seriously adduce as proofs that the divinity of Jesus was recognised by the ecclesia at Rome in the first century. In ch. ii. occurs the passage : " And ye were all lowly in mind . . . . and content with the provisions which God supplieth. And giving heed unto His words, ye laid them up diligently in your hearts, and His sufferings were before your eyes" (Lightfoot's translation). It is contended that in this passage 'God' means Jesus, because the 'sufferings' of the latter are referred to. It appears to me that the word 'sufferings' is incongruous with the sense of the context. The meaning of the writer was evidently that the words of God were remembered and followed. The Greek word $\pi\alpha\theta\acute{\eta}\mu\alpha\tau\alpha$, translated 'sufferings,' is very closely similar to $\mu\alpha\theta\acute{\eta}\mu\alpha\tau\alpha$, teachings or maxims, and it is very likely that the scribe, either by mistake or intentionally, wrote the letter π instead of μ (see note to this passage in Jacobson's edition). The other passage occurs in ch. xvi. : " The sceptre [of the majesty] of God, even our Lord Jesus Christ, came not in the pomp of arrogance or of pride, though he might have done so, but in lowliness of mind." This passage is said to indicate divinity, as Jesus voluntarily chose to come in a lowly position when he possessed the power of coming in pomp. This is an interpretation that is far-fetched and characteristic of the old school-men. Suppose Joe Smith be substituted in the passage for Jesus, no one would interpret it in the sense that Joe Smith possessed the power of choosing how he should come into the world. I am glad to be able to add that no English theologian has accepted this extraordinary interpretation of the passage.

The strong and predominating Jewish character of the epistle indicates that the society or ecclesia at Rome was mainly composed of Jews. Further, with thé exception of the allusions to Peter and Paul and the original disciples of Jesus, there is no mention of Apostles in Bishop Lightfoot's translation, leaving the impression on the mind that this class of officials did not exist in the Roman society or ecclesia of Christians. I think, however, ch. lxv. clearly mentions Apostles. The passage is thus rendered by Bishop Lightfoot: " Now, send ye back speedily unto us our messengers, Claudius Ephebus and Valerius Bito, together with Fortunatus also, in peace and with joy, to the end that they may the more quickly report the peace and concord which is prayed for and earnestly desired by us," etc. I should substitute 'Apostles' for the word 'messengers,' employed by the learned Bishop as a correct rendering of the Greek words, τοὺς ἀπεσταλμένους. These apostles bore Roman names, and may have been Pagans, and if Pagans, they remained Pagans, although members and apostles of the ecclesia, because Paul specially objected to the Pagans being Judaised. The Latin names they bore does not, of course, necessarily imply that they were not Jews, as the latter assumed Greek and Latin names.

The amiable society or ecclesia of Christians who observed the teaching of Jesus very early became the prey of designing knaves and rogues. The practical observation of the precepts of kindness, benevolence, hospitality, submission to injuries, etc., exposed them to the inroads of unscrupulous men. Even in the days of Paul, when the scattered Christian associations were comparatively poor, there were many who corrupted, or, as literally translated in the Revised Version, " made merchandise of the Word of God " (2 Cor. ii. 17, margin). The nature of the operations of knaves upon the gentle disciples of Jesus is thus simply described in the *Didache*, or teaching of the Apostles, a work written at the close of the first century or beginning of the second, by Christian Jews of Palestine or Syria, as Dr Lightfoot concludes : " Concerning Apostles and prophets, do thus according to the teaching of the Gospel. Let every apostle who comes to you be received as the Lord ; he shall remain but one day, but if there be need, another also ; but if he remains three days, he is a false prophet. When the Apostle leaves, let him receive nothing but bread until where he stops (*i.e.*, to his next halting-place) ; but if he asks for money, he is a false prophet. And every prophet speaking in the Spirit ye shall not try nor judge ; for every sin shall be forgiven, but this sin shall not be forgiven. Not every one that speaks in the Spirit is a prophet, but only if he have the manners of the Lord. From his manners shall the false prophet and the prophet be known. And no prophet who appoints a table in the Spirit shall eat of it ; otherwise he is a false prophet. And every prophet who teaches the truth, if he does not what he teaches, is a false prophet. And every prophet approved true who makes a worldly (or material) thing of the assembly (or association) into a mystery,[1] and teaches you not to do all that he does, shall not be judged by you; for he has judgment with God; for in like manner also did the ancient prophets. And whosoever shall say in the Spirit: Give me money or something else, ye shall not listen to him; but if he tell you to give on account of others in want, let no man judge him.

"But let every one that cometh in the name of the Lord be received; and then, having approved, ye shall know him: for ye shall have right and left knowledge. If the comer is a wayfarer, assist him as much as ye are able: but he shall not stay with you more than two or three days, if it be necessary. But if he wishes to have his abode with you, being a craftsman, let him work and eat. But if he has no craft, take ye thought according to your knowledge, how not in idleness he shall live with you a Christian. But if he will not do so, he is a Christ-merchant ($\chi\rho\iota\sigma\tau\acute{\epsilon}\mu\pi\rho\rho\sigma$). (Bishop Lightfoot: he is trafficking upon Christ.) Beware of such men."

Bishop Lightfoot describes the *Didache* as "a Church manual of primitive Christianity, or of some section of it," consisting of two parts, the first part being "a moral treatise," and "the second part gives directions affecting Church rites and orders." This view of the *Didache* appears to my mind to be that of a man having a thorough ecclesiastical or theological mind, whose vision is deeply coloured by his theological preconceptions: in other words, it is the view of a man who habitually wears theological spectacles. My own theological preconceptions have been a source of error and embarrassment to me, and I can thoroughly understand and sympathise with the practical difficulty of professional theologians laying aside the theological spectacles. Setting aside theological preconceptions, and removing theological spectacles, the *Didache* may be justly described as the Rules and Regulations of the

---

[1] I do not understand on what grounds Bishop Lightfoot translates this clause: ποιῶν εἰς μυστήριον κοσμικὸν ἐκκλησίας, "if he doeth aught as an outward mystery typical of the Church." My translation is a simple and exact rendering of the Greek words.

Society of Christians of the Jewish Faith.[1] Although the corruptions of Jesus' moral system had made some progress, they had not yet advanced sufficiently far as to justify the inference that a new religion had become established. The function of baptism, although performed in the name of the Father, Son, and Holy Ghost;[2] the eating of the Memorial Supper, although preceded and followed by prayer; the observance of fasting on certain days of the week; the expectation of the second advent and of the limited resurrection of the dead,[3] were not enough to constitute a new religion; and in point of fact, these observances and beliefs were not inconsistent with Judaism. It is to be marked that the *Didache* makes no statement on the subject of the divinity and incarnation or virgin birth and resurrection of Jesus, or of his crucifixion being an expiatory sacrifice, the two latter omissions being proof that these views, inculcated by Paul, had not found general acceptance amongst Christians in the first century. Other views of Paul, such as justification by faith and predestination, are also unnoticed.

The powerful influence of the itinerant preachers, or teachers, or apostles, or prophets, for they were called by all these designations, is very markedly seen in the *Didache*. Distrust of them and withholding of hospitality to apostles or prophets was regarded as an unpardonable offence (ch. xi.).

[1] Anyone who will take the trouble to refer to the word ecclesia in Smith's *Dictionary of Antiquities* will find that it means "the General Assembly of the citizens of Athens, in which they met to discuss and determine upon matters of public interest." The word did not mean a church or place of worship, or an association for purposes of worship, till the second century was well advanced, and only amongst Christians. The word *ecclesia* meant an association, assembly, or congregation in the first century, and it is used in that sense in the Christian writings of the first century, *i.e.*, it had no religious meaning, such as the word *church* now has. That the *Didache* was a Jewish work seems to me clear from the following passages:—Ch. i.: "Do not even the Gentiles the same." Ch. x.: "Hosanna to the God of David." Ch. xi.: "In like manner did the ancient prophets." Ch. viii.: "Keep your fast on the preparation."

[2] The function of the graduation of students at the universities is not a religious rite—though each student, even Indian, Chinese, and Japanese students—receives his degree *in nomine Patris, Filii et Sancti Spiritus*.

[3] The learned theologian, and oft Prime Minister, the late Mr W. E. Gladstone, is said to have thought that this was only certain in the case of a good believer in Christ, just as the early Christians did.

They were to be received as the Lord : but as sad experience had made the gracious society aware of the existence of knaves and rogues under the guise of apostles, precaution was necessary. The true prophets who desired to settle amongst the scattered brotherhoods were to be allowed to do so ; and their reward was the first fruits or practically a tithe, or 10 per cent., of the produce of every description of an industrious community—good pay and stimulus to the apostles and prophets for the encouragement of historical investigations for "the increase of righteousness and the knowledge of the Lord" (ch. xi.).

I am of opinion that the *Didache* refers to a written Gospel in two passages in ch. xv., "as ye have in the Gospel"; and again, "as ye have in the Gospel of our Lord"; and that the moral section of it is a rude summary, or perhaps only a selection from this Gospel. A few of the phrases and sentences employed are very similar to certain passages in the Synoptic Gospels. The conclusion may be drawn that this primitive Gospel, doubtless a very meagre one, formed part of the material employed by the Synoptic writers. The evidence in the *Didache*, so far as it goes, indicates that this primitive Gospel consisted of short epigrammatic precepts or λόγια. There is a Gospel precept in the *Didache* that has not been utilised in the Synoptics: " Let thine alms sweat into thine hands, until thou shalt have learnt to whom to give." I have also remarked that the *Didache* contains no Gospel precept on the subject of divorce, or the putting away of a wife and of not marrying another. Whether this primitive Gospel was the λόγια written in Hebrew by Matthew, to which Papias refers (Eusebius, *Eccl. Hist.*, iii. 39), cannot be ascertained.

A matter of information of great importance derived from the *Didache* is that the apostles or prophets of the period had begun the practice of converting material or ordinary things of the assembly into mysteries. For example, as I understand the passage, the bread and wine of the Memorial Supper, ordinary articles employed in the assembly or ecclesia, were made by the apostles or prophets into the mystery of the body and blood of Jesus. The society of Christians obviously.

did not approve of the making of mysteries, but left the judgment of it to God, who, however, never interferes in such matters. One mystery appears to have taken root: the breaking of bread appears to have been mystified into a sacrifice, θυσία (ch. xiv.). I do not understand the application of the clause in ch. xi., "teacheth you not to do all that he himself doeth." A point to be borne in mind is that bishops and deacons were chosen by vote, by raising the hands (χειροτονήσατε, ch. xv.), a practice used by the Greeks and Romans of old, and still in use by us in public assemblies, but not in use by the Church: *but hands were not laid upon them*.[1] The bishops and deacons also performed the office of the apostles or prophets, or teachers, the latter only, however, being reported as paid (in kind) for their services; the bishops and deacons were not to be 'lovers of money,' and were not to be despised; and as the apostles and prophets disappear from history in the second century, the natural inference is that they were gradually superseded by the bishops and deacons, who with the full office took the stipend, or 10 per cent., of the apostles.

The famous letter of Pliny the younger to Trajan, written at the beginning of the second century (*c.* 110 or 111), throws a little light upon the subject we are discussing, *i.e.*, the status of early Christianity, whether a secular system of morality or a religion. The letter is a puzzle to me, for neither Pliny, nor the emperor in his reply, gives us any insight into the reasons that brought the Christians under the cognisance of the magistrate. The former acknowledges his ignorance of the subject: he had never been present at legal proceedings against the Christians; he knew not why or to what extent it was usual to punish or proceed against them; he was in doubt whether age and physical weakness should make any difference in their punishment, whether the penitent may be pardoned, whether it would suffice for the Christian to drop the name,

---

[1] The custom of laying on of hands did not exist in the first century. I can gather no evidence of its existence before the second century. There is no mention of it in the Epistle of James in dealing with the sick (v. 14, 15), nor in the appointment of Matthias as an Apostle in Acts i. 24-26. All the subsequent occasions are recorded in writings of the second century, and are hence very suspicious. The *Didache* proves that it was not practised at the close of the first century.

although it was free from crime, or whether the crimes attributed to the name should be punished. In this dilemma of ignorance his *interim* procedure was to ask the accused, Were they Christians? He repeated the inquiry two and three times, threatening punishment. If they persisted in confessing themselves Christians, he ordered them to be led to execution. This strange and cruel proceeding he thought justifiable, because he had no doubt that, whatever it was which they professed, contumacy and inflexible obstinacy ought to be punished. It would appear, then, that Pliny punished these Christians for an offence which we might call 'contempt of court.' The above were the only Christians punished.[1] The others who were accused denied that they are or were Christians, proclaimed the gods, to the dictation of the magistrate, offered oblations of incense and wine to the statue of the emperor and the images of the gods, and besides spoke ill of Christ, all which those who were real Christians, it was said, could not be found to do. But they declared that the chief part of their fault or error was that they had the habit, on an appointed day, to assemble before daybreak and to say in turns amongst themselves a form of words or *carmen*, to Christ, *quasi* god, that they would not bind themselves by an oath to any crime, but would neither commit theft, robbery, nor adultery; they would not break their faith, nor when called upon deny a deposit; which being got over, it was their practice to disperse, and to assemble again for the purpose of taking food, but of a common and innocent kind. Pliny examined, under torture, two maid-servants, who, he says, were called *ministræ*—probably deaconesses?—but he ascertained nothing beyond a foolish and intemperate superstition (*superstitionem pravam et immodicam*). The above facts, as they are stated in Pliny's letter to Trajan, gives me the impression that the Roman governor regarded the Christians as a society or association, rather than as people professing

[1] The falsification of early Christian history by Eusebius is apparent in this historical circumstance. He says (*Eccl. Hist.*, Bk. III. 33) that Pliny, "moved by the number of martyrs, communicated with the emperor respecting the multitudes that were put to death for their faith." The letter of Pliny, on the contrary, proves that few Christians were put to death, and those not on account of their 'faith.'

a new religion. A new religion was no subject of offence to the Romans, who had a very broad religious tolerance. He prohibited the assemblies in the early morning and later in the day, on the ground that they came under the decrees of the emperor against the formation of *hetæriæ*, or political clubs or societies, which were considered to be dangerous to the order of the province. The above occurrences took place in the Asiatic province of Pontica, in Asia Minor, of which Pliny was appointed prætor by Trajan; and they exhibit to us a society of Christians of the Pagan faith. The readiness with which the Christians offered incense and wine to the images of the gods, and the alacrity with which they returned to the temples, which had been deserted, resumed the sacred rites which had been long intermitted, and bought up the victims, who had hardly a purchaser, indicates that they had not broken with Paganism. It was different after Christianity had grown into a new religion and all connection with Paganism had been severed. The Christians, or many of them, then inflexibly refused to offer incense to idols or to worship in heathen temples.

Read with theological spectacles, the letter of Pliny affords proof to the theological mind that Christianity was regarded as a religion, and that the divinity of Christ was clearly recognised by the Roman governor. The passage, "*carmenque Christo, quasi deo, dicere secum invicem, seque sacramento non in scelus aliquod obstringere*," is theologically understood to mean "to sing a hymn antiphonally to Christ as God, and to bind themselves by the sacrament to no crime." The translation seems perfectly natural to many simple people. It should be remembered, however, that these words were written by a Pagan, whose mind was filled with Pagan conceptions, and should be understood accordingly. '*Carmen dicere Christo*' does not mean to sing a song or hymn to Christ,[1] for which the expression would be '*carmen canere*,' but to say or repeat a verse or form of words. This was the Pagan view of the repeating or reading of the epigrammatic

---

[1] I regret to find the brilliant historian, Dean Milman, translates the words of Pliny, "Singing a hymn to Christ as God."—*History of Christianity*, ii. 6, p. 93 of vol. 2, new edition.

moral precepts or λόγια of the Gospel. The early Christian made no oath, and the Lord's Memorial Supper was not regarded by them as a sacrament, but a material or cosmical meal. To the puzzled mind of Pliny, Christ seemed a '*quasi* god.' It is plain that the Roman governor was in perplexity regarding the essential nature of the Christian society; he was uncertain whether it was a religion in which Christ was a *quasi* god, or an association possibly for political purposes, or *hetæria*; but his mind rather inclined to the latter view, and his magisterial action was regulated by it. The fact that a highly-educated Roman, like Pliny the younger, who had officially investigated the subject, was uncertain whether Christianity was a religion should be pondered by modern Christians.

It should be remarked that the gospel of the Society of Christian Pagans of Pontica was of the same nature as that of the Christian Jews of Syria or Palestine, and that the want of distinct religious characteristics was common to both societies. Pliny does not speak of apostles, prophets and teachers, not even of bishops and deacons; the maid-servants, examined under torture, were slaves: they are described as *ministræ*, and may have been employed as deaconesses to assist at the baptism of female candidates on admission to the Christian assembly or ecclesia.

With the exception of the glimpse of the Christian Pagans of Pontica above given, and of the martyrdom of Ignatius, the details of which are unreliable and its literature falsified, the history of Christianity for the first quarter of the second century is a blank. But there were forces in silent operation, the manifestation of which in the second quarter showed their power and importance. One of these was the steady extension of what I may call Christian knowledge derived from the historical investigations of the stipendiary, and perhaps also of the itinerant apostles and prophets, or teachers, of the Christian Society of Jews. The result of these historical investigations, to which were added numerous inventions or fabrications, was the conversion of Christianity into a religious system, and the consequent conflict which now first arose between Christianism and Judaism. A learned Jewish writer says that, on the destruction of the temple of Jerusalem, Judaism ceased to be a 'political commonwealth,' and became a 'church without priests,' or, rather, a synagogue. Judaism was now in need of "a new religious centre, not only to replace the temple, but also to bring about a greater solidarity of view." This was a time of special excitement, aggravated by the rise of Christianism and its aggressiveness to Judaism. "The student of the Talmud finds that such marvels as predicting the future, reviving the dead, casting out demons, crossing rivers dry-shod, curing the sick by a touch or prayer, were the order of the day, and performed by scores of rabbis. Voices from heaven were often heard, and strange visions were frequently beheld." These miracles obviously were devices resorted to by ambitious rabbis to obtain acceptance for their interpretations of the Law; but they failed to secure this object, for when the honest and wiser rabbis saw the dangerous consequences, they insisted that miracles should have no influence "on the interpretation and development of the Law." One of the great rabbis failed to prove the justice of his case by the intervention of miracles, and even the Bath-Kol, or celestial voice, which declared itself in his favour, was ignored (see *Studies in Judaism*, by A. Schechter, M.A., reader in Talmudic in the University of Cambridge, 1896, pp. 229-231).[1] The latter occurrence is dated 120 A.D. It is no great straining of historical probability to presume that similar excitement and activity prevailed at this period among the apostles and prophets of the Christian Societies of Jews. The gift of the interpretation of Hebrew prophecy was always claimed by the early Christian Jews, but histories to accommodate these interpretations were now invented and added as supplements to the simple Gospel of moral precepts delivered by Jesus. The reader will remark the similarity of the miracles named by Mr Schechter to those that now for the first time begin to appear in the Christian writings of the second century. Every supernatural occurrence to be found in our Canonical and Apocryphal Gospels is mentioned in his list; and those that are not found in the list, such as the

[1] Mr Schechter has been recently appointed Professor of Hebrew in the University of London.

miraculous births of Jesus and John the Baptist, are merely modifications of Jewish legends recorded in the Old Testament. The publication and preaching of those new additions to the Gospel may perhaps be set down as done at the close of the second or beginning of the third decade of the second century.

It is of essential importance to discover the intentions which impelled the Christian apostles and prophets or teachers to the publication and preaching of these additions to the simple gospel of moral precepts delivered by Jesus : additions of which there is no record in such Christian writings that survive of the first century. In this investigation we have no surer guide than the universal experience of mankind. No man—Jew, Christian, or Gentile—would hesitate to attribute the assertion of miraculous powers and supernatural agency by the Jewish rabbis in support of their superior claims to the interpretation of the Torah, or Mosaic Law, to personal self-interest. I do not think that it would be reasonable or just to attribute self-interest as the purpose of the conduct of these dishonest rabbis, and to abstain from applying the same human experience which gives this verdict to the conduct of the Christian apostles. If to self-interest human experience assigns the conduct of the Jewish rabbis, to the same motive must logically be ascribed the corresponding conduct of the Christian apostles. The extension of the area of 10 per cent. of the produce of an industrious people was a sufficient consideration to prevail upon clever knaves and rogues, in the guise of Christian apostles, to construct alluring tales regarding the Founder of Christianity to attract the unthinking mob to attach themselves to the Christian society. The results of the same conduct in both sets of men, success in the one case and failure in the other, cannot change the nature of the impelling purpose. The opposition and foresight of the honest rabbis frustrated the designs of the rogue rabbis, but the remonstrances of honest Christians unfortunately failed to suppress the attractive and interesting narratives, an ingenious mixture of truth and falsehood, fabricated by rogue apostles. I have already displayed (page 21) the remonstrances of honest Christians ; the cautions, "not to give heed to fables and endless genealogies" (1 Tim. i. 4); to "refuse profane and old wives' fables" (1 Tim. iv. 7); to "avoid profane and vain babblings" (1 Tim. vi. 20, and 2 Tim. ii. 16); not "to give heed to Jewish fables" (Titus i. 14), and the suggestion that "cunningly devised fables are abroad" (2 Peter i. 16). The existence of these remonstrances in the surviving Christian writings of the first half of the second century are documentary proofs of the knavery and roguery of the false apostles, prophets, and teachers to whom the supernatural tales in the New Testament Gospels have now been traced. That these remonstrances failed may probably have been due to their having been made too late, after the fabricated narratives had taken deep root amongst the Christian communities.[1]

The first distinct pronouncement that Christianity was a religion, so far as documents in our possession indicate past history, is to be found in the *Apology of Aristides*, dated A.D. 125 or thereabouts (see page 19). In Professor Rendel Harris' translation of the Syriac version of the *Apology*, the sentence occurs : " The Christians reckon the beginning of their religion from Jesus Christ " (*Texts and Studies, Contributions to Biblical and Patristic Literature*. Ed. by J. Armitage Robinson, B.D., vol. i. No. 1. *Apology of Aristides*, p. 36). The word 'religion' is not found in the Armenian fragment (*op. cit.*, pp. 29 and 32), where the word translated *genus* and *race* is used, nor in the *History of Barlaam and Josaphat* (p. 110); but the essential characteristics of a religion are clearly stated. The Founder of Christianity is described as the physiological son of God ; "it is said that God came down from heaven, and from a Hebrew virgin took and clad Himself with flesh, and in a daughter of man there dwelt the Son of God. . . . . He died and was buried ; and they say that after three days he rose and ascended to heaven ; and then these twelve disciples[2] went forth into the known parts of the

[1] The epistles to Timothy and Titus are falsely attributed to Paul. They are second century writings ; there are no other reasonable grounds on which these allusions to fabricated Jewish narratives can be explained. There are other cogent reasons for dating these epistles in the second century.

[2] It is clear that from the number *twelve* being noted, that Aristides, writing in A.D. 125, was ignorant of the story of Judas Iscariot.

world, and taught concerning his greatness with all humility and sobriety; and on this account those also who believe in this preaching are called Christians, who are well known" (pp. 36, 37). The conversion of a system of morality into a system of religion based upon the divine person of Jesus was complete. There can be no mistake now that Jesus was God; no ground for perplexity, such as Pliny experienced when he spoke of him as '*quasi* god.'

The simple gospel of moral precepts or λόγια now became the gospel of a religion, and contained the above statements in a more amplified form. The date of this new gospel may be gathered from Aristides' words : " This is taught from that gospel which a little while ago was spoken among them as being preached ; wherein if ye also read, ye will comprehend the power that is upon it " (p. 36). The new religious accretions were reduced to writing, and there was a multiplicity of these writings. "Their sayings and their ordinances, O King, and the glory of their service, and the expectation of their recompense of reward, according to the doing of each one of them, which they expect in another world, thou art able to know from their writings. . . . . Take now their writings and read in them, and lo! ye will find that not of myself have I brought these things forward, nor as their advocate have I said them, but as I have read in their writings, these things I firmly believe, and those things that are to come" (p. 50). "Thus far, O King, it is I that have spoken. For as to what remains, as was said above, there are found in their other writings words which are difficult to speak, or that one should repeat them; things which are not only said, but actually done " (p. 51). The latter statements regarding the 'other writings' manifestly refer to the miracles and other stories of the new religion, 'things actually done,' which Aristides, like Justin, later on, found difficult to repeat. Both these writers were Greek philosophers, who were acquainted with the miracles of Apollonius of Tyana, of Simon Magus, and other impostors of the age, and they were naturally reluctant to repeat the miracles attributed in the new writings to Jesus; though it must be sadly concluded they assented to them, and made no attempt to controvert them.

It would be a mistake, I think, to condemn the whole contents of these new writings as fictitious. Their writers, the stipendiary apostles, were men of some education, which raised them above their fellows, and they had ample leisure, seeing that the generous brethren supplied all their needs with the first-fruits or tithe of their earnings. They had the capacity and means of studying the Christian literature existing in the first century, and they doubtless collected the facts available regarding the personal history of the Great Master and of his immediate followers, and utilised them in the new writings. The Christian writings available for historical investigation in the first century were truthful and honest, for I have found no reason to distrust them, but only the interpolations made in them in the second century. The stipendiary apostles had before them the writings of Paul (four epistles), of James, of the unknown authors of the Epistle to the Hebrews and First Epistle of John, possibly Jude, of Cerinthus, of John of the Apocalypse, of Clement of Rome, of Philip, called in the second century the evangelist (Acts xxi. 8), and of Matthew and Mark, and perhaps of many others now lost.[1] I see no reason to reject Papias' statement that the Apostle Matthew wrote a book of λόγια in Hebrew, and that Mark, the interpreter of the Apostle Peter, who was ignorant of Greek and Latin, wrote a cursory and disconnected account of things said and done by Jesus (Eusebius, *Eccl. Hist.*, iii. 39). The facts, personal to Jesus and his Apostles, found in these various writings, were incor-

---

[1] I do not think the First Epistle of Peter existed in the first century. The writer was not one of the twelve, but a 10 per cent. or stipendiary apostle and presbyter or elder of the second century, as he himself declares (1 Peter i. 1, and v. 1), just as Paul, the writer of the Epistles to the Ephesians, Philippians, and Colossians, was a stipendiary apostle and deacon of the second century (see page 102). In the early age of Peter and Paul, the Apostles of the Lord, there were no bishops, presbyters, or deacons (1 Cor. xii. 28), who were officers instituted at a later age. Peter, one of the twelve, was an illiterate Galilean fisherman, and we have no proof of his ability to write a letter in Greek. The writer of the First Epistle of Peter speaks of shepherds or pastors, bishops, and elders, all which are technical expressions of a later age. The writer of the Second Epistle was a gross impostor of the second century. The advanced theology of these two writers clearly points to a later age than the first century.

porated with considerable embellishment, as is the practice of many historians in all ages, in the new histories. The names of the parents of Jesus, the industry followed by his father and himself, that of village carpenters, his brothers and sisters, the names of the twelve Apostles, their occupations as fishermen and publicans, the disputes with the Scribes and Pharisees, his attachment to the sisters Mary and Martha, the plots to seize him, his arrest, trial, crucifixion, and supposed resurrection, his discourses and moral precepts, and much other information can be trustfully accepted, shorn of their embellishments. Whatever can be inferred or proved to have been unknown in the first century, such as the miracles, the parables, the story of Judas, the story of the miraculous birth of Jesus, and the whole story of John the Baptist in its alleged connection with Jesus, the story of Herod's cruelty to the little children of Bethlehem, and the story of the birth of Jesus at Bethlehem, the ascension, Pentecost, and much more may be reasonably set down as fabrications of the second and subsequent centuries. Profane history, which, however, was not such to the Jewish stipendiary apostles, such as the writings of Josephus, was obviously also utilised. I acquit these later apostles of the authorship of the parables, which on the whole were beyond their mental capacity, as I find no mention of them, except of one, in the Christian writings of the first half of the second century. Justin Martyr quotes, as said by the Lord, a very succinct statement of the parable: "A sower went forth to sow the seed; and some fell by the wayside, and some among thorns, and some on stony ground, and some on good ground"[1] (*Trypho*, cxxv., Ante-Nicene Christian Library). Hippolytus states that the Naasseni made use of this parable, which they quoted in a more extended form, to enforce their pretensions (*Hippolytus*, Ante-Nicene Christian Library, vol. i. p. 144). The parables were the chief contributions to the Gospels made in the second half of the second century: but the two brightest

---

[1] Bishop Westcott thinks that the incoherent statement immediately following the above in Justin's *Trypho* indicates the parable of the Talents (Matt. xxv. 14-30; Luke xix. 11-28). I am unable to identify the parable. The passage has been tampered with. It is nonsense as it stands.

gems amongst them, the parable of the Good Samaritan and the Prodigal Son, were not added to the Gospel of Luke till after the second century.[1] I make this statement on the authority of

[1] Irenæus, in Bk. III. 17, 3, refers to a story very similar to the parable of the Good Samaritan, but it is not the same. He speaks of it, not as a parable, but as an actual incident in the life of Jesus, in which the Lord himself took a personal part. It is clear that Irenæus derived the story from an unknown Apocryphal Gospel, but not from the Canonical Gospel of Luke. I can find no trace of the existence of this parable in the Canonical Gospel in the second and third centuries and greater part of the fourth till after the time of Epiphanius. From the silence of Tertullian regarding it, it is clear that it did not exist in Marcion's Gospel; and from his abstinence of remark that Marcion had erased it, it follows that it did not exist in the Canonical Gospel. The same observations are applicable to the silence of Epiphanius regarding the parable. The parable was absent both in Marcion's Gospel and in the Canonical Gospel of Luke of that period, and hence the dead silence regarding it of both these great denouncers of Marcion. Regarding the parable of the Prodigal Son, Irenæus speaks of it in Bk. IV. 14, 2, and again in Bk. IV. 36, 7; and there can be no doubt that the parable which he describes was identical with Luke xv. 11-32, although he does not attribute it to Luke. Clement of Alexandria, perhaps, makes an obscure allusion to it, "after the image of the rich man's son in the Gospel" (*Pæd.*, II. 1, 9), while deprecating disorderly living. One would naturally conclude, from these references to the parable, that the latter had been admitted into the Canonical Gospel in the interval between the publication of the third and fourth Books of Irenæus' great work. But against such a conclusion is the fact of the dead silence regarding this parable maintained by Tertullian in his close criticism of Marcion's Gospel in Bk. IV. of Anti-Marcion. The only inference that can be drawn from Tertullian's silence is that the parable was absent from both Marcion's Gospel and the Canonical Gospel of Luke. There is no doubt that the parable was wanting in Marcion's Gospel; but it is hard to believe that, if it existed in the Canonical Gospel, a close and hostile critic like Tertullian, who notes the omission or change of single words in the two Gospels, would have silently let slip the great opportunity of pointing out the deletion of the finest parable in the Gospel of Luke and of assigning suitable reasons for the erasure. I therefore conclude that Irenæus derived his knowledge of the parable, which he omits in his statement of the contents of Luke's Gospel, from an unknown Apocryphal Gospel, current in his time. Tertullian refers elsewhere (*De patientia*, xii., and *De penitentia*, viii.) to the parable of the Prodigal Son, but he does not mention the source of his information. The parable was probably introduced late in the third century, or in the fourth century, into the Canonical Gospel of Luke. It is referred to in the *Apostolic Constitutions*, ii. 41, but is put into the mouth of the Apostle Matthew. Epiphanius says that it was cut out by Marcion (*Scholion*, xlii.); the real fact, however, was that the parable was

Irenæus, who omits these two parables, incomparably the finest in the whole collection, in the running table of contents which he gives of the Gospel of Luke of his day (Irenæus, III. xiv. 3). The talent in the Church in the second century was not so great as in the third century, in which were found men of the intellectual calibre of Clement of Alexandria, Tertullian, and Origen. Marcion may possibly have composed these two parables for his gospel, but it is hardly probable that the ecclesiastical compilers, who made his gospel the foundation of the Gospel of Luke, would have dropped two of the very brightest gems. Marcion, with all his errors, was a man deeply imbued with the essence of the morality which Jesus had taught.

The chief and most deplorable corruption introduced by the Christian Jews was the remuneration or payment of their apostles and prophets. Had they adhered to their original plan, observed for a century, of simply providing board and lodging for a few days, they would have maintained the integrity and honesty of the apostles. Knaves and rogues of the clever sort would never have thought it worth their while to intrude into their society. Ten per cent., with an ever-widening area, which they could extend by their personal exertions, was a great temptation to unscrupulous men. These nameless rogues and knaves, under the guise of apostles and prophets, were the founders of ecclesiastical Christianity; and on them should be directed the execration of mankind. Judaism had a narrow escape from the fate that had overtaken the system of morality inculcated by Jesus. The institution of apostles, which had been established by Jesus and had continued in the first century, was later on overthrown by the usurpation by the presbytery of the functions of the former. The beginning of this change is indicated in ch. xv. of the *Didache*;[1] and the completion of the struggle for

absent in both Gospels, but was latterly put into the Canonical Gospel of Luke, and not cut out in Marcion's Gospel.

[1] "Appoint for yourselves therefore bishops and deacons worthy of the Lord, men who are meek and not lovers of money, and true and approved; for unto you they also perform the service of the prophets and teachers. Therefore despise them not; for they are your honourable men along with the prophets and teachers" (*Didache*, xv., Lightfoot's translation). Instead

supremacy, and to the claim to the apostolic 10 per cent., is sufficiently clear in the falsified letters of Ignatius. The main object of the falsification of these letters by ecclesiastical rogues appears to me to have been to justify and blazon the suppression of the apostles, a class instituted by Jesus, and the elevation of the presbytery to their now lucrative office. The glorification of the bishops and presbytery is the key-note of the falsified letters. The extension of the system of morality inculcated by Jesus was already considerable in the first century, as testified to by Pliny, who found, in the populous Roman province under his government, that the temples were deserted, the rites of religion neglected, and victims for sacrifice without purchasers. It is to be deeply deplored that this prosperous spread of the moral system of Jesus had been interfered with by apostolic and episcopal knavery, and converted into a growth of ecclesiastical superstition and gain. A few more centuries of the development of the morality of Jesus amongst the civilised nations of the world would indeed have ushered in the Kingdom of God, which Jesus had passionately contemplated.

We are now in a position to comprehend the sources of Justin's information. The documents which he utilised were 'the other writings' to which Aristides refers. Justin's *Memoirs of the Apostles* were the writings of the stipendiary or 10 per cent. apostles, accredited members of the Parent Church or body of Christians. The confusion between the twelve Apostles, the personal disciples of the Lord, and the itinerant and stipendiary apostles at the conclusion of the first and beginning of the second century is the cause of much chronological perplexity in the perusal of the writings of the second century. Various individuals are styled disciples of apostles, such as Quadratus, Papias, Polycarp, Hegesippus, and others: they were, in fact, disciples of the stipendiary and itinerant apostles. The longevity of the Hebrew Patriarchs would be needed to make them disciples of the twelve. I make the statement with reserve, as I have not sufficiently investigated the subject of the Synoptic Gospels, that the word 'gospel' in

of 'appoint' I should translate 'Vote by raising your hands.' The 'laying on of hands' was a practice which originated in the second century.

the first half of the second century, and throughout the first century, was always used in the singular number and applied exclusively to the general Gospel or teaching of Jesus, the moral precepts or *logia*, which alone were meant by the term. The only exception to this custom that I remember is in Justin's *First Apology*, lxvi., where is a parenthetical clause in explanation of the *Memoirs of the Apostles*, "which are called Gospels," and this may very well be considered a gloss subsequently added. To this custom may have been due the use by Justin of the expression, 'Memoirs of the Apostles.' The custom certainly did not prevail in the second half of the second century, and we find Irenæus, in a moment of triumph when he was obviously off his guard, using the expression, 'Gospels of the Apostles,' which I take to be the same as Justin's 'Memoirs of the Apostles.' Speaking of the Valentinians, Irenæus remarks: "They have advanced to such a pitch of daring as to entitle a book which was composed by them not long since the *Gospel of Truth*, though it accords in no respects with the Gospels of the Apostles; so that the Gospel in fact cannot exist among them without blasphemy. For if that which they bring forward is the Gospel of Truth, and still is unlike those which are delivered to us by the Apostles—they who please can learn *how* from the writings themselves—it is shown at once that that which is delivered to us by the Apostles is not the Gospel of Truth" (Irenæus, III. xi. 9, Westcott's translation, *Canon of the New Testament*, Part I. iv. p. 301 of 6th ed.). The expressions 'Gospels of the Apostles' and 'the Apostles' cannot possibly mean the four Canonical Gospels and 'the twelve Apostles'; but they accord strictly with the facts that I have gathered from early Christian records, regarding the writings of the itinerant and stipendiary apostles. I should not, however, be surprised if theologians seize this correspondence between Justin's 'Memoirs of the Apostles' and Irenæus' 'Gospels of the Apostles' to maintain that Justin's Memoirs are identical with the Canonical Gospels, which Irenæus, they will say, meant, although only two of the latter were hypothetically regarded to have been written by members of the twelve—the Gospels *according* to John and *according* to Matthew, and the other two were neither written nor delivered by any of the twelve Apostles. I have to add that there can be no doubt that the literary productions of the itinerant and stipendiary apostles, prophets, or teachers or masters, for they are called by all these names, were recognised and accredited by the Church, for Justin writes: "On the day called of the sun there is an assembly in the same place of all dwelling in the cities or country, and the *Memoirs of the Apostles* and the writings of the prophets are read as long as practicable. Then the reader ceasing, he who presides admonishes and exhorts to the imitation of these excellent things" (*First Apology*, lxvii.).

A striking confirmation of the fact that ecclesiastical Christianity, as we have it now, was founded, not in the first century upon the teaching of Jesus and of the twelve, but in the second century on the writings of nameless apostles, prophets, and teachers, is to be found in the writing called the Epistle to the Ephesians. This is a writing of the second century, falsely attributed to Paul the Apostle, and erroneously antedated about three-fourths or nearly a full century. The expressions and ideas of Gnosticism are so numerous in the Epistles to the Ephesians, Philippians, and Colossians that they justify the rejection of Paul the Apostle as their author, and clearly indicate their date to be the second century. They give one the impression of being writings, not of several, but of one author, who was not the Apostle Paul. The writer declares himself to be Paul the deacon, and hence he could not have been Paul the Apostle, who never was a deacon. The reader of English will never be able to find this out, either from the Authorised or Revised versions, because the translation is not the exact rendering of the Greek original. If a French writer should declare himself to be a captain in the army, and his English translator should convert *captain* into *officer*, the English reader would not know that the French writer was not a *general*. A deacon was a distinct grade in the ancient Church, and hence the Greek word διάκονος should be justly translated *deacon* and not *minister*, which is a general term. In the Epistle to the Colossians occurs the following passage: "If ye continue in the faith grounded and settled, and be not moved away from the hope of the Gospel, which ye have heard, *and* which was preached to every creature which is under heaven; whereof I Paul am made a minister; who now rejoice in my sufferings for you, and fill up that which is behind of the afflictions of Christ in my flesh for his body's sake, which is the church: whereof I am made a minister, according to the dispensation of God" (Col. i. 23–25, Authorised Version). In the Revised Version the tense is correctly altered in accordance with the Greek: "I Paul was made a minister" in both passages; but it is sad to find that the word *deacon* was not substituted for *minister*, as it ought to have been to suit the Greek word διάκονος in the original. The writer likewise speaks of Tychicus, a deacon (erroneously translated minister), and fellow servant of his (Col. iv. 7). In Ephesians iii. 7 the writer again speaks of himself as a deacon, erroneously translated minister. It was the easiest thing in the world, if it was deemed necessary, to change the word *deacon* in the exordium of the Epistles to the Ephesians and Colossians to *apostle*: in the Epistle to the Philippians, the descriptive word used is *servant*. Paul, the apostle of the first century, was tenacious of his title of apostle, and never failed to use it. It should be borne in mind that deacons in the second century discharged, in addition to their especial duties, the office of apostle or teacher, as stated in the *Didache*, ch. xvi., so that the deacon Paul had the right of writing epistles to churches, and of styling himself an apostle. The words: "The Gospel which was preached to every creature which is under heaven," could not have been written by Paul the Apostle, in whose days the spread of the Gospel was very limited. There are also a few other indications of a second century date, very small in themselves, but, like the trouser button or piece of rag torn off the clothes, affording valuable clues to the detective officer. In Ephesians iii. 14 occurs the passage, "I bow my knees unto the Father," and in Philippians ii. 10, "At the name of Jesus every knee should bow." Now, kneeling was not practised in the first century, in which the attitude of prayer was standing amongst Christians, Jews, and Pagans. In Ephesians iv. 11, 'evangelists' are spoken of. I can find no trace of 'gospels' in the plural, in the first century, certainly not in the days of Paul, and hence there were no evangelists or writers of gospels; but their number was legion in the second century. The personage, 'Luke the evangelist,' is said to have been Paul's companion. But there is no evidence that Paul had a companion of that name. The Lucius (Λούκιος) spoken of in the very doubtfully authentic ch. xvi. of Romans, verse 21, is as different from Luke (Λουκᾶς) the beloved physician of Paul the deacon (Col. iv. 14) as Jones from Robinson—they were different persons, living in different epochs. The Luke in Philemon 24 may have been the same as the above Luke, but may also have been another fellow. In Philippians i. 1, bishops and deacons are spoken of. There were neither deacons nor bishops in Paul's day (1 Cor. xii. 28). The first trace of bishops appears in Clement's Epistle and in the *Didache*, ch. xvi., about the close of the first century or beginning of the second. The Epistles to Titus and Timothy, in which bishops are spoken of, are second century writings. The Epistle to the Ephesians being a second century writing, the following passages which occur in it clearly indicate the certain fact that the ecclesiastical faith of the second century was founded, not on the teaching of Jesus and the twelve Apostles, but on the writings of the stipendiary or 10 per cent. apostles and prophets, or 'after-apostles,' *post apostoli*, as they were called by Tertullian. "And are built upon the foundation of the apostles and prophets, Jesus Christ being the chief corner *stone*..... Whereby, when ye read, ye may understand my knowledge in the mystery of Christ; which, in other ages, was not made known unto the sons of men, as it is now revealed unto his holy apostles and prophets by the Spirit" (Eph. i. 20; ii. 4, 5). Paul, the deacon and apostle, was the writer of the Epistles to the Ephesians, Philippians, and Colossians. He was probably a deacon of the Church of Marcion, to whom we owe the preservation of these three Epistles.

The Jewish corruptions of the moral Gospel of Jesus above spoken of are incidentally connected with my subject: the Greek corruptions are directly and prominently connected with the Fourth Gospel, which was originally a Gnostic or Greek writing. The dove of Cerinthus, the divine æon that descended from above and occupied the body of Jesus, was early seized upon, as already stated, p. 67, by the Jewish stipendiary apostles and prophets, and worked up in their memoirs into a story of the baptism of Jesus by John the Baptist, about whom they obtained information from Josephus and perhaps other writers extant in their days. Hence the dove has gained a permanent position in ecclesiastical faith, and cannot be dislodged without an earthquake or other great catastrophe, though modern divines show a disposition to regard the ethereal bird with their blind eye alone. The dove or æon of Cerinthus is not, however, the only conception of Greek metaphysical theology which has found a permanent place in ecclesiastical religion. I am deeply grieved to state that my investigation has constrained me to form the conclusion that one of the most sacred objects of Christian faith, which has become associated with the tenderest feelings of millions of simple Christians in the many troubles of life, known to them as the Comforter or Paraclete, was unknown to Jesus, and was unknown to orthodox Christians before the second half of the second century. Like the dove, which was an æon of Cerinthus, Paraclete was an æon of the metaphysical theology of Valentinus the Gnostic (A.D. 140), grafted into the ecclesiastical system of religion, disguised as the Holy Spirit or Holy Ghost.

The theology of Valentinus is most complex and difficult of comprehension, but the complete understanding of it is not necessary for our subject. It is sufficient to know that the system of Valentinus consisted of thirty æons, of which Paraclete was one. Irenæus gives an account of the Valentinian æon, named Paraclete, which runs startlingly close to the account of the Spirit of the same name in the Fourth Gospel: " He (Christ) having returned to the Pleroma (or Gnostic heaven), being, as it seems, loth to descend a second time, sent forth Paraclete, that is the Saviour, the Father endowing him with all power, and placing everything under his authority" (Irenæus, I. iv. 5). Compare this with ch. xiv. 16, 26; xv. 26; xvi. 7-11, of the Fourth Gospel; in these verses the proper name Paraclete is translated Comforter in the Authorised Version, but in the margin of the Revised Version other translations of the proper name are given, and Greek Paraclete is added. The Christians of the first century and of the first half of the second were familiar with the Holy

Ghost or Holy Spirit, whose name and functions abound in the authentic writings of the period. Clement of Rome (*c.* 95 A.D.) says, " Have we not one God and one Christ, and one Spirit of Grace that was shed upon us ? " (*First Ep.*, 46). Paul also says, " Now there are diversities of gifts, but the same Spirit, and there are diversities of administrations, but the same Lord. And there are diversities of operations, but it is the same God which worketh all in all " (1 Cor. xii. 4–6). Let any one who cares to do so read Paul's Epistle to the Romans, viii. 1–27. This is a passage of Scripture that contains more spirits than any other of similar length that I know of. The word Spirit occurs nineteen times, and it will not be possible to make out more than one with a personality, and some people will find even one such with difficulty. The first twenty chapters of the Fourth Gospel have the word Spirit twenty-two times, counting Paraclete, translated Comforter, as Spirit. From this number four can be identified as possessing separate personalities. God is defined as a Spirit in ch. iv. 24 ; the Holy Ghost is referred to by name at the conclusion of ch. i. 33, and also in ch. iii. 5, 6, 8, 34, and xx. 22, and there is the Spirit that descended from heaven in the form of a dove (ch. i. 33). The first two Spirits were well known to Jewish Christians of the first century, and descended to them from the Old Testament dispensation ; and the third Spirit I have already discussed. The fourth Spirit is Paraclete. This Spirit is introduced in a pathetic scene and address to the disciples when Jesus announces his approaching departure from them : " Let not your heart be troubled. . . . . In my Father's house are many mansions. . . . . I go to prepare a place for you. . . . . If ye love me, keep my commandments, and I will pray the Father, and he will give you Paraclete, that he may abide with you for ever ; even the Spirit of Truth. . . . . I will not leave you orphans: I will come to you. . . . . He that hath my commandments, and keepeth them, he it is that loveth me ; and he that loveth me shall be loved of my Father, and I will love him. . . . . These things have I spoken unto you, being yet present with you. But that Spirit, Paraclete, whom the Father will send in my name, he shall teach you all things, and bring all things to your remembrance whatsoever I have said unto you. . . . . Let not your heart be troubled, neither let it be afraid. . . . . These things I command you, that ye love one another. If the world hate you, ye know that it hated me before it hated you. . . . . But when Paraclete is come, whom I will send unto you from the Father, he shall testify of me : and ye also shall bear witness, because ye have been with me from the beginning. . . . . But now I go unto him that sent me. . . . . But because I have said these things unto you, sorrow hath filled your heart. Nevertheless I tell you the truth ; it is expedient for you that I go away : for if I go not away, Paraclete will not come unto you ; but if I depart, I will send him unto you."

Now in the perusal of this affectionate address, I find it impracticable to identify Paraclete with the well-known Holy Ghost of Christian literature. A Spirit that has always been with mankind, according to Jewish-Christian ideas, cannot be the same as the Spirit Paraclete, which was to come only after the departure of Jesus from earth, and for whose coming the departure of Jesus was a necessary condition. The proper name Paraclete is not found in any other Christian writing of the first century and first half of the second century. The word παράκλητος, used by the writer of the First Epistle of John ii. 1, is not a proper name, but a descriptive or adjective noun applied, not to the Holy Ghost, but to Jesus.[1] In the Fourth Gospel, Paraclete is a proper name, and to translate it is as foolish as to translate the respectable name of Mr Smith into Mr Worker-in-Metals. In the Vulgate the name is not translated ; nor in the Syriac of Mrs Lewis's Gospels, according to her marginal notes. In this interesting palimpsest, the reading of ch. xiv. 26 is : "But that Spirit, Paraclete, whom my Father will send unto you in my name" ; and this reading I have adopted in my quotation as consistent with the context. The received Greek text, which is correct, has been manifestly wrenched in the translation of this passage

---

[1] The word is also used in the writing called the Second Epistle of Clement, ch. vi., and the passage is translated by Bishop Lightfoot : "Or who shall be our advocate, unless we be found having holy and righteous works" ; the allusion being to Christ, not to the Holy Spirit.

in order to convert Paraclete into the familiar Holy Ghost of Christians; it is thus rendered: "But the Comforter, which is the Holy Ghost, whom the Father will send in my name." In ch. vii. 39, a verse explanatory of a most strange passage, said to be a quotation from the Scriptures, but which cannot be found in them, is another transparent effort of the translators to convert Paraclete into the Holy Ghost. The verse reads: "But this spake he of the Spirit, which they that believe should receive; for the Holy Ghost was not yet *given*; because that Jesus was not yet glorified." In the Revised Version the verse is more correctly translated, but the word *given* is retained, although it is not found in the Greek text. The exact and true translation of the Greek text is: "But this spake he of the Spirit which they believing on him were to receive: for the Spirit was not yet, because that Jesus was not yet glorified." Taking the initial words of the Prologue, "in the beginning *of the Gospel*," as fixing the chronology of the Fourth Gospel, the understanding of this passage is clear and easy. In the beginning of the Gospel, the Word was; in the beginning of the Gospel the Spirit or Paraclete, which they believing on him were to receive, was not. A non-existent Spirit at the beginning of the Gospel is not the Holy Ghost of Christians. There can be no doubt that this future-coming Spirit spoken of in ch. vii. 39 was Paraclete, which was not to come, for it had no existence before sent forth as an emanation, till after Jesus had suffered, or, in evangelical language, had been glorified, and was the same Spirit mentioned in ch. xiv. 16 and 26, and ch. xv. 26. The Holy Ghost of Christians was always in existence, in the Old Testament as well as in the New.

I think there was confusion in the ancient Christian mind caused by the intrusion of the Johannine theology, which was Gnostic and alien, into the conventional and Synoptic theology, which was Jewish. Paraclete was a new Gnostic Spirit, but the Holy Ghost or Spirit was an ancient Jewish Spirit, and the old and the new Spirits could not very well mix and amalgamate into one. We have seen that Paraclete was not to descend to the disciples till after the return exoterically, that is, according to the words of the text, of

Jesus to the Father, *i.e.*, after the Ascension, but esoterically, that is, the hidden or secret meaning was, the return of the æon Christ (the dove) to the pleroma or Gnostic heaven. It appears to me that sometimes the one meaning and sometimes the other was taken in the third century. In ch. xxi. 21 and 22 of the Fourth Gospel, after the resurrection, Jesus is represented as breathing the Holy Ghost upon the disciples: this representation (an interpolation made in the third century, see p. 306, ff.) is in accordance with the esoteric meaning of the text, *i.e.*, after the return of the æon or dove. In the Acts of the Apostles, the ascension of Jesus, which is omitted in all the Gospels (written and revised in the second century), is first described (ch. i. 9), and then is delineated the scene in which the Holy Ghost descends upon the Christian assembly (ch. ii. 1-4). This is the proper sequel of the narrative in the Fourth Gospel, and I believe was originally so intended. It is to be observed that it is in accord with the exoteric meaning of the text, for this meaning required, as a preliminary event, the ascension of Jesus Himself. Origen, in his *Commentary on Matthew*, ch. 40, remarking on the Transfiguration, says: "John taught in the Gospel that, before the resurrection of the Saviour, no one had the Holy Spirit, saying: 'For the Spirit was not yet, because Jesus was not glorified'" (see additional vol., Ante-Nicene Christian Library, p. 471). This was not in accord with the Jewish conception of the Holy Spirit, as set forth in the Synoptic Gospels, in which the Holy Ghost is represented as in active operation throughout the Gospel story. In the development of the doctrine of the miraculous conception, the Holy Ghost is represented as overshadowing the Virgin Mary some thirty-one years before the beginning of the Gospel, and a longer period before the return to the Father, whether the latter event be understood esoterically or exoterically, after which only Paraclete was to descend to the earth. It is clear that Paraclete of the Fourth Gospel is not the same Spirit as the Holy Ghost of the Synoptic Gospels. The Gnostic Spirit cannot be assimilated to the Jewish Spirit—chronology is hostile to the fusion.

The theology of the Gnostics, as represented, or rather

perhaps wilfully misrepresented, in the pages of Irenæus and Hippolytus and others of the Fathers, is an unintelligible mass of metaphysical conceptions of divinity, comparable to the lucubrations of the inmates of a lunatic asylum, and it has not the appearance of being a marketable commodity. Yet, strange to say, there is the authority of Irenæus, who regarded the Gnostic theology and its *personnel* with hatred and all unrighteousness, for the fact that the Gnostics obtained a high price for imparting the knowledge of their profound mysteries (Irenæus, I. iv. 3).

The Jewish and Gnostic or Greek Christians interchanged their corruptions, the Jewish Christians appropriating some of the Gnostic corruptions, and the Gnostics some of the Jewish, and the Parent Church finished by appropriating some of both. We have seen that the earlier Ebionite sects, who were Jews, appropriated the dove of Cerinthus, but they gave it a Jewish flavour so as to accommodate it to Jewish digestion. The æon of Cerinthus was interpreted as an angel which dwelt in Christ—a view agreeable to Jewish notions. The Gnostics, or many of them—markedly the Valentinians, but not the Marcionites—received the Jewish story of the miraculous birth of Jesus, but they interpreted it in an ingenious manner, purifying it from its material grossness, which was repulsive to the Greek metaphysical mind. Jesus, they said, was not *of* the Virgin's womb but *in* it, and passed *through* it like water through a tube, without taking up any of the carnal impurity of the Virgin's womb in his transit through it. These humorous views were questions of life and death, of money or no money, in the second century; but we of the nineteenth century should not be too censorious in our condemnation of them, seeing that we ourselves, with all our additional enlightenment, the growth of centuries, are in conflict with each other on the great question whether a wheaten loaf, eaten in the Eucharist, is or is not the real human body of the Lord—a question on which the destination of large amounts of money, the produce of industry and thieving, depends.

CHAPTER V.

THE FIRST EPISTLE OF JOHN, AND THE REVELATIONS.

I THINK it desirable to make a few remarks regarding the connection between the Fourth Gospel and the writing known as the First Epistle of John. This epistle is anonymous, but professes to be written by a contemporary of Jesus, and there is no reason to disbelieve this statement. The approximative date can be ascertained from ch. ii. 13 and 14. The epistle is addressed to fathers, who were contemporaries of Jesus and knew him personally, to young men, and to little children. I take this to indicate three generations, and that the epistle was written when the third generation was still young, *i.e.*, about A.D. 75 or 85, or thereabouts. Although I have no reason to doubt that the writer was a contemporary and disciple of Jesus, as he describes himself to have been, yet I have found no reason to believe that he was the Apostle John. He does not state his name, as Peter and James, Jude and Paul, and the writer of the Revelations do, and as Matthew and Mark probably did. The so-called traditions of the Church are often ridiculous and generally untrustworthy, and the Church itself was too active in the perpetration of acts usually condoned as 'pious frauds,' but which are better described as rogueries, to be a safe guide. The name of the Apostle John has been falsely used to cover and give credit to the great forgery of the Fourth Gospel: and a Church that can do that has no claim to be believed in its attribution of the First Epistle of John to the Apostle of that name, without collateral corroboration, and that does not exist.

Place aux forgeurs. As in the study of all early Christian writings of any importance, preliminary precautions must be taken to detect and evict falsifications in the First Epistle of John. The unction or ointment verses, ch. ii. 20 and 27, should be expunged; and if verse 21 be also an ointment verse, it should follow. The practice of applying oil or ointment as a part of the religious ceremony of baptism was a Pagan usage adopted by Christians in the second century;[1] and the acquirement of knowledge foolishly and superstitiously attributed to the application of the ointment is incongruous with the sensible and pure morality of the first century, but quite in harmony with the growth of superstition amongst Christians in the second century. This practice has died out in Christian churches, the priesthood having, I conclude, become ashamed of it. In Marriott's *Vestiarium Christianum* is a quaint picture of "a bishop administering the chrism in infant baptism, from a MS. of the ninth century" (Plate XXXVII.). In the Roman Church its place has seemingly been taken by the practice of covertly inserting into the mouth of the infant at baptism some salt dissolved in the saliva of the officiating priest. I am not sure that this disgusting practice is on the wane, or that Ritualists have introduced it into the Anglican churches. Irenæus quotes the passage from verse 18 to verse 22, but he omits the unction verse 20 altogether, and verse 21 is greatly modified, and verse 22 is unfairly quoted, and shall be spoken of further on (III. xvi. 5). Verse 20 being an interpolation, verse 27 must be so also, as it is exactly of the same nature. Both these verses are anachronisms in a Christian writing of the first century, and are hence most certainly interpolations of a later period. I rejoice that I have been able to produce some documentary evidence of deceit in this instance, but it is not essential. If in a book of the eighteenth century a statement

---

[1] The following passage occurs in the well-known letter of the Emperor Hadrian (A.D. 117 to 137) on the Christians in Egypt: "Those who worship Serapis are Christians, and those who call themselves Christian bishops are worshippers of Serapis. There is no ruler of a Jewish synagogue, no Samaritan, no Christian bishop, who is not an astrologer, an interpreter of prodigies, and an anointer." See also Theophilus, *Ad Autolycum*, i. 12, where the source of the practice is clearly indicated.

should be found regarding railway travelling, electric telegraphic and telephonic communication, or bicycles, we should be justified in summarily pronouncing such statement to be an interpolation of the nineteenth century, without any further warrant but the historical fact that railways, electric telegraph and telephone and bicycles were not invented and used till the nineteenth century had made some advance. The third verse of chapter iv. affords an instance of alteration of original about which the two great Churches of Roman Catholics and Protestants are not agreed. In the Vulgate, or Roman Catholic Bible, the reading is, "*Omnis spiritus, qui solvit Jesum, ex Deo non est*," *i.e.*, every spirit, or individual, that dissolves, or separates, or analyses, or disintegrates, or decomposes Jesus is not of God. Irenæus has a slight but important modification, '*Jesum Christum*' (III. xvi. 8), and in this change he is followed by Jerome. The Protestant Bibles have the same verse thus: "Every spirit that confesseth not that Jesus Christ is come in the flesh is not of God." Tischendorf, in his critical text of the New Testament, curtails the verse thus: "Every spirit that confesses not Jesus is not of God." There exists a passage in the Epistle of Polycarp (ch. vii.) which closely resembles the text: "For every one who shall not confess that Jesus Christ is come in the flesh is Antichrist." Socrates, a Greek ecclesiastical historian of the fifth century, states (*Eccl. Hist.*, vii. 32) that "in the old copies of the Catholic Epistle of John it was written, 'Every spirit that dissolveth Jesus is not from God.' But thus thought those who wished to separate the divinity from the economy (or system, or constitution) of a man erased from the old copies." Archbishop Alexander of Armagh, who is the commentator on this Epistle in the *Speaker's Commentary*, considers this historian the only Greek evidence who remains, and that the reading is of Latin origin. "Its aim," he continues, "is clearly polemical against heretics, who distinguished between the Man Jesus and the Divine Æon, Christ—or the Divine and Human Nature—and who, as thus isolating the true Humanity, might be said to separate the Man Jesus from Christ as God, and as it were to 'dissolve' him. This became inserted into the text." Irenæus, who, however, was a Greek authority, made great use of this verse, especially against Cerinthus, whom he accused of comminuting Jesus, *i.e.*, breaking him into pieces. The reading against dissolving or comminuting Jesus was, in fact, in Dr Alexander's judgment, needed for the strange discussions against Gnostics in the second century, and thus in fact it came into being, exactly as in my judgment the clause "and the world was made by him" found its way into the tenth verse of the Prologue of the Fourth Gospel. I am glad to remark that an archbishop clearly perceives a source of corruption of the sacred text that is also patent to me. In the course of time the Gnostics disappeared, the need for the verse against dissolving was not urgent, and its presence became inconvenient, as theologians found it necessary to discriminate between the human necessities of Jesus and his divine nature; as in the very early instance of Irenæus, who, in explaining the descent of the dove at the baptism, says, "inasmuch as the Word of God was man," anointed the latter, and continues, "but inasmuch as He was God, He did not judge according to glory, nor reprove after the manner of speech" (III. ix. 3), the meaning of which language I do not pretend to understand. The earlier and original reading of ch. iv. 3 was hence with a considerable consensus restored to the Epistle.

In connection with the changes made in ch. iv. 3, it is evident that the reading '*qui solvit Jesum*' was specially introduced into the sacred text to denounce Cerinthus, who certainly made a clear distinction between the man Jesus and the divine æon Christ. The corrupted text denounced Cerinthus; the genuine text, that quoted by Polycarp and followed in our Protestant Bibles, did not, for Cerinthus maintained that Jesus came in the flesh. In this verse time has rendered justice to Cerinthus. In another verse, however, which was also a forgery introduced for the purpose of vituperating Cerinthus, time has not yet rendered justice to the great Gnostic. The forged verse, ii. 22, was directly aimed at Cerinthus, as was the forged verse, iv. 3, '*qui solvit Jesum.*' Just as in the latter verse Cerinthus was charged with splitting or dissolving Jesus, and declared to be not of God, but inferentially of the devil; so, in ii. 22, he was charged with denying Jesus to be the Christ, and abused as a liar. No one has put this matter in a clearer light than Irenæus. I have already alluded to his quotation of this verse above. If the quotation in Irenæus be seen in juxtaposition with the reading of our received version, the force of the following remarks will be the better understood.

RECEIVED VERSION, ii. 22.   IRENÆUS, III. xvi. 5.

Who is a liar but he that denieth that Jesus is the Christ? He is Antichrist, that denieth the Father and the Son.

Who is a liar but he that denieth that Jesus is the Christ? This is Antichrist.

Irenæus, in the passage in which he makes this quotation, was speaking of the heresy of Cerinthus, and remarked that the Gospel " knew no Christ who flew away from Jesus before the Passion " ; so that there can be no mistake regarding the person whom he stigmatised as liar and Antichrist. The disciple of the Lord, who wrote the Epistle, declares that " he is Antichrist that denies the Father and the Son." Now Cerinthus did not deny the Father and Son, and so is not Antichrist. Here the unfairness and roguery of Irenæus in short quoting the passage become apparent. The first clause of the verse is couched in coarse language unbecoming the disciple of the Lord, whose language elsewhere is decent. The first clause of the verse is alien to the subject which the disciple of the Lord is discussing, viz., that of Antichrists. These two considerations alone, apart from others, justify me in pronouncing this clause to be an interpolation, which in all probability Irenæus knew to be a forgery, if he was not the forger himself. The vulgar language and base mind of the forger is apparent in the clause. The forgery, further, does not state the truth, for though Cerinthus imagined the æon Christ, he did not deny that Jesus was the Jewish Messiah or the Christ, which is the synonym of Messiah in Greek. That is a subject on which we have no evidence that Cerinthus expressed any contrary opinion: and in his account of Cerinthus' heresy (Bk. I. xxvi. 1) Irenæus does not bring the accusation against him.

The next passage which comes under condemnation may be called collectively the liquidation verses, viz., ch. v. 6–11, inclusive. Verse 7 has already been expunged from the Revised Version. All these verses are obviously the outcome of the transmutation of the dove into water at the crucifixion, as already explained. Their object is now transparent: they were interpolated in order to support and corroborate the forgery of the Fourth Gospel, and make believe that the writer of the Epistle, who was alleged to be the Apostle John, knew of the gush of water and blood from the wound inflicted by the soldier's spear on the body of Jesus, and drew from the incident a few profound religious truths which puzzled the learned brain of Bishop Lightfoot. I have endeavoured to ascertain, but without success, how and why the order of the two words is blood and water in the Fourth Gospel, and water and blood in the Epistle. I regret that I am not satisfied with Dr Alexander's explanation, " The *water* and *blood* is the ideal, mystical, sacramental, *subjective* order; the *blood* and *water* is the historical and *objective* order. The first, therefore, is appropriately adopted in the Epistle; the second in the Gospel." The learned archbishop was not aware, when he penned these thoughts, that there was 'liquidation' but no water in question, so that he formed his opinion without a full knowledge of the facts. In Irenæus (III. xxii. 2) the order is *blood and water*, and also in the *Diatessaron* of Tatian and in the Apocryphal Gospel of Nicodemus, or *Acta Pilati*, which Tischendorf regarded as a writing of the second century; but in every other known passage in which these words are quoted in ancient days, the order is *water and blood*. My belief is that the original order in the forged Fourth Gospel was *water and blood*, the order in fact which was followed in the interpolation of the Epistle, and in the Vatican and Sinaitic versions of Matthew; but in course of time the order was changed in the Fourth Gospel with some design that is not apparent, but probably to prevent or embarrass the re-discovery of the original word for which water was substituted.

To the above I feel disposed to add two other verses as interpolations. It will be noticed that throughout the Epistle there is no mention made of the Holy Ghost. This circumstance appeared propitious to the creation of another connecting link with the Fourth Gospel besides the liquidation verses. Thus two verses were interpolated: they were utterly superfluous, not being necessary to the sense: in the language dear to theologians, subjectively they were surplusage, objectively they were useful connecting links or coincidences, and also as supports of the forged Fourth Gospel: they were otherwise harmless. These two verses are ch. iii. 24, the concluding sentence only, and ch. iv. 13. "And hereby we know that he abideth in us by the Spirit which he hath given us." "Hereby know we that we dwell in him, and he in us, because he has given us of his Spirit." The Spirit, or Paraclete, of the Fourth Gospel was thus introduced into the Epistle: but it is foreign matter, and does not amalgamate with it. To keep God's word, to walk righteously, to confess that Jesus is the Son of God, and to dwell in love are far better tests, natural, simple, and sensible, of fellowship than a mythical spirit (ch. ii. 5, 6; ch. iv. 15, 16).

Not only has the Greek text been "deceitfully dealt with," as Socrates, the Greek ecclesiastical historian, declares, but even the translation has been falsified, perhaps unconsciously, and as the consequence of preconception. I believe the words 'that is' introduced into the translation of the 13th and 14th verses of the second chapter are a mistranslation designed to change the meaning of the author. "I write unto you, fathers, because ye have known him from the beginning"—a literal translation of the Greek text—is a clear and intelligent statement that the fathers were acquainted with Jesus from the beginning of the Gospel, and nothing else. "I write unto you, fathers, because ye have known him *that is* from the beginning," as translated in the Authorised and Revised versions, is designed to mean that the fathers knew Jesus had existed from eternity, and in fact that he was God. This is a tortured interpretation that raises a smile. The thought of the divinity of Jesus is forced into the Epistle wherever it is possible to do so. A very marked instance of this proclivity on the part of the translators is to be found in ch. iii. 16, which is thus rendered in the Authorised Version: "Hereby perceive we the love *of God*, because he laid down his life for us." The words in italics are an interpolation of the translators, as corresponding words do not exist in the Greek received text. These interpolated words in the Authorised Version are very properly expunged in the Revised Version: one proof of the divinity of Jesus, in the minds of numbers of simple people, being thus annulled by a stroke of the pen. The climax is reached in the 20th verse of the 5th chapter: "And we know that the Son of God is come, and hath given us an understanding that we may know Him that is true: and we are in Him that is true, *even* in His Son Jesus Christ. This is the true God and eternal life." As thus rendered, the meaning is clear that Jesus is God, and the true God. The commentator on the Epistle in the *Speaker's Commentary* (Dr Alexander, Archbishop of Armagh) sums up the contents of the Epistle in these words: "Concerning the Word, who is the Life, that which we have seen and heard declare we unto you. This is the true God and Eternal Life" (Introduction, ii. 4, p. 281). Can there be any doubt that in Dr Alexander's opinion the prime conclusion to be drawn from the Epistle is that Jesus is the true God? Nevertheless we find the late Bishop Thorold of Winchester in his Commentary on the Epistle (published by the Society for the Promotion of Christian Knowledge) has for comment on the clause, "This is the true God" (ch. v. 20), nothing but the curt remark, "That is, God the Father." And further, we find the Rev. A. Plummer, D.D., in his comment on this same verse (Cambridge Bible, edited by Bishop Perowne of Worcester), saying, "Omit *even* [in the clause '*even* in His Son Jesus Christ'] which has been inserted in the Authorised Version and Revised Version to make 'in Him that is true' refer to Christ. This last clause explains how it is that we are in the Father, viz., by being in the Son (*Comp.*, ii. 23; John i. 18; xvii. 21, 23). Tyndale boldly turns the second 'in' into 'through'; 'we are in Him that is true, through His Son Jesu Christ.' We have had similar explanatory additions in verses 13, 16.". And again, commenting on the clause, "This is the true God," Dr Plummer remarks, "It is impossible to determine with certainty whether 'This' (οὗτος) refers to the Father, the *principal* substantive of the previous sentence, or to

Jesus Christ, the *nearest* substantive." He then adds that the question need not be discussed with heat, as a proof more or less of the divinity of Christ is of no consequence. He then gives four considerations for regarding the 'True God' to be Jesus, and five considerations for the Father: a majority of one for the Father. Now it must be obvious to people of common sense that the original verse of the Epistle had been "deceitfully dealt with," as Socrates declares; that the words of the writer had been tampered with and muddled—a device of the forger; with the result of modifying and rendering his meaning the reverse of what he intended, or of rendering it so obscure that it is difficult, if not impossible, to ascertain with precision what the meaning is. The key to the right meaning of the writer of the Epistle in this passage is to be found in the work of a contemporary writer who had made the Epistle his guide and pattern, Cerinthus, the author of the Fourth Gospel, who follows this passage in ch. xvii. 3, in Jesus' prayer to the Father: "And this is life eternal, that they might know Thee the only true God, and Jesus Christ whom Thou hast sent." Cerinthus thus helps to display to us the real object and intention of the writer of the First Epistle of John. As in the fourth verse of the Prologue of the Fourth Gospel, the Greek preposition ἐν has been wrongly translated; it has here an instrumental meaning (with, by, by means of, through). It is also probable that the two clauses preceding: "This is the true God and eternal life," are interpolations introduced with the design of changing or obscuring the meaning of the writer, so as to suit the views of the forgers.

Besides the introduction of foreign material and falsification in translation, the critical student has further to guard against false interpretation. In reading the preamble of the Epistle, the unsophisticated student would not think of understanding the familiar phrase, 'from the beginning,' otherwise than as the beginning of the Gospel, until the thought is put into his mind by the commentator that the phrase means 'from the beginning of the world.' The natural sense of the beginning of the Gospel is attached to every clause of the first verse. "That which was from the beginning, which we have heard *from the beginning*, which we have seen with our eyes *from the beginning*, which we have looked upon *from the beginning*, and our hands have handled *from the beginning*, of the word of life." Theologians, however, inculcate that the phrase 'from the beginning' here means from 'eternity, or at least from the beginning of the world,' and that its force is limited to the first clause only, 'that which was from the beginning'; all the other clauses having a different chronology. The remarks of Dr Alexander, Archbishop of Armagh, on this subject ought to be regarded with respect, and doubtless they are influential, but they are not persuasive. He gives three reasons in support of the view that 'from the beginning' here means the beginning of the world. 1st. "*The analogy of the proœmium of the Gospel.*" He quotes Dionysius, Bishop of Alexandria (Eusebius, *Eccl. Hist.*, vii. 25). "The Gospel and the Epistle of John are in harmony and begin similarly. The former says, *In the beginning was the Word*; the latter, *That which was from the beginning*. These are the first notes in the strain." As Dionysius does not say how he understood the current colloquial expression, 'in the beginning,' this witness is certainly unprofitable for Dr Alexander's purpose. 2nd. "*The elevated tone of the whole context.*" The passage, we are told, "is prefaced and brought in with more magnificent ceremony than any one passage of Scripture; the very length of the sentence testifies to the emotion of the writer; the sublimity of the passage gives a proportional elevation to each single clause, and makes the highest sense also the most natural." There are possibly simple people who may be convinced by this reasoning, or rather rhetorical statement, but I regret to say that I am not convinced by it. Does Dr Alexander mean that the highest, and hence the most natural and, I suppose, correct sense, is to throw back the chronology of each single clause of this verse to the beginning of the world or of time? 3rd. "*The context seems to be almost inconsistent with the second interpretation*, viz., the beginning of the ministry of Christ, or the '*initium rei Christianæ.*'" "How could the Apostle be said," demands the archbishop, "not only to have heard, but to have seen and handled the commencement of the Gospel message?" The illusory nature of this reasoning will be best perceived by quoting the verse as follows: "That which was from the beginning *of the Gospel*, which we have heard, which we have seen with our eyes, which we have looked upon, and our hands have handled, of the Word of life."

When the factitious accretions of downright forgery, of mistranslation and misinterpretation are eliminated, the real purport of the First Epistle of John becomes apparent. The main object of the writer was to vindicate the pure humanity of Jesus. He gives his testimony as a contemporary of Jesus from the beginning of his public career, as one who had seen him, had heard him, and had handled him : the best testimony that can be offered. The writer declares explicitly that Jesus was a man and nothing more. "Every spirit (or individual) that confesseth that Jesus Christ is come in the flesh, is of God." This is a clear statement in the evangelical language of the period that he was born and came into the world like other men ; and I can discover no statement in the purified Epistle ascribing divinity to Jesus, or of his miraculous conception by a virgin. Unfortunately, we are helpless against the forgery of omission. It is probable that definite statements that Jesus was not a deity, although employed by God on a divine mission, were made in the Epistle, but had been simply eradicated. The Epistle bears internal testimony that it was partly polemical, and aimed at those who had formed and were teaching perverted notions of the person of Jesus; chiefly those who denied his humanity and worshipped him as God. The writer says that now there are "many Antichrists" (ii. 18) and "false prophets" (iv. 1). Some deny the "Father and the Son" (ii. 22). Others again deny that Jesus was a man, or, in the mannerism of the period, "confess not that Jesus Christ is come in the flesh" (iv. 3). Cerinthus adopted this Epistle as his pattern and guide. He was out of sympathy with an obscure or vague opinion then cropping up amongst the Christian communities, that Jesus was not man. As already explained, there is no evidence in the writings of the first century of the inauguration of the doctrine of the miraculous conception, and of the idea that Jesus was a godman, or of dual nature. Cerinthus appears to be the first who made a viable compromise between the two views, *i.e.*, the view that Jesus was man and nothing else, and the view that he was God and not man. Cerinthus made Jesus a man, in whom an emanation of the deity, the æon Christ in the form of a dove, took up its residence temporarily at the beginning of the Gospel, leaving him at the crucifixion. The view was embodied in the Fourth Gospel. This work, written with the hand of a master, in which the morality and general religious ideas of the writer of the Epistle, a disciple of the Lord, were incorporated, was apparently accepted by the local Christian community. We get the first glimpse of its peculiar Christology from the account of the martyrdom of Polycarp written by the presbyters of the Christian community at Smyrna, at the beginning of the second half of the second century, A.D. 155 or 156.

The concluding verse of the First Epistle of John I regard as prophetic. The aged disciple of the Lord warns the younger members of the Christian community "to keep themselves from idols"; these idols being the results of speculation on the nature of Jesus. The wrong ideas formed of the nature of Jesus have led to Jesus being converted into a deity, and from this parent error has flowed the stream of speculative and practical idolatry that is now almost universal in Christendom. Jesus being regarded as a god, his mother, grandmother, shirt, handkerchief, hair, wood of cross, blood, sweat, heart, even his prepuce or foreskin, and what not, are revered as divine and worthy of adoration. Images of him and of his mother, molten, engraved, carved, or painted, are made objects of prayer and aids to devotion. Bits of bread at fourpence a pound, and wine at half-a-crown or more a bottle, are consecrated by a clergyman or sacrificing priest, and worshipped as his actual flesh and blood, or as material objects which are sanctified by his real presence, and are then devoured. These are the idols against which the foresight of the aged disciple of the Lord cautioned the young Christian community whom he addressed in the Epistle.

Regarding the Revelations, which are in theological opinion associated with the Fourth Gospel and the First Epistle of John as writings of the same author, I have to remark that I do not perceive this connection or authorship. The Revelations are a composition which I am unable to understand. I believe it is the universal experience of civilised mankind for the last eighteen centuries that the Revelations are unintelligible. The Christian Church has had amongst its members and ministers many of the acutest of minds, and none of them have been able to understand the Revelations. It is not possible, in fact, for the sane intellect to comprehend the incoherent and grotesque descriptions in the Revelations. My conclusion is that the Revelations are the production of a lunatic, and of one indifferently instructed in Christianity. The representation of Jesus as a lamb with its throat as if cut, ὡς ἐσφαγμένον, and the strange new song in which Jesus is informed that his throat was cut, ὅτι ἐσφάγης (Rev. v. 6, 9),[1] are clear evidences of the writer's ignorance of the mode in which Jesus died, and throw suspicion on the clause in ch. xi. 8,[2] in which the crucifixion is parenthetically introduced as the work of a Christian interpolator. The Greek verb σφάζω is the exact equivalent of the French verb *égorger*, to cut the throat. The French translator of the Revelations must have had some qualms of conscience when he substituted the word *immolé* for *égorgé* in the rendering of this passage. In the German translation, Luther used the word *erwürget*, which means strangled or throttled. In the Vulgate, *occisus* is used; and in the Authorised and Revised versions the word *slain*. The representation of God in the Revelations, "like a jasper and a sardine stone" (Rev. iv. 3), like the idol in the Temple of Somnath, indicates an indifferent weaning from Paganism. It was surely an insane and unbalanced mind only that could introduce into a serious composition so quizzical a metaphor as the Lamb's wife (Rev. xix. 7 and

[1] The translation of these verses is incorrect in both the Authorised and Revised versions. The clause in verse 6, "stood a lamb as it had been slain," should be literally translated thus, "stood a lamb as if cut in the throat." In verse 9 the clause, "for thou wast slain," should be "for thy throat was cut."

[2] I quote this verse as an illustration of the incoherency of the writer: "And their bodies *shall lie* in the street of the great city, which sp'ritually is called Sodom and Egypt, where also our Lord was crucified."

xxi. 9), which is of the same order of ideas as the grasshopper's granddaughter, and "Will you walk into my parlour, said the spider to the fly."[1] The circumstance that the Revelations were written at the end of the first or beginning of the second century by a quasi-Christian lunatic is, however, no obstacle to the work being of historical interest and value, apart from its unintelligibility. It is significant that the Revelations are excluded from the Peschito, or Bible of the Syrian Church, the most ancient, I believe, of the Christian Churches, and one likely to be a good judge of the authenticity of ancient sacred writings.

[1] This amusing metaphor of the 'Lamb's wife' is one of which the Church is proud, and considers of importance, although preference is shown to the very much modified and uncanonical metaphor of 'Spouse of Christ.' It may probably have been to the influence, at anyrate in part, of this metaphor that the adoption of female millinery by the clergy of the Anglican Church was due. The surplice and stole, which form the foundation of clerical dress, are lineal descendants of female garments worn in the early centuries of the Christian era, so far as I have been able to trace them. The dress of the inferior clergy is essentially feminine in its superstructure, the surplice and stole. The dress of the Anglican bishops is singularly feminine: nothing can be more effeminate than the lawn sleeves and lawn robes of the officiating costume; and the silk apron of the ordinary dress is also feminine. The thought pervading clerical dress appears to be the assimilation of the units of the clergy to the female, in order to give an apparent practical application to the metaphor of the lunatic canonical writer, 'Lamb's wife.' The adoption of the female cut or style of the *tunica talaris* and *orarium* (the modern surplice and stole) by the Roman Christian priests in the fourth century, was in all probability an imitation of the female costume worn by the priests of Isis, the counterpart of Mary, and was part of the wholesale adoption of Pagan ritual by the corrupted Christian Church.

CHAPTER VI.

AN ATTEMPT TO RESTORE THE ORIGINAL WRITING OF CERINTHUS.

THE facts and considerations set forth in this work are in my judgment sufficiently strong to justify the conclusion that Cerinthus was the author of the original Fourth Gospel. Every point in the discussion, with the exception of one, has the support of the authority of ancient authors of good repute. Many of the original sentences of the Prologue have been discovered in the writings of Theophilus, and Irenæus, and Tertullian. The study of the authentic Christian literature of the first century and the beginning of the second century reveals the startling fact that the authors of that literature were ignorant of the miraculous conception, never mention by name the mother of Jesus, and were utterly unconscious of her virginity, and had no knowledge whatever of the name by which she has been known to later centuries, of the Virgin Mary. This great fact must have an influence over other minds as it has had on mine. The crucial test of the return flight of the dove at the crucifixion has been satisfactorily met. The identical ancient writing which has supplied a great Anglican divine with proof of the early date of the Fourth Gospel, has also supplied me with the most important clue to the authorship of the Fourth Gospel. By means of the ancient account of the martyrdom of Polycarp, I have been enabled to discover and lay before the reader the *corpus delicti*, as it were, of a long-suspected forgery; a fact of such great intrinsic importance that of itself it would have sufficed to establish the authorship of the Fourth

Gospel, for history indicates none but Cerinthus as the author of the dove exodus. I have even succeeded in overcoming the contrivances adopted by the forger, or committee of forgers, for the concealment and confirmation of their forgery, and for the purpose of embarrassing the discovery of the original text, by the help of the corruptions made in the text of the ancient Christian Scripture known as the First Epistle of John, and of the Sinaitic and Vatican codices of the New Testament. Classical literature of the second century has also supplied corroboration of the great fact of the dove exodus having been in the original Fourth Gospel. The single point for which I have not been able to bring documentary proof is the interpolation of the clause, "the world was made by him," in the tenth verse of the Prologue of the Fourth Gospel. In the face, however, of all the other facts that have been discovered and set forth, the theological statement that the Palestinian Jew, Jesus, the son of Joseph the carpenter, and of his wife Mary, said to have been a female barber, created the universe, may be left unnoticed in its folly.

Up to this point, therefore, the investigation has progressed on stable ground. I regret that my future steps will advance on what I must admit is unstable ground, and that my guides will no longer be, for the most part, the positive clues obtained from ancient and genuine writings, but chiefly such directions and indications as may be derived from reasonable conjecture. Some useful hints have been received upon the subject of the art of gospel-manufacture from the careful comparison of Marcion's Gospel with the Gospel according to Luke, and of the *Diatessaron* with the Four Gospels. In these two groups of writings the student has the opportunity of viewing in what manner gospel-material had been manipulated by early Christian editors. Cerinthus being the author of the Fourth Gospel, or rather the principal author of the Fourth Gospel, the investigation will now turn upon the question of what portion or how much of it he contributed. It is reasonable to think that he wrote no more of it than was essential for the enunciation of his doctrine, which, according to Irenæus, consisted of the following points:—" That Jesus was the son of Joseph and Mary according to the ordinary course of human generation; that he was more righteous, prudent, and wise than other men; that, after his baptism, Christ descended upon him in the form of a dove from the Supreme Ruler, and that then he proclaimed the unknown Father and perfected his virtues; that at last Christ departed from Jesus, and that then Jesus suffered and rose again, while Christ remained impassible, inasmuch as he was a spiritual being." As Cerinthus elected to explain his doctrine in a narrative form it is reasonable to conclude that the incidents he would relate have some direct or indirect bearing on his doctrine, and that he introduced no extraneous or unnecessary matter, or as little of it as possible. It must be borne in mind that Cerinthus was a Greek and no Jew, and that it is highly improbable that he respected Jewish law or theology, or gave thought to the alleged predictions of the Jewish prophets, or that he accepted the so-called fulfilment of prophecy. The belief in miracles had not originated in the first century amongst Christians, and hence the intrusion of miracles into the Fourth Gospel was an anachronism not likely to have been perpetrated by Cerinthus. The fact that Jesus was regarded by Cerinthus as purely a human being should never be forgotten, and hence the ascription of divine attributes, such as supernatural power and knowledge, to Jesus was alien to his opinions. These are the canons that have guided me in sifting the Fourth Gospel of its foreign material. In the detection of omissions and of minor alterations of the original text I am almost helpless:[1] in these matters recourse to pure conjecture is unavoidable, and I have not been able to do more than merely to indicate their probable existence.

In studying the first chapter of the Fourth Gospel, from verses 15–34, a portion that consists of four sections or paragraphs (verses 15, 19, 29, 32), the student will remark that each section relates what a certain individual named John

---

[1] A passage in the original Gospel, not to be found in the present Gospel, is perhaps alluded to by Clement of Alexandria (*Prot.*, iv. 59). "They," according to John, "are not of those who are beneath, but have learned all from him who came from above."

said or did. In two paragraphs (15 and 32) this individual bears witness, in the other two paragraphs (19 and 29) he baptises; but the two functions of bearing witness and baptising are conjointly assigned to this individual in verses 31 and 33. The unnecessary prolixity with which all this is narrated raises the suspicion in my mind that the name John covers two separate individuals, whom the forger or committee of forgers desired to amalgamate into one. Why he or they did not proceed to effect this design in a direct manner may probably be due to the fact that it was not possible to do so at the time without immediate detection, and that the amalgamation was effected not at one stroke but gradually. In verse 6 of the Prologue reference is made to a John who was sent from God to bear witness, and I identify this individual with the John of verse 32. The John spoken of in verses 15, 19, and 29 is not the same, but another individual, known in profane history of the first century, and in ecclesiastical history of the second century, as John the Baptist, whom the forger or committee of forgers desired to identify with the witness-bearing John.[1] In their respective sections these two Johns are fairly distinct, but they are ingeniously confounded together in verses 15, 30, and 31, and again in verse 33. I strongly suspect that verse 15 was interpolated, and that verse 16 was in the original text linked to verse 14 of the Prologue, with which it is in sense completely in accord. The clause in verse 17, "the law was given by Moses," was perhaps also an interpolation. These interpolations should be cut out. In verse 33 the clause "He that sent me to baptise with water" was manifestly substituted for "He that sent me to bear wit-

---

[1] Matthew Arnold, writing in the *Contemporary Review* for May 1875, knew nothing of my exegesis of this passage, but this is how he wrote on John of the sixth verse:—"The solemn and mystical way in which John the Baptist is introduced, 'There was a man sent from God whose name was John,' how unlike the matter-of-fact, historical way in which John the Baptist is introduced by Jewish writers who had probably seen him, like the writer of the First Gospel, who at any rate were familiar with him, knew all about him! 'In those days came John the Baptist, preaching in the wilderness of Judæa.' How much more is the Fourth Gospel's way of speaking about John the Baptist the way that would be used about a wonderful stranger, an unknown."

ness," as stated in verses 6 and 7 of the Prologue. Assuming these conjectures to be reasonable, the two middle paragraphs from verses 19 to 31 should be deleted as not belonging to the original composition of Cerinthus. John, who was sent by God to bear witness, was a stranger to Jesus, 'knew him not' (verse 33), had never seen him before, and hence could not have been John the Baptist who was a near relation of Jesus, if the account of Luke be credible, and whose mother was on terms of intimacy with the mother of Jesus. John the Baptist further cannot be credited with saying, as in verse 16, "and of his fulness have all we received and grace for grace," which is the phraseology of a devout Gnostic Christian, such as Cerinthus undoubtedly was, actually using a Gnostic theological expression, $\pi\lambda\acute{\eta}\rho\omega\mu\alpha$ or fulness. I regard this John, "who was sent by God to bear witness," to be the eye-witness of the escape flight of the dove spoken of in ch. xix. 35, as he was of the descent of the dove in ch. i. 32; and here is another reason, of the nature called *alibi* in law, that John the Baptist was not the John who 'bore witness,' as the former had been executed anterior to the crucifixion, and hence could not have been a witness to the return flight of the dove. I think this legal reason for separating the two Johns is more reliable than that derived from the asserted relationship of John the Baptist to Jesus, which I do not believe to have been the fact. It is probable that the verse, xix. 35, in the original was couched in similar terms as i. 32, 33, 34, the name John being mentioned, and the statement made in the first person; but this was altered in order to permit of the authorship being attributed to another John who is not named, owing to his 'incomparable modesty,' but is inferred, according to a devout modern theorist. Who the John of Cerinthus was there are no means of ascertaining. He is the person referred to by Jesus in ch. v. 32–36, not as a minister of baptism but only as a witness, and was apparently a person of consideration. In spite of the successful endeavour of the forger or the committee of forgers to amalgamate him with John the Baptist, there appear to me to be sufficient reasons for disentangling the two individuals. It seems to me, further, that John the Baptist was not of much account amongst Christians in the first century; there is no mention made of him by any Christian writer of the first century, nor is there any allusion whatever to Jesus being baptised at all, or baptised by John the Baptist, in any of the first century writers, including Cerinthus. In the Fourth Gospel Jesus is unbaptised. It is not improbable that Jesus never came in contact with John the Baptist, and that the latter did not introduce him to his own disciples, who received his baptism. A colony of 'certain disciples' of John are represented in the Acts of the Apostles, ch. xix. 4, 5, as hearing for the first time from the lips of Paul of the name of Jesus. On such strong considerations as the above, I believe I am justified in not regarding a single reference to John the Baptist in the Fourth Gospel to have existed in Cerinthus' contribution. Hence, in addition to those already deleted, the following passage should be scored out: ch. iii. 23-30, which, with verse 22, have been wedged into the midst of a discourse of Jesus. In connection with the subject of baptism I am constrained to suspect two other passages as accretions. No statement can be more distinct, clear, and definite that Jesus baptised than that in ch. iii. 22, and repeated in ch. iv. 1. There is no mention of this alleged fact in the Synoptic Gospels, nor in any Christian writings of the first century, and the statement itself is corrected in ch. iv. 2. To me it appears very extraordinary that a statement should be made and immediately contradicted. The contradiction was unknown to Origen (*Commentary*, x. 6); but it was known to Tertullian (*De Bapt.*, 11), though both writers were contemporaries, or not far apart in epoch. It is clear that the statement and its contradiction were not written by the same hand; and, as the statement itself was erroneous and utterly irrelevant to Cerinthus' purpose, it was presumably not made by him. Ch. iii. 22 and ch. iv. 1, 2 should be scored out for the above reasons. The careful reader will further notice another contradiction between these interpolated passages and the original text. In the former, great popularity is attributed to Jesus; in ch. iii. 22 he 'tarried' or made a prolonged stay in Judæa in order to baptise, the impression being left on the mind that he tarried on account of the number of people who flocked to him to be baptised, and in ch. iv. 2, the numbers baptised by Jesus are stated to have exceeded John's baptisms. These statements are not in accord with the despairing tone adopted by Jesus in ch. iii. 11, 12, and again in ch. iii. 32, in speaking of his rejection by the people, which was most disheartening to him.

It can hardly be considered probable that Cerinthus had any interest in demonstrating that Jesus was the Paschal Lamb, and it was not possible that he had any part in the Paschal controversy that took place in the second half of the second century. The doctrine of the identity of Jesus with the Paschal Lamb runs through the Fourth Gospel. John, who was sent to bear witness, takes no part in the Paschal scheme. John, who came to baptise, cries in ch. i. 29, "Behold the Lamb of God which taketh away the sin of the world"; again the same John, identified by his having disciples, says in ch. i. 36, "Behold the Lamb of God!" In this passage the Apostles Andrew and John (the latter, as is alleged, not named, by reason of his 'incomparable modesty') are represented to have been disciples of John the Baptist before they followed Jesus—an alleged fact not alluded to by any Christian writer of the first century, and not found in the Synoptic Gospels.

The Paschal doctrine covertly crops up again in ch. xii. 1–9, in which is an interesting anecdote of how Mary, the sister of Lazarus, anointed Jesus "six days before the Passover." Bishop Westcott, in his commentary on this passage, says: "The act of anointing was symbolic of consecration to a divine work," which Mary, he remarks, felt by a 'divine intuition' to be imminent. I regret that I cannot concur in Bishop Westcott's date of the anointing, which he says was "apparently on the 8th Nisan." I consider Dr Martineau's chronology, explained in his great work, *The Seat of Authority in Religion*, Bk. II. ch. ii. sec. 2, D., as strictly accurate. Six days before the Passover, 15th Nisan, is the 10th Nisan, both days on which the events occurred being computed, as undoubtedly was the evangelical custom. Sunday, the day of the resurrection, is called the third day or three days after Friday, the day of the crucifixion; so inversely Friday would be computed as three days before Sunday. Counting after this fashion, three days before the 15th would be the 13th, four days the 12th, five days the 11th, six days the 10th Nisan. The exact date being ascertained, the motive of the anecdote becomes apparent. The tenth of the month was the day on which the Paschal lamb was chosen (Exodus xii. 3-7). And thus an alleged event which, in the mind of a devout theologian and learned bishop, was due to the 'divine intuition' of one of the actors, appears to my mind in the prosaic light of a very definite fabrication of a forger or committee of forgers for a set purpose. Hence I should expunge the entire passage, ch. xii. 1-9, as not contributed by Cerinthus.

The Paschal Lamb doctrine finally reappears at the crucifixion, in which, by dexterous omissions and additions to the text, Jesus is set forth in the Fourth Gospel as the Lamb slain on the 14th Nisan. In order to effect this object it was necessary to ignore ecclesiastical history, for ecclesiastical history records that Jesus kept the Passover on the 14th Nisan, the evening preceding the crucifixion.

Eusebius states the question of the Paschal controversy, which took place in the second half of the second century, with some impartiality, seeing that he himself took the Roman side, but not clearly. "The Churches of all Asia," he says (*Eccl. Hist.*, v. 23), "according to a remoter tradition, supposed that they ought to keep the fourteenth day of the moon for the festival of the Saviour's passover, on which day the Jews were commanded to kill the paschal lamb: and that they ought to terminate the fast on this day, on whatever day of the week it should happen to fall" (see also Cruse's translation, Bohn). The meaning of this passage is that the Eastern Churches, in the second half of the second century, when the Paschal controversy was started, used to break the fast which was practised at this season on the evening of the 14th Nisan, "for the festival of the Saviour's passover," by which terms I understand that the Saviour kept the festival, and eat the paschal lamb that was slain. In the subsequent chapter (Bk. v. 24), Eusebius quotes Irenæus as relating that when Polycarp went to Rome in the time of Anicetus, Bishop of Rome, "they had a little difference amongst themselves likewise respecting other matters, not disputing much with one another on this head. For neither could Anicetus persuade Polycarp not to observe it, since he had always observed it with John the disciple of our Lord, and the rest of the apostles, with whom he associated." The meaning of this passage is that John, the apostle, and other apostles with whom he associated, kept the "festival of the Saviour's passover" on the 14th Nisan, when the paschal lamb was slain. Further, Eusebius quotes the statement of Polycrates, Bishop of Ephesus, who headed the bishops of Asia in the paschal controversy, who wrote (*Eccl. Hist.*, v. 24) : " We therefore observe the genuine day ; neither adding thereto nor taking therefrom. For in Asia great elements have been struck down, which shall rise again in the day of the Lord's coming, in which he will arrive with glory from heaven, and will raise up all the saints ; Philip, one of the twelve Apostles, who was struck down in Hierapolis, and his two aged virgin daughters. His other daughter, also, who having lived in the Holy Ghost, now likewise rests in Ephesus. Moreover, John, who laid upon the bosom of our Lord, who also was a priest bearing the petalon, both a martyr and teacher. He was struck down in Ephesus. Also Polycarp of Smyrna, both bishop and martyr. Thraseas, also, Bishop and martyr of Eumenia, who was struck down at Smyrna. Why should I mention Sagaris, bishop and martyr, who rests at Laodicea ? Moreover, the blessed Papirius ; and Melito, the eunuch, who lived altogether in the Holy Spirit, who now rests at Sardis, awaiting the episcopate from heaven, when he shall rise from the dead. All these observed the fourteenth day of the Passover according to the Gospel, deviating in no respect, but following the rule or canon of the faith. Moreover, I, Polycrates, who am the least of you, according to the tradition of my relatives, some of whom I have followed. For there were seven of my relatives bishops, and I am the eighth ; and my relatives always observed the day when the people (*i.e.*, the Jews) threw away the leaven."

It will be observed from these two quotations that the 'festival of the Saviour's passover,' by which term was meant the anniversary of the Passover eaten by the Saviour on the evening previous to his crucifixion, was observed by the

Apostles John and Philip and by other apostles who may have been contemporaries of the Lord, by the three aged daughters of the Apostle Philip, who were probably also contemporaries, and by a long line of bishops. If the above testimony be credible, and there is no reason for disbelieving it, it is plain that Jesus eat the Passover before he suffered. There is no evidence, and Eusebius provides none, on the opposite side in favour of the story found in the Fourth Gospel that Jesus suffered on the 14th Nisan, and did not eat the Passover. It should finally be mentioned in this connection that the three Synoptic Gospels clearly narrate that Jesus eat the Passover before he suffered, and that bishops of the Eastern Churches insist that their practice was in accordance with the Gospel, and they make no allusion to the divergence in the Fourth Gospel. For the above reasons I am disposed to regard as interpolations all those clauses and verses in which there is direct or indirect allusion to Jesus not having eaten the Passover, but to have been himself the paschal lamb that was slain on the 14th Nisan, viz., the clause "but that they might eat the passover," in ch. xviii. 28; "and it was the preparation of the passover," xix. 14. The crurifragium, or the breaking of the legs, must also come under condemnation, as this scene had manifestly been introduced to give support to the paschal lamb theory; thus xix. 31, 32, 33, and 36 should be deleted. Another reason is also assignable for the introduction of this episode, namely, the factitious fulfilment of prophecy and of an ordinance of the Mosaic Law; both the prophecy and the Mosaic Law being, as was supposed by the forger or committee of forgers, ingeniously and dexterously blended with the Roman usage at crucifixions, from the operation of which, however, it was necessary to find a reason for exempting Jesus. The alleged prophecy (Ps. xxxiv. 20 [1]) is no prophecy at all, but merely a pious declamation that God takes care of the righteous man, delivers him from affliction, and "keeps all his bones: not one of them is broken." If this be a prophecy, it was not fulfilled, for it would be a curious mode of taking care of a righteous man to allow him to be scourged, tortured with thorns and

---

[1] I believe this prophecy was a modern find (see p. 262).

crucified, but to be careful of his bones! The quaint expression of the Psalmist is surely only an Eastern and metaphorical way of saying that the righteous man will be safe-guarded by God; but there was assuredly no safe-guarding of Jesus at the crucifixion. The forger, or committee of forgers, were here playing to the ignorant and credulous mob. But, as a matter of anatomical fact, it is very questionable whether the alleged prophecy was fulfilled and the Mosaic ordinance observed in this instance. The great bones of Jesus' legs were indeed exempted from the crurifragium, according to the fabricated narrative, but it was overlooked that the smaller bones of his hands and feet could not have escaped fracture from the great nails that were hammered through them. I am not aware that the discrepancy between this supposed prophecy and its alleged fulfilment has ever before been brought to the notice of theologians.

It has been argued that, as Paul refers to Jesus as the 'Passover sacrificed for us' (1 Cor. v. 7), he gives support to the narrative of the Fourth Gospel. This, however, is an error. Justin Martyr also calls Jesus the Passover, but it is quite clear from his remarks that he did not believe that he was the Paschal Lamb, slain on the 14th Nisan. He says: "For the Passover was Christ, who was afterwards sacrificed, as also Isaiah said, 'He was led as a sheep to the slaughter.' And it is written that on the day of the passover you seized him, and that also during the passover you crucified him. And as the blood of the passover saved those who were in Egypt, so also the blood of Christ will deliver from death those who have believed" (*Trypho*, cxi., Ante-Nicene Christian Library). Jesus was regarded by the early Christians in a general sense, but not in all details, as the Passover, to which sentiment no historical objection can be taken, and from which no inference can be drawn in support of the false history of the Fourth Gospel. It is to be remarked in the passage quoted that Justin asserts that Jesus was seized on the 14th Nisan, the day of the Passover, and crucified during the Passover.[1]

---

[1] Here, perhaps, is a proper place to give publicity to a private opinion expressed by the late Dr Hort, the learned coadjutor of Bishop Westcott, on the subject of the Paschal Lamb as applied to Jesus in the

In the course of this investigation I have been obliged to yield to the conviction that the Fourth Gospel had been manipulated by more than a single individual or committee, and at different epochs, and to effect various objects. In my remarks on the subject of baptism I pointed out the obvious fact that the statement that Jesus baptised and its contradiction was penned by two hands, and at different times, and that neither the statement nor its contradiction was made by Cerinthus, whose statement bearing indirectly on this subject is altogether of a different import. I have been strongly impressed by this fact in the investigation of the last supper. There is, I think, hardly a single incident in the biography of Jesus that is better attested, owing to the Paschal controversy, than the fact that Jesus eat the Passover before he suffered.[1]

Fourth Gospel. It is taken from a letter, dated 25th August 1877, addressed to the Rev. Dr Milligan, found on p. 221 of the second volume of the *Life and Letters of Fenton John Anthony Hort*, by his son. "To begin with, I wish I could see as clearly as you do that St John treats our Lord as the Paschal Lamb at all. Why are the quotations so little distinctive?—xix. 36 may be paschal or it may not; xix. 37 strikes me as not paschal at all; even the 'first-born' is surely of doubtful reference, and I see no reference to the Jewish festival or deliverance over against the Ægyptian calamity. The four passages referred to (24, 28, 36, 37) are from prophetic works; the Law is nowhere. So also in i. 29 the paschal lamb may possibly be *included*, but the direct reference seems to me to be clearly to Isaiah liii. It is to me very difficult to imagine the *absence* of the Paschal Lamb from St John's conception, and I am very far from denying it, but the want of clear evidence is to me most perplexing."

[1] A further proof of the fact that Jesus eat the Passover before he suffered is derived from Bede's *Ecclesiastical History*. This historian records that Augustine, the Roman missionary to England in the sixth century, entered into a conflict with the earlier Christian Churches of Britain (Wales), Ireland, and Scotland (Iona), similar to the Paschal controversy described by Eusebius as having occurred in the second century. The early Christian Churches of Britain, Ireland, and Scotland broke the fast at Easter on the 14th Nisan, just as the Churches of Asia Minor did, while the Roman missionaries to England observed the Roman practice. Colman, Bishop of Lindisfarne (an offshoot of Iona), defended his observance of Easter on the authority of his elders, who had sent him to be bishop, and who had received the custom from their fathers, as derived from John the Apostle. This ancient custom, undoubtedly the original one, disappeared in the Asiatic Churches about the fourth century, but was retained by the Irish and Ionan Churches of Northern England and Scotland to the beginning of the eighth, and lingered in the early British and

This fact, in my judgment, is better attested than the crucifixion, of which there may be pardonable doubt, seeing that there exist in ecclesiastical history no less than four methods alleged by which Jesus suffered: namely, by crucifixion; hanging on a tree; cutting of the throat, as alleged by apostles and pseudo-apostles in the New Testament; and by stoning to death followed by hanging, according to the Talmud, which latter accords with one apostolical account (Acts v. 30 and x. 39). I believe that all accounts agree in recording that Jesus eat a supper in company with his twelve disciples on the evening before the crucifixion. This supper, unlike various alleged incidents in the history of Jesus, was known to Christians in the first century, and it was marked in Christian history as the occasion on which Jesus instituted the solemn religious function known as the Eucharist, or the Sacrament of the Lord's Supper (1 Cor. xi. 23-26). The Eucharist was celebrated by Christians of the first century, and there is no reason for concluding that Cerinthus was unacquainted with it and with the occasion of its institution. One is not, however, able to say with certainty that he recorded the supper and the institution of the Eucharist in his gospel, but the presumption is that he did not omit to record a solemn incident in the story of Jesus which was well known to the Christians of his day. But it is utterly improbable that the forger or committee of forgers who appropriated Cerinthus' writings had omitted the institution of the Eucharist, seeing that a supper was recorded by them as eaten in company with the disciples on the evening preceding the crucifixion. Christian people are accustomed to read the sacred writings with deadened intellectual faculties, with far too much reverence, or with the opposite feeling of far too much indifference, to be in the frame of mind to detect flaws and inconsistencies in the narrative; and the efforts of theologians are directed chiefly to explain away, or divert attention from and conceal in clouds of learned dust, the defects which abound in the Scriptures. Now, in ch. xiii. 1-30, there is ostensibly an account of a single meal, but a careful

Welsh Churches to the end of that century (Martineau's *Church History of England*, ch. iv.).

perusal of the passage will reveal the strange fact that it is rather an account of two meals knocked into one. The preamble in verses 1 and 3 is of an exalted nature, and has no homogeneity with the useless and ignoble scene that follows. 'When Jesus knew that his hour was come that he should depart out of this world unto the Father, having loved his own which were in the world, he loved them unto the end; .... knowing that the Father had given all things into his hands, and that he was come from God and went to God, he riseth from supper, and laid aside *his* garments, and took a towel and girded himself," and proceeded to wash the feet of his twelve disciples, a most incongruous descent in fact from the dignity and elevation of the sentiment in the preamble. Such a prologue would be more befitting the account of the inauguration of the Eucharist than as a preamble to the ignoble story of the feet-washing.[1] While the successor of the first forgers or committee of forgers ejected the account of the institution of the Eucharist, "the sinew and marrow-bone of the Christian faith," the story of Judas was considered of too great importance to be passed over; and in order to bring it in, Jesus is replaced at table, and, although the supper was ended, and an hour occupied in the feet-washing, allowing five minutes for each disciple, the feast is resumed (ch. xiii. 12, 26).

Theologians appear to have recently perceived that the supper in ch. xiii. of the Fourth Gospel was an amalgamation of two meals, and they have proceeded to make a rectification. The translation is declared to be incorrect; the Greek words καὶ δείπνου γενομένου, translated in the Authorised Version, 'and supper being ended,' have been re-translated in the Revised Version, 'and during supper.' The zeal for accuracy has even gone so far as to declare that the correct translation is 'when supper-time had arrived,' or 'supper having been

[1] I will simply bring to notice in this place that Bishop Westcott regards this manifestly-fabricated story of the feet-washing as exhibiting "the love of the Lord revealed in its highest form," and "as the crowning display of love." See his commentary on John xiii. I believe the pope exhibits an annual sham show of this scene as a religious function, in which he performs in public the feet-washing of persons whose feet had been previously well washed. Cardinal Vaughan has in England this year imitated this religious function of the pope.

served,' on the plea that the washing of the feet took place at the beginning, not at the end, of the feast. This is adopting the view that the object of the washing was sanitary; but how would the case stand if it was doctrinal, as might have been the intention of the forger, seeing that none of the twelve had been baptised into the Christian Church, and only two are alleged to have received John's baptism? The Christian Churches of all shades of opinion have for seventeen centuries understood the passage to mean 'when supper was ended or over.' The translation of the Vulgate is '*cæna facta*,' of Luther '*nach dem Abendessen*,' of the French '*après le souper*,' all meaning after supper. The Latin translation in the *Codex Bezæ* is '*cum cæna fieretur*,' which also means when supper was done or over, in the past tense. This, in fact, was a point in which all previous translators were in harmony, and there is no grammatical reason for dissenting from them. It is idle to say that the story of the institution of the Eucharist, being well known, was omitted by the anonymous author of 'incomparable modesty,'[1] because the story of Judas Iscariot was equally well known in the second half of the second century, but had not been so omitted. The successor of the first forgers or committee of forgers appears to have considered the doctrine of Jesus as the Paschal Lamb more important than the Eucharist: but this was a mere feint, I suspect, to cover a deliberate stratagem for meeting the necessities of the Paschal controversy, and thus allaying the violence of the animosities aroused by that famous dispute. Ample evidence has already been given to prove that Jesus did eat the passover before suffering; but to that may now be added the clear testimony of Irenæus, that the Fourth Gospel once contained the history of the eating of the passover by our Lord. In his great work, *Against Heresies* (II. xxii. 3), Irenæus gives a partial table of contents of the Fourth Gospel, and he thus writes with reference to the final passover: "Then, when he had

[1] What would be thought of a biography of Napoleon which did not give an account of the campaign in Egypt or of the battle of Austerlitz; or of Wellington, which omitted the history of the Peninsular campaign or of Waterloo; or of Lord Roberts, which omitted the Afghan campaign or the march to Candahar, on the plea that these events were well known and fully described in other biographies?

raised Lazarus from the dead, and plots were formed against him by the Pharisees, he withdrew to a city called Ephraim; and from that place, as it is written, 'he came to Bethany six days before the passover,' and going from Bethany to Jerusalem, he there eat the passover, and suffered on the following day." My conjecture is that Cerinthus did contribute a narrative of the last supper, in which the paschal lamb was eaten by Jesus, and that verses 1 and 3 were an appropriate introduction to the solemn scene; verse 2, however, was not his, and instead of the time being before the passover, as stated in the first verse, it was the hour of the passover. Whether Cerinthus' account of the Last Supper agreed in all its details with the account given by Paul and the Synoptics I have no data for stating—possibly it did not —and that might have been an additional reason which in the forger's mind recommended the substitution of the fabricated feet-washing, which function in primitive Christian times was performed by women (1 Tim. v. 10).

I might conveniently in this connection discuss the subject of the apparent discrepancy between the Fourth Gospel and the Synoptics in the number of Passovers which intervened between the descent of the dove on Jesus and his crucifixion; that is to say, the duration of his public ministry. The number of Passovers in the Fourth Gospel is usually reckoned to be three, viz., those mentioned in ch. ii. 13, vi. 4, xi. 55; to these some theologians add the 'feast of the Jews' spoken of in ch. v. i., thus making four years; a third view is that of Tatian in the *Diatessaron*, where the first Passover (ch. ii. 13) is simply withdrawn as a separate Passover but thrown into the final Passover in the unceremonious manner practised by second century theologians; but the 'feast of the Jews' is counted a Passover, thus retaining the period of three years. Irenæus ignored the Passover in vi. 4, but considered the feast of the Jews (v. 1) a Passover, thus retaining three Passovers (*Ad Her.*, ii. 22-3).[1]

---

[1] Origen's view is not very clearly indicated in his *Commentary on John*, Bk. x. 15. It may be that he recognised only two passovers in the Fourth Gospel, viz., those in ch. ii. 13 and xi. 55, the intermediate passover or passovers being unnoticed. He maintains, however, at the close of the

My opinion is that no discrepancy was intended by the forgers; but that the period of about one year, or several months, was the actual duration of the public career of Jesus. The seeming discrepancy was brought about, I am constrained to conclude, by negligence and the remarkable indifference to accurate chronology displayed by most second century theologians. Irenæus may, perhaps, be brought forward with advantage as an example of utter indifference to the sequence of events. In his great work, *Against Heresies*, he confuses the order in which the great Heresiarchs flourished, confounding together second and first century men and sects. In the same manner the various forgers or the committee of forgers of the Fourth Gospel introduced confusion into the chronology of the narrative by simple carelessness and want of thought. The interesting anecdote with which each apparently new Passover was illustrated was either separately composed or extracted from other gospels or books of pious stories, and the statement made in each separately that the Passover was at hand referred to the single Passover in which the year of Jesus' public ministry terminated. These interesting anecdotes were larded into the narrative of the Fourth Gospel at what were considered the most suitable places; but the forgers forgot to strike out the clause in each in which the approach of the Passover was stated, and thus it happened that the single Passover was unwittingly multiplied. If the deletion of these superfluous clauses be now made, it will be seen that the continuity of the narrative will not suffer; the clauses are, "And the Jews' passover was at hand," ch. ii. 13; "at the passover, on the feast day," ch. ii. 23; "After this there was a feast of the Jews," ch. v. 1; "And the passover, a feast of the Jews, was nigh," ch. vi. 4; and the Fourth Gospel will not be a penny the worse, but rather the better, for the excision of these forgotten-to-be-removed words.

I have no doubt my readers have admired the clever

chapter, that the Synoptic Gospels relate the incidents which are supposed to be the same as those described by John in connection with one visit of Jesus to Jerusalem, while John places them in connection with two visits widely separated from each other, and declares that the discrepancy cannot be overlooked.

manner in which the doctrine of the Paschal Lamb has been worked into the Fourth Gospel from the beginning right through to the end. The ingenious forger who accomplished this unscrupulous piece of work shared the chronological slovenliness of his age, and failed to take note of the three superfluous clauses indicated above. A man of his quality would never have allowed his work to be made null and void for the sake of a few small clauses which could be well spared. He evidently did not perceive that the Fourth Gospel extended the public ministry of Jesus over three or four years. The term of the public life of the Lord, in his estimation and that of Christians of his time, and previous to his time, was a year or under,[1] and it was an absolute necessity for his purpose that this period should not be exceeded. For the Paschal Lamb, according to the ordinance of the Mosaic Law, must be a male of the first year (Exod. xii. 5).

The story of the treachery of Judas was a fiction invented in the second century by the strange sect called Cainites, spoken of by Irenæus. "They declare that Judas the traitor . . . . accomplished the mystery of the betrayal; by him all things, both earthly and heavenly, were thus thrown into confusion. They produce a fictitious history of this kind, which they style the Gospel of Judas" (*Ad Her.*, I. xxxi. I). The story of Judas was unknown in the first century, and is not noticed by any Christian writer of the first century. Paul's testimony is practically a direct denial of the alleged betrayal by Judas and of the tragical fate of this Apostle. He says that Jesus after the resurrection was seen by 'the twelve,' and again on another occasion by 'all the Apostles' (1 Cor. xv. 5, 7). This distinct and definite statement by a well-known writer in a genuine writing, and the complete silence regarding Judas of every authentic Christian writer of the first century, is ample reason for concluding that the story of Judas was unknown in the first century, for the story of Judas in the Gospels and Acts asserts his death before the resurrec-

---

[1] Irenæus was the first writer who pointed out the increased number of Passovers. His object was to prolong the life of the Lord, who he said was an old man when he was crucified. This subject will be discussed further on.

tion, and in Acts the election of Matthias was subsequent to the ascension. It is remarkable that Justin Martyr, who was familiar with most of the details of the evangelical biography of Jesus, is absolutely silent on the subject of Judas, although there were many opportunities in his writings for his referring to the betrayal, if he only knew of it, or believed it. The only passage that I can call to mind in which the simple reader of the New Testament, outside the Gospels and Acts, may think he finds a reference to Judas and his alleged crime, is in 1 Cor. xi. 23, in which it is stated, "That the Lord Jesus the *same* night in which he was betrayed (παρεδίδοτο) took bread," etc. The word *betrayed* is a mistranslation in this passage, under preconceived notions, of the Greek verb παραδίδωμι, which means, according to Liddell and Scott, "to give or hand over; to commit, consign. 2. To give into another's hands *as an hostage*, to deliver up, surrender; to hand over to justice; *also* to betray," etc. The Greek word mistranslated in this passage by translators who fancied that they saw in it a reference to Judas, is correctly translated in Romans viii. 32. "He that spared not his own Son, but delivered (παρέδωκεν) him up for us all, how shall he not with him also freely give us all things?" I feel justified in declaring that in the previous passage Paul's meaning was that Jesus was not '*betrayed* (by Judas),' of whose alleged crime he knew nothing, but was 'delivered up (by God).' I have already given a few instances in which the translators of the New Testament, unconsciously under mistaken preconceptions, have wrongly rendered certain passages.

Like some other events in the sacred biography, the treachery of Judas was the fruit of prophecy. The character of Judas was clearly the invention of the Gnostic sect of the Cainites, who required him for the purposes of their strange theology, as indicated by Irenæus. The character was eventually adopted by the Parent Church, on the discovery of a suitable prophecy which appeared to call for its production, and once introduced into the evangelical narratives, it was natural that amplifications and accessory incidents associated with the fictitious personage of the traitor-apostle should have followed. It was necessary that 'the Scripture be fulfilled', is the reason assigned for the treachery of Judas, and put into the mouth of Jesus, who is further made to quote the altered prophecy: "He that eateth bread with me hath lifted up his heel against me" (ch. xiii. 18). This, however, was not the whole prophecy, but only the portion that was appropriated and provided for. The complete prophecy will be found in Psalms xli. 9: "Yea, mine own familiar friend, in whom I trusted, which did eat of my bread, hath lifted up *his* heel against me." The first part of the prophecy did not apply to the fictitious Judas, but only the latter part; the first part, however, was applicable to Peter, or to 'the beloved disciple,' neither of whom from their known history could have been selected as the traitor; for this character an obscure apostle named Judas was hence chosen. The prophecy, however, is no prophecy at all, and not a syllable of Psalm xli. is prophetic.

For the reasons above assigned, I should strike out the whole account of this double meal and its incidents, *i.e.*, the whole ch. xiii., retaining only verses 1 (changing the word *before* for *at*) and 3, which, from the dignity and elevation of tone evident in them, appear to me to have been penned by Cerinthus as an appropriate introduction to the institution of the Eucharist: and also verses 33, 34, and 35, which appear to be genuine, and, the two latter, a reproduction of the sentiments of the writer of the so-called First Epistle of John, whom Cerinthus worthily followed as his guide and pattern.

To return again to the consideration of the first chapter, from which the discussion of the Paschal Lamb doctrine and the Passovers started, although I consider the portion regarding John the Baptist to be an interpolation, I see no reason for rejecting the remainder of the chapter, which is simple narrative. I prefer the reading of verse 34 of Mrs Lewis' Syriac Gospel, which corresponds on this point with the Cureton Syriac manuscript, of 'chosen one of God' to 'Son of God.' This change affords spontaneously the reason why those who heard John speak immediately regarded Jesus as the Messiah, whom the Hebrew Scriptures had foretold, and who apparently was expected by the common people of the Jews. I also prefer the reading of verse 45 as rendered by

Mrs Lewis, viz., "He of whom Moses wrote, and the prophets, we have found him, that he is Jesus the son of Joseph of Nazareth," instead of the reading in our received version: "We have found him of whom Moses in the law, and the prophets, did write, Jesus of Nazareth, the son of Joseph." Moses and the prophets wrote of a Messiah, not of Jesus of Nazareth, the son of Joseph. Verses 35 and 36 should be deleted for reasons already assigned: in verse 37 the reading should be 'and two men heard John speak'; and verse 51 is an extravagancy added by some foolish editor.

The story of the marriage in Cana I regard as a pure fabrication of the second century. I may say once for all that there is no trace of miracles in the genuine Christian writings of the first century. To have represented Jesus in the first century as a worker of miracles would have been equivalent to placing him on the same level as Simon Magus, Apollonius of Tyana, and common sorcerers, such as Bar-jesus or Elymas (Acts xiii. 6, 8), and to have practically condemned him in the eyes of the Christian communities as an impostor. The proofs of the occurrence of miracles in the first century are derived from a stupendous development of the system of interpretation ridiculed by Dean Swift, by which words and phrases originally used in one sense by the writers are interpreted in a different sense. I emphatically state that I have not succeeded in discovering in the genuine Christian writings of the first century any references to the numerous miracles asserted in the Gospels, including the Fourth, to have been wrought by Jesus. It is in the power of any person who doubts this statement to investigate the subject for himself: and this can be done in a few weeks by reading, with an especial look out for miracles or allusions to them, the Christian writings catalogued on page 16. The only alleged allusions to miracles are in reality misinterpretations of certain passages in the writings of the Apostle Paul: the principal of these passages are the following:—(1) "Through mighty signs and wonders, by the power of the Spirit of God; so that from Jerusalem, and round about Illyricum, I have fully preached the Gospel of Christ" (Rom. xv. 19). In the Revised Version the rendering is: "In the power of signs and wonders, in

K

the power of the Holy Ghost," etc. (2) "Truly the signs of an apostle were wrought among you in all patience, in signs, and wonders, and mighty deeds" (2 Cor. xii. 12). (3) "But the manifestation of the Spirit is given to every man to profit withal. For to one is given by the Spirit the word of wisdom; to another the word of knowledge by the same Spirit; to another faith by the same Spirit; to another the working of miracles; to another prophecy; to another discerning of Spirits; to another *divers* kinds of tongues; to another the interpretation of tongues" (1 Cor. xii. 7–10). The translation of this passage in the Revised Version differs mainly in the translation of the prepositions associated with the Spirit: but the clause bearing on miracles is rendered 'and to another workings of miracles,' with a second translation in the margin, 'Gr. powers.' The next quotation is similar to the preceding: (4) "And God hath set some in the church, first apostles, secondarily prophets, thirdly teachers, after that miracles, then gifts of healing, helps, governments, diversities of tongues. *Are* all apostles? *are* all prophets? *are* all teachers? *are* all workers of miracles?" (1 Cor. xii. 28, 29). The Revised Version is almost verbatim like the above, with the addition of a second translation for 'miracles' in the margin, 'Gr. powers,' and the words '*workers of*' in italics, to indicate that there are no corresponding words in the Greek text, and that the words have been introduced by the translators. (5) "He that ministereth to you the Spirit, and worketh miracles among you" (Gal. iii. 5, Revised Version, a second translation for miracles, 'Gr. powers'). The above passages represent the nature of the alleged references to miracles to be found in the entire body of Christian literature of the first century: and it is to be noted that none of these passages refer to the alleged miracles wrought by Jesus. The first two are deliberately brought forward by two leading English theologians (Bishops Lightfoot and Westcott) as proofs that Paul personally wrought miracles: and the two latter passages are generally regarded by theologians as proofs that some of Paul's saints had the power or gift of working miracles. Now the Greek words from which have been deduced these astounding conclusions are the three following: σημεῖον and τέρας, translated in the passages quoted above, *sign* and *wonder*, and δυνάμεις, translated *miracles*. Turning to Liddell and Scott's Lexicon, it will be found that none of these words had a meaning corresponding to our sense of miracles. The meaning of the Greek word σημεῖον is as follows:—"A mark, sign, or token by which something is known: a trace, track; (2) a sign from the gods, an omen; (3) a sign or signal to do anything: the signal for battle; (4) a flag or ensign *on the admiral's ship, or on the general's tent*: *generally*, a standard, ensign; (5) a device upon a shield; *also on a seal*; a seal *itself*. II. *In reasoning*, a sign or proof." Τέρας: "a sign, wonder, marvel, portent. II. Anything that serves as an omen; a monster, strange creature, Lat. *monstrum*; (2) *like Lat. signum*, a sign in the heavens, a constellation, meteor; *cf.* τείρεα": on turning to which word in the Lexicon the meaning is given, "the heavenly bodies, signs." Δύναμις: "strength, might, power, ability: κατὰ δύναμιν, *to* the best of one's power, Lat. *pro virile*; παρὰ δύναμιν or ὑπὲρ δύναμιν, *beyond* one's power; (2) a force for war, forces, Lat. *copiæ*; (3) a quantity, Lat. *vis*, *e.g.*, χρημάτων; (4) the force of a word, etc., meaning, Lat. *vis*; (5) a faculty, power: *hence* a faculty, art, *as Logic*; (6) worth, value, *as of money*." To derive from the passages above quoted the meaning which theologians desired, it was necessary to construct a special theological lexicon; and the beginnings of such a lexicon are traceable to the second century, but not further back. If Paul had desired to say that the 'working of miracles' was a gift possessed by his saints (he does not claim it for himself, like the gift of tongues) he would not have used the words ἐνεργήματα δυνάμεων, which mean, not the *working of miracles*, but the *effect or operation of powers*, but rather τερατουργία or θαυματουργία, which means the *working of wonders*, a synonyme for jugglery, or performing juggler's tricks. The meaning of the Greek word δυνάμεις,[1] as employed by Paul in the passages quoted, is practically lost: it can only be guessed at, like that of his 'angels,' because of whom women were to be veiled; and his stake, or "thorn in the side," which theologians

---

[1] The word may mean the peculiar power of effecting faith cures (see page 173).

have much exercised themselves in discussing whether it meant the sexual passion, sore eyes, dyspepsia, stammering, epilepsy, malarial fever, short stature, a scolding wife, or what not. The signs and wonders that Paul speaks of mean nothing miraculous, but are a mere mannerism of exaggerated speech adopted by all theologians from the days of Paul the apostle to those of the Rev. William Booth, the Salvation Army General. The signs and wonders spoken of by Paul were far inferior in magnitude and extent to those great operations, with their concomitants, managed by General Booth and his assistants, which are reported in the same style of extravagant phraseology; and we know that miracles form no part of the latter's work.

The condemnation of the story of the marriage at Cana as a fabrication[1] is less serious than the accusation that it grossly misrepresents Jesus, by attributing to him unfilial language and the encouragement of intemperance in wine. In every language, living or dead, the words, "Woman, what have I to do with thee? mine hour is not yet come," are disrespectful when addressed to a mother by her grown-up son. The same sense could easily have been communicated to her by her son in becoming and respectful language. There are occasions when the address 'woman' is certainly not disrespectful, but never can that expression with the words associated with it, as in this alleged speech of Jesus to his mother, be other than arrogant and rude. Theologians have, in general, a familiar acquaintance with the classical languages and are well read in classical literature: they maintain that this address of Jesus is not disrespectful. Bishop Westcott says that it means "courteous respect and even tenderness." Classical literature has without doubt been ransacked for the purpose of discovering speeches in which the address woman has been employed without disrespect being intended. Such a search has apparently resulted in the find of a single passage, the only one that I am aware of brought forward by theologians, and it is amusing to find them repeating it one after the other. In Dion Cassius, *Hist.*, li. 12, Augustus thus addresses Cleopatra: "Take

---

[1] It will be seen further on (p. 236) that I have traced this miracle to the Ophites or Naasseni, the Gnostic sect of snake-worshippers.

courage, woman, and keep a good heart." The address of a conqueror to a captive, a royal prostitute whose conduct scandalised Pagan society in Rome, is brought forward by theologians as justifying a rude speech to his mother put into the mouth of Jesus. Such a defence is discreditable to theologians. The same address 'woman' is put into the mouth of Jesus at the crucifixion (xix. 26). Although the words accompanying the address on this occasion are not offensive, the address itself is unbecoming when uttered by a son. Eastern people, in their conversation, are extravagantly polite in the expressions they use towards each other; such an address as 'woman' would never be used in the East by a son to his mother. The expression would not be rude in any language when employed by a superior in addressing a woman of inferior social status, or by an equal to an equal. The word that ought to have been put into the mouth of Jesus is 'mother' or perhaps 'lady,' κυρία, which was the respectful form of addressing a woman. (See 2 John i. 1, 5; Shepherd of Hermas, *Vision*, i. 1, 3, and elsewhere.) It is sad to think that the necessities of their position have persuaded theologians to regard and represent bad manners as "courteous respect and even tenderness."

The unfilial speech put into the mouth of Jesus is surpassed in moral aberration by the encouragement which Jesus is represented to have given to the guests at the marriage in Cana to intemperate indulgence in wine. The speech of the governor of the feast in ch. ii. 10 gives one the impression that the society in which he moved was not select. I understand it to mean that the custom at feasts of which the governor had experience was to intoxicate the guests with good wine, and then to bring in bad wine: but that on this occasion the usual order had been reversed, the guests being first intoxicated with bad wine, and then good wine was brought in. The English translators have evidently attempted to conceal the condition of the guests: the Greek word translated 'well drunk' in the Authorised Version, and 'drunk freely' in the Revised Version, means drunken or intoxicated. The French translation is more straightforward, '*beaucoup bu.*' The Vulgate is honest, the translation being '*cum inebriati sunt,*' and so is the German, '*trunken geworden sind.*' It is for these drunken guests that the alleged miracle was wrought. The supplemental quantity of miraculous wine was considerable. The six water pots of stone, which were used not merely for the washing of hands and cups and brazen vessels and couches, but for bathing purposes also, and for washing clothes, are said by Bishop Westcott to have contained 8¾ gallons each, so that the total quantity of additional wine would have amounted to 52½ gallons, or 210 quart bottles, a quantity that would suffice to intoxicate two companies of soldiers with their officers. Bishop Westcott quotes with approval Dr D. E. Clark's *Travels*, in which the traveller estimates the contents of the large stone pots found by him in the ruins of the village of Cana, each holding from 18 to 27 gallons. If the ancient water pots at the marriage of Cana were of similar capacity, the amount of miraculous wine in the six pots was from 108 to 162 gallons, equivalent to from 432 to 648 quart bottles. The former quantity would suffice to intoxicate about two-thirds of a British regiment, and the latter quantity an entire British regiment when not of full war strength.

The above is the most natural view to take of the story of the conversion of water into wine, so far as the quantity of wine is concerned: and theologians have doubtless had such a view before their minds, and have made similar arithmetical calculations. The quantity of wine was undoubtedly much in excess of the needs of the marriage feast: and hence it was believed necessary to account for the disposal of the surplus. And this is how the theological mind has explained the exuberant profusion of wine. The family was poor and pious, notwithstanding it kept servants, and the deficiency of wine, although the guests were already drunk, was a proof of great poverty: and hence the Redeemer desired not only to relieve a present necessity, notwithstanding the guests were already intoxicated, but to give, as a wedding present, to him who had just married, a quantity of wine, "*ut diuturnum testimonium ac monimentum esset facti miraculi*" (Maldonatus), that it might be an everlasting testimony and monument of the miracle that had been made. This is the view that Luther favoured, and the great reformer innocently explained further that the wine was given by Christ, by whom the world and all the treasures therein were created, because perchance he had no gold nor jewel to offer. Can any one imagine a great religious leader, say an Archbishop of Westminster, presenting a poor couple on their wedding with a large cellar of wine! but perhaps the parallel is here strained, as the archbishop has the alternative of gold and jewels to offer. This view of the disposal of the exuberance of wine is not referred to by Bishop Westcott in his commentary on the Fourth Gospel, and is, perchance, not approved by him. He has a theory of his own: and that is, if I understand him correctly, that the traditional view that the water in the six large stone pots was converted into wine is a mistake, but that the water in the well was converted into wine. The learned bishop founds his theory on the two commands of Jesus to the servants: "Fill the water pots with water," and "Draw out now, and bear unto the governor of the feast." The insignificant word 'now' is the key of the position: "It seems to mark," the bishop explains, "the continuance of the same action of drawing as before, but with a different end. Hitherto they had drawn to fill the vessels of purification: they were charged *now* to 'draw and bear to the governor of the feast.' It seems most unlikely that water taken from the vessels of purification could have been employed for the purpose of the miracle": the probability, in the bishop's matured judgment, is greater that the water in the well was so used, as the word 'draw' in the original Greek, contrary to the usage in modern hotels, is applied most naturally to drawing water from the well, and not from a vessel like the water-pot. The water in the well was water when poured into the vessels of purification, but "became wine when borne in faith to minister to the needs" of the guests, and, the bishop euphemistically adds, to their "superfluous requirements." The only flaw that I can perceive in the bishop's admirable theory is the introduction, without ceremony, of the element of 'faith,' of which there is no record or implication in the text of the Fourth Gospel: the speech of the governor is absolutely free from faith, as he was ignorant of the facts of the case, and the condition of the guests debarred them from exercising that or any other mental faculty. The flaw, which is fatal, as when 'faith' is introduced there can be no longer 'miracle,' is regrettable, as the learned bishop's theory is elastic, and admits of being applied to the water in the pots as well as to the water in the well. Although the fact is not directly stated in the text of the Gospel that the water was changed into wine, according to the purpose for which it was drawn, the bishop thinks: "This view that the change in the water was determined by its destination for use at the feast can be held equally if the water so used, and limited to that which was used, were 'drawn' from the vessels, and not from the well." The simplicity of the theory would have been a great recommendation: water from the well wanted for washing purposes was water, but when wanted to drink was wine. There was no limitation of time, however, and hence it might have been an embarrassment to the newly married couple to have nothing but wine to drink. The bishop, however, does not demand acceptance of his theory: and he would as lief take the traditional view of the miracle, as, in his opinion, "no real difficulty can be felt in the magnitude of the marriage gift with which Christ endowed the house of a friend."

In general, theologians indulge in pæans on the liberality and generosity of the miracle of Cana; in their opinion, apparently, the more the quantity of wine the greater was the manifestation of divine power and of divine benevolence. Modern society, however, deprecates gifts of this nature to poor and pious people: the legislature of most civilised States punishes the publican who dispenses liquor to drunken men, and the Postmaster-General of England annually at Christmas issues a proclamation deprecating donations of wine and similar intoxicating liquids to postmen. The modern view is tardily and with great effort penetrating the theological intellect, and the theory of Bishop Westcott, although in the present state of theological opinion he puts no stress upon it, is a quarter step in the direction of running into the current of secular opinion on this subject. It is a satisfaction to the common-sense of mankind that, barring ecclesiastics and the more choice specimens of the sheep of their flocks, the great majority of civilised society does not accept the ecclesiastical stories of miracles that are found in the Gospels.

It is clear that the overbearing and unseemly language

towards his mother put into the mouth of Jesus, and the extravagant profusion of wine that he is related to have produced at Cana, are conceptions of a vulgar mind, that can only realise divine grandeur and benevolence in arrogance of speech and quantity of performance. The divinity of Jesus was paramount in the mind of the base forger, and the story of the marriage at Cana was the offspring of this idea. But Cerinthus did not inculcate the divinity of Jesus; throughout his Gospel Jesus is but a man and the son of human parents, of the same nature as his fellow men, and such is Irenæus' account of his view. It is manifest that the story of the miracle at Cana was an accretion to the original work of Cerinthus, and should therefore be deleted.[1]

[1] I have not thought it necessary in this work to refer to continental theologians, but I think I am justified in making an exception of Professor Godet's commentary on this immoral miracle of the changing of water into wine for the delectation of drunken guests. Godet's influence on the English clergy is great, and I can perceive the partiality felt for him by our great theologian, Bishop Westcott. Godet's theological enthusiasm and professional admiration of this miracle has led him into sad extravagancies of opinion. Every reader of Godet will be willing to concede that he is a most learned and sensible writer, and of deep piety: and no reflection is here intended either against his learning or piety. But the religious obligation which theologians foolishly consider binding on them to write up every thing, even what is false and absurd and even worse, found in the canonical writings, constantly warps his learned and judicious judgment. Speaking of this miracle, Godet says : " Mais ensuite il faut se representer l'etât d'exaltation dans lequel devait se trouver en ce moment toute cette société, Marie surtout. . . . . Elle voit déja, à l'occasion de ce manque de vin, le ciel s'ouvrir, l'ange monter et descendre." (But then we ought to picture to ourselves the state of exaltation in which the whole company must have been in at this moment, especially Mary. . . . . She sees already, on the occasion of this want of wine, the sky open and the angel ascending and descending.") Verse 10 of the second chapter, in the original Greek, gives only the idea that the company was in the condition that may be described as spirituous exaltation, *i.e.*, intoxication, from the imbibition of inferior wine. There is no statement in the Gospel referring specially to Mary's state : but according to M. Godet, Mary was more tipsy than the others, and he gives a remarkably strong proof of her vinous exaltation. M. Godet does not, however, mean to say this, although that is the meaning which his language, compared with the text of the Gospel, conveys to my mind, from my point of view. The learned French theologian did not calculate upon people who understand the evangelical text not in the conventional manner, but exactly in the sense which the actual language of the Greek text conveys. M. Godet innocently meant not spirituous or vinous exaltation, which is the sense of

The going down to Capernaum (verse 12), where Jesus did nothing, appears to be a superfluity. Though it is a perfectly neutral statement, I hardly think it could have been in the original Gospel. The visit to this town is mentioned in Luke iv. 31 : and hence on Eusebius' authority it ought not to be in the Fourth Gospel. It is omitted in Tatian's *Diatessaron*.

The next incident in the narrative that calls for remark is what theologians euphemistically call "the purification of the temple," that is, the expulsion of the traders and money changers, with their commodities, from the temple. There is nothing improbable in the story, as in the previous one of the miracle at Cana. It was certainly not a dignified or justifiable proceeding, but it is represented to have occurred in the earlier part of the public life of Jesus, when his experience was forming and his zeal ran riot. One is at a loss to account for the non-resistance of the Jews, a rather turbulent people at that

the evangelical text, but spiritual exaltation, which is the conventional theological sense in which the Gospel text is interpreted.

Again, M. Godet refers to the solitary example in which, in the whole volume of classical literature, theologians have discovered the word 'woman' employed in an address. "Dans Dion Cassius, une reine est abordée par Auguste avec cette expression." (In Dion Cassius, a queen is accosted by Augustus with this expression.) M. Godet appears to me to be not ingenuous here, but to have unwittingly stooped to what I consider a paltry device. Some theological students and a great many of his lay readers will be ignorant of the telling fact that this 'queen' was a very disreputable character and the most notorious harlot in classical history. M. Godet unconsciously omitted to state that the 'queen' was Cleopatra. That a Roman emperor addressed a captive harlot as 'woman' is, in M. Godet's opinion, a justification for Jesus' use of that expression to his mother.

Further, I must denounce, as utterly immoral, the opinion expressed by M. Godet, that the use of the word 'woman' by Jesus to his mother was designed to indicate that his filial relation to her had ceased, and that she was no longer to him anything but an ordinary woman : "Elle n'est plus pour lui qu'une simple femme." No good man or woman, no civilised community, will acquiesce in such an immoral view. These extravagancies of theologians are perhaps harmless in our age : but there cannot be a doubt that there was a long period in the history of Christian nations in which theological opinions were of great power in influencing the conduct and character of the people. It may be that the striking contrast between Christian and non-Christian nations in the practice of the virtues of sobriety and filial piety, has a connection with the views inculcated by theologians and priests regarding a god, the Christian model of morality, creating drink for the use of drunken guests, and the same god treating his mother with disrespectful language.

time, and by no means disposed to submit to unjust violence. The chronicler makes no attempt to glorify Jesus' performance, like the vulgar forger of the wine miracle (ii. 11), but rather apologises for it: he says the disciples remembered that it was written, "The zeal of thine house hath eaten me up," which is a sentence purely apologetic and deprecative of reproach, and only prophetic in the sense of being a quotation from the Hebrew Scriptures. There was undoubtedly a strong craving in the Christian mind during those early times for prophecies and parallelisms or coincidences with the history of Jesus out of the Hebrew Scriptures, and the writer yielded to this popular taste. On the other hand, a Gnostic would hardly quote the Hebrew Scriptures. The anecdote is in keeping with Cerinthus' fundamental view that Jesus was a man and was subject to human imperfections and faults. It is also consistent with Irenæus' account, who states that, after the descent of the dove upon him, Jesus perfected his virtues ('*virtutes perfecisse*'[1]— *Ad Her.*, I. xxvi. 1). There is no statement in the subsequent part of the history in the Fourth Gospel that Jesus again resorted to physical violence; as his experience grew he moderated the impetuosity of his early zeal, and in this respect there was improvement in the conduct of Jesus, and progress in the perfection of his virtues. On these considerations one feels inclined to regard this episode as contributed by Cerinthus.

An alternative view, however, presents itself that "the purification of the temple" was an anecdote written separately, or extracted from a popular gospel, and larded into the Fourth Gospel at this place, without the introductory clause, "and the Jews' passover was at hand," being previously removed. Eusebius gives us an account of a supposed tradition in which John the Apostle is said to have undertaken the composition of the Fourth Gospel in order to write "the account of the time not recorded by the former evangelists, and the deeds done by our Saviour, which they have passed by." As the 'former evangelists,' *i.e.*, the Synoptics, do relate this incident, a justi-

[1] In the Ante-Nicene Christian Library these words are rendered, 'performed miracles.' To a translation so unjustifiable as this is, Dean Swift's satire applies. The late Canon Liddon correctly translated the words in his great work on the *Divinity of Our Lord*, sect. v. 2, exactly as they are in my text.

fiable inference is that the same incident was not repeated in the original Fourth Gospel. Further, in Irenæus' great work (II. xxii. 3) is a running table of contents of the passover narratives of the Fourth Gospel, in which the purification of the temple has no place. I feel constrained to sacrifice, on account of the evidence of Eusebius and Irenæus, a picturesque incident, not in itself improbable, perfectly consistent with the sketch given by Irenæus of the views regarding the Saviour put forth by Cerinthus, and explained by the chronicler in a rational and modest manner, and without theological extravagance of laudation. The incident is omitted at this early stage in Tatian's *Diatessaron*.

I am unable to accept the verses that follow this anecdote as genuine. They have the flat ring of the forger; they attribute the power of prophecy to Jesus, they make him perform miracles which attract to him many disciples in whom he places no confidence, but utterly distrusts. From verse 18 to 25 of the second chapter ought to be deleted: the vulgarity of the passage is sufficient to condemn it as spurious in my judgment.

The visit to Jerusalem need not have been made on account of the passover; it is reasonable to conclude that Jesus went to Jerusalem to disseminate his doctrines. Verses 23–25 have the look of a cutting from a popular gospel inserted by mistake in this early part of the story, without previous removal of the words "at the passover, in the feast."

The interview of Nicodemus with Jesus appears to me to be genuine, but the narrative suffers from omissions and additions. The translation of the Authorised Version must of course be altered in verse 2; 'miracles' is an unjustifiable translation: 'signs' must be substituted as correct, and is in fact the translation of the Revised Version. There is some controversy among theologians as to the correct rendering of the word $ἄνωθεν$ in verses 3 and 5; to me the natural translation is 'from above,' *i.e.*, from heaven or of God: and here Cerinthus clearly indicates the source from which he derived the thought. The conception 'born from above' of Cerinthus is essentially the same as that of 'born of God,' which is repeatedly employed by his guide and pattern, the disciple of the Lord, who wrote the so-called First Epistle of John (1 John iii. 9; iv. 7; v. 1, 4, 18). One could justly say and believe that the thought originally emanated from Jesus, being worthy of him, and was committed to writing by his personal disciple, from whom Cerinthus obtained it. Justin Martyr (c. 150 A.D.) quotes this passage without understanding it correctly in the sense in which the disciple of the Lord and Cerinthus meant. The sense of Cerinthus and of his master was obviously a change of the heart, or disposition, or feelings in harmony with the divine will, or in evangelical language, a spiritual birth or regeneration. Justin misunderstood the expression to mean 'baptism,' and his reference occurs in his description of the rite. He says: "As many as are persuaded and believe that what we teach and say to be true, and promise to be able to live accordingly, are instructed to pray, and, fasting, to entreat God for the remission of their former sins, we praying and fasting with them. Then they are brought by us where there is water, and are regenerated in the same manner in which we were ourselves regenerated (ἀναγεννήθημεν and ἀναγεννῶνται). For, in the name of God, the Father and Lord of all things, and of our Saviour Jesus Christ, and of the Holy Spirit, they then perform the washing in the water. For Christ also said, 'Except ye be born again (ἀναγεννηθῆτε), ye shall not enter into the kingdom of heaven.' Now, that it is impossible for those who have once been born to enter into their mothers' wombs, is manifest to all. And how those who have sinned and repent shall escape their sins, is declared by Esaias the prophet, as I wrote above; he thus speaks: 'Wash you, become clean; put away the evil of your doings from your souls'" (see also Ante-Nicene Christian Library, *First Ap.*, 61). It is clear that Justin misunderstood the expression 'born from above' or 'born again or anew,' as some translate, to mean the ceremony of baptism.[1] This being Justin's view, it is remarkable that the quotation which he brings in support of the rite has no mention of water: notwithstanding in the Fourth

---

[1] This inaccurate notion, that regeneration or being born again was simply the ceremony of baptism, gained strength as time advanced, for we find Tertullian declaring that the Lord said, "Unless one be born of water, he hath not life". (*On Baptism*, xii.).

Gospel, as it has come down to us, the expression 'born of water' is to be found in ch. iii. 5. The inference from these two facts is that the words 'of water' were interpolated since Justin's days: and that the original form of verse 5 was, "Except a man be born of the Spirit, he cannot enter into the kingdom of heaven." This conclusion is supported by the explanatory words which follow, and from which no allusion, expressed or implied, to water can be made out. With the above exception and the modification of the translation pointed out, the passage from verse 1 to verse 8 of the third chapter appears to be the genuine text of Cerinthus.

The verses that follow are incongruous and relevant to nothing in particular; and verse 13 is simple nonsense. " No man hath ascended up to heaven" is an absolute fact (always excepting balloonists), but sounds odd when put into the mouth of the Jew Jesus, who may be assumed to have been a believer in Jewish sacred history, in which two men, Enoch and Elijah, are declared to have gone up to heaven. But the general assertion is made in order to show that there was an exception, namely, he that came down from heaven, even the son of man who is in heaven. It is impossible to believe that such a foolish statement could have emanated from Cerinthus, who undoubtedly represents the son of man to be in reality what these words indicate. The passage beginning at verse 9 should be cut out, but it is not clear how far the excision should extend. I shall limit it at a venture at verse 15, and shall consider the verses that follow not as utterances of Jesus, but as special observations made by the writer, in the midst of which, at verse 22 up to 30, have been interpolated certain statements about baptism by Jesus and a speech of John the Baptist, regarding which I have already spoken. Verse 35 should perhaps be deleted, if the latter clause implies the governance of the universe.

The interview with the woman of Samaria appears to my mind to be a genuine production of Cerinthus, as during it Jesus declared the pith and marrow of his theology: "God is a Spirit: and they that worship him must worship him in spirit and in truth." "The hour cometh, when ye shall neither in this mountain, nor yet at Jerusalem, worship the

Father," which may be simply interpreted in modern language to mean that the worship of the Father consists not in rites and ceremonials, in prostration of the body and bowing of the head, processions, the wearing of vestments, the burning of incense and candles, the reading of prayers and of chapters of the Scriptures, and the singing of psalms and hymns, at St Peter's at Rome nor yet at St Paul's in London, nor even in the late Mr Spurgeon's tabernacle. Jesus did not foresee the worship of his mother nor of his cross, clothes, and other articles, and hence made no reference to them directly or indirectly. The forger, or committee of forgers, did not fail to enter in and spoil this fine episode by intruding into it their ideas of the attributes of divinity. Verses 15-18 are obvious and paltry interpolations introduced with the pitiful object of attributing omniscience to Jesus. These verses being cut out, the narrative proceeds without interruption from verses 19-26; but verse 22 should be omitted, as containing a sentiment which a Gnostic would not entertain. The rest of the narrative requires considerable weeding. The pretence is introduced that Jesus could do without food, clearly not a Cerinthian notion, and that his body could be nourished by doing his Father's work. The description of this work, which I suppose verses 35-38 to be, is simply unintelligible. The language and ideas are confused, and it is not possible to extract a clear meaning out of the passage without supplementing the language and thought. As it stands in the text it must be declared meaningless; and the whole passage from verses 31-38 should be cut away as spurious. The remaining verses of the episode were doubtless trimmed to suit the passage, verses 15-18, already condemned, and hence such trimming needs to be removed. The earliest transcript of verse 42 will be found in Irenæus (Bk. IV. ii. 7), in which the word 'Christ' is omitted. Theologians have vainly used their ingenuity to explain how the evangelist obtained information of the exact words of the conversation between Jesus and the woman of Samaria, seeing that there was no third party present at the interview to take notes.[1] If they

[1] Bishop Westcott's attempted explanation of this mystery is the following: "Perhaps St John remained with Christ. The narrative is

would read a modern work of fiction they would perceive that the writer always accurately reports the private conversations between persons introduced in the story, and is acquainted even with their most intimate thoughts. Ancient writers of fiction possessed the same faculty.

The narrative is continued at ch. iv. 43. Here occurs a statement which in my judgment corroborates my view that the development of the story of the birth of Jesus that took place in the second century was unknown to Cerinthus. On his return from Jerusalem through Samaria, Jesus did not proceed to Nazareth, his home, but to other parts of Galilee; and the reason for his avoidance of his home is given, viz., "a prophet hath no honour in his own country" (verse 44). Second century chroniclers, viz., the writers of the three Synoptic Gospels, concur in referring this saying of the Lord to Nazareth, the birthplace and home of Jesus (see Matt. xiii. 57; Mark vi. 4; Luke iv. 24). This is a point on which the four Gospels are in agreement. Theologians, however, are opposed to this harmony. The words employed, 'ἡ ἰδία πατρίς,' mean native country, the place where one is born; but unfortunately the second century development of the story of the birth of Jesus, being founded on prophecy and not on fact, assigns Bethlehem of Judæa as the birthplace of Jesus. Hence arises the opposition of theologians. Bishop Westcott maintains that Nazareth was not the 'own country' of Jesus. "Both by fact, and by the current interpretation of prophecy," he says, "Judæa alone could receive that title.

_{more like that of an eye-witness than a secondary account derived from the woman, or even from the Lord himself. Yet it may be urged that verse 33 naturally suggests that the Lord had been left alone." So after all the gentle bishop leaves the mystery unexplained. I do not know whether the following extract from Bishop Lightfoot's Lecture on the Fourth Gospel can be taken as the explanation of the mystery offered by that powerful writer. "Either you have here, as we are constantly reminded, in an uncritical age and among an uncritical people, the most masterly piece of romance-writing which the genius and learning of man ever penned in any age, or you have (what universal tradition represents it to be) a genuine work of an eye-witness and companion of our Lord. Which of these two suppositions does less violence to historical probability I will leave to yourselves to determine." I for one vote for the former view, without the florid exaggeration of the great bishop.}

Moreover, Judæa is naturally suggested by the circumstances"; and he proceeds to make various statements of Jesus not having been duly honoured in Jerusalem, his Messianic claims being denied, etc., which circumstances stand equally good with reference to Nazareth. If Judæa was referred to, the proper place for stating the reason for leaving it was at verse 3; but it is clear that the 'own country' referred to in verses 43 and 44, at a period when the narrative had reached an advanced stage, was Nazareth. This passage is in harmony, not only with the Synoptics *quoad* Nazareth, but also with ch. vii. 41, in which the objection made to the acceptance of Jesus as the Christ, that he came out of Galilee, was not contradicted. With the trimmings removed, *i.e.*, the allusion to the feast, verses 43, 44, and 45 appear to me to be genuine, and also the introductory clause in verse 46: "So Jesus came into Cana of Galilee."

The miracle of the healing of the nobleman's son, recounted in ch. iv. 46–54, must necessarily be cut out, for the reason already assigned, that the miracles of Jesus were not invented in the first century. In verse 54 it is stated that this was the second miracle wrought by Jesus: the first being the conversion of water into wine. This statement at once gives the denial to the statement in ch. ii. 23, that Jesus performed miracles at Jerusalem in the interval between these two miracles. Theologians are to be greatly commiserated on the ungrateful and difficult, if not impossible, task often devolving upon them of reconciling contradictory passages. The earliest attempt to remove the present contradiction was the addition of the gloss, "when he was come out of Judæa into Galilee." The futility of such a transparent attempt at reconciliation becomes obvious when one reflects that it imputes to the evangelist the design to keep arithmetical score of the miracles performed in Cana of Galilee, and not to take into account the miracles alleged to be wrought elsewhere. Further, the gloss does not necessarily limit the miracles counted to Galilee, nor does it imply that the first miracle was wrought in Galilee; that is to say, if the record of the conversion of water into wine had been lost, the gloss could not lead to a presumption that the first

L

miracle had been wrought in Cana of Galilee and not elsewhere. That the gloss was an addition by another hand is manifest. "The point," says Bishop Westcott, "lies in the relation of the two miracles as marking two visits to Cana, separated by a visit to Jerusalem." The point rather is that this was the second alleged miracle simply, but it awkwardly limited the fertility of miracle manufacture.

The miracle following (ch. v. 1-18) should for the same reason be removed. The statement made in verse 16, that the Jews persecuted and sought to kill Jesus because he had miraculously cured on the Sabbath an unfortunate man, who had an infirmity for thirty-eight years, is incredible, and belies human nature. A second hand has made the attempt to modify the impossible libel on human nature, in verses 17 and 18, by introducing at the tail of the story a speech of Jesus, "My Father worketh hitherto, and I work," and thus creating another plausible cause of offence, viz., "making himself equal with God." The modification was silly, as the Jews were familiar with the idea that Jehovah was their Father (see viii. 41). This foolish representation of the effect of a miracle on the Jews stamps the whole story as a fabrication. The incarnate God is represented as having miscalculated the effect which his alleged miracles were wrought to accomplish.

The speech of Jesus, from verse 19 to 23, is egotistic and pompous, and obviously designed to raise Jesus above the human level, and place him on a plane of equality with God. Such an apotheosis of Jesus was no part of Cerinthus' plan. This passage must therefore be regarded as a subsequent accretion.

The remaining verses of the fifth chapter appear to me to be genuine, but the forgers have added touches here and there. Thus verse 33, which is superfluous, has been inserted to turn attention to John the Baptist, an individual whose name is not mentioned in the Christian literature of the first century. I should reverse the order of verses 34 and 35. Verse 27 is also suspicious, as it confers divine power on Jesus; and verse 39 is unlikely to have been written by a Gnostic who despised the Hebrew Scriptures. For this reason also, the concluding verses, 45-47, should be erased. The passage must be linked to the first clause of iv. 46; and the address be regarded as delivered at Cana to the Galileans.

After the address, Jesus is, in ch. vi. 1, made to go across the Sea of Galilee. It is to be remarked here that from Jerusalem, where in the Gospel we last see Jesus (ch. v. 1), to over the Sea of Galilee is a long stride. In my correction of the Gospel, on reasonable grounds, I have evicted the story of the miraculous cure of the paralytic man (ch. v.) at the market pool in Jerusalem; and thus Jesus is enabled to pass from Cana of Galilee to over the Sea of Galilee, which is a reasonable movement. Theologians have remarked this geographical discrepancy, and have endeavoured to account for it. On this point Bishop Westcott remarks that it has been "suggested that chaps. v. and vi. were transposed accidentally, perhaps at the time when chaps. vi., xxi.— episodes of the Galilæan lake—were added on the last review of the Gospel." I think the first three verses of ch. vi. may be retained, only the second clause of verse 2, regarding miracles or signs, being excised. Verse 4 announces the approach of another Passover very close upon the preceding one in ch. v. 1. Bishop Westcott wisely says that "the chronology cannot be settled with absolute certainty." Irenæus (II. xxii. 3) takes no notice whatever of this passover. Bishop Westcott says that "Some have supposed that the words τὸ πάσχα (vi. 4) are a very early and erroneous gloss." My own view is that these clauses regarding the Passover were parts of the interesting anecdotes which they introduce, that they all refer to the same passover, but were forgotten to be removed when the interesting anecdotes were larded into the Fourth Gospel. Verse 4, and the whole story of the miracle of the feeding of five thousand men with five loaves and two small fishes, with twelve baskets filled with the remnants, are utterly incompatible with Cerinthus' times and ideas, and should therefore be cut out. With the above should follow the succeeding miracle of Jesus walking on the sea, as well as the utterly useless and improbable details up to verse 26.

The only further remark worth making regarding the above spurious passages is, that the feeding of the five thousand has a sacramental semblance. In verse 11 it is stated that "Jesus took the loaves, and when he had given thanks, he distributed to the disciples, and the disciples to them that were set down." Attention is specially drawn to the ceremonial later on, in verse 23, where, to indicate the locality, it is said, " the place where they did eat bread, after that the Lord had given thanks." The passage from verse 4–26 has been wedged in between verse 3 and verse 27, and it is probable that the introductory words of the latter verse suggested the part as a suitable place for inserting the miracle of the feeding of the multitude. As it is most improbable that a multitude of five thousand people could be simultaneously transported across the Sea of Galilee in the few fishing boats that plied in that water, it would be reasonable to conclude that on the mountain spoken of in verse 3 Jesus delivered the address beginning at verse 27 to an audience of Galileans, and that that was the purpose for which this great multitude was assembled. This discourse seems to me to be genuine. In verse 29 is a reflection of Cerinthus' guide and pattern (1 John iii. 23). In verse 30 is the very clearest indication that all the miracles recounted in the previous chapters—the conversion of water into wine, the miraculous healing of the nobleman's distant son, the feeding of the five thousand, etc.—were quite unknown to the vast audience, denizens of the very places and their neighbourhood where these miracles were alleged to have been wrought, and participators in the last miracle. Say the multitude to Jesus, " What sign showest thou then, that we may see and believe thee? What dost thou work?" Were not these astounding miracles, signs and wonderful work? Such proofs as these displayed in modern times, provided there was no suspicion of imposture, would have satisfied a great multitude of people. But bishops are not satisfied. Bishop Westcott says that in the demand of the multitude for some clear attestation of Jesus' claims, " there is nothing inconsistent with the effect which the feeding of the multitude had produced on some. Great as that work was, their history taught them to look for greater." Bishop Walsham How says the Jews rejected " the late miracle of the feeding of the five thousand as being a small thing in comparison with the miraculous feeding of the Israelites, numbering more than a hundred times as many, for forty years in the wilderness." I have no doubt the whole bench of bishops will follow suit. The Jews did not ask Jesus for a miracle, but for some proof or attestation of the truth of his mission; and they simply inquire, "What dost thou work?" which implies that he had done nothing extraordinary—nothing that can be regarded as a proof. The theological mind is saturated with the thought that a sign or proof is a miracle. In verse 33 the translation of the Authorised Version is incorrect: the Revised Version gives the correct translation, which is, "The bread of God is that which cometh down out of heaven." There is no implication that Jesus came down from heaven in this verse, looked at from Cerinthus' point of view, which was that the Spirit came down from heaven. The misunderstanding of the statement by the Jews in verse 41 is, however, quite natural. There is nothing here like the grossness of the thought in ch. iii. 13, where Jesus is made to represent himself as having come down bodily from heaven in the same manner as he was alleged to have subsequently ascended bodily to heaven. In verse 39 of this discourse is a statement which involves the inference that Cerinthus knew nothing of Judas' alleged misconduct and fate. Jesus says that it was the Father's will, "that of all which he hath given me I should lose nothing." The forgers manifestly overlooked this passage, and failed to put in the exception, "but the son of perdition," as in ch. xvii. 12. It is remarkable that no theologian has directed attention to this omission. The concluding clauses of verses 39, 40, and 44 must necessarily be modified.[1] Verse 42 of this chapter is fatal to the doctrine of the miraculous birth of Jesus promulgated in the Gospels according to Matthew and Luke, and in these writings only in the New Testament. The inhabi-

---

[1] It appears to me that the concluding clauses of these three verses were not an addition to, but a modification of the original text. The original may have been that God, and not Jesus, will raise up the believer at the last day. The Christian belief regarding the resurrection appears to have been, *in the first century*, that the resurrection was limited to believers, and was not enjoyed by Jews and Pagans, who were not believers.

tants of Nazareth, Cana, Capernaum, and other parts of Galilee, who were likely to have a personal knowledge of Jesus, said, "Is not this Jesus, the son of Joseph, whose father and mother we know? How is it, then, that he saith, I came down from heaven?" Cerinthus would never have given a place in his writings to such a statement if he had a knowledge of and accepted the doctrine of the miraculous conception, and nowhere in this Gospel is a contradiction to be found. It seems remarkable to me that the forgers did not apply a corrective. The initial clause of verse 45 should be omitted. The long passage from the concluding clause of verse 51–57 is alien to Cerinthus' style and thought, and is the grossest and most repulsive form in which the doctrine of the Eucharist is presented in Christian literature. It reminds me of a corresponding passage in Ignatius. The foisting of this passage into the discourse at Galilee, which is on the subject of bread from heaven, metaphorically treated, is introduced by the strange statement, unceremonious like many another enunciated in the second century, that bread is flesh. Christian people are accustomed to read the Scriptures with prepossessed or indifferent or paralysed minds, and hence an unsavoury and barbaric passage like the one under notice makes no impression upon them. I quote the passage in full, to enable the reader to judge whether my opinion of it, just expressed, is not justifiable: "The bread that I will give is my flesh, which I will give for the life of the world. 52. The Jews therefore strove amongst themselves, saying, How can this man give us *his* flesh to eat? 53. Then Jesus said unto them, Verily, verily, I say unto you, Except ye eat the flesh of the Son of man, and drink his blood, ye have no life in you. 54. Whoso eateth my flesh and drinketh my blood, hath eternal life; and I will raise him up at the last day. 55. For my flesh is meat indeed, and my blood is drink indeed. 56. He that eateth my flesh and drinketh my blood, dwelleth in me and I in him. 57. As the living Father hath sent me, and I live by the Father; so he that eateth me, even he shall live by me." The zest with which the writer repeats the elements of the feast, the eating of human flesh and the drinking of human blood, is remarkable. The translators have smoothed down the coarseness in this connection of the Greek words ὁ τρώγων, in verses 56 and 57, which mean 'he who gnaws or eats raw.'[1] Compare the above with the delicacy of the language and thought of Paul, in describing the origin of this sacrament: "The Lord Jesus . . . . took bread, and when he had given thanks, he brake it, and said, Take, eat: [this is my body, which is broken for you:] this do in remembrance of me. After the same manner also *he took* the cup, when he had supped, saying, [This cup is the new testament in my blood:] this do ye, [as oft as ye drink *it*,] in remembrance of me. For as often as ye eat this bread and drink this cup, ye do show the Lord's death till he come" (1 Cor. xi. 23-26).[2] The second century

---

[1] Further on (p. 237), the reader will ascertain that I regard the Naasseni, or Christian Snake-worshipping Gnostics, as the probable contributors of this passage. Clement of Alexandria says that the bacchanals celebrated their orgies crowned with snakes and eating raw flesh (*Exhortation to the Heathen*, ii). In his quaint and, in parts, piously amusing *Commentary on the Fourth Gospel*, Origen, commenting on this passage (vi. 48-57), says amongst other remarks, "We are not, however, to eat the flesh of the Lamb raw, as those do who are slaves of the letter, like irrational animals, etc., but we must strive to convert the rawness of Scripture into well-cooked food" (x. 13). Origen, however, does not show how this was to be done, or in what way the process of cooking Scripture was to be managed, so that a Pagan rite may be converted into a Christian one. He, indeed, quotes Jeremiah v. 14 and Luke xxiv. 32, but there are no instructions regarding cooking to be found in these texts. Origen's *Commentary on the Fourth Gospel*, though rather tedious, is well worth perusal. It contains much sound common sense, unusual theological honesty, and several delicious bits of pious amusement for devout readers. It is translated in the additional volume of the Ante-Nicene Christian Library.

[2] I have a strong suspicion that the clauses which I have inclosed in brackets were second century interpolations. In no other writings of the first century, a list of which I have drawn up on page 16, do I remember a word said about the body and blood of Jesus in connection with the Eucharist. In the *Didache*, a writing of the first or early part of the second century, the simple ceremony of the Eucharist is described, and the prayers used at the commencement and conclusion of the meal are given in full. There is not a word in these prayers about the body and blood of Jesus. The body of Jesus was not broken, nor was his blood shed. These facts justify my suspicion. I think the Eucharist or memorial supper of the Christians, in the earlier part of the first century, was annual, and celebrated only once in the year, in the evening at the Jewish passover. In

conception of the Eucharist, as expressed in the Fourth Gospel, is vulgar, gross, and unreasonable, a conception that would revolt many educated Pagans of those early days. The first century conception as expressed by Paul was refined, affectionate, and reasonable, the Eucharist being represented as a memorial repast, like a Waterloo or Lucknow dinner. It is remarkable that accretions to Jesus' discourses are always made in the body of the discourse and not tacked on at the end. The objectionable passage under discussion has been wedged between the body of the discourse and the last sentence of it. Verse 58 is the proper continuation of the discourse after the second clause of verse 51. The remaining verses of the chapter, from 59 to 71, are paltry additions, showing the natural results on the audience of the repulsive ideas of eating human flesh and of drinking human blood, imputing omniscience to Jesus (verse 64), and forcibly dragging in Judas Iscariot. These verses should be excised.

Much of the succeeding chapter (vii.) is of a neutral character, and hence might be left alone, a precaution being given against the theological misinterpretation of certain words, *e.g.*, the word 'works' with reference to Jesus, in ch. vii. 3, being

our times the Presbyterians and the Dutch Kirche observe the ceremonial twice in the year: the Roman and Anglican Churches a hundred times or more, as often, I believe, as six or seven times in the week, and even three or four times on Sundays. The memorial Lord's Supper of the Christians of the first century has been practically reduced to a pious farce by a progressive ecclesiasticism. In the fragments from the lost writings of Irenæus, collected in Stieren's edition, and translated in the Ante-Nicene Christian Library (*Irenæus*, vol. ii.), is one numbered xxxvii. in the latter, and xxxviii. in the former, occurs the following sentence: "Those who have followed the subsequent constitutions of the apostles (ταῖς δευτέραις διατάξεσι) know that the Lord in the New Testament instituted a new oblation according to the word of the prophet Malachi." As neither the twelve Apostles nor Paul instituted subsequent constitutions, the expression "subsequent constitutions of the apostles" can only refer to the innovations introduced by the stipendiary apostles. We learn from the *Didache*, ch. xi., that the stipendiary apostles made mysteries of material things, and the conclusion is reasonable that the stipendiary apostles mystified the bread and wine of the Eucharist into the body and blood of Jesus (see *ante*, page 87). Transubstantiation and the real presence were not ideas entertained by Christians in the first century.

explained by theologians as 'miracles,' but the same word, with reference to the world, in verse 7, as works only but not miracles. Some passages, however, which are not of a neutral tint, such as verses 21-24 and verse 31, should be cut out. In verses 41-43, the Jesus of fact, a native of Galilee and of unknown ancestry, is contrasted with the Christ or Messiah of prophecy, a native of Judæa, and of the seed of David. The concluding clause of verse 42, "and out of the town of Bethlehem, where David was," is a second century gloss, and must be deleted. " It seems strange," says Bishop Westcott, "that any one should have argued from this passage that the writer of the Gospel was unacquainted with Christ's birth at Bethlehem. He simply relates the words of the multitude who were unacquainted with it." To which remark it may be replied that it seems strange that not only the multitude at Jerusalem was unacquainted with this alleged fact, but there is no evidence that any Christian writer of the first century was acquainted with it. Justin Martyr, who wrote about the middle of the second century, is the first writer who mentions Bethlehem as the birthplace of Jesus (*Trypho*, lxxviii.). Paul, indeed, says that Jesus was of the " seed of David according to the flesh " (Rom. i. 3); the writer of the Epistle to the Hebrews makes the inferential proposition, " it is evident that our Lord sprang out of Juda " (Heb. vii. 14) ; and the writer of the Revelations repeats both statements : " behold the Lion of the tribe of Juda, the Root of David " (Rev. v. 5), but these statements are not at all inconsistent with the fact that Nazareth was Jesus' native place. No writer of the first century has gone the length of stating that Jesus was born in Bethlehem, a theological statement founded on Micah v. 2. The statements of Paul and the other writers were made in faith, relying absolutely on known prophecy (Gen. xlix. 9, 10 ; Isa. xi. 1 ; Jer. xxiii. 5) regarding the Messiah ; but the details of the birth of Jesus were unknown until the second century was well advanced, and the prophecies of Micah and other prophets were discovered. The writer of the Fourth Gospel had in the passage in question a good opportunity of stating in direct terms an important fact, relevant to his subject, but he did not make the statement. It is quite as legitimate to infer from that omission that he was unacquainted with the theological fact, founded on prophecy, as to express surprise, like Bishop Westcott, that anyone should suspect his knowledge of it. History cannot be made out of notes of exclamation. The Fourth Gospel is very consistent on the subject of the birthplace of Jesus. In ch. i. 45, Philip speaks of "Jesus of Nazareth, the son of Joseph"; and again in ch. xix. 29, the writing set up by Pilate was "Jesus of Nazareth the King of the Jews."

The final verse of ch. vii., and the initial verses of ch. viii. from 1-11, are known interpolations, being omitted in "most of the ancient authorities," as stated in the margin of the Revised Version. It is possible that the story of the woman taken in adultery is the same as "the history of a woman who had been accused of many sins before the Lord," spoken of by Eusebius (*Eccl. Hist.*, iii. 39), as related by Papias in the second century, and "which is also contained in the Gospel according to the Hebrews." It is probable that the other interesting anecdotes in the Fourth Gospel were derived from the same or similar sources. The story of the woman taken in adultery was conceived by a person who had thoroughly imbibed the spirit of the moral teaching of Jesus. *Si non e vero, e ben trovato.* Of the remaining verses of ch. viii., I should excise verse 28, in which Jesus is made to utter a paltry prophecy; and verses 56-59, in which Jesus is made to utter some nonsense about his great antiquity. The concluding clauses of verses 44 and 55 seem to me to smack of the coarseness of language indulged in by forgers of the second century.

The whole chapter ix., in which the performance of a miracle and some incidents consequent on it are related, is manifestly an accretion, for I perceive nothing Cerinthian in it. The working of a miracle, and the worship of Jesus by the man cured of congenital blindness (verse 38), sufficiently indicate the whole chapter to be a forgery. Strictly speaking, the healing of the blind man was not a miracle, for the means whereby the cure was effected are stated. Jesus "spat on the ground and made clay of the spittle, and he anointed the eyes of the blind man with the clay, and said to him, Go, wash in the pool of Siloam." These are means similar to those used by a physician, who may apply belladonna or other medicament to the eyes, and direct the patient to wash off the medicament after an interval of time. The resulting cure would not be a miracle. The real miracle, if one strictly followed the words of the narrative, was the conversion of Jesus' saliva into clay: "He made clay of the spittle." It is remarkable that no theologian has perceived the true miracle that was performed on this occasion : one analogous to the conversion of water into wine. Following, however, the traditional interpretation of the story, the cure was effected by the mixture of saliva and clay. Of these two ingredients, Bishop Westcott says : "The application of spittle to the eyes was considered very salutary." There is no doubt that in early times the saliva was credited with some efficacy in diseases of the eye, and the notion has not become extinct in these days amongst the English poor, though the medical profession gives it no support. Clay also has been credited with salutary effects. In India, special varieties of clay are eaten by the natives as aids to digestion ; and in European countries there exist great establishments in which mud or clay baths are employed for medical purposes.

I have a very strong suspicion that the miracles of the cure of the blind man in ch. ix., and of the cure of the impotent man in ch. v., are imitations of the *miracles* actually performed by the Roman Emperor Vespasian, in Alexandria, in A.D. 70. That Vespasian accomplished the instantaneous cure of a blind man and of a paralytic man there can be no reasonable doubt. The account of Tacitus is most explicit, and is well worth reading in connection with these miracles of the Fourth Gospel, with a view to the perception of the obvious relationship of the classical and evangelical miracles. "During the months," says Tacitus, "when Vespasian was detained at Alexandria, waiting for the season of the summer winds and of sure navigation, many miracles took place, by which the favour of heaven and a certain amount of partiality of the gods towards Vespasian was displayed. One of the Alexandrian·common people, well known on account of a disease of the eyes, embraced the emperor's knees, demanding with a groan the cure of blindness, on the instigation of the god Serapis, whom a people given to superstition worship beyond all others; he implored the prince to deign to besprinkle his eyelids and the globes of his eyes with the excrement of his mouth. Another man, ailing in his hand, inspired by the same god, begged that he might be trodden upon by the foot of Cæsar. Vespasian at first smiled, refused, and these persisting, at one time he feared a reputation for vanity, at another time he was persuaded into hope by the entreaties of the wretches and by the words of flatterers; finally, he orders that it should be considered by the medical men whether such blindness and debility might be overcome by human aid. The medical men made various declarations: that to the one man the power of vision was not worn out, and would return if obstacles were removed; that, to the other man, the limbs that had gone bad could be restored, if a salutary power be employed. That perhaps the prince was chosen by the gods for this divine service; finally, that the glory of an accomplished cure would be with Cæsar; that the ridicule of failure would be with the wretches. Thereupon, Vespasian, believing that all things were open to his fortune, and that nothing was incredible, performed what was demanded with a pleasant countenance, the multitude which stood by being intently expectant. Immediately the hand was restored to use, and the daylight shone again to the blind man. Those who were present still recount both events, although there is no longer any reward for lying" (*Hist.*, iv. 81). Suetonius (*Vespas.*, 7) refers to these same incidents, with the unimportant difference that the afflicted limb was a leg.

Similar instantaneous cures are well known to the public of these days and to the medical profession, and they were also known in ancient pre-Christian times. Professor Charcot, of Paris, has written a popular article on the subjects in the *New Review* for January 1893. He says: "The instantaneous cure produced directly by faith-healing, which is commonly known in medicine by the name of 'miracle,' is, as may be shown in the majority of cases, a natural phenomenon which is produced at all times, in the most different degrees of civilisation, and among the most various religions, and is as irregular in its manifestation as it is diffused in latitude. The so-called miraculous facts—I make no pretence here to express any new opinion—have a double character: they are engendered by a special disposition on the part of the patient; a confidence, a credulity, a receptivity of suggestion, as it is called now-a-days, favourable to the faith cure, which may be brought to bear in various ways. On the other hand, the domain of faith healing is limited; to produce its effects it must be applied to those cases which demand for their cure no intervention beyond the power which the mind has over the body—cases which Hack Tuke[1] has analysed so excellently in his remarkable work. No intervention can make it pass these bounds, for we are powerless against natural laws. For example, no instance can be found amongst the records sacred to so-called miraculous cures where the faith cure has availed to restore an amputated limb. On the other hand, there are hundreds of cases of the cure of paralysis, but I think these have all partaken of the nature of those which Professor Russell Reynolds[2] has classified under the heading of paralysis 'dependent on idea.'"

Professor Charcot further remarks: "The methods by which the faith cure works, then, are the same at all times, in all latitudes; the same among Pagans and Christians as among Mussulmans—one and all wear the same characteristics. The shrines and propitiatory rites are analogous. The healing god, indeed, varies, but the human mind, which is always the same in its great manifestations, ascribes to each and all identical functions."

The professor states that he has himself sent patients for their cure to Lourdes and other shrines now in vogue, over whom he had no ability "to inspire the operation of the faith cure." This ability to effect faith cures may perhaps be the explication of the mysterious gift called by Paul '$\delta\upsilon\nu\acute{\alpha}\mu\epsilon\iota\varsigma$.' That Jesus possessed the power or influence to effect faith

[1] *Illustrations of the Influence of the Mind upon the Body in Health and Disease, designed to elucidate the Action of the Imagination.* London: Churchill, 1872.

[2] "Remarks on Paralysis and other Disorders of Motion and Sensation dependent on Idea," read to the Medical Section of the British Medical Association, Leeds, July 1869, in *British Medical Journal*, November 1869.

cures is nowhere mentioned in the genuine Christian writings of the first century: but it is clear from the Gospels, including the Fourth, that this singular faculty was attributed to him in the second century, and that it was further falsely and deceitfully distorted and magnified into a power to raise the dead, to walk on water, to still storms, and to instantaneously multiply inanimate and dead objects, to effect their transubstantiation, and to catch a fish with a piece of money in its mouth.

In chapter x. the allegory of the good shepherd is apparently genuine: and verse 8, in which Jesus says, "All that came before me are thieves and robbers," is in harmony with the Gnostic rejection of Jewish religious leaders and doctrines. Verses 17 and 18 are manifestly interpolations, as they attribute divine power to Jesus, which was no part of Cerinthus' design. It was silly to put into the mouth of Jesus the assertion that he laid down his life without compulsion, and that he had power to take it up again. The clause in verse 15, "and I lay down my life for the sheep," is suspicious, if it be regarded not as a strong statement of his devotion to his disciples, but as a prophecy. The verses 19, 20, and 21, describing the strife that arose amongst the Jews in consequence of Jesus' utterances about giving up his life at pleasure and taking it up again, should be excised. Further excision is necessary in the remainder of this chapter. The concluding clause of verse 25, "the works that I do in my Father's name, they bear witness of me," is an interpolation attributing the working of miracles to Jesus; and the same objection applies to verses 37 and 38, which require to be cut out. After much consideration I have come to the conclusion that the long passage from verse 30–36 is not genuine. The passage is inconsistent with Irenæus' account of Cerinthus' doctrine. It was no design of Cerinthus to equalise Jesus to God: Jesus' great function was to declare the Father, not to declare his own attributes. The singular reasoning by which he is made to endeavour to justify his godhead, or apparent godhead, is pure sophistry. The reference to the Jewish law is far-fetched. The quotation, "Ye are gods," does not occur in the alleged writings of Moses, but in those of David. Psalm lxxxii., from which the quotation is made, is fragmentary, disjointed, and incoherent. It seems to me to be a collection of fragments or detached sentences, whose connection with each is not apparent. In the first verse, God is said "to judge amongst the gods," or Elohim. The meaning is obscure, as we are instructed that the Jews were monotheists: but here is a passage which clearly implies the existence of other gods. Theologians interpret the words Elohim, or gods, to mean in this passage 'judges': but the mind immediately reverts to the Venerable Dean Swift's satire on interpretation. Unfortunately for the interpretation, Jesus in this passage is made to use the word gods in the quotation "Ye are gods" in the sense of gods or divinities, not of judges; and in this sense alone can the quotation be employed to justify the statement that he was a god and one with the Father. The statement made is not that Jesus was a nominal, titular, representative, or complementary god, but an essential god and one with the Father. Such a statement is utterly inconsistent with Cerinthus' views, and hence it is not possible that it was written by him. The sense in which Cerinthus used the expression "Son of God" was not physiological, but spiritual, and is sufficiently explained in ch. i. 12: "But as many as received him, to them gave he the right to become children of God, *even* to them that believe on his name." This was the sense in which his guide and pattern employed the phrase (1 John iii. 1, 2, 10, etc.). Cerinthus ignored the Jewish law, and the Jewish God was not the Father which he represented Jesus to declare in the Gospel of Christ. I should here remark that Tertullian quotes verse 30, "I and my Father are one," as contained in the Lord's answer to Philip, in ch. xiv. 7-11 (see Tertullian, *Ad Praxeam*, xx.).

In verses 40 and 41 John the Baptist is again obtruded into the narrative, and hence these two verses, with the exception of the introductory clause of verse 40, should be cut out. The pertinacity with which John the Baptist, a man unnoticed in the genuine Christian writings of the first century, is introduced in various passages of the forged Fourth Gospel is remarkable, and raises a suspicion that there was some strong reason or motive for such persistency. That all these passages referring to John the Baptist are accretions is sufficiently clear, and hence it is legitimate to inquire for what purpose they were inserted. I think an inquiry into the early history of the rite of baptism may lead us to the discovery of this purpose. There is no evidence that Jesus introduced the rite, nor that he and his disciples were baptised. The statements on this subject to be found in the four Gospels are false. That the ceremony existed in Paul's Christian experience is evident, as he himself administered baptism on two occasions (1 Cor. i. 14, 16); but he takes care to show that he attached no importance to the ceremony, and repudiates the idea that baptising was any function of his, the greatest of Christian apostles and missionaries. Nothing can be more unmistakable than his clear statement, "Christ sent me not to baptise, but to preach the gospel" (1 Cor. i. 17).[1] I feel that I can justly draw the inference that the members of the Churches planted by this greatest of Christian missionaries were unbaptised. The practice of baptism in the apostolic communities of Christians must have sprung up spontaneously, and nothing can be more probable, as history indicates, than that it was an imitation of Pagan baptism. It was a harmless practice, and hence may be found the reason why the broad-minded Paul made no objection to it, and even occasionally performed it himself, although he considered baptism to be no part of his mission. Baptism was, in fact, a ceremonial common to almost all the ancient cults, and hence the early converts were familiar with it, and, I may also say, were attached to it. The indiscriminate abuse of Paganism by Christian writers and preachers is not justifiable, for the ancient religious systems, or some of them, were not altogether divested of what was high and noble and appealed to the best feelings of mankind, and the early converts felt that. It appears to me that they showed more attachment to the Mithraic religion than to any of the other prevailing systems

---

[1] This statement of Paul unmistakably discredits the command put into the mouth of Jesus in Matt. xxviii. 19, "Go ye, therefore, and teach all nations, baptising them in the name of the Father, and of the Son, and of the Holy Ghost." There are other strong reasons for declaring this verse to be spurious and false.

of Paganism. As already stated, there is no evidence that the founder of Christianity instituted baptism, and it must be remembered that it was not a Jewish rite during the lifetime of Jesus. Paul, the next great historical Christian leader in the first century, markedly repudiated baptism as no business of his. There is no evidence from the literature of the first century that any Christian leader inculcated the rite. Hence the inference is justifiable that baptism was spontaneously introduced or grafted into Christian practice by the members of the Church, the laity, who were strongly attached to the ceremony. It is certain that it was not universal and not obligatory on the Christian communities in Paul's days; and I further conclude, from Paul's writings, that it was the Mithraic conception of baptism that was introduced into Christian thought. No detailed account of the Mithraic initiation has survived to our days; but we know that the neophyte simulated death, and was resuscitated by the rite of baptism. The obvious import of the Mithraic baptism was a rising to a new life after death in the old life. The ordinary Pagan import of baptism was a cleansing or purification by washing from sin, the ideas of death and resuscitation forming no element in it. I am unaware of the exact form of the Mithraic baptism, and hence I am unable to say that Christian baptism took the Mithraic form; but there can be no doubt that Paul favoured the Mithraic conception of the rite, and permitted amongst converts the ordinary Pagan immersion. In Romans vi. 2–11 Paul gives a Christian turn or significance to the Mithraic conception of baptism; but it will be remarked that he makes no allusion to cleansing or purification or washing from sin, while the words, "so many of us as were baptised,"[1] clearly indicate that the rite was not

---

[1] I must here take exception to the translation of this passage in the Revised Version, "Are ye ignorant that all we who were baptised into Jesus Christ were baptised unto his death?" The received text is, "Ἢ ἀγνοεῖτε ὅτι ὅσοι ἐβαπτίσθημεν εἰς Χριστὸν Ἰησοῦν, εἰς τὸν θάνατον αὐτοῦ ἐβαπτίσθημεν." The Authorised Version translates accurately, "so many of us as were baptised.". If the Revised Version had translated "all of us who were baptised," there would be no objection, as the meaning then would be limited to those only who were baptised of the whole number addressed. A lecturer addressing an audience in England might say, "All of us who have

general, and hence not obligatory. Compare Galatians iii. 26 and 27: "How shall we, that are dead to sin, live any longer therein? Know ye not, that so many of us as were baptised into Jesus Christ were baptised into his death? Therefore we are buried with him by baptism into death; that like as Christ was raised up from the dead by the glory of the Father, even so we also should walk in the newness of life. For if we have been planted together in the likeness of his death, we shall be also *in the likeness* of *his* resurrection. Knowing this, that our old man is crucified with *him*, that the body of sin might be destroyed, that henceforth we should not serve sin. For he that is dead is freed (justified) from sin. Now if we be dead with Christ, we believe that we also live with him: knowing that Christ being raised from the dead dieth no more; death hath no dominion over him. For in that he died, he died unto sin once; but in that he liveth, he liveth unto God. Likewise reckon ye also yourselves to be dead indeed unto sin, but alive unto God through Jesus Christ our Lord." The confused and involved thought and language of this passage indicate that the fundamental idea, which is the simple, clear, and definite Mithraic conception of baptism, could not readily be worked into the Pauline mould. Paul's forced and tortured explication of the rite did not maintain its ground in the second century.[1] The writer of the Epistle

resided in South Africa must have felt the delicious softness of the climate," and would thus limit his meaning to actual former residents. But "all we who have resided," etc., would include every individual. The Vulgate has translated correctly, "*An ignoratis quia quicumque baptizati sumus in Christo Jesu, in morte ipsius baptizati sumus?*" The French version is correct, the German doubtful. The Revised Version is not only incorrect, but inelegant and not idiomatic. "All we who were baptised" is not good English; "we who were all baptised" is. Irenæus translates, "*quotquot baptizati sumus*" (III. xvi. 9).

[1] In the *Shepherd of Hermas*, S. ix. 16, the Mithraic doctrine of baptism is more explicit than in Paul's writings. "'It was necessary for them,' saith he, 'to rise up through water, that they might be made alive; for otherwise they could not enter into the kingdom of God, except they had put aside the deadness of their [former] life. .... For before a man.' saith he, 'has borne the name of [the Son of] God, he is dead; but when he has received the seal, he layeth aside his deadness, and resumeth life. The seal then is the water; so they go down into the water dead, and they come up alive'" (Lightfoot's translation).

to Titus (iii. 5) speaks of the 'water of regeneration,' which implies Justin's view of being born again in baptism, and not Paul's view of death and resurrection. In another passage Justin speaks of the purifying power of baptism : " By reason, therefore, of this laver of repentance and knowledge of God, which has been ordained on account of the transgression of God's people, as Isaiah cries, we have believed, and testify that that very baptism which he announced is alone able to purify those who have repented; and this is the water of life " (*Trypho*, ch. xiv.). The same view reappears in Theophilus, who says "that men were to receive repentance and remission of sins by water and washing of regeneration " (*Ad Autolycum*, ii. 16). One is perhaps justified in concluding that the popular gospels of the second century propagated the same view. The prophecy of Isaiah regarding a forerunner, which escaped notice in the first century, was discovered in the second, and applied to John the Baptist, " The voice of one crying in the wilderness, Prepare ye the way of the Lord, make his paths straight." Of John the Baptist, Josephus says, he "was a good man, and commanded the Jews to exercise virtue, both as to righteousness towards one another, and piety towards God, and so to come to baptism : for that the washing would be acceptable to him, if they made use of it, not in order to the putting away of some sins, but for the purification of the body, supposing still that the soul was thoroughly purified beforehand by righteousness. Now, when others came in crowds about him, for they were greatly moved by hearing his words," etc. (Whiston's *Josephus' Antiquities*, xviii. 2). The preachings and doings of this man were woven into the sacred history by the stipendiary apostles, prophets, and popular evangelists, and it was made to appear that the rite of baptism was derived from him. The *soi-disant* forerunner of Jesus was a more reputable source of the rite of baptism than any of the religious systems prevalent amongst the heathen or unconverted. It was unlikely, however, that Paul's Gentile converts knew anything of John the Baptist; and it would appear from Acts xix. 1–5 that some at least of John's disciples had not heard of Jesus and the Christian *quasi* theology.[1]

---

[1] In connection with my remark that the Pauline import of baptism was

The whole story of the raising of Lazarus, in ch. xi., is a manifest fabrication, and, notwithstanding a certain dramatic force in the narrative, a foolish fabrication. In the preliminary by-play Jesus is represented as really making sundry mistakes derived from Mithraism, I feel bound to say that this statement is only a reasonable conjecture. There are no writings extant in which the doctrines or mysteries and rites of Mithraism are described, and our knowledge of these subjects is obtained from a few casual remarks by ancient writers (such as the early Christian fathers), and from a reasonable interpretation of pictorial illustrations on cones, cylinders, and seals, and of bas-reliefs. From these sources of information several points of analogy and common religious ideas and modes of thought have been perceived between the Mithraic and the Christian religion, and it must always be borne in mind that the former was the more ancient of the two. The rites of Mithras were baptism, confession of sins, bloody sacrifices, communion, offerings, etc. The Christian rites are similar, except that an unintelligible metaphysical and not a realistic bloody sacrifice is practised. Jesus Christ, the sun of righteousness and the light of the world, was the Christian analogue of Mithras, the sun-god, the son of Ormuzd or God, the mediator between Ormuzd and mankind, the redeemer and saviour of men, the model for imitation offered by Ormuzd to mortals who aspire to the salvation of their souls (John iii. 16, 17); the disciple of Mithras was called a soldier of Mithras, and was armed (metaphorically), and received instruction and precepts to overcome the carnal passions: these ideas have passed into the Christian religion. The most common representation of Mithras was the performance by him of the act of redemption by the sacrifice of a bull, which, interpreted by most competent judges, is the sacrifice of the material life, under the symbol of a bull, intending thereby to inculcate the sacrifice of carnal passions. The crucifix or the cross (the latter instituted late in the second century or early in the third) is the analogue of this representation. The early Christian attitude of prayer, *i.e.*, uplifted hands, kneeling, and the laying on of hands in confirmation and ordination, were derived from Mithraic usages. The halo placed around the head in pictorial representations of Christian saints was an obvious imitation of the aureole placed on the heads of disciples of Mithras who attained the grade of Helios, or the Sun, an advanced stage in the Mithraic religious life. The birthday of Mithras was adopted as the birthday of Jesus, 25th December. The Mithraic prayers and litanies, as found in the Zend-Avesta, may have been the models of the Christian liturgies. On the whole, the influence of the Mithraic religion on Christianity was beneficial, and the ideas and practices borrowed by Christianity from Mithraism may be regarded as good and not unwholesome. It is regrettable that Christianity did not appropriate the official equality of the sexes that was a prominent feature of the Mithraic religion, which admitted competent and qualified women to every grade and even to the priesthood. There were Mithraic priestesses and archpriestesses, or arch-magesses. In this matter the Mithraic religion had the pre-eminence.

and slips. When informed of the sickness of Lazarus, his beloved friend, by a message from the sisters Mary and Martha, he exclaims that the sickness was not unto death, and he abode still two days in the region beyond Jordan, instead of forthwith hurrying to the bedside of his sick friend. He then announced his intention of proceeding to Judæa, apparently to assist his sick friend; and when reminded by his disciples of the danger of stoning by the Jews, his reply to them, contained in verses 9 and 10 of ch. xi., is to me a Delphic enigma. " Jesus answered, Are there not twelve hours in the day? If any man walk in the day, he stumbleth not, because he seeth the light of this world. But if a man walk in the night, he stumbleth, because there is no light in him. These things said he." As general propositions, these verses are intelligible: but what puzzles one is their relevancy to the danger of stoning by the Jews pointed out by the disciples. Consulting Bishop Westcott's commentary, I find that in his serious opinion "the answer is, as a whole, a parable of human action," and then follow further remarks which do not help one to perceive the relevancy of the answer to the danger of stoning. Reference to other theologians brought no satisfactory result. Jesus then announces to his disciples that Lazarus was asleep, and his disciples say that then he shall do well. But Jesus immediately says that Lazarus is dead, a result that he did not anticipate on the arrival of the intelligence of the illness of Lazarus, and expresses his gladness that "he was not there, to the intent ye may believe." One would have thought that his disciples at that advanced period of his ministry were not unbelieving. The whole party now proceed to Bethany, and Jesus on arrival found that Lazarus had lain already four days in the cave which was used as a tomb. There are no means of ascertaining from the details given whether the announcement of Lazarus' death made by Jesus to his disciples was synchronous with the event. The two sisters on meeting Jesus express sorrow that he was not there, or their brother had not died: but are assured by Jesus that he will rise again, not at the last day, but immediately. Even after such an assurance there was no abatement of their grief. On perceiving the continued grief of the sisters and their friends, Jesus, according to the Authorised Version, "groaned in the spirit, and was troubled": the Revised Version gives a second marginal translation, "was moved with indignation in the spirit," and "troubled himself." A colloquial translation would be "was annoyed or vexed and upset." He immediately inquired where Lazarus was laid, and the text directly adds "Jesus wept." The emotion of vexation and resentment that nobody seemed to have the least hope of Lazarus' return to life by his means is inconsistent with the emotion of uncontrollable grief or the shedding of tears by a full-grown man. . Hence, I suspect, these words "Jesus wept," over which tens of thousands of sympathetic preachers and believers have shed tears, may have been a gloss[1] to the interpolations. It is most certainly foreign and incongruous to the context. The succeeding verse 36 was a happy thought of a subsequent editor. Both verses may be omitted without the text being a penny the worse. On arrival at the cave in which the body of Lazarus had been laid, Jesus commanded that the stone covering the entrance should be removed, and is remonstrated with by Martha in language more practical than refined. The stone, however, is removed, and Jesus is then represented as uttering a prayer to the Father which surpasses in pious folly the renowned prayer of the Scotch minister, "Lord give us all a good conceit of ourselves." Jesus' prayer was "Father, I thank thee that thou hast heard me. And I knew that thou hearest me always; but because of the people that stand by I said *it*, that they may believe that thou hast sent me." The second portion of the prayer is surely objectionable, *cela va sans dire*. Thanks uttered to the Father, not because reverently due to him, but that the bystanders might hear, and that the hearing might persuade them to believe. In fact, the thanksgiving to the Father was a mean and vulgar trick to obtain the belief of the people. Such a scene as this could not have been penned by Cerinthus, but by a paltry and vulgar-minded forger. It is in passages such as this one sees with pity and regret the sad necessity

---

[1] A gloss is a marginal remark, introduced by the next copyist of the manuscript into the body of the text.

imposed upon learned and devout theologians to defend or explain away, if they can, what is really wrong and objectionable—the crude and vulgar conceptions of forgers and interpolators. Bishop Westcott's comment on this passage is: "At the close of verse 41 we must make a pause. The reflection which follows is spoken as a self-revelation to the disciples": a remark that does not improve the position. Bishop Walsham How's commentary is no better; that Jesus uttered "the wonderful words of this verse, possibly in a lower voice, and so as to be heard chiefly by His believing disciples." And his paraphrase of the prayer is six and half-a-dozen. And so we might go through a score of commentaries by bishops. These learned gentlemen, the teachers of morality, are incapable, from their education and mode of thinking, of perceiving that the sentiment of this prayer, or 'self-revelation,' or whatever else it may be called, is inherently wrong, whether uttered aloud or in a low voice, whether heard by the Father, or by believing disciples, or the unbelieving multitude. Let us be thankful that this prayer, though eulogised by bishops, is not followed as a pattern by the clergy and laity. The whole passage from verse 1–46 should be excised. There is no serious objection to the remainder of ch. xi., except the concluding clause of verse 47, which should be cut out.

Of chapter xii., I have already spoken of the anointing of the feet of Jesus by Mary six days before the Passover, and have rejected the story as a fabrication wrought for a very definite purpose. The visit to Bethany is mentioned by Irenæus, but not the interesting anecdote of the anointing (*Ad Her.*, III. xxii. 3). The next story of the triumphal procession of Jesus mounted on an ass, and accompanied by a multitude bearing branches of palm trees and chanting hosannas, is an amplification of the commonplace circumstance that Jesus proceeded to Jerusalem at the Passover, very clearly founded upon prophecy, as declared in the passage. All these verses, therefore, from verse 1–19 should be deleted, retaining merely the fact that Jesus had arrived at Jerusalem before the Passover. The interview with the Greeks is not improbable; but that interview is described in verses 20–22, and verses 44–50, verse 45 being deleted. The intermediate verses, from 23–43, are an accretion which I attribute to the same hand which produced the objectionable prayer in the preceding chapter. The same moral homogeneity is perceptible in the explanation of the voice from heaven, which came for the behoof of the multitude. A further illustration of the sad fact that learned and conscientious theologians feel obliged to maintain the crude notions of forgers as truths, as far as they can possibly manage to do so, is found in their comments on this interpolation. No greater nonsense could have been put into the mouth of Jesus than verse 24: "Verily, verily, I say unto you, except a corn of wheat fall into the ground and die, it abideth alone: but if it die, it bringeth forth much fruit." The very reverse of this statement is the fact, and modern theologians are surely as well informed on this matter as any gardener or farmer's hind. Yet in Bishop Westcott's comments there is no trace of a sense of the falsity of the statement. On the contrary, one feels ashamed to say, knowing the worth and talent of the eminent prelate, that Bishop Westcott's comments support the passage. These are his main remarks on verse 24: "The law of life through death is shown in the simplest analogy. Every nobler form of being presupposes the loss of that which precedes." "The general truth of verse 24 is presented in its final antithesis in relation to human life. Sacrifice, self-surrender, death is the condition of the highest life; selfishness is the destruction of life. The language is closely parallel to words recorded by the Synoptists: Matt. x. 38 f.; Luke xvii. 33." On referring to these texts, I find not a word bearing upon the statement that a dead seed germinates. Bishop Walsham How's comment on verse 24 is: "Christ compares Himself to the grain of corn. The grain by dying (as it were) in the ground brings forth much fruit. Christ by dying wins a rich harvest of souls." The bishop clearly had a sense of the falseness of the statement, and ought to have been deterred from enforcing a false fact. But he bravely proceeds to use it; but is it not clear that the terms of his comparison are wrongly stated? The second clause should also have the parenthetical qualification. The late Professor Jowett, Master of Balliol, lamented the 'love of pious frauds' prevalent amongst the clergy. He says of the latter, their "tyranny is very great on education and opinion."

I have already spoken of the substitution of the feet washing scene for the institution of the Eucharist in ch. xiii. (see p. 138). Of the remaining verses of that chapter I should excise verses 31 and 32 (retaining merely the words 'Jesus said' as an introduction to the address that follows), and verse 38 (with the exception of the first clause), in which a prophecy of a low order is put into the mouth of Jesus. Verses 31 and 32, in which the son of man is primarily glorified and the Father secondarily glorified, do not indicate the Cerinthian sense in which Jesus is not set up as a rival to God. These verses read like the composition of a schoolman displaying his skill in tautology.

In the discourses that follow, the guide to the discovery of interpolations is the obvious intent of Cerinthus, as explained by Irenæus, to limit the part of Jesus to human functions, and not to elevate him to the Godhead. The interruption of Thomas in ch. xiv. 5 may be an interpolation, but it is of a neutral character, and may be allowed to stand. The interruption of Philip is, however, a manifest interpolation, as it leads to the statement that Jesus is the equal of the Father, whom he had been commissioned to declare. Verses 7-11 should be excised; also verses 13 and 14. I have already spoken of Paraclete, translated Comforter in ch. xiv. 16, and in the other passages of the Fourth Gospel where the name occurs. The name Paraclete does not occur in any other Christian writing of the first century, and hence I feel justified in concluding that it was an unknown name to the Christians of that period. The expression 'another Paraclete' in the text of the Fourth Gospel, however, clearly implies that there was a Paraclete previously known to Christians; but of this there is not a particle of evidence. Justin Martyr is silent regarding Paraclete. The name first occurs in Christian literature in the letter from the Churches of Lyons and Vienna to the Churches in Asia and Phrygia (Eusebius, *Eccl. Hist.*, v. 1), detailing the persecution in Gaul during the reign of Marcus Aurelius and Verus, A.D. 161-180. I feel, therefore, justified in declaring the word 'other' in the text to be an interpolation requiring excision. But the motive which actuated the interpolator to speak of 'another Paraclete' will become apparent on referring to the writing called the First Epistle of John, ch. ii. 1, "and if any man sin we have an advocate with the Father, Jesus Christ the righteous," the Greek word translated 'advocate' being παράκλητος. The Greek word in the Epistle is not a proper name, and the attempt to use it as a proper name will simply render the passage unintelligible. The translation of the word in another language was essential to convey a meaning, and the English word 'advocate' employed is a correct rendering of the original. But in the Fourth Gospel the word is a proper name, and the translation of it will be an act of folly similar to translating the proper names Smith, White, or Bacon.[1]

But the committee of forgers found it useful to identify the proper name Paraclete of the Fourth Gospel with the descriptive word παράκλητος employed in the Epistle, and thus they in a measure formed a connecting link between the Fourth Gospel and the First Epistle of John, and upon this founded the assertion of identity of authorship. This design of the committee of forgers has been frustrated by the diverse translation in the English version of the proper name in the Gospel as 'Comforter,' and of the descriptive word in the Epistle as 'Advocate.' Bishop Lightfoot was strongly in favour of assimilating the translation in Gospel and Epistle, and his argument in support of this view was a genuine one of a modern advocate, based less upon right than on its advantage for attaining the main chance. He says: "The language of the Gospel will thus be linked in the English version, as it is in the original, with the language of the Epistle. In this there will be a twofold advantage. We shall see fresh force in the words thus rendered, 'He will give you

---

[1] Translation of proper names would render identification of individuals exceedingly difficult, if not impossible. The bearers of these names, Messrs Smith, White, and Bacon, would hardly recognise themselves in a French translation as Messieurs Forgeron, Blanc, and Lard, or in a German translation as Herren Schmied, Weiss, and Speck. Compound proper names would fare roughly. Thus Mr Cunningham would be rendered Monsieur Jambon-rusé or Sly-bacon in French, and Herr Schlau-Schinken in German.

another advocate,' when we remember that our Lord is styled by St John an 'advocate': the advocacy of Christ illustrating and being illustrated by the advocacy of the Spirit. At the same time we shall bring out another of the many coincidences, tending to establish an identity of authorship in the Gospel and Epistle, and thus to make valid for the former all the evidences external and internal which may be adduced to prove the genuineness of the latter" (*On a fresh revision of the English New Testament*, by J. B. Lightfoot, D.D., 1872). The authors of the Revised Version were probably swayed by sentiment in retaining the current translation or rather mistranslation, as it had been influentially urged that "so many sacred associations have connected themselves for generation after generation with the name of *The Comforter*, that it would seem something like an act of sacrilege to change it." Bishop Lightfoot's powerful advocacy was not, however, without result, as the revisers placed the translation 'advocate' in the margin. The word 'advocate,' though a correct rendering of the common noun παράκλητος, incorrectly indicates the function and purpose of Paraclete. In the Fourth Gospel Paraclete is not stated to be an advocate, but his functions are clearly indicated in several passages. In ch. xiv. 26, he is described as a teacher and a remembrancer: "he shall teach you all things, and bring all things to your remembrance, whatsoever I have said unto you." In ch. xv. 26 he is to be a witness: "he shall testify of me." In ch. xvi. 8 he is to be a judge or reprover: "he will reprove (or convict, Revised Version) the world of sin, and of righteousness, and of judgment"; and in verse 13 he is to be a guide: "he will guide you into all truth." From the above statements taken from the Fourth Gospel, I am unable to perceive that advocacy is any part of the functions assigned by Jesus to Paraclete, or that the expression 'advocate,' as applied to Jesus in the Epistle, was appropriate to Paraclete in the Gospel: "If any man sin, we have an advocate with the Father, Jesus Christ the righteous" (1 John ii. 1). But I regret to say that theologians are not above the use of pious sophistry. Bishop Lightfoot says, "If 'advocate' is the only sense which παράκλητος can properly bear, it is also (as I cannot but think) the sense which the context suggests whenever the word is used in the Gospel. . . . . And generally it may be said that the Holy Spirit, the Paraclete, is represented in these passages as the advocate, the counsel, who suggests true reasonings to our minds and true courses of action for our lives, who convicts our adversary the world of wrong, and who pleads our cause before God our Father." The reader has before him the passages in the Fourth Gospel in which the part to be played by Paraclete is declared, and is in a position to judge whether this great divine was justified in using rhetoric of this description.[1] Believing my view of the origin of the Fourth Gospel to be the true one, these eager pleadings of the distinguished and learned Anglican prelate, to appropriate a Gnostic æon as the third member of the Trinity, appear to me to be singularly grotesque.

The above remarks refer only to the English version, the received Greek text being correct. The word 'Comforter' should be scored out of the English version, and the proper name[2] Paraclete substituted, and this step is actually indi-

[1] Tertullian says: '*Quæ est ergo Paracleti administratio nisi hæc, quod disciplina dirigitur, quod Scripturæ revelantur, quod intellectus reformatur, quod ad meliora proficitur*" (*De Virginibus velandis*, 1). What, then, are the functions of Paraclete but these, that discipline be directed, that the Scriptures be revealed, that the mind be reformed, that progress be made to better things. None of these functions is discharged by an advocate; the third century theologian, himself a barrister or advocate, is clearly in this matter ahead of the nineteenth century bishop. Origen, who certainly knew Greek better than an English bishop of the nineteenth century, says that the word Paraclete means both advocate or intercessor and comforter, παρακλησις, being termed in Latin *consolatio*, and he distinctly says that the latter is the meaning in the Fourth Gospel. (See *De Principiis*, vii. 4, and Ante-Nicene Christian Library, *Origen*, vol. i. p. 117.)

[2] Bishop Westcott and Bishop Ellicot in their commentaries have collected tons of learned dust on the subject of the 'comforter' or 'advocate,' by which the eyes and minds of their readers have been blinded. While they have exhausted all the learning of Pagan, Jewish, and Christian writers, they have passed over the Christian Gnostics on this subject. Any one who will take the trouble of reading the article on Valentinus in the *Encyclopædia Britannica* will become sensible that this great theologian was entitled to be quoted in the discussion of this subject. The Valentinian Paraclete is worthy of consideration. It would be preposterous to charge these uncommonly learned gentlemen with unacquaintance with the Valentinian theology. The omission to notice it was obviously by design.

cated in the margin of the Revised Version. Verse 18 in the original Greek may not, perhaps, accurately describe the bereaved disciples of a moral teacher as 'orphans,' but this is no excuse for the substitution of the word 'comfortless' in the translation. "I will not leave you comfortless or desolate" is not equivalent to "I will not leave you orphans," which is the accurate translation of the Greek text. 'Orphans' is given in the margin of the Revised Version, and should be substituted for the word 'comfortless' or 'desolate.' The Vulgate has accurately translated the passage. The verses that follow are mystical, and not uniformly intelligible, and are fair subjects of suspicion if not of condemnation. I should strike out the two concluding clauses of verse 19, verse 20, the concluding clause of verse 21, verse 22 (Judas' interruption), the initial clause of verse 23, and the concluding clause of the same verse. What remains of the passage from verse 19–23 is clear and intelligible, with no suspicious meaning, but fair and above board, and may be justly regarded as portions of the original. In verse 26 I have already explained that the original text had here been 'deceitfully used' so as to identify Paraclete with the well known Holy Ghost of Christians. Mrs Lewis' Syriac Gospels supplies the correct original, which is 'that Spirit Paraclete,' which should be substituted for the word 'Comforter (Paraclete) which is the Holy Ghost,' which is not the correct translation even of the received Greek text. The vulgarity of verse 29 condemns it as the interpolation of a base soul. Verse 30 does not convey any intelligible idea, and hence may be scored out.

The parable of the vine in chapter xv. is a separate composition, not in keeping with the address preceding or following, interpo'ated into the discourse. It is markedly egotistic and minatory, and hence not in harmony with the pathetic feeling pre-eminent in Jesus' valedictory words. The continuation of the discourse is at verse 9. In the concluding clause of verse 16, an objectionable touch has been given to Jesus' words, and hence it should be struck out. Verses 22–25 appear to be an interpolation requiring excision. In verse 26 the Greek text is doubtless genuine, but the English version needs correction to the extent of substituting the proper name Paraclete for the erroneous translation 'the Comforter.'

In chapter xvi. the interpolations are of much the same general character as in the preceding chapters. Verse 4 is of the same base nature as xiv. 29, and should be deleted. The translation of Paraclete is of course objectionable in verse 7, and hence the proper name is to be retained, and 'the Comforter' cut out. Verses 14 and 15 are opposed to the Cerinthian sense, in which Jesus is only a human teacher, and hence they should be scored out. For the same reason verse 23–26 should be deleted. Verses 29, 30, and 31 seem to be foolish, redundant, and without *raison d'être*.

The prayer to the Father in chapter xvii. also has been tampered with, and needs weeding. In verse 2, the clause 'over all flesh' is redundant, and probably was intended to mean more than the moderate power assigned to Jesus by Cerinthus. Verse 5 is *primâ facie* an interpolation, for in Cerinthus' view Jesus was a simple human being (see Irenæus, *Ad Her.*, IV. xiv. 1). In verse 9 the clause "I pray not for the world" embodies a view which I do not think genuine Christians would ever have willingly endorsed. In verse 12 the clause referring to the fabulous story of Judas the traitor, and the fulfilment of the Scripture, must necessarily be deleted. I do not think the remainder of this chapter has been interpolated, with the exception of the concluding clause of verse 24.

The four chapters which we have been just discussing, xiv.–xvii., form the glory of the Fourth Gospel. The simple beauty of the language and the pathos of the sentiment are most touching. It is probably to these four chapters that we owe the conservation of this Gnostic composition. The parting address of Jesus to his disciples is a natural and tender farewell to faithful disciples. The expectation of his coming doom by Jesus was ordinary and reasonable foresight and inference from the hostile relations narrated between the Jews and himself; and it was shared by the disciples. One can well understand that the early Christian sects would not willingly let this Gospel die, and hence it was taken in hand by various sects and by several orthodox Churches, and

modified from time to time, till, under skilled editing, it
acquired the form in which it has come down to us. But for
the clue to its origin revealed by Bishop Lightfoot's successful
inquiry into the antiquity of this Gospel, it may have run
another course of many years without detection, and perhaps
have baffled for ever the critical ingenuity of man.

In examining the next two chapters, xviii. and xix., in
which the arrest and trial of Jesus are related, we are met
with the great difficulty that there are no earlier authentic
detailed accounts of these events. With the exception of the
barest reference there is no mention made of them in the
surviving Christian literature of the first century. In the
writing called the First Epistle to Timothy an allusion to
Pontius Pilate is made in ch. vi. 13, but this allusion is
subject to the suspicion that it is a late gloss, being parenthetical; and further, the language is obscure, and may be
translated in at least two ways, and hence is not quite satisfactory as a historical guide. And the date of the writing is
doubtful—it was probably written in the first half of the
second century after some of the Gospel stories had been
invented and had become current. The next mention of
Pontius Pilate is in the Gospel of Nicodemus or *Acta Pilati*,
and by Justin Martyr, both in the early half of the second
century. I should have considered myself justified, from the
absence of evidence, in doubting whether there were any
judicial proceedings in connection with Jesus' arrest and
execution, but for one remark of a genuine and reliable
witness, the Apostle Paul. In 1 Cor. ii. 8, Paul, speaking of
the mysterious ways of God, says that none of the "princes
of this world" know them, for otherwise "they would not
have crucified the Lord of glory." I accept this casual
remark of Paul as giving some historical corroboration, the
only one available, to the account in the Fourth Gospel of
the arrest and condemnation of Jesus by Caiaphas, the High
Priest, and Pontius Pilate, the Roman Procurator, great
officials who might well be called by Paul 'princes of this
world.' These high personages can hardly be regarded as
concerned in the death of Jesus otherwise than as officials
and magistrates acting in their public capacity; and hence

we must conclude that there were judicial proceedings of some sort. In checking the details of the judicial proceedings one is obliged to have recourse to common sense.

In revising chapter xviii., the participation of Judas in the arrest must be cut out as utterly false, the existence of Judas being without any corroboration in the writings of the first century and first half of the second century. The first clause of verse 2 should hence be struck out, and also the words in verse 3, "Judas then having received." In verse 4, the clause "knowing all things that should come upon him," states much beyond what is justifiable to say of any human person's sagacity, and hence should be deleted as not likely to have been in the original. The concluding clause of verse 5 must of course be struck out; and also verse 6, as it appears generally to be understood by theologians that the alleged falling to the ground of the band of men and officers was supernatural, and shows, or as Bishop Westcott says, "seems to show, at any rate, that the Lord purposed to declare openly to the disciples (comp. Matt. xxvi. 53) that it was of his own free choice that He gave Himself up." Cerinthus was unlikely to lend himself to any silly notion of this sort. Ideas of the foolish nature of the reference given by Bishop Westcott of 'twelve legions of angels' being available for the rescue, if desired, was not the sort that Cerinthus gave encouragement to. It must be remarked that the assertion is amazing that a cohort of Roman soldiers with a military tribune (translated captain) at its head, fell down before Jesus. This is a statement that is of exactly the same nature as an interesting anecdote related in the Gospel of Nicodemus or *Acts of Pilate*, the most famous of the New Testament Apocrypha, and said by Tischendorf to date from the second century. The subject is the judicial examination of Jesus. An officer was sent to bring in Jesus: "And when Jesus entered, and the standard bearers holding the standards, the tops of the standards bowed down and worshipped Jesus. And when the Jews saw the manner of the standards, how they bowed down and worshipped Jesus, they cried out exceedingly against the standard bearers. And Pilate said to the Jews, Do ye not marvel how the banners bowed down and worshipped Jesus? The Jews said to Pilate, We saw how the standard bearers bowed and worshipped him. And the governor called the standard bearers and said to them, Why did ye do so? They said to Pilate, We are Greeks, and wait upon the gods, how could we worship him? but as we were holding the banners they bowed down of themselves and worshipped him." A test was applied by Pilate to ascertain whether the standards spontaneously bowed, or were lowered by the bearers, and it was proved beyond a doubt that the standards bowed! (*The Apocryphal Gospels*, by B. H. Cowper, "Gospel of Nicodemus," ch. 1). The concluding clause of verse 8 and the whole of verse 9, the interpolation being self-declared, should be struck out. Now follows some confusion in the narrative, from which the inference is justifiable that the passage had been tampered with. Jesus, when captured, was taken first to Annas, who, although deposed by the Romans, was recognised by the Jews as high priest (see Luke iii. 2, and Acts iv. 6). A disciple, spoken of as 'another disciple,' who was known to the high priest, introduced Peter into the court of the high priest's residence, and there Peter perpetrated his first denial of his master, and stood and warmed himself before the fire. In verse 24 the statement is made that Annas sent on Jesus to Caiaphas, who had been appointed high priest by the Romans. And then follows the story of the second and third denials of Peter. The reader would naturally conclude that the first denial was made in the court of Annas, and the second and third in the court of Caiaphas: but it is singular that Peter is represented as doing *chez* Caiaphas in verse 25, exactly what he is represented as doing *chez* Annas in verse 18: standing and warming himself before the fire, as if he had not stirred the whole time from the court of Annas. It appears to me that the second clause of verse 13, and the whole of verse 14 is an explanatory gloss, and may be struck out as unnecessary and superfluous to the narrative. The interesting anecdote regarding the denials of Peter and the crowing of the cock was probably extracted from some pious story-book, and should be summarily struck out. Verse 24 should be linked to the first clause of verse 13.

It was natural and legally necessary that the deposed high priest should send on the prisoner to the high priest appointed and recognised by the Roman Government. The examination spoken of in verse 19 was made by Caiaphas, the high priest in power, and the narrative proceeds to verse 23, and is resumed in verse 28. The concluding clauses of this verse, "lest they should be defiled; but that they might eat the passover," should be deleted for reasons already given, and the text of Mrs Lewis' Syriac Gospel substituted: "that they should not be defiled whilst they were eating the unleavened bread." The narrative continues from verse 29, but is here specially of an unsatisfactory nature, as no definite charge or accusation is made in reply to Pilate's inquiry. Verse 32, I am inclined to think, was a gloss, and should be omitted. Pilate's examination of Jesus is very limited, but probably only the most important part of it was recorded. I consider it utterly impossible that a Roman magistrate would openly declare a prisoner to be absolutely innocent, and then promptly proceed to execute him. Under the circumstances it would have been simple prudence for him to hold his tongue. I should, therefore, delete the clause "I find in him no fault at all."

In chapter xix. I consider the verses 2-5 relate proceedings that were improbable. We have no parallel case of a Roman magistrate dealing with a prisoner in the manner detailed in these verses, and it must be remembered that Pilate is implied as having ordered and permitted these disorderly proceedings. They amount to a *dedecus imperii*, which no Roman emperor would permit. These are second century extravagancies, and cannot be attributed to Cerinthus. These verses should be deleted. After the scourging, which was a regular judicial proceeding of those times, the narrative finds a natural continuation in the concluding clause of verse 5 and verse 6, in which Pilate pronounces sentence of crucifixion. The concluding clause of verse 6 should be deleted. Verse 7 may stand; but the whole passage from verse 8-15, being foolish and redundant, and hence not fairly attributable to a writer of the high stamp of Cerinthus, should be bodily struck out. It is unlikely that a Roman governor would submit to the dictation of a Jewish mob. On pronouncing sentence, after which no further examination or pleading was necessary or permissible, Pilate delivered the prisoner for execution, as stated in verse 16. At the crucifixion, the division of the clothing amongst the soldiers who carried out the punishment was quite natural, and may stand; but the story of the casting of lots for the seamless coat was a pious fabrication in fulfilment of prophecy, and hence the second half of verse 23 and verse 24 should be scored out.

The passage from verse 25-27 should be scored out. The object for which this incident was contrived was the aggrandisement of the beloved disciple, the reputed author of the Fourth Gospel. The nameless beloved disciple was a creation of the second half of the second century, for he is unknown in the Christian literature of the first hundred and fifty years and more of the Christian era. Even Justin Martyr is silent about him. The beloved disciple made his *debut* in the Fourth Gospel in connection with the story of Judas Iscariot — a very bad association — in ch. xiii., and, as a considerable portion of that chapter was declared spurious, the story of the beloved disciple was scored out, and did not come up for remark. Some eminent theologians maintain that in the Fourth Gospel the writer takes pains to set John, who is supposed to be the beloved disciple, over Peter, and various incidents in the Gospel are mentioned in which stress is laid upon this pre-eminence. For instance, in ch. xiii., the description, 'whom Jesus loved' (verse 23), at once sets up John on a pinnacle. So again, in ch. xx., on the information given by Mary Magdalene, Peter and the beloved disciple ran to the sepulchre, and the latter outran Peter and arrived first at the sepulchre. And further instances are given in which Peter is depreciated otherwise. There naturally appears design in all these instances. Bishop Westcott, however, considers that John did not claim pre-eminence over Peter, but, on the contrary, set himself second to him, and he founds this opinion on the position at table of John at the last supper. On the authority of Bishop Lightfoot, he states that the guests reclined at meals resting on their left arms, stretched obliquely, "so that the back of the head of one guest lay in the bosom of the dress of the guest above him. If three reclined together the centre was the place of honour, the second place that above (to the left), the third that below (to the right)" (*Commentary on St John*, xiii. 23). Bishop Westcott assigns quite correctly the third place to the beloved disciple; but he assumes, I hardly think correctly, that Peter occupied the second place on the left of the Lord. In this situation, I do not understand how Peter could have caught the attention of the beloved disciple by beckoning to the back or top of his head. To enable him to beckon to the beloved Apostle, Peter's position must have been on the other side of the table. We cannot imagine Cerinthus to have been swayed by any predilection for the disciple who in the second century was set up as the author of the former's own work. The design of elevating John is, however, very apparent in several passages, of which the passage under notice is one; hence I feel justified in condemning all these passages as the interpolations of a forger. The expression 'woman' (verse 26) put into the mouth of Jesus in addressing his mother from the cross is bad manners in Eastern countries, and clearly indicates the base mind of a forger, who considered haughtiness of tone and rudeness of speech as proper adjuncts of a superior and divine person. In the verses that follow much deletion is necessary and some transposition. In verse 28 the parenthetical clause, "knowing that all things were now accomplished, that the Scripture might be fulfilled," must of course be cut out. Verse 34 should be amended as already demonstrated, *i.e.*, the words 'blood and water' expunged, and the original words, 'a dove and blood,' substituted, and verse 35 should follow verse 29. It is highly probable that in verse 35 the original was not anonymous, but that the name of the witness, John, was recorded: thus, "John that saw it bare record," etc.; or the first person may have been employed, thus: "I, John, that saw it, bear record, and my record is true; and I know that I say true, that ye might believe." However, taking the Greek text as it stands, I prefer the translation of Dr Martineau and Matthew Arnold, both accomplished Greek scholars and men of genius: "that man knoweth that he saith true" (see *Seat of Authority in Religion*, Bk. II. ch. ii. 13, and

Contemporary Review for May 1875). The corresponding statement of the descent of the dove, in ch. i. 32, is not declared anonymously, and as the witness is the same in both instances, it is reasonable to conclude that Cerinthus did not employ a periphrasis and the third person when describing the return flight of the dove. The purpose or intent of the employment of a periphrasis and the third person is very obvious: it gives good cover for conveying the impression that the witness who saw the descent of the dove was not the same person as the witness who saw the ascension of the dove. I have already explained that the forgers or committee of forgers had fixed upon John the Baptist as the witness of the descending dove, and in this passage was the first step taken for fixing upon the anonymous beloved disciple as the witness of the ascending dove (or of the water and blood), the same individual being boldly declared subsequently (ch. xxi. 24) to be the writer of the Gospel. The continuation of the narrative will be found in verse 30, in which the words "he said, It is finished: and" must be deleted. The following three verses, 31, 32, and 33, were manifestly introduced in the interests of the Paschal Lamb doctrine, as already explained, and should be cut out. Verses 36 and 37, in which the fulfilment of prophecy is spoken of, must necessarily be excised. The story continues unbroken to verse 42, in which the clause regarding the preparation need not be struck out, as the allusion is to the Sabbath Day and not to the passover.

Before proceeding to the examination of the twentieth or final chapter of the original Fourth Gospel, it is desirable that I should submit a few ideas that I have gathered from the perusal of the Christian writings of the first century on the subjects of the resurrection and ascension of Jesus. It is unquestionable that it was the belief amongst Christians of the first century that Jesus rose from the dead. On this subject we may take the testimony of Paul as a genuine, honest, and credible witness. Throughout his epistles he insists on this fact with all the fervour and eloquence that he was capable of. In Romans i. 4 he says that Jesus was "declared to be the Son of God with power, according to the spirit of holiness, by the resurrection from the dead." In 1 Cor. xv. 3-9 he gives proofs of the resurrection of Jesus by naming the witnesses who saw Jesus after the resurrection, and by declaring that he himself saw him after the resurrection, although he had not seen him before. "I delivered unto you first of all that which I also received, how that Christ died for our sins, according to the Scriptures; and that he was buried, and that he rose again the third day, according to the Scriptures; and that he was seen of Cephas, then of the twelve; after that, he was seen of above five hundred brethren at once; of whom the greater part remain unto this present, but some are fallen asleep. After that he was seen of James; then of all the apostles. And last of all he was seen of me also, as of one born out of due time. For I am the least of the apostles, that am not meet to be called an apostle, because I persecuted the Church of God." The most important point of Paul's evidence is his clear and unmistakable statement that he himself saw the risen Lord. I can see no reason for discrediting or explaining away Paul's emphasised and repeated (1 Cor. ix. 1) testimony that he saw the Lord after the crucifixion, although theologians concur in not accepting the distinct and unmistakable evidence of a trustworthy witness. I say advisedly that theologians reject Paul's evidence on this point, for to say that Paul saw the risen Lord in the mythical story related in Acts ix. 3-9, xxii. 6-11, xxvi. 13-18, is tantamount to denying and rejecting the validity of the evidence of a credible witness. The story of the heavenly vision related in the Acts is impossible and unhistorical, a fabrication to which Paul gives no countenance in his writings. In the statement given in 1 Cor. xv. 3-9, Paul saw the risen Lord under the same mundane circumstances and conditions as the other witnesses. That Paul and other witnesses saw the Lord after the crucifixion does not imply that the Lord had undergone the final doom of humanity; it most certainly implies and proves the contrary. If Jesus had died on the cross, it is against common sense that he could have been seen living afterwards. The events of the crucifixion, as related in the Gospel of Cerinthus, are consistent with the circumstance that death did not occur. Crucifixion for a few hours is not necessarily fatal. The wound from the soldier's spear can hardly be regarded as mortal, if it had been inflicted on the right side of the chest, as all great painters depict it in their paintings. The apparently dead body of Jesus was deposited in a clean and cool cave, or newly-constructed sepulchre, in which the latent energies of life revived. In all this there was nothing supernatural, but a natural though unusual and unexpected result. Had the circumstances been otherwise, life could not have revived. Had the crucifixion been prolonged and the wound been inflicted on the left side, and the heart pierced, had the body of Jesus been deposited in a grave six feet deep and ten tons of earth piled over it, resuscitation would have been impossible. That ignorant people, whose usual experience of crucifixion was that death followed, should firmly and honestly believe that death had occurred and that their Lord and Master had risen from the dead, and that this belief spread and influenced the minds of many, is natural and credible. There is no reason for supposing that Cerinthus had no belief in the resurrection of the Lord after the crucifixion.

Regarding the ascension of Jesus, I believe that I can justly speak with the same decision. There is no evidence in the Christian literature of the first century that Jesus corporeally ascended from the earth into the upper atmosphere. There are no witnesses of such ascension recorded by our best historian, Paul, and there is no trace of a belief in the first century that such an event had occurred. I am distinctly of opinion that a belief prevailed in the first century, amongst some Christians at least, that Jesus, having risen from the dead, would be immortal on earth. In Romans vi. 9, 10, Paul unequivocally says : " Knowing that Christ being raised from the dead dieth no more ; death hath no more dominion over him. For in that he died, he died unto sin once ; but in that he liveth, he liveth unto God." I understand these words to mean that Paul believed that Jesus was living on earth at that moment, and had become immortal on earth (see Acts xxv. 19). In this point Jesus differed from all other men, who though immortal in the next world were doomed to death on earth. Ignatius, in the Epistle to the

Smyrnæans (ch. iii.) expresses a similar belief. This passage is probably genuine, as the belief expressed in it did not prevail later in the second century. There is a considerable difference in the interpretation of this passage by various translators. The ancient Latin translation of the passage (given in Jacobson's edition) is "*Ego enim et post resurrectionem in carne ipsum vidi, et credo existentem,*" which I translate: "For I saw him in the flesh even after the resurrection and I believe he is still existing or living," i.e., in the beginning of the second century (*circa* 107 A.D.), the date of the Epistle. In the Greek original the word 'know' takes the place of 'saw,' but in other respects, especially the final clause, which on this point is of importance, the Latin is a literal rendering. Bishop Lightfoot, however, translates the Greek differently, thus: "For I know and believe that He was in the flesh even after the resurrection"; the important word ὄντα is in this translation simply passed over.[1] Archbishop Wake's translation is more accurate: "But I know that even after his resurrection he was in the flesh; and I believe that he is still so." It must be remembered that Ignatius wrote these words in the beginning of the second century. The original is: Ἐγὼ γὰρ καὶ μετὰ τὴν ἀνάστασιν ἐν σαρκὶ αὐτὸν οἶδα καὶ πιστεύω ὄντα, which I translate literally, preserving the textual sequence of the words: "For I even after the resurrection know him in the flesh, and I believe him existing or living." The point of these quotations from Paul and Ignatius is that there was in the first century a belief (partial and limited probably) in the continued existence of Jesus on earth."[2] In the passages that I have quoted I do

---

[1] In the Essays on *Supernatural Religion*, Bishop Lightfoot translates the passage thus: "And I myself know and believe that He exists in the flesh after the resurrection."

[2] In addition to Paul and Ignatius, I ought to add the insane writer of the Revelations to the number of those who believed in the immortality of Jesus on earth after the resurrection. This lunatic relates an interview with Jesus "in the Spirit on the Lord's day," in the island of Patmos. Jesus is represented as an aged man: "his head and *his* hairs *were* white like wool, as white as snow" (Rev. i. 14), and as saying, "behold I am alive for evermore" (verse 18). See also Rev. ii. 8, in which passage Jesus is again represented to be alive, *i.e.*, at the end of the first century or beginning of

not perceive any consciousness on the part of the writers that Jesus was not on earth at the time those passages were written. Paul, in saying of Jesus in his Epistle to the Romans, he "dieth no more: death hath no more dominion over him: . . . . but in that he liveth, he liveth unto God," could only mean that Jesus was at that time on earth, and not in heaven, in which region death has no place. No Christian in the first century needed to have been told that a resident in heaven is deathless and immortal. Later on Paul was apparently embarrassed in his belief in the continued life of Jesus on earth by the non-appearance or disappearance of the Lord. He had met the Lord, and had been instructed by him (as we must understand him to say in the first chapter of the Epistle to the Galatians),[1] but had lost sight of him since. We should

the second, whatever may be supposed to be the date of the Revelations. I must refer in this connection to Irenæus' remarkable statements on the age of Jesus in his work, *Ad Her.*, II. xxii. 3-6. This great divine was convinced that Jesus attained old age, and he founded this belief on the testimony of the elders, who were familiar in Asia with John and other apostles, who communicated this information to them. Having stated a fact on good authority, Irenæus directly stultifies himself by pretending to prove that Jesus attained old age before the crucifixion! The well-attested fact is unaffected by Irenæus' foolish exposition. That Jesus lived to old age after the crucifixion is thus proved. There are not wanting testimonies to the ultimate death of Jesus. In James v. 11, 'the end of the Lord' is spoken of as having been seen by his audience; Job and Jesus being brought forward as examples of ultimate happiness after calamity. This passage, however, has been otherwise interpreted, in a perverse sense, I think. In Ignatius' letter to the Ephesians (19), the reference to the silence or mystery connected with the ultimate death of Jesus is unmistakable. "And hidden from the prince of this world were the virginity of Mary and her child-bearing, and likewise also the death of the Lord—three mysteries to be cried aloud [three mysteries of the Shout]—the which were wrought in the silence of God" (Lightfoot). The death on the cross cannot surely be regarded a mystery wrought in silence. It is unlikely that this singular and peculiar passage was forged. Both Paul and Ignatius appear to have held the same belief: that Jesus was immortal on earth and yet mysteriously disappeared.

[1] There are verbal difficulties in the first chapter of Galatians, which, without doubt, influence many worthy people, who in general take accurate common-sense views of things. Paul says in Gal. i. 13, 14, that he was at first a fierce persecutor of the Christians; but he continues that it pleased God to "reveal his Son in him ($\dot{\epsilon}\nu$ $\dot{\epsilon}\mu oί$, or to him, or perhaps by means of him), that he might preach him among the heathen." In verse 11 he says

have expected that had he known of the corporeal ascension of Jesus, he would have spoken of it; but he is markedly silent on that subject. The fifth chapter of Second Corinthians is a mysterious disquisition which I cannot clearly comprehend, in which is a remarkable statement of Paul having known Jesus after the flesh, but now knowing him henceforth no more (verse 16). Paul here supplies a metaphysical explanation of the disappearance of Jesus. It is exceedingly difficult to follow and acquiesce in the reasoning. The steps of the argument appear to be the following:—

Jesus died for all: then all were dead.

Therefore henceforth we know no man after the flesh or living on earth.

"that the gospel which was preached of me is not of men : for I neither received it of man, neither was I taught it, but by the revelation of Jesus Christ." These singular statements must be read in connection with verse 16, in which Paul states that he conferred not with flesh and blood, went not up to Jerusalem where the apostles were till after three years, and then he saw Peter for fifteen days. In Acts ix. 26 and 27, it is related when Paul (or Saul as he was then called) visited Jerusalem after the three years, the disciples were afraid of him naturally from his reputation as a persecutor; but Barnabas took him in hand, and introduced him to the apostles, and declared to them "how he had seen the Lord on the way, and that he had spoken to him, and how he had preached boldly at Damascus in the name of Jesus." There is nothing in the statement of Barnabas which clashes with Paul's own statements in the Galatians, though more detailed and precise information is given. It is a simple, prosaic, and natural statement, which may be accepted as truthful, as it was by the disciples : whereas the story of the heavenly vision is an obvious invention unworthy of belief by sensible men, and it is clear that the apostles knew nothing about it, or the disciples would not have been afraid of Saul. I put Paul's evangelical language into colloquial English as follows : Saul (afterwards called Paul) was a fierce persecutor of the disciples of Jesus, and pursued them by the authority of the Sanhedrim from Jerusalem to Damascus. On the way he met Jesus himself amongst the fugitives : who spoke to him and won him over to his side, and instructed him in the moral principles he taught. Saul was so much impressed by the excellence of the teaching, which was far ahead of what was professed and practised in those days, that he considered this gospel disclosed to him by Jesus as derived from God. Paul had doubtless peculiar notions about Jesus, of which I have noted one in the text. His knowledge of Christianity, and of events in the ministry of Jesus, was obtained direct from Jesus himself, and not from his disciples. In his second visit to Jerusalem he was anxious to compare his gospel or teaching with that of the apostles (Gal. ii. 2).

Therefore we know Jesus after the flesh, or living on earth, no more.

This reasoning will be found in verses 14 and 16. In verse 15 is an intercalary statement that is redundant to the argument, which finally proceeds to show that 'we,' *i.e.*, the apostles or ministers, are the ambassadors or representatives or substitutes of Jesus in the work of reconciliation on earth. In Romans viii. 34, in the same epistle in which Paul expresses his belief in the perpetual dwelling on earth of Jesus (Rom. vi. 9 and 10), is a contradictory statement that Jesus is at the right hand of God, making intercession for us. These two consecutive parenthetical clauses, "who is even at the right hand of God, who also maketh intercession for us," are obvious glosses. Besides being contradictory to Paul's beliefs on both points, they are redundant and encumber the rhythm of the sentence, they spoil the fine passage, and interrupt the ecstatic feeling of the writer by the introduction of extraneous ideas. The first mention of the ascension of Jesus in Christian literature is found in the *Apology* of Aristides (*c.* 125), who evidently did not believe it, and merely mentions the subject as an *on dit*: "and they say that after three days he rose and ascended into heaven" (see Rendel Harris' Syriac translation). The popular report was that the resurrection and ascension were on the same day. The next reference is in the Epistle of Barnabas, who says (ch. xv.) : " Wherefore also we keep the eighth day for rejoicing, in the which also Jesus rose from the dead, and having been manifested, ascended into the heavens " (Lightfoot's translation). The exact date of this Christian composition is unknown : Bishop Lightfoot says, " the possible limits are A.D. 70 and A.D. 132," but he is disposed to place the date between A.D. 70–79. The epistle is full of the Christian mythology which is conspicuously absent in the undisputed Christian writings of the first century ; and it is sadly deficient in the refinement of thought and language which characterises the Christian literature of the first century. I am thus constrained to refer it to the early years of the second century, before the Christian mythology had crystallised into the form in which it has come down to us. It will be remarked that the resurrection and ascension are on the same day, Sunday, as in Luke's

Gospel, a belief that was modified as the years ran on in the second century. Doubtless the subject of the ascension was previously dealt with in the numerous popular writings and pious story-books that abounded in the first half of the second century: and Barnabas obtained his information on the subject from these sources, for there is no source discoverable in the Christian writings of the first century. Some of the Christian writings contemporary with the Epistle of Barnabas and even much earlier contain no allusions to an ascension, but speak of Jesus as "passed into the heavens" (Heb. iv. 14); "sat down on the right hand of the Majesty on high" (Heb. i. 3); "sat down on the right hand of God" (Heb. x. 12); "set him at his own right hand in the heavenly places" (Eph. i. 20); "gone into heaven, and is on the right hand of God" (1 Peter iii. 22); "received up into glory" (1 Tim. iii. 16), and there are other similar passages. These writers, I conclude, accepted neither Paul's (and Ignatius') view of the perpetual residence on earth of Jesus, nor yet the popular story-book account of the undefined and vague ascension into heaven: but they adopted an intermediate view, founded on Psalms cx. 1: "The Lord saith unto my lord, Sit thou at my right hand, until I make thy enemies thy footstool." This second view I regard as antecedent in date to Barnabas' view, being without the grossness characteristic of second century Christian mythological ideas. I hope sincerely that I am not making an unjustifiable statement when I say that I do not think that the writer of the Epistle to the Hebrews (falsely and foolishly said by the Fathers, or some of them, to be Paul, and so taught to children and older persons in the present day by the Churches) believed in the resurrection of Jesus, and hence he could not have believed in a bodily ascension. Throughout the Epistle to the Hebrews the event of the resurrection is passed over on every occasion when it naturally comes up for mention: see Heb. i. 3; ii. 9; iv. 14; vi. 1 and 2; x. 12; xii. 2. In ix. 16-18, it is stated that where there is a testament, there must of necessity be the death of the testator, for then only the testament is of force; but the writer does not consider the apposite question, whether on the resurrection of the dead testator the testament retains its force. After realising the fact that the writer of the

Epistle to the Hebrews disbelieved the resurrection of Jesus, the parenthetical clause in xiii. 20, "that brought again from the dead our Lord Jesus," etc., is clearly perceived to be a gloss, if not a designed interpolation, the author of which may almost summarily be detected. This gloss being removed, the subject of the resurrection of Jesus is conspicuous by its absence from the Epistle to the Hebrews: and a justifiable inference from such omission is that the writer did not believe it. It should, moreover, be understood that persons who disbelieved in the resurrection were tenderly dealt with in the first two centuries, and were by no means regarded as heretical. I draw this conclusion from the very gentle manner in which Irenæus speaks of such persons, who, nevertheless, he says are reckoned to be orthodox, "*qui putantur recte credidisse*" (*Ad Her.*, v. xxxi. and xxxii.). Amongst Paul's Corinthian saints there were a few who disbelieved in the resurrection of Jesus from the dead, on the general ground that there can be no resurrection from the dead (1 Cor. xv. 12 ff.).

In chapter xx. the running contest between Peter and John, from verse 2–10, must be excised; it is part of the scheme for elevating John over Peter, in which Cerinthus had no interest. In verse 11 the final clause, "she stooped down and looked into the sepulchre," and verses 12 and 13, and the initial clause of verse 14, "and when she had thus said," ought to be cut out, for the reason frequently acted on hitherto that there are no traces of a belief in supernatural appearances to be found in the genuine Christian writings of the first century. The continuity of the narrative will be found intact when this interpolation is removed. I believe verse 17 is an interpolation: as there was no knowledge of an ascension amongst Christians of the first century, Cerinthus could not have written the verse. There is no serious objection, however, to the first clause: "Jesus saith unto her, Touch me not." The rest of the conversation with Jesus is not stated, and may have been excised by the committee of forgers. Verses 22 and 23 are without doubt an interpolation, for they attribute a power and authority which it is obvious Cerinthus did not invest Jesus with. The mean and paltry mode, with the whiff of the conjurer, of imparting the Holy Ghost, indicates the base mind of a forger.

The shutting of the doors in verses 19 and 26 cannot reasonably be understood to convey the meaning that Jesus passed through shut doors, which would be simple nonsense. The exclamation of Thomas in verse 28 must not be understood to mean anything more than an ordinary exclamation of surprise or horror, such as the one in common use in Germany and elsewhere in the present day.

As previously stated in an earlier part of this work, I am disposed to consider that the Fourth Gospel was known at the date of the martyrdom of Polycarp as "the Gospel of Christ" (see *Martyrdom of Polycarp*, ch. xix.). The name Christ had already been given to Jesus, and was accepted by all Christians. There is no evidence that any person disputed the title. Jesus was accepted by Jewish Christians as the Messiah of the Hebrew prophets, and by the Gentiles, or such of them as denied the authority of the Jewish Scriptures, like the Gnostics, as the Christ, 'the chosen one of God,' the phrase employed in Cureton's and in Mrs Lewis' Syriac Gospels, and also, as I think, in the original Fourth Gospel. By acknowledging Jesus as the Christ, Cerinthus in no way interfered with his main doctrine, in which we may assume lay his deepest interest. The acceptance of Jesus as the Christ did not commit anyone to a belief in his divinity: and it harmonised very well with the main doctrine of Cerinthus, that Jesus was a human being, and not a god, but one specially chosen by God for the divine mission of declaring the Father. For this reason I have not considered it justifiable to cut out various passages in the Fourth Gospel in which Jesus is spoken of by Jews as the Messiah, or Christ, such as i. 41, 45; vii. 41, 42. It is plain that Cerinthus had a direct interest in encouraging and supporting the belief in the Messiah, or Christ, an interest which was wanting with regard to the literal Paschal Lamb doctrine, or the endeavour to display John as all-round, even in the use of his legs, a superior person to Peter. The æon Christ was not put forward in the "Gospel of Christ," but was concealed under the term Spirit, the esoteric meaning of which expression was known only to the initiated. The æon Christ was a distinct individuality from Jesus Christ. The Christian Church in the second century accepted the advent of the dove or Spirit (or æon Christ) with a wonderful unanimity, as is apparent from a perusal of the four Gospels. But there is no direct evidence that, if not the entire Church, a considerable section of it, did not also accept the exodus of the Spirit (or æon Christ) at the crucifixion : for the advent and exit of the dove or æon Christ originally were bound together. The story of the martyrdom of Polycarp gives ground for the presumption that the Church of Smyrna, and perhaps of Asia Minor generally, accepted in the second century both the advent and flight of the dove or Spirit (or æon Christ). There was no confusion between Jesus Christ and the Spirit in the form of a dove, esoterically understood by one school of Gnostics to be the æon Christ. For the above reasons I do not think any interference with the text of the final verse of ch. xx. is called for.

Chapter xxi. of the present Fourth Gospel was no part of the original work, which ended at ch. xx., and hence does not come up for investigation here.

It is necessary finally to consider again the Prologue. I find it difficult to regard the first section as the work of Cerinthus. He was no more concerned with the Logos doctrine than with the Paschal Lamb doctrine, or the excellence of John and Peter. I should have been disposed to think that the original Gospel, as it emerged from the hands of Cerinthus, began at the sixth verse, but for the abrupt manner in which the subject of verses 14 and 32 is introduced, which gives me the impression that there was something premised regarding it. I feel it is not now possible to restore this omission, and I must simply abandon the attempt. I must, however, plead for the retention of the first verse with a little change. It does not seem to be improbable that the original Gospel began with a statement regarding the Spirit spoken of in ch. i. 32 and 33, and that the forger or the committee changed the Spirit into the Word, both in the first verse and also in the fourteenth. In support of this conjecture, for I cannot claim anything more than reasonable probability, I may refer to a passage in an ancient writing described by Bishop Lightfoot "as the earliest Christian homily extant," which he assigns to the first half of the second century, about

A.D. 120–140. This writing has hitherto been known as the Second Epistle of Clement of Rome, but it has no right to assume such authorship. Its author does not speak of Jesus as the Logos, but in two or three passages refers to him as the Spirit. He appears to me to have seen the Fourth Gospel before it had been exploited by Valentinus, as I shall explain further on. A few expressions and sentiments from the Fourth Gospel are also employed by him. He quotes freely from a gospel, or from gospels, or rather writings, unknown to us. The special passage to which I allude is the following in ch. ix.: Εἰ Χριστὸς ὁ Κύριος, ὁ σώσας ἡμᾶς, ὢν μὲν τὸ πρῶτον πνεῦμα, ἐγένετο σὰρξ καὶ οὕτως ἡμᾶς ἐκάλεσεν, κ.τ.λ. If Christ the Lord who saved us, being the first spirit, became flesh and so called us, etc.[1] Again, in ch. xiv., Christ is repeatedly spoken of as the Spirit, never as the Logos. I think this unknown writer is unique in second century Christian literature in speaking of Christ as the Spirit, and not as the Logos. If this conjecture, that the Spirit stood in the original where the Word now stands in the forged Gospel, be reasonable, the parenthetical clause in the fourteenth verse, "the glory of the only begotten of the Father," being conventionally applicable to Jesus, but not to the Spirit, must be deleted.

It must always be borne in mind that the alterations and additions to the original "Gospel of Christ" were effected in succession, and at different epochs and with varying designs, and not all at the same time and all for the same purpose; and that changes and interpolations were made from time to time in previous alterations and interpolations of the text, and that various individuals and a committee were the forgers.

[1] I feel justified in considering Bishop Lightfoot's translation of this passage as an incorrect rendering. He translates: "If Christ the Lord who saved us, being first spirit, then became flesh, and so called us."

CHAPTER VII.

THE RESTORED WRITING OF CERINTHUS, THE ORIGINAL
OF THE "GOSPEL ACCORDING TO JOHN."

I. IN the beginning was the Spirit and the Spirit was with God, and the Spirit was God. . . . .

There was a man sent from God, whose name was John. The same came for a witness to bear witness of the Light, that all men through him might believe. He was not that Light, but *came* that he might bear witness of that Light. He was the true Light who lighteth every man that cometh into the world. He was in the world and the world knew him not: he came unto his own, and his own received him not. But as many as received him, to them gave he the right to become the sons of God, *even* to them that believe on his name.

Not of blood, nor of the will of the flesh, nor of the will of man, but of God, was the Spirit made flesh, and tented amongst us, and we beheld his glory, full of grace and truth. And of his fulness have we all received, and grace for grace, for grace and truth came by Jesus Christ.

No man hath seen God at any time; the only begotten Son, which is in the bosom of the Father, he hath declared him.

And John bare witness, saying, I saw the Spirit descending from heaven like a dove, and it abode upon him. And I knew him not; but he that sent me to bear witness, the same said unto me, Upon whom thou shalt see the Spirit descending, and remaining on him, the same is he which baptiseth with the Holy Ghost. And I saw and bare witness that this is the chosen one of God.

And two men heard John speak, and they followed Jesus. Then Jesus turned, and saw them following, and saith unto them, What seek ye? They said unto him, Rabbi (which is to say, being interpreted, Master), where dwellest thou? He saith unto them, Come and see. They came and saw where he dwelt, and abode with him that day: for it was about the tenth hour. One of the two which heard John *speak*, and followed him, was Andrew, Simon Peter's brother. He first findeth his own brother Simon, and saith unto him, We have found the Messiah, and he brought him to Jesus. And when Jesus beheld him, he said, Thou art Simon, the son of Jonah: thou shalt be called Cephas, which is, being interpreted into Greek, Peter.

The day following Jesus would go forth into Galilee, and findeth Philip, and saith unto him, Follow me. Now Philip was of Bethsaida, the city of Andrew and Peter. Philip findeth Nathaniel, and saith unto him, He of whom Moses wrote, and the prophets, we have found him, that he is Jesus of Nazareth, the son of Joseph. And Nathaniel said unto him, Can any good thing be from Nazareth? Philip saith unto him, Come and see. Jesus saw Nathaniel coming to him and saith of him, Behold an Israelite indeed, in whom is no guile! Nathaniel saith unto him, Whence knowest thou me? Jesus answered and said unto him, Before that Philip called thee, when thou wast under the fig tree, I saw thee. Nathaniel answered and saith unto him, Rabbi, thou art the Son of God; thou art the King of Israel. Jesus answered and said unto him, Because I said unto thee, I saw thee under the fig tree, believest thou? thou shalt see greater things than these.

II. And Jesus went up to Jerusalem. III. There was a man of the Pharisees, named Nicodemus, a ruler of the Jews; the same came to Jesus by night, and said unto him, "Rabbi, we know thou art a teacher come from God." Jesus answered and said unto him, "Verily, verily, I say unto you, Except a man be born from above, he cannot see the kingdom of God." Nicodemus saith unto him, "How can a man be born when he is old? can he enter the second time into his mother's womb, and be born?" Jesus answered, "Verily, verily, I say unto thee, Except a man be born of the Spirit, he cannot enter into the kingdom of God. That which is born of the flesh is flesh; and that which is born of the Spirit is spirit. Marvel not that I said unto thee, Ye must be born from above. The wind bloweth where it listeth, and thou hearest the sound thereof, but canst not tell whence it cometh, and whither it goeth: so is every one that is born of the Spirit."

God so loved the world, that he gave his only begotten Son that whosoever believeth in him should not perish, but have everlasting life. For God sent not his Son into the world to condemn the world; but that the world through him might be saved. He that believeth in him is not condemned: but he that believeth not is condemned already, because he hath not believed in the name of the only begotten Son of God. And this is the condemnation, that light is come into the world, and men loved darkness rather than light, because their deeds were evil. For every one that doeth evil hateth the light, neither cometh to the light, lest his deeds should be reproved. But he that doeth truth cometh to the light, that his deeds may be made manifest, that they are wrought in God. He that cometh from above is above all: he that is of the earth is earthly, and speaketh of the earth: he that cometh from heaven is above all. And what he hath seen and heard that he testifieth; and no man receiveth his testimony. He that hath received his testimony hath set to his seal that God is true. For he whom God hath sent speaketh the words of God: for God giveth not the Spirit by measure *unto him*. He that believeth on the Son hath everlasting life: and he that believeth not the Son shall not see life; but the wrath of God abideth in him.

IV. He left Judæa and departed again into Galilee, and he must needs go through Samaria. Then cometh he to a city of Samaria, which is called Sychar, near to the parcel of ground that Jacob gave to his son Joseph. Now Jacob's well was there. Jesus, therefore, being wearied with *his* journey, sat thus on the well: and it was about the sixth hour. There cometh a woman of Samaria to draw water: Jesus saith unto her, Give me to drink. For his disciples were gone away unto the city to buy meat. Then saith the woman of Samaria unto him, How is it that thou, being a Jew, askest drink of me, which am a woman of Samaria? for the Jews have no dealings with the Samaritans. Jesus answered and said unto her, If thou knewest the gift of God, and who it is that saith to thee, Give me to drink; thou wouldest have asked of him, and he would have given thee living water. The woman saith unto him, Sir, thou hast nothing to draw with, and the well is deep: from whence then hast thou that living water? Art thou greater than our father Jacob, which gave us the well, and drank thereof himself, and his children and his cattle? Jesus answered and said unto her, Whosoever drinketh of this water shall thirst again : but whosoever drinketh of the water that I shall give him shall never thirst; but the water that I shall give him shall be in him a well of water springing up into everlasting life. The woman saith unto him, Sir, I perceive that thou art a prophet. Our fathers worshipped on this mountain; and ye say, that in Jerusalem is the place where men ought to worship. Jesus saith to her, Woman, believe me, the hour cometh, when ye shall neither in this mountain, nor yet at Jerusalem, worship the Father. But the hour cometh, and now is, when the true worshippers shall worship the Father in spirit and in truth, for the Father seeketh such to worship him. God is a Spirit: and they that worship him must worship *him* in spirit and in truth. The woman saith unto him, I know that Messias cometh, which is called Christ: when he is come, he will tell us all things. Jesus saith unto her, I that speak unto thee am *he*. And at this moment came his disciples, and marvelled that he talked with the woman: yet no man said, What seekest thou? or Why talkest thou with her? The woman then left her water pot, and went her way into the city, and told the men. So when the Samaritans were come unto him, they besought that he would tarry with them : and he abode there two days. And many believed because of his word; and said unto the woman, Now we believe, not because of thy saying: for we have heard *him* ourselves, and know that this is indeed the Saviour of the world.

Now after two days he departed thence and went into Galilee. For Jesus himself testified that a prophet has no honour in his own country. Then when he was come into Galilee, the Galilæans received him. So Jesus came unto Cana of Galilee.

V. . . . , " Verily, verily, I say unto you, He that heareth my word and believeth on him that sent me, hath everlasting life, and shall not come into condemnation, but is passed from death unto life. Verily, verily, I say unto you, the hour is coming and now is, when the dead shall hear the voice of the Son of God : and they that hear shall live. For as the Father hath life in himself, so hath he given to the Son to have life in himself. Marvel not at this, for the hour is coming, in the which all that are in the graves shall hear his voice, and shall come forth ; they that have done good, unto the resurrection of life ; and they that have done evil, unto the resurrection of damnation. I can of myself do nothing: as I hear, I judge : and my judgment is just; because I seek not mine own will, but the will of the Father which hath sent me. If I bear witness of myself, my witness is not true. There is another that beareth witness of me ; and I know that the witness which he beareth of me is true. He was a burning and a shining light : and ye were willing to rejoice in his light. But I receive not testimony from man : but these things I say that ye may be saved. But I have a greater witness than *that* of John ; for the works which my Father hath given me to finish, the same works that I do, bear witness of me, that the Father hath sent me. And the Father himself, which hath sent me, hath borne witness of me. Ye have neither heard his voice at any time, nor seen his shape. And ye have not his word abiding in you : for whom he hath sent, him ye believe not. And ye will not come to me, that ye might have life. I receive not honour from men. But I know you, that ye have not the love of God in you. I am come in my Father's name, and ye receive me not ; if another shall come in his own name, him ye will receive. How can ye believe, which receive honour one of another, and seek not the honour that *cometh* from God only."

VI. After these things Jesus went over the sea of Galilee, which is the sea of Tiberias. And a great multitude followed him. And Jesus went up into a mountain, and there he sat with his disciples. Jesus answered them, and said, Labour not for the meat which perisheth, but for that meat which endureth unto everlasting life, which the Son of man shall give unto you : for him hath God the Father sealed. Then said they unto him, What shall we do, that we might work the works of God ? Jesus answered and said unto them, This is the work of God, that ye believe on him whom he hath sent. They said therefore unto him, What sign showest thou then, that we may see and believe thee ? What dost thou work ? Our fathers did eat manna in the desert. Then Jesus said unto them, My Father giveth you the true bread from heaven. For the bread of God is that which cometh down from heaven, and giveth life unto the world. Then said they unto him, Lord, evermore give us this bread. And Jesus said unto them, I am the bread of life: he that cometh to me shall never hunger ; and he that believeth on me shall never thirst. But I said unto you, That ye also have seen me, and believe not. All that the Father giveth to me shall come to me; and him that cometh to me I will in no wise cast out. For I came down from heaven, not to do mine own will, but the will of him that sent me. And this is the Father's will which hath sent me, that of all which he hath given me I should lose nothing. And this is the will of him that sent me, that every one which seeth the Son, and believeth on him, may have everlasting life, and he will raise him up on the last day. The Jews then murmured at him, because he said, I am the bread which came down from heaven. And they said, Is not this Jesus, the son of Joseph, whose father and mother we know ? How is it then that he saith, I came down from heaven ? Jesus therefore answered and said unto them, Murmur not among yourselves. No man can come to me, except the Father which hath sent me draw him, and he will raise him up at the last day. Every man therefore that hath heard, and hath learned of the Father, cometh unto me. Not that any man hath seen the Father, save he which is of God, he hath seen the Father. Verily, verily, I say unto you, He that believeth on me hath everlasting life. I am that bread of life. Your fathers did eat manna in the wilderness, and are dead. This is the bread which cometh down from heaven, that a man may eat thereof, and not die. I am the living bread which came down from heaven; if any man eat of this bread he shall live for ever. This is that bread which came down from heaven: he that eateth of this bread shall live for ever.

VII. After these things Jesus walked in Galilee: for he would not walk in Jewry, because the Jews sought to kill him. Now the Jews' feast of tabernacles was at hand. His brethren therefore said unto him, Depart hence and go into Judæa, that thy disciples also may see the works that thou doest. For *there is* no man *that* doeth any thing in secret, and he himself seeketh to be known openly. If thou do these things, show thyself to the world. For neither did his brethren believe in him. Then Jesus said unto them, My time is not yet come: but your time is alway ready. The world cannot hate you: but me it hateth, because I testify of it, that the works thereof are evil. Go ye up unto this feast: I go not up unto this feast; for my time is not yet full come. When he said these words, he abode *still* in Galilee. But when his brethren were gone up, then went he also up unto the feast, not openly, but as it were in secret. Then the Jews sought him at the feast and said, Where is he? And there was much murmuring among the people concerning him: for some said, He is a good man; others said, Nay; but he deceiveth the people. Howbeit no man spake openly of him for fear of the Jews. Now about the midst of the feast Jesus went up into the temple and taught. And the Jews marvelled, saying, How knoweth this man letters, having never learned? Jesus answered them, and said, My doctrine is not mine, but his that sent me. If any man will do his will, he shall know of the doctrine, whether it be of God, or *whether* I speak of myself. He that speaketh of himself seeketh his own glory: but he that seeketh his glory that sent him, the same is true, and no unrighteousness is in him. Did not Moses give you the law, and *yet* none of you keepeth the law? Why go ye about to kill me? The people answered and said, Thou hast a devil: who goeth about to kill you ? Then said some of them of Jerusalem, Is not this he whom they seek to kill? But, lo, he speaketh boldly, and they say nothing unto him. Do the rulers know that this is truly the Christ? Howbeit we know this man whence he is: but when Christ cometh, no man knoweth whence he is. Then cried Jesus in the temple as he taught, saying, Ye both know me, and ye know whence I am : and I am not come of myself, but he that sent me is true, whom ye know not. But I know him : for I am from him, and he hath sent me. Then they sought to take him : but no man laid hands on him, because his hour was not yet come. The Pharisees heard that the people murmured such things concerning him ; and the Pharisees and the chief priests sent officers to take him. Then Jesus said unto them, Yet a little while am I with you, and *then* I go unto him that sent me. Ye shall seek me, and shall not find *me* : and where I am, *thither* ye cannot come. Then said the Jews among themselves, Whither will he go, that we shall not find him ? Will he go unto the dispersed among the Gentiles, and teach the Gentiles ? What *manner* of saying is this that he said, Ye shall seek me, and shall not find *me* : and where I am *thither* ye cannot come. In the last day, that great day of the feast, Jesus stood and cried, saying, If any man thirst, let him come unto me and drink. He that believeth on me, as the Scripture hath said, out of his belly shall flow rivers of living water. Many of the people therefore, when they heard this saying, said, Of a truth this is the Prophet. Others said, This is the Christ. But some said, Shall Christ come out of Galilee ? Hath not the Scripture said, That Christ cometh of the seed of David ? So there was a division among the people because of him. And some of them would have taken him ; but no man laid hands on him. Then came the officers to the chief priests and Pharisees ; and they said unto him, Why have ye not brought him ? The officers answered, Never man spake like this man. Then answered them the Pharisees, Are ye also deceived ? Have any of the rulers or of the Pharisees believed on him ? But this people who knoweth not the law are cursed. Nicodemus saith unto them (he that came to Jesus by night, being one of them), Doth our law judge *any* man before it hear him, and know what he doeth? They answered and said unto him, Art thou also of Galilee? Search and look; for out of Galilee ariseth no prophet.

VIII. Then spake Jesus again unto them, saying, I am the light of the world: he that followeth me shall not walk in darkness, but shall have the light of life. The Pharisees therefore said unto him, Thou bearest record of thyself; thy record is not true. Jesus answered and said unto them, Though I bear record of myself, *yet* my record is true: for I know whence I came, and whither I go; but ye cannot tell whence I come, and whither I go. Ye judge after the flesh; I judge no man. And yet if I judge, my judgment is true: for I am not alone, but I and the Father that sent me. It is also written in your law, that the testimony of two men is true. I am one that bear witness of myself, and the Father that sent me beareth witness of me. Then said they unto him, Where is thy Father? Jesus answered, Ye neither know me, nor my Father: if ye had known me, ye should have known my Father also. These words spake Jesus in the treasury: and no man laid hands on him; for his hour was not yet come. Then said Jesus again unto them, I go my way, and ye shall seek me, and shall die in your sins; whither I go ye cannot come. Then said the Jews, Will he kill himself? because he saith, Whither I go ye cannot come. And he said unto them, Ye are from beneath; I am from above: ye are of this world; I am not of this world. I said therefore unto you, that ye shall die in your sins: for if ye believe not that I am *he*, ye shall die in your sins. Then said they unto him, Who art thou? And Jesus saith unto them, Even the *same* that I said unto you from the beginning. I have many things to say and judge of you: but he that sent me is true; and I speak to the world those things which I have heard of him. They understood not that he spake to them of the Father. And he that sent me is with me: the Father hath not left me alone; for I do always those things that please him. As he spake these words, many believed on him. Then said Jesus to those Jews that believed on him, If ye continue in my word, *then* are ye my disciples indeed; and ye shall know the truth, and the truth shall make you free. They answered him, We be Abraham's seed, and were never in bondage to any man; how sayest thou, Ye shall be made free? Jesus answered them, Verily, verily, I say unto you, Whosoever committeth sin is a slave, and the slave abideth not in the house for ever. If the Son therefore make you free, ye shall be free, and the truth shall make you free.[1] I know that ye are Abraham's seed; but ye seek to kill me, because my word hath no place in you. I speak that which I have seen with my Father: and ye do that which ye have seen with your father. They answered and said unto him, Abraham is our father. Jesus saith unto them, If ye were Abraham's children, ye would do the works of Abraham. But now ye seek to kill me, a man that hath told you the truth, which I have heard of God: this did not Abraham. Ye do the deeds of your father. Then said they unto him, We be not born of fornication; we have one Father, *even* God. Jesus said unto them, If God were your Father, ye would love me: for I proceeded forth and came from God; neither came I of myself, but he sent me. Why do ye not understand my speech? *even* because ye cannot hear my word. Ye are of *your* father the devil, and the lusts of your father ye will do. And because I tell you the truth, ye believe me not. Which of you convinceth me of sin? And if I say the truth, why do ye not believe me? He that is God heareth God's words: ye therefore hear *them* not, because ye are not of God. Then answered the Jews, and said unto him, Say we not well that thou art a Samaritan, and hast a devil? Jesus answered, I have not a devil; but I honour my Father, and ye do dishonour me. And I seek not mine own glory: there is one that seeketh and judgeth. Verily, verily, I say unto you, If a man keep my saying, he shall never see death. Then said the Jews unto him, Now we know thou hast a devil. Abraham is dead and the prophets; and thou sayest, If a man keep my saying, he shall never taste of death. Art thou greater than our father Abraham, which is dead? and the prophets are dead: whom makest thou thyself? Jesus answered, If I honour myself my honour is nothing: it is my Father that honoureth me; of whom ye say, that he is your

---

[1] Clement of Alexandria, *Stromateis*, ii. 5.

God: yet ye have not known him; but I know him and keep his saying.

IX. Verily, verily, I say unto you, He that entereth not by the door into the sheepfold, but climbeth some other way, the same is a thief and a robber. But he that entereth in by the door is the shepherd of the sheep. To him the porter openeth; and the sheep hear his voice: and he calleth his own sheep by name, and leadeth them out. And when he putteth forth his own sheep, he goeth before them and the sheep follow him: for they know his voice. And, a stranger will they not follow, but will flee from him: for they know not the voice of strangers. This parable spake Jesus unto them: but they understood not what things they were which he spake unto them. Then said Jesus unto them again, Verily, verily, I say unto you, I am the door of the sheep. All that came before me are thieves and robbers; but the sheep did not hear them. I am the door; by me if any man enter in, he shall be saved, and shall go in and out, and find pasture. The thief cometh not, but for to steal, and to kill, and to destroy; I am come that they might have life, and that they might have *it* more abundantly. I am the good shepherd: the good shepherd giveth his life for the sheep. But he that is an hireling, and not the shepherd, whose own the sheep are not, seeth the wolf coming, and leaveth the sheep, and fleeth: and the wolf catcheth them, and scattereth the sheep. The hireling fleeth, because he is an hireling, and careth not for the sheep. I am the good shepherd and know my *sheep*, and am known of mine. As the Father knoweth me, even so know I the Father: and I lay down my life for the sheep. And other sheep I have, which are not of this fold: them also I must bring, and they shall hear my voice; and there shall be one fold, *and* one shepherd.

And it was at Jerusalem the feast of the dedication, and it was winter. And Jesus walked in the temple in Solomon's porch. Then came the Jews round about him, and said unto him, How long dost thou make us to doubt? If thou be the Christ, tell us plainly. Jesus answered them, I told you, and ye believed not. But ye believe not, because ye are not of my sheep, as I said unto you. My sheep hear my voice, and

I know them, and they follow me: and I give unto them eternal life: and they shall never perish, neither shall any *man* pluck them out of my hand. My Father, which gave *them* me, is greater than all; and no *man* is able to pluck *them* out of my Father's hand. . . . . Therefore they sought again to take him: but he escaped out of their hand, and went away again beyond Jordan, and there he abode. And many believed on him there.

XI. Then gathered the chief priests and the Pharisees a council and said, What do we? If we let him thus alone, all *men* will believe on him: and the Romans shall come and take away both our place and nation. And one of them, *named* Caiaphas, being the high priest that same year, said unto them, Ye know nothing at all, nor consider that it is expedient for us that one man should die for the people, and that the whole nation perish not. And this spake he not of himself: but being high priest that year, he prophesied that Jesus should die for that nation; and not for that nation only, but that also he should gather together in one the children of God that were scattered abroad. Then from that day forth they took counsel together for to put him to death. Jesus therefore walked no more openly among the Jews; but went thence unto a country near to the wilderness, unto a city called Ephraim, and there continued with his disciples. And the Jews' passover was at hand: and many went out of the country up to Jerusalem before the passover, to purify themselves. Then sought they for Jesus, and spake among themselves, as they stood in the temple, What think ye, that he will not come to the feast? Now both the chief priests and the Pharisees had given a commandment, that, if any man knew where he were, he should show *it*, that they might take him.

.   .   .   .

(*Jesus and his disciples at this time proceeded to Jerusalem for the passover.*)

XII. And there were certain Greeks among them that came up to worship at the feast: the same came up therefore to Philip, which was of Bethsaida of Galilee, and desired him, saying, Sir, we would see Jesus. Philip cometh and telleth

Andrew: and again Andrew and Philip tell Jesus. . . . . Jesus cried and said, He that believeth on me, believeth not on me, but on him that sent me. I am come a light into the world, that whosoever believeth on me should not abide in darkness. And if any man hear my words, and believe not, I judge him not: for I came not to judge the world, but to save the world. He that rejecteth me, and receiveth not my words, hath one that judgeth him: the word that I have spoken, the same shall judge him in the last day. For I have not spoken of myself; but the Father which sent me, he gave me a commandment, what I should say, and what I should speak. And I know that his commandment is life everlasting: whatsoever I speak therefore, even as the Father said unto me, so I speak.

XIII. Now at the feast of the passover, when Jesus knew that his hour was come that he should depart out of this world unto the Father, having loved his own which were in the world, he loved them unto the end. . . . . And supper being ended, Jesus knowing . . . . that he was come from God and went to God . . . . Jesus said, Little children, yet a little while I am with you. Ye shall seek me: and as I said unto the Jews, Whither I go ye cannot come; so now I say to you. A new commandment I give unto you, That ye love one another; as I have loved you, that ye also love one another. By this shall all *men* know that ye are my disciples, if ye have love one to another. Simon Peter said unto him, Lord, whither goest thou? Jesus answereth him, Whither I go, thou canst not follow me now; but thou shalt follow me afterwards. Peter said unto him, Lord, why cannot I follow thee now? I will lay down my life for thy sake. Jesus answered him :—

XIV. Let not your heart be troubled: ye believe in God, believe also in me. In my Father's house are many mansions: if it *were* not *so*, I would have told you. I go to prepare a place for you. And if I go and prepare a place for you, I will come again, and receive you unto myself; that where I am, *there* ye may be also. And whither I go ye know, and the way ye know. Thomas saith unto him, Lord, we know not whither thou goest; and how can we know the way? Jesus

saith unto him, I am the way, the truth and the life: no man
cometh unto the Father but by me. Verily, verily, I say unto
you, He that believeth on me, the works that I do shall he do
also; and greater *works* than these shall he do; because I go
unto the Father. If ye love me, keep my commandments.
I will not leave you orphans: I will come to you. Yet a
little while, and the world seeth me no more. He that hath
my commandments, and keepeth them, he it is that loveth
me: and he that loveth me shall be loved of my Father, and
I will love him. If a man love me, he will keep my words:
and my Father will love him. He that loveth me not keepeth
not my sayings: and the word which ye hear is not mine, but
the Father's which sent me. Peace I leave with you, my
peace I give unto you: not as the world giveth, give I unto
you. Let not your heart be troubled, neither let it be afraid.
Ye have heard how I said unto you, I go away, and come
again unto you. If ye loved me, ye would rejoice because I
said I go unto the Father: for my Father is greater than I.
But that the world may know that I love the Father; and as
the Father gave me commandment, *even·so I do*. Arise, let
us go hence.

XV. As the Father hath loved me, so have I loved you: continue ye in my love. If ye keep my commandments, ye shall
abide in my love; even as I have kept my Father's commandments, and abide in his love. These things have I spoken
unto you, that my joy might remain in you, and *that* your
joy might be full. This is my commandment, That ye love
one another, as I have loved you. Greater love hath no
man than this, that a man lay down his life for his friends.
Ye are my friends, if ye do whatsoever I command you.
Henceforth I call you not servants; for the servant knoweth
not what his lord doeth: but I have called you friends; for
all things that I have heard of my Father I have made
known unto you. Ye have not chosen me, but I have chosen
you, and ordained you, that ye should go and bring forth
fruit, and *that* your fruit should remain. These things I
command you, that ye love one another. If the world hate
you, ye know that it hated me before it *hated* you. If ye
were of the world, the world would love its own: but because

ye are not of the world, but I have chosen you out of the world, therefore the world hateth you. Remember the word that I said unto you, The servant is not greater than his lord. If they have persecuted me, they will also persecute you: if they have kept my saying, they will keep yours also. But all these things will they do unto you for my name's sake, because they know not him that sent me. And ye shall bear witness, because ye have been with me from the beginning.

XVI. These things have I spoken unto you, that ye should not be offended. They shall put you out of the synagogues: yea, the time cometh, that whosoever killeth you will think that he doeth God service. And these things they will do unto you, because they have not known the Father, nor me. And these things I said not unto you at the beginning, because I was with you. But now I go my way to him that sent me; and none of you asketh me, Whither goest thou? But because I have said these things unto you, sorrow hath filled your heart. Nevertheless I tell you the truth. I have yet many things to say unto you, but ye cannot hear them now. A little while, and ye shall not see me: and again, a little while, and ye shall see me, because I go to my Father. Then said *some* of his disciples, What is this that he saith unto us, A little while, and ye shall not see me: and again, a little while, and ye shall see me: and Because I go to the Father? They said therefore, What is this that he saith, A little while? we cannot tell what he saith. Now Jesus knew that they were desirous to ask him, and said unto them, Do ye inquire among yourselves of that I said, A little while, and ye shall not see me: and again, a little while, and ye shall see me? Verily, verily, I say unto you, that ye shall weep and lament, but the world shall rejoice: and ye shall be sorrowful, but your sorrow shall be turned into joy. A woman when she is in travail hath sorrow, because her hour is come: but as soon as she is delivered of the child, she remembereth no more the anguish, for joy that a man is born into the world. And ye now have sorrow: but I will see you again, and your heart shall rejoice, and your joy no man taketh from you. For the Father himself loveth you, because ye have loved me, and have believed that I came out from

God. I came forth from the Father, and am come into the world: again, I leave the world, and go to the Father. Behold the hour cometh, yea, is now come, that ye shall be scattered, every man to his own, and shall leave me alone: and yet I am not alone, because the Father is with me. These things I have spoken unto you, that in me ye might have peace. In the world ye shall have tribulation: but be of good cheer; I have overcome the world.

XVII. These words spake Jesus, and lifted up his eyes to heaven, and said, Father, the hour is come; glorify thy Son, that thy Son also may glorify thee: As thou hast given him power that he should give eternal life to as many as thou hast given him. And this is life eternal, that they might know thee the only true God, and Jesus Christ whom thou hast sent. I have glorified thee on earth; I have finished the work which thou gavest me to do. I have manifested thy name unto the men which thou gavest me out of the world: thine they were, and thou gavest them me; and they have kept thy word. Now they have known that all things whatsoever that thou hast given me are of thee. For I have given unto them the words which thou gavest me; and they have received *them*, and have known surely that I came out from thee, and they have believed that thou didst send me. I pray for them which thou hast given me; for they are thine. And all mine are thine, and thine are mine; and I am glorified in them. And now I am no more in the world, but these are in the world, and I come to thee. Holy Father, keep through thine own name those whom thou hast given me, that they may be one, as we *are*. While I was in the world, I kept them in thy name: those that thou gavest me I have kept, and none of them is lost. And now come I to thee; and these things I speak in the world, that they might have my joy fulfilled in themselves. I have given them thy word; and the world hath hated them, because they are not of the world, even as I am not of the world. I pray not that thou shouldest take them out of the world, but that thou shouldest keep them from evil. They are not of the world, even as I am not of the world. Sanctify them through thy truth: thy word is truth. As thou hast sent me into the world, even so have I also sent them into the world. And for their sakes I sanctify myself, that they also may be sanctified through the truth. Neither pray I for these alone, but for them also which shall believe on me through their word; that they all may be one; as thou, Father, *art* in me, and I in thee, that they also may be one in us: that the world may believe that thou hast sent me. And the glory which thou gavest me I have given them, that they may be one, even as we are one: I in them and thou in me, that they may be made perfect in one; and that the world may know that thou hast sent me, and hast loved them, as thou hast loved me. Father, I will that they also, whom thou hast given me, be with me where I am; that they may behold my glory, which thou hast given me. O righteous Father, the world hath not known thee: but I have known thee, and these have known that thou hast sent me. And I have declared unto them thy name, and will declare *it*: that the love wherewith thou hast loved me may be in them, and I in them.

XVIII. When Jesus had spoken these words, he went forth with his disciples over the brook Cedron, where was a garden, into the which he entered and his disciples; for Jesus ofttimes resorted thither with his disciples. A band *of men* and officers from the chief priests and Pharisees, cometh thither with lanterns and torches and weapons. Jesus, therefore, went forth, and said unto them, Whom seek ye? They answered him, Jesus of Nazareth. Jesus saith unto them, I am *he*. Then asked he them again, Whom seek ye? And they said, Jesus of Nazareth. Jesus answered, I have told you that I am *he*. Then Simon Peter having a sword drew it, and smote the high priest's servant, and cut off his ear. The servant's name was Malchus. Then said Jesus unto Peter, Put up thy sword into the sheath: the cup which my Father hath given me, shall I not drink it? Then the band and the captain and officers of the Jews took Jesus and bound him. And led him away to Annas first. Now Annas sent him bound unto Caiaphas, the high priest. The high priest then asked Jesus of his disciples and of his doctrine. Jesus answered him, I spake openly to the world; I ever taught in the synagogue, and in the temple, whither the Jews always resort; and in secret have I said nothing. Why askest thou me? ask them which heard me, what I have said unto them: behold, they know what I said. And when he had thus spoken, one of the officers which stood by struck Jesus with the palm of his hand, saying, Answerest thou the high priest so? Jesus answered him, If I have spoken evil, bear witness of the evil; but if well, why smitest thou me? Then led they Jesus from Caiaphas unto the hall of judgment: and it was early; and they themselves went not into the judgment hall, that they should not be defiled whilst they were eating the unleavened bread. Pilate then went out to them, and said, What accusation bring ye against this man? They answered and said unto him, If he were not a malefactor, we would not have delivered him unto thee. Then said Pilate unto them, Take ye him, and judge him according to your law. The Jews therefore said unto him, It is not lawful for us to put any man to death. Then Pilate entered into the judgment hall again, and called Jesus, and said unto him, Art thou the King of the Jews? Jesus answered him, Sayest thou this of thyself, or did others tell it thee of me? Pilate answered, Am I a Jew? Thine own nation and the chief priests have delivered thee unto me: what hast thou done? Jesus answered, My kingdom is not of this world: if my kingdom were of this world, then would my servants fight, that I should not be delivered to the Jews: but now is my kingdom not from hence. Pilate therefore said unto him, Art thou a king then? Jesus answered, Thou sayest that I am a king. To this end was I born, and for this cause came I into the world, that I should bear witness unto the truth. Every one that is of the truth heareth my voice. Pilate saith unto him, What is truth? And when he had said this, he went out again unto the Jews, and saith unto them, Ye have a custom, that I should release unto you one at the passover: will ye therefore that I release unto you the King of the Jews? Then cried they all again, Not this man, but Barabbas. Now Barabbas was a robber.

XIX. Then Pilate therefore took Jesus, and scourged him. And *Pilate* saith unto them, Behold the man! When the chief priests therefore and officers saw him, they cried out, saying, Crucify *him*, crucify *him*. Pilate saith unto them, Take ye him and crucify *him*. The Jews answered him, We have a law, and by our law he ought to die, because he made himself the son of God. Then delivered he him therefore unto them to be crucified. And they took Jesus and led *him* away. And he bearing his cross went forth into a place called *the place* of a skull, which is called in Hebrew Golgotha: where they crucified him, and two others with him, on either side, one, and Jesus in the midst. And Pilate wrote a title, and put *it* on the cross. And the writing was, JESUS OF NAZARETH THE KING OF THE JEWS. This title then read many of the Jews: for the place where Jesus was crucified was nigh to the city: and it was written in Hebrew, *and* Greek, *and* Latin. Then said the chief priests to Pilate, Write not, The King of the Jews; but that he said, I am King of the Jews. Pilate answered, What I have written I have written.

Then the soldiers, when they had crucified Jesus, took his garments, and made four parts, to every soldier a part. After this, Jesus saith, I thirst. Now there was a vessel full of vinegar: and they filled a spunge with vinegar, and put *it* upon hyssop, and put it to his mouth. But one of the soldiers with a spear pierced his side, and forthwith came there out a dove and blood. And John that saw it bare record, and his record is true; and that man knoweth that he saith true, that ye might believe. When Jesus therefore had received the vinegar, he bowed his head, and gave up the ghost.

And after this Joseph of Arimathæa, being a disciple of Jesus, but secretly for fear of the Jews, besought Pilate that he might take away the body of Jesus: and Pilate gave him leave. He came, therefore, and took the body of Jesus. And there came also Nicodemus, which at the first came to Jesus by night, and brought a mixture of myrrh and aloes, about an hundred pound *weight*. Then took they away the body of Jesus, and wound it in linen clothes with the spices, as the manner of the Jews is to bury. Now in the place where he was crucified there was a garden; and in the garden a new sepulchre, wherein was never man yet laid. There laid they Jesus therefore because of the Jews' preparation day, for the sepulchre was nigh at hand.

XX. The first *day* of the week cometh Mary Magdalene, early, when it was yet dark, unto the sepulchre, and seeth the stone taken away from the sepulchre. But Mary stood without at the sepulchre weeping: and as she wept, she turned herself back, and saw Jesus standing, and knew not that it was Jesus. Jesus saith unto her, Woman, why weepest thou? She, supposing him to be the gardener, saith unto him, Sir, if thou have borne him hence, tell me where thou hast laid him, and I will take him away. Jesus saith unto her, Mary. She turned herself, and saith unto him, Rabboni; which is to say, Master. Jesus saith unto her, Touch me not. Mary Magdalene came and told the disciples that she had seen the Lord, and *that* he had spoken unto her. Then the same day at evening, being the first day of the week, when the doors were shut where the disciples were assembled for fear of the Jews, came Jesus and stood in the midst, and saith unto them, Peace be unto you. And when he had so said, he showed them *his* hands and his side. Then were the disciples glad, when they saw the Lord. Then said Jesus to them again, Peace *be* unto you: as *my* Father hath sent me, even so send I you. But Thomas, one of the twelve, called Didymus, was not with them when Jesus came. The other disciples therefore said unto him, We have seen the Lord. But he said unto them, Except I shall see in his hands the print of the nails, and put my finger into the print of the nails, and thrust my hand into his side, I will not believe. And after eight days again his disciples were within, and Thomas with them: *then* came Jesus, the doors being shut, and stood in the midst, and said, Peace *be* unto you. Then saith he to Thomas, Reach hither thy finger, and behold my hands; and reach hither thy hand, and thrust *it* into my side: and be not faithless, but believing. And Thomas answered and said, My Lord and my God. Jesus saith unto him, Thomas, because thou hast seen me, thou hast believed: blessed *are* they that have not seen, and *yet* have believed.

And many other signs truly did Jesus in the presence of his disciples, which are not written in this book. But these are written that ye might believe that Jesus is the Christ, the Son of God; and that believing ye might have life through his name.

CHAPTER VIII.

INTERPOLATIONS MADE IN THE REVISED FOURTH GOSPEL OF THE SECOND CENTURY, SUBSEQUENT TO ITS PUBLICATION. KNAVERY AND ROGUERY OF BISHOPS ZEPHYRINUS AND CALLISTUS, POPES OF ROME.

I THINK it is possible, out of the facts that I have been able to gather from the writings of the Fathers, to form some reasonable conjectures, and even in a few instances some positive conclusions, regarding the approximative dates, and even regarding the authors of the numerous alterations and additions that were made in the original text of the Gospel of Christ, now known as the Fourth Gospel, or Gospel according to John, and also of the circumstances under which some of these were fabricated. It must always, however, be borne in mind that the statements that I shall make are altogether dependent on the facts available, and further, on the interpretation that I put on these facts. More knowledge, *i.e.*, more facts and a different interpretation, may necessitate a change of opinion, and consequently of statement. My conjectures and conclusions are absolutely based upon my present knowledge and interpretation of the facts.

I am inclined to attribute the first section of the Prologue to the early Gnostic sects. The first heretics known to history were Simon Magus and his followers. This great heresiarch is described in Acts viii. 9-11: "There was a certain man, called Simon, which before time in the same city used sorcery and bewitched the people of Samaria, giving out that himself was some great one; 'to whom they all gave heed, from the least to the greatest, saying, This man is the great power of God. And to him they had regard, because that of long time he had bewitched them with sorceries." This account of Simon is confirmed by Irenæus, Hippolytus, and others. Irenæus thus speaks of him: "This man was glorified by many as if he were a god; and he taught that it was himself who appeared among the Jews as the Son, but descended in Samaria as the Father, while he came to other nations in the character of the Holy Ghost. He represented himself, in a word, as being the loftiest of all powers—that is, the Being who is the Father over all—and he allowed himself to be called by whatsoever title men were pleased to address him" (*Ad Hær.*, I. xxiii. 1). Hippolytus also says that Simon was "an adept in sorceries," and that "he attempted to deify himself" (*Refutation*, vi. 2). Justin Martyr also, writing in the middle of the second century, says that Simon "did mighty acts of magic" in Rome itself, and was there considered a god: "and almost all the Samaritans, and a few even of other nations, worship him, and acknowledge him as the first god" (*First Apology*, xxvi.). We find further that Hippolytus, in the work quoted, vi. 4 (either he or the followers of Simon), even ventured so far as to draw a comparison between the heresiarch and Jesus. And we have the authority of Jerome (see Matt. xxiv. 5) that Simon said of himself, "*Ego sum sermo Dei*": I am the Word of God, or in Greek the Logos of God. In these facts I perceive the origin of the Prologue of the Fourth Gospel. Simon Magus was the first individual in history to whom the Logos doctrine of Philo was practically applied in a concrete form. We have no record in Christian literature of the epithet and attributes of the Logos, or Word of God, having been applied to Jesus in the first century. So far as I can ascertain from the sparse records of the period, while the Simonians of the first century styled their founder Logos, rival Gnostic sects of the second century applied the epithet to Jesus; and this epithet became popularised in the second century, and we find Justin Martyr very familiar with it. "The Logos himself," says Justin Martyr, "took shape and became man, and was called Jesus Christ" (*First Apology*, v.);

and the Logos as Jesus is repeatedly referred to in chaps. xii., xxi., xlvi. of Justin's *First Apology*; in chaps. vi., viii., xiii. of the *Second Apology*; in ch. cxxviii. of the *Dialogue with Trypho*, and ch. v. of the *Discourse to the Greeks*. Justin does not say that he derived his knowledge of the use of the epithet Logos from the *Memoirs of the Apostles*;[1] but the frequent use made of the epithet by him is proof of the popular currency of the application of the Logos doctrine of Philo to Jesus in Justin's days.

The credit of the concrete application of Philo's doctrine to Jesus should perhaps be divided between the Greek sects of the first half of the second century; but the sects that appear to have the best claim to this honour are those specially named by Irenæus and Hippolytus, viz., the Ophites (including the Naasseni) and the Valentinians. These sects are the first to whom Christian writers have attributed the use of the Prologue of the Fourth Gospel. The process of reasoning by which I arrive at the tentative conclusion that the Prologue of the Fourth Gospel was probably the composition of Gnostic sects is simple. The Christian writers of the first century make no allusion to the Logos doctrine. A Christian writer of the first half of the second century is familiar with the Christian Logos doctrine, but he makes no allusion to the Prologue of the Fourth Gospel or other source from which he derived it, and he does not claim the invention of the doctrine for himself. The Christian writers of the second half of the second and beginning of the third century are familiar with the Prologue of the Fourth Gospel, and they speak of it as used by Gnostic sects of the first half of the second century, but as misinterpreted by them. From the above facts, postulating that they are not controvertible, the rational inference is justifiable that the Gnostic sects were the authors of the Prologue. Unfortunately, it is open to dispute whether the Gnostic

---

[1] I surmise, however, that Justin obtained his knowledge of the Logos from the corrupted Fourth Gospel, directly or second-hand. He says, in *Trypho*, cxxviiii., " They call him the Word, because he carries tidings from the Father to men." This is clearly an idea which is embodied in the Fourth Gospel (ch. i. 18, and *passim*).

sects used the Prologue in the first half or in the second half of the second century. Both Irenæus and Hippolytus, in introducing quotations from the Prologue, which quotations were employed by the Gnostic sects, use the words 'he says' and 'they say,' and it is not clear who the 'he' is, so that the chronology becomes misty. If the 'he' is understood to be the founder of the sect, the date of the quotation would be necessarily the first half of the century; but it may be reasonably contended that the expression does not specify any person in particular, and is equivalent to the French '*on dit*,' or the German '*man spricht*,' in which case there is no clue available to determine the date. Assuming that the Prologue was employed by the Gnostic sects in the first half of the second century, and hence conjecturally composed by them, certain limitations must be made. In the first verse it should be understood that the word 'Spirit,' which I take to have been in the original text, was changed into the 'Word'; and that only the third, fourth, and fifth verses were composed *de novo* by the Gnostics. The second verse was not added to the text till after the time of Theophilus (*c.* 168), who was the first Christian writer who quoted the Prologue, but with the second verse omitted.[1] It may be that Valentinus was the author of these three verses of the Prologue; and, according to Irenæus, I. viii. 5, Valentinus limited the meaning of these verses to the peculiarities of his own theological system. In this connection Irenæus is singularly curt in rendering the Valentinian signification of the second verse, of which he only says, "this clause discloses the order of production," and raises the suspicion in my mind that Valentinus rendered no explication of a verse which, from the evidence available, was not existent in his time. The Valentinian meaning of the third verse is very important, for it differs materially from the orthodox interpretation to such an extent that, were it not the original, the most ancient, and hence most influential signification of the verse, there would have been no necessity for the subsequent interpolation of the clause, "the world was made by him," in the

[1] In Hippolytus' *Treatise against the Heresy of Noetus*, ch. 12, it is singular to find in the prologue quoted the second verse omitted.

tenth verse. "'All things were made by him, and without him was nothing made'; for the Word was the author of form and beginning to all the æons that came into existence after him." The same verse is discussed by Irenæus in Bk. III. xi. 1, where he thus contends against this meaning: "'All things,' he says, 'were made by Him'; therefore, in 'all things' this creation of ours is [included], for we cannot concede to these men that [the words] 'all things' are spoken in reference to those within their Pleroma. For if their Pleroma do indeed contain these, this creation, as being such, is not outside, as I have demonstrated in the preceding book; but if they are outside the Pleroma, which indeed appeared impossible, it follows, in that case, that their Pleroma cannot be 'all things': therefore this vast creation is not outside [the Pleroma]." The same subject is more fully discussed by Irenæus in the 'preceding book,' viz., II. i. 1–5. Notwithstanding all this large amount of argumentation on the meaning of a text of the orthodox Scriptures, in opposition to a heretical interpretation of the same passage, John, who flourished in the first century in utter ignorance of the Valentinian system of theology, and of the Valentinian misinterpretation of his writings, "does himself put this matter beyond all controversy on our part," as Irenæus says, by conveniently introducing the clause "and the world was made by him" into the tenth verse (*Ad Hær.*, III. xi. 2), thus extending the signification of 'all things' to objects existing both within and without the Pleroma or the Gnostic heaven. A remarkable circumstance is that Irenæus omits to state whether the Valentinians admitted the authenticity of this clause, which was specially introduced for their behoof by the beloved disciple, or had it in their recension of the Gospel.[1]

The next verse, 4, is thus given by Irenæus: "What was made in Him is life, and the life was the light of men." The exegesis of Valentinus of this verse is thus stated

---

[1] The Valentinians understood 'all things,' in verse 3, to comprise only the contents of the Pleroma or the Gnostic heaven. This limitation did not suit the Christian theology, hence the clause, "the world was made by him," was introduced into verse 10, in order to extend the meaning of 'all things.'

by Irenæus: "Here again he indicated conjunction; for all things, he said, were made *by* Him, but *in* Him was life. This then, which is in Him, is more closely connected with Him than those things which were simply made by Him, for it exists along with Him, and is developed by Him. When, again, he adds, 'And the life was the light of men,' while thus mentioning ·Anthropos, he indicated also Ecclesia by that one expression," and so on, dealing with speculative ideas which are incomprehensible to us moderns. The upshot of the exegesis of Valentinus I take to be that 'life' and 'light' indicate 'the Saviour,' as stated a few lines lower down, " he says that He is the fruit of the entire Pleroma. For he styles him a 'light which shineth in darkness, and which was not comprehended'" (*Ad Hær.*, I. viii. 5).[1]

To Valentinus also I ascribe the separation of verse 13 of the Prologue from verse 14, and its attachment to verse 12. Tertullian attributes the tampering of this passage presumably to Valentinus and Marcion and their congeners (see *ante*, p. 12). The birth of Jesus from a woman is said to have been a notion which to the devout mind of Marcion was abomination and blasphemy: for in his view, as Tertullian represents it, Jesus descended as an adult from heaven. Valentinus, however, accepted the doctrine that Jesus was born of a virgin: and hence to him and his congeners should be attributed the tampering with the original text, which changed the columbine incarnation of the Spirit of Cerinthus into the implied immaculate conception of the Virgin.

It appears to be a fact that the Fourth Gospel was very much, if not altogether, in the hands of the Gnostic sects in the earlier part of the second century. This fact is well

---

[1] It will be interesting to know how this passage was understood by other Gnostic sects. The Naasseni, according to Hippolytus (*Refutation*, v. 3), held the following view: "This, says he (*i.e.*, perhaps the sectary), is the life, the ineffable generation of perfect men, which was not known by preceding generations." Further on in the same chapter, a 'perfect man' is explained to be one "that is born again—of water and the Spirit not carnal." The Peratæ, a later offshoot of the Ophites, understood 'life' to be "Eve, mother of all living—a common nature, that is, of gods, angels, immortals, mortals, irrational creatures and rational ones" (*Ibid.*, v. 1.1).

brought out in the late Canon Liddon's great work on *The Divinity of our Lord and Saviour Jesus Christ*, being the Oxford Bampton Lectures of 1866. After tracing the Fourth Gospel to the times of Justin Martyr, the eloquent and learned author has recourse to the testimony of 'contemporary heretics,' such as Valentinus (whose system, he states, on the authority of Irenæus, "was mainly based upon a perversion of St John's Gospel") and Marcion, Basilides, and the Ophitic Gnostics, the Naassenians, and the Peratæ; and he comes to the conclusion that St John's Gospel "was thus already, we may say in the year 110, a recognised authority amongst sects external to the Catholic Church." The learned author was unable to indicate any trace in the early half of the second century of a knowledge of the Fourth Gospel amongst 'orthodox Christians,' except perhaps an allusion to the flesh and blood of Jesus as meat and drink in the letter of Ignatius to the Romans (ch. 7), a suspected and interpolated writing, and a quotation from the letter called the First Epistle of John by Polycarp (ch. 7, Epistle to the Philippians), which is not evidence of the Fourth Gospel. After having stated so much, I doubt whether the pious author was justified in remarking, as he unfortunately does, that "this evidence might be largely reinforced from other quarters," while he abstains from giving us further evidence from this foolishly-asserted, but non-existent, large reinforcement of it.

In the first half of the second century the Ophites, or snake worshippers, including the Naasseni, greatly used the Fourth Gospel. These sectaries assuredly had a much larger infusion of pure Paganism in their tenets than the Valentinians. "The older sectarians," says King, in his work on the *Gnostics*, p. 32, "retaining the Ægyptian veneration for the Agatho-dæmon, the Chnuphis serpent, regarded Ophis as identical with Achamoth, or with Christos. Thus they employed a live serpent, even when Epiphanius wrote [fourth century], to encircle and consecrate the loaves to be eaten in their Eucharistic supper."[1] They worshipped the serpent as the

[1] "They kept a tame serpent in a *cista*, or sacred ark, and when celebrating their mysteries piled loaves on a table before it, and then invoked

author of all knowledge, and they associated the adoration of this reptile with the Christian religion. They derived support for their system not only from Æygpt, but from Phrygian Paganism and the mysteries of Isis (Hippolytus, *Refutation of all Heresies*, v. 2). Their religious books were the gospel "according to the Ægyptians," that "according to Thomas," the Old Testament, the Fourth Gospel, and some of the Pauline epistles, which they quoted. This strange sect most probably made additions in those early times to the Fourth Gospel. Their Christology corresponded in some particulars with that of Cerinthus. The Ophites, according to Irenæus, I. xxx. 13, believed in the existence of a celestial personage, Christ, the offspring of the Father-of-all, and also of Jesus, "begotten of the Virgin through the agency of God," *i.e.*, of Ialdaboth, a secondary God: "Christ united to Sophia descended into him, and thus Jesus Christ was produced. They affirm that many of his disciples were not aware of the descent of Christ into him; but that, when Christ did descend on Jesus, he began to perfect his virtues,[1] and heal, and announce the unknown Father, and openly to confess himself the son of the first man." The first notice of the miracle of Cana in Christian literature is in connection with the Ophites. Hippolytus (*Refutation*, v. 3) thus quotes the mysterious 'he' in his account of the Naasseni. "This, he says, is the mighty and true beginning of miracles which Jesus performed in Cana of Galilee, and manifested the kingdom of heaven." The invention of this miracle, and its insertion into the text of the Fourth Gospel, may perhaps be attributed to these half-Pagan, half-Christian sectarians. There appears to have been some secret connection between this miracle and the "great and ineffable mystery of the Samothracians," to which the unknown 'he' immediately after refers in Hippolytus' incoherent account, and also between the said Samothracian

the serpent to come forth. Whereupon, opening of himself the ark, he would come forth, mount upon the table, and twine round the loaves, which they then broke in pieces and distributed amongst the worshippers, calling this the 'Perfect Sacrifice,' and their 'Eucharist'" (Epiphan., *Hæres.*, xxxvii. Quoted from King's *Gnostics*, p. 85).

[1] The Ante-Nicene Christian Library translation has 'to work miracles,' instead of the literal translation of the words '*virtutes perficere.*'

mysteries and the parody, in John vi. 51-57, of Paul's account of the last supper (verse 53 of which is quoted in the same connection), both apparently declared by 'him' to be identical. It is perhaps within the limits of what is justifiable to describe this passage in the Fourth Gospel as a Pagan sacramental parody of the last supper or passover eaten by Jesus in company with his disciples. The savage conception of acquiring the qualities of a slain hero by eating his body was early in the history of the human race introduced into religious ceremonial, if it is not to be considered the latter from its inception. This conception was still fresh and green in the early centuries of our era. Clement of Alexandria was a convert from Paganism, and had been initiated into the Pagan mysteries. The Pagan doctrine announced in this passage of the Fourth Gospel was familiar, and seemed natural to him, and in no way did it jar upon his nerves. The explication, by this learned and eminent Father, of the Christian Sacrament is startling to a thinking member of modern society. He says (*Pæd.*, ii. 2), " to drink the blood of Jesus is to get a share of or to be partaker of the Lord's immortality,"[1] exactly the intention of the corresponding Pagan rite. His explication of the Mosaic prohibition to the eating of the hare and hyæna, or coney of our Authorised Version, is on the same lines: to avoid acquiring the singularly depraved qualities of these animals (*Pæd.*, ii. 10). As civilisation advanced, eating and drinking an edible or potable representative of a god became a solemn sacramental rite in the religious worship of the god, whereby the worshipper acquired the attributes and qualities of the god. When the god was a corn god, corn represented his body; when he was a vine god, the juice of the grape represented his blood; and by eating the bread and drinking the wine the worshipper was understood to partake of the flesh and blood of his god, and thereby to acquire the

[1] Irenæus' explication is less clear. Let any one refer to Bk. IV. xviii. 4-6, or to the translation in the Ante-Nicene Christian Library, vol. i. pp. 434 and 435, and see what he can make out of the exuberant verbosity of this writer. I understand it that the bodies of devout communicants are rendered incorruptible by partaking of the Eucharist, for which view there is no Scriptural authority except this passage in the Fourth Gospel, which I conjecture to be a Pagan interpolation.

qualities of the latter.[1] This passage in the Fourth Gospel may be regarded as a contribution from the Naasseni. Verses 14 and 15 of the third chapter, in which the brazen serpent of Moses is referred to, may also have been an interpolation made by the same sect.

The introduction of the story of John the Baptist was probably due to Valentinus, as we find Origen referring to Heracleon, a renowned Valentinian, who wrote a *Commentary* on the Fourth Gospel, as accepting the passage in ch. i. 19 ff., containing the speech of the deputation from the Pharisees. Heracleon, it appears, maintained that the office of baptism belonged to Christ and to Elijah and every prophet: so that one would be justified in concluding that such was the view of Valentinus, and thus would become apparent the reason of the preponderance of statements regarding baptism in the Fourth Gospel (Origen, *Commentary on John*, vi. 12, 13). It would also appear, in a dim and obscure way, from the same work, that the incident known as the purging or purification of the temple was introduced into the Fourth Gospel by Valentinus. The passage is quoted in full, with the introductory clause, "And the Jews' passover was at hand," omitted, from verse 13-17, and this passage was accepted and commented upon by Heracleon (see Origen's *Commentary on John*, x. 14, 15, 19). The quotation was perhaps made from Heracleon's copy of the Fourth Gospel, on which supposition the omission of the introductory clause will be of importance, and will justify the conclusion that in Heracleon's gospel there was only one passover related, the purging of the temple being narrated as occurring in the single passover. It should never be forgotten that Origen admitted only two passovers: thus the one passover in excess will be accounted for. The continuation of the Gospel narrative from verse 18-22 appears also to have been accepted by Heracleon, as Origen comments on the mistake, 'in three days' instead of 'on the third day,' which he attributes to Heracleon's not having examined the point (see ch. xxi. of Origen's *Commentary on John*). Heracleon's gospel was probably an earlier recension than our revised gospel of the second century, with less matter in it.

[1] See *Pioneers of Evolution*, by Edward Clodd.

THE FOURTH GOSPEL

I shall now refer to the histories, or rather theories, of the origin of the Fourth Gospel given by ancient Christian writers. The oldest of these is derived from the Muratorian fragment. This is a manuscript discovered in the Ambrosian Library at Milan, which originally belonged to Columban's great monastery at Bobbio. It was first published by Muratori in 1740. Bishop Westcott (in the *Canon of the New Testament*) gives an interesting description of it. He says that it is mutilated at beginning and end; is disfigured throughout by remarkable barbarisms, due in part to the ignorance of the transcriber, and in part to the translator of the original text, for the bishop has little doubt that the fragment is a version from the Greek. Bunsen thinks that it is a translation from the historical work of Hegisippus. The date of the fragment is ascertained from the allusion made in it to Hermas, the author of the ancient writing called the *Shepherd of Hermas*; it claims to have been written by a contemporary of Pius, and Bishop Westcott on that statement assigns it a date not much later than 170 A.D. He further adds that the fragment may be regarded as a summary of the opinion of the Western Church on the Canon shortly after the middle of the second century.

The following is the account of the Fourth Gospel given in this fragment, with the spelling retained, but with the punctuation indicated, and a gap filled in with a word happily suggested by Bishop Westcott.

"Quarti Euangeliorum Johannis ex discipolis, cohortantibus condescipulis et episcopis suis dixit: conjejunate mihi hodie triduo, et quid cuique fuerit revelatum alterutrum nobis ennarremus. eadem nocte revelatum Andreæ ex apostolis, ut recogniscentibus cunctis, Johannis suo nomine cuncta describeret. Et ideo licit varia singulis euangeliorum libris principia doceantur nihil tamen differt credentium fidei, cum uno ac principali spiritu declarata sint in omnibus omnia de nativitate, de passione, de resurrectione, de conversatione cum decipulis suis, ac de gemino ejus adventu primo in humilitate dispectus, quod [fuit, Westcott] secundum potestate regali præclarum, quod foturum est. Quid ergo mirum si Johannes tam constanter singula etiam in epistulis suis proferat dicens in semeipsu : *Quæ vidimus oculis nostris, et auribus audivimus, et manus nostræ palpaverunt, hæc scripsimus vobis.* Sic enim non solum visurem, sed et auditorem, sed et scriptorem omnium mirabilium domini per ordinem profetetur."

The following is a verbatim translation of the above :—The fellow-disciples of John of the fourth of the Gospels, *one* of the disciples, and his bishops exhorting him, he said : Fast to me to-day for three days, and what shall have been revealed to each, let us narrate to one another. In the same night it was revealed to Andrew one of the apostles, that John should write everything in his own name, all acknowledging (or certifying or recognising him as the author). And so, although various principles are taught in the individual books of the Gospels, yet it makes no difference to the faith of believers, since by one supreme Spirit have been declared in them all things regarding the nativity, the passion, the resurrection, intercourse with his disciples and regarding his double advent, the first in the humility of despisal, which was; the second splendid with regal power, which is to be. What wonder then if John so firmly puts forth each thing in his Epistles, saying regarding himself : What we have seen with our eyes, and have heard with our ears, and our hands have handled, these things we have written to you. For so he professes himself not only an eye-witness and a hearer, but also a writer of all the wonderful things of the Lord in order.

Though the above account is stated by Bishop Westcott, and also by Bishop Lightfoot, to date from about 170 A.D., a later date, about the first quarter or half of the third century, has been assigned to it by others, for reasons that influenced them. The next theory or history of the Gospel is that quoted by Eusebius (*Eccl. Hist.*, vi. 14) from the *Hypotyposes*, a lost work of Clement of Alexandria. "But John, last of all, perceiving that what had reference to the body in the Gospel of our Saviour, was sufficiently detailed, and being encouraged by his familiar friends, and urged by the Spirit, he wrote a spiritual Gospel" (Crusé, Bohn's Library). I do not think it gives support to the previous theory, according to my understanding of the latter, in which the Fourth Gospel is stated to have been conjointly composed by several and perhaps numerous individuals, namely, by apostles of the Lord, of whom Andrew is named, and by John's bishops, whose number is not stated. John, however, reduced the oral contributions of all to writing, and the product, the Fourth Gospel, was published in his name, the various contributors acknowledging him as the author. John proposed that, after a fast of three days, his fellow-disciples and his bishops should relate what shall have been revealed to each. Andrew's proposal was not an amendment in supersession of John's proposal, but in addition to it, that is, that the revelation of each member should be written down by John in his own name, and that all should acknowledge him as the author. Clement's account omits to state the active co-operation in the production of the Fourth Gospel of the apostles and bishops mentioned in the Muratorian fragment: but theologians conclude that Clement confirms the Muratorian theory or history simply because this author speaks of the encouragement offered by John's familiar friends. Eusebius, who wrote in the earlier part of the fourth century, gives a third theory or history, which he introduces with the unsatisfactory expression, 'they say,' which can only be interpreted to mean that the theory or history which he relates was popularly current in his days. It seems that, on some indefinite date and occasion, the three Synoptic Gospels having been distributed to the company present, and also handed to John, the latter admitted them as true narratives, but stated that they were defective in not containing an account of the things done by Jesus at the commencement of his ministry, before the imprisonment of John the Baptist. Being then entreated to undertake to supply the omissions, John wrote the account of the time not recorded by the Synoptic evangelists, and of the deeds done by Jesus, which they had passed over (*Eccl. Hist.*, iii. 24). It will be perceived here that Eusebius' account is altogether at variance with the Muratorian theory, and gives no hint that the historian had seen or had given credit to the latter.[1] A

---

[1] Eusebius was acquainted with the history of Hegisippus, and quoted from it. If the Muratorian fragment was a translation of Hegisippus, as the Chevalier Bunsen declares, Eusebius would have known it; but he shows

fourth theory was a late one, found in a note attached to a manuscript of the *Apostolical Constitutions*, and is to be seen in Whiston's translation of these writings, republished in the Ante-Nicene Christian Library, VIII. iii. It is there stated by some unknown person that John composed the Gospel according to him in the island of Patmos, to which he was banished by Domitian ; and that he died a natural death in the third year of Trajan's reign in Ephesus. I need hardly remark that according to my view, of which the present treatise is the exposition, all these diverging theories or histories are false. The earliest of them, the Muratorian fragment, was not in existence, and it must be observed that it refers to no authority, till perhaps over seventy years after the production of the Fourth Gospel, beyond the personal knowledge of any person living at the time. I regard it, however, as a garbled and modified version of a fact. Although John and other apostles of the twelve, and John's bishops, were not the joint authors of the Fourth Gospel, I draw the conclusion that the Muratorian account indicates that the writing of Cerinthus, which was the foundation of the Fourth Gospel, underwent revision and enlargement and rechristening by a committee of Church dignitaries, *i.e.*, of stipendiary apostles and bishops,[1] of whom two of the former may have borne the names of John and Andrew.

no consciousness of the Muratorian story of the origin of the Fourth Gospel. If he was aware of it, he would have adopted it, as its nature exactly suited a man of his kidney.

[1] Some eminent scholars hold the view that in the second half of the second century a selection and revision of the Gospels was made, because there is a marked difference between the manner of quotation of evangelical passages in the first half and in the second half of the second century. I conjecture that the basis or starting-point of the statement made in the Muratorian fragment was the fact that there was an influential committee for the revision of the Fourth Gospel. The colophon at the conclusion of Mrs Lewis' Syriac Gospels begins thus : " Here endeth the Gospel of *Mĕpharrĕshē* four books." The amiable and learned lady says that the word *Mĕpharrĕshē* is of uncertain meaning. Bernstein suggested division into lections or lessons for reading throughout the year : a meaning which Mrs Lewis does not accept. She seems to think better of Dr Wright's suggestion "of the interpreters or translators," and also of the meaning being 'separate,' as distinct from 'mixed.' I respectfully and humbly suggest that the Syriac word admits of being translated 'of the revisers.'

The date on which the committee assembled for this work was within the memory of men contemporary with the writer of the Muratorian fragment ; but I doubt if it could be pushed further back than a little after the middle of the second century, for Justin Martyr, who wrote at that period, names no Gospel according to John or any other person. I may perhaps with justice contend that the date was subsequent to the martyrdom of Polycarp (*c.* 155 or 156), which event occurred while the original verse, xix. 34, of the Fourth Gospel, containing the story of the flight of the dove out of the wound inflicted upon the side of Jesus, was still read in the churches at Smyrna and elsewhere in Asia Minor. Perhaps I may venture without strain to advance the date to after the perpetration of Lucian's great joke (*c.* 166 A.D.), which may have been the lever which moved the Christians of that period to put their historical literature in order, and to fix a limit to the excursions of religious fancy and invention. Perhaps the year 168, when appeared Theophilus' work, *Ad Autolycum*, in which occurs the first quotation from the Fourth Gospel in connection with John's name, may be taken as the time-boundary of the work of this important committee, so that the interval between A.D. 166 and 168 was the period of its operation. The above are a few gleams of light that remain to assist us to peer into the abyss of darkness in which the building up of ecclesiastical Christianity was carried on. I am ready to admit, a fact I believe which few will be bold enough to deny, that literary transactions of the nature of those here conjectured to have been undertaken by a committee of Church dignitaries, of frequent occurrence in early Christian times, were not regarded as indicating serious moral turpitude, and were perhaps in certain instances deemed even laudable in a sense. There was, nevertheless, a consciousness on the part of the operators of personal culpability, as these proceedings were always done in secrecy, and, at our remote age, a secrecy that is impenetrable. We have seen how Tertullian and others accused the Gnostic leaders of tampering with the sacred text ; and from the force of facts one cannot refrain from imputing similar conduct to the orthodox leaders.

The Fourth Gospel, as it has come down to our times, at

least in its main outlines, was the outcome of the labours of this committee. The original writing of Cerinthus, with such additions and alterations as may have happened to it at the hands of the various sects who were known to have used it, came before the committee, it is conjectured, for the purpose of revision and elaboration. It may reasonably be imagined that all ideas that were incurably unorthodox were simply expunged. Such thoughts, whether original to Cerinthus or added by interpolators, which favoured the views of the committee or could be altered to accord with their views, were retained. Interesting anecdotes were probably added to enliven the narrative. Doubtless opportunity was taken to enforce and accentuate doctrinal points, but I am conscious of an inability to adequately explore this part of the subject, which I must leave to more competent hands. Considerable effort of the committee, I am of opinion, was directed to the aggrandisement of the Apostle John, which appeared to require the abasement to a partial extent of the Apostle Peter. If I am right in this view, a clue is obtained to the geographical site of the committee, viz., Ephesus, where John resided, and not Rome, where Peter's reputation was probably paramount. At this epoch there were three compositions extant, which were regarded, if not universally by the whole Catholic Church, at least by certain Churches or individuals, as works of great sanctity. Justin Martyr refers to the Revelations apparently as the work of the Apostle John, if the parenthetical sentence, "one of the Apostles of Christ," in *Trypho*, l. xxxi., be not a gloss, and it must be concluded, although he does not quote a verse of the sacred work, that he regarded it with due veneration. The Church at Smyrna, of which Polycarp was a little before that time bishop, without doubt publicly read the Gospel of Christ, in which were mentioned both the descent and ascent of the Cerinthian dove. The third writing was the Epistle now known as the First Epistle of John. The two latter were works of literary merit: the first, though incoherent and unintelligible, had somehow acquired the reputation of being the work of the Apostle John. The committee, to judge of their procedure from the results of their work which are apparent in the present day, conceived the idea of attributing all three works to the Apostle, and they accordingly proceeded to assimilate them as far as was practicable in the details of thought, doctrine, and story. With regard to the two superior writings, the Gospel and the Epistle, their work was much facilitated by the evident fact that the author of the Gospel chose the Epistle as his guide and pattern. In dealing with the Gospel, the Committee were able to give scope to their invention, and to introduce remarks, circumstances, and scenes which would materially serve to achieve their object of aggrandising John.

I imagine the first real difficulty the committee had to overcome was in connection with the name John, which was found both in the Gospel and in the Revelations, and was popularly supposed to indicate the Apostle of that name. I form this conclusion from the vague statements of Caius and Dionysius recorded by Eusebius (*Eccl. Hist.*, iii. 28), from which I infer that there was an impression that Cerinthus pretended that his 'forgery' (one is puzzled to ascertain, from the chapter of Eusebius quoted, whether the Revelations or the Gospel, or both, were so considered) was written by a great Apostle, and that he designedly used the name John. This may indeed have been a device of Cerinthus to give *éclat* to his writing. The John of Revelations is certainly akin to the John of the Gospel: "John, who bare record of the Word of God," in Rev. i. 2, is apparently identical with John who "bare record, saying I saw the Spirit descending from heaven like a dove," for the Cerinthian Spirit was probably the same as the Valentinian Word, as I have already explained. There is no doubt, moreover, that the Valentinians encouraged the belief that John the Apostle was the author of the Gospel, which they took under their wings (Irenæus, *Ad Hær.*, I. viii. 5), and they made great pretensions of deriving their theological notions from purer sources than other sects. The object in view was thus already seemingly in their hands, viz., that both works were written by the same John. Unfortunately, while it was evident to the reader of Revelations that a man named John was the writer, it was not clearly evident to the reader of the Gospel that John was its author, but only an actor in two scenes, viz., the descent of the dove and its ascent at the crucifixion. The John of the Gospel is not introduced as author, but only as a personage in the history. To add to this dilemma, the popular story writers, of whom there were tons at that epoch, had appropriated the descent of the Cerinthian dove as an incident of the assumed baptism of Jesus, and John who bare record had thus already slid past redemption into John the Baptist. But for this unlucky diversion of John by the popular writers, the labours of the committee to effect their object might have been greatly facilitated, for by simply prefixing the personal pronoun I to John in verse 32 of the first chapter, with perhaps the addition of the words "which testifieth of these things and wrote these things," xxi. 24, would have sufficed to satisfy the Christians that the Apostle was also the author of the Gospel, as well as of the Revelations, as was perhaps the general opinion with respect to the latter.

But circumstances not being in favour of this simple proceeding, the committee boldly followed in the wake of the popular story writers, so far as John of verse 32 of the first chapter was concerned, since it was hopeless to contend against the deeply set current of popular belief; but they took care to dissociate the witness of the descent of the dove, now metamorphosed into John the Baptist, from the witness of the ascent of the dove at the crucifixion, who could not be represented to be John the Baptist, who had been executed previously to the crucifixion. The verbal change made in xix. 35 (of the Fourth Gospel) from the original words, was perhaps in itself insufficient to indicate a clear difference from the John of i. 32, and v. 32 and 33, but the oral teaching and interpretation of the verse which followed in the schools and churches was certainly very effective, for I am unaware that any person has hitherto suspected the identity of the two personages who bare record of these two events. The numerous interpolations of statements regarding John the Baptist, and of alleged speeches of his, were probably the work of this committee, though perhaps not the whole of those in the first chapter, as Valentinus may have had a hand in the work. The repetitions in the first chapter are remarkable:

verse 15, the initial clause of verse 27, and verse 30 reiterate the same statements; and the expression, "Lamb of God which taketh away the sin of the world," precedes the statement in verse 30. These scattered statements appear to have been condensed into one in the Gospel as it issued from the committee, for Irenæus thus quotes them: "John made known, saying, Behold the lamb of God who taketh away the sin of the world. This is he of whom I said, After me cometh a man who was made before me; because he was prior to me: and of his fulness have we all received" (*Ad Her.*, III. x. 3). There can be no doubt from the final clause that this passage occupied the position of verses 15 and 16: and as the passage contains all that is essential in the repetitions, it appears to me probable that the whole passage which follows, from verse 19 to verse 31, which has the look of cuttings or extracts from various popular gospels, was not put in by the committee, but inserted subsequently to the date of Irenæus' work. But at the same time, as there are no serious objections against it, the passage may have been inserted by the committee, and Irenæus' version was afterwards constructed. The literary structure of the passage from verse 15 to verse 31 is very patchy. Verse 2 of ch. iv., in which the statement made in the previous verse that Jesus baptised is corrected, is manifestly the insertion of a later hand.

I conclude the committee mainly relied on the employment of the same epithets applied to Jesus in the two writings being taken as proof of identity of authorship. In the Revelations Jesus is called the Lamb of God repeatedly in twenty-eight different passages. In the second half of the second century, by virtue of the publicity given to him in the popular Gospels as the personage who had administered baptism to the Lord, John the Baptist had doubtless acquired considerable sanctity and influence amongst Gentile Christians. This epithet so frequently employed in the Revelations is put into John's mouth: and the difference of the word ἀμνός in the Gospel, and of ἀρνίον in the Revelations is insignificant, as both words are allied. The epithets, 'Son of God' and 'Son of Man' are frequent in the Gospel, and are also occasionally employed in the Revelations. Under Valentinian auspices, as I conjecture, Jesus was called the Word in the Gospel in two verses: and in three verses in the Revelations the same epithet is applied to him, viz., in i. 2 and 9, and again in xix. 13. Of these three latter verses it may be remarked that the clauses in them referring to the Word of God may be omitted without the Revelations being a penny the worse for the loss of them, and this remarkable character of surplusage indicates the tampering of the forger. These proofs of identity will strike the reader as hardly convincing, but it should be remembered that the identity of authorship of these two writings was enforced upon the people by the teaching and preaching in the schools and churches, and also by the writings of learned bishops and others, such as Clement of Alexandria. I should, however, here direct attention to the statement of Dionysius, Bishop of Alexandria, on the subject of the author of the Revelations, who he says is not the same as the author of the Gospel and Epistle. I have already quoted (p. 38) the remarks of this learned prelate, pointing out the similarity in the thoughts and expressions of the two latter works; he continues, "Very otherwise and alien from this is the Apocalypse, which touches or resembles almost nothing of them, and so to say has not a syllable in common with them" (see also Crusé's translation, Bohn's Eccl. Library). This statement must be taken as endorsed by Eusebius, who quotes the Bishop of Alexandria's opinions with approval. The conclusion is inevitable that the words and expressions that exist in our version of the Revelations did not exist in the Apocalypse in the times of Dionysius and Eusebius. The accommodations in the Apocalypse above referred to were thus not made by the second century revision committee, but by forgers of the fourth century.

The difficulties offered by the Epistle were less, as the Epistle was clearly followed by Cerinthus in many points, as I have already shown. The parts of greatest difficulty in assimilating the Gospel and the Epistle were those which formed specially the singular theology of Cerinthus, viz., the dove or the columbine incarnation of the Spirit or æon Christ, and in a far less degree the Valentinian æon Paraclete.

The descent of the dove, however, as already shown, gave no difficulty, as the popular evangelists had fully appropriated this pretty idea which had now passed into orthodox theology, and learned theologians discussed the descent of the dove as an ultimate theological fact, universally accepted. The descending dove still maintains a place in Christian theology, as it is not possible to erase it from the sacred writings without a convulsion of the universe or the extinction of the sun. The revision committee of the nineteenth century was not composed of men who possessed the grit and valour of the apostles and bishops (according to the Muratorian fragment) who formed the revision committee of the second century. Modern theologians may be divided into three classes on the question of the descent of the dove. *First.* Those who believe it as a veritable fact, and say so. This class is not numerous, and amongst Anglicans I can only call to mind Bishop Ellicott and Dean Alford.[1] *Second.* Those who do not believe it, and say so. Of this class, which is in the formative stage, I am not aware of a single individual; but the learned and very able Professor Sanday of Oxford, if I understand him rightly, is very near coming under this category. *Third.* Those who do not believe it, but do not say so. Unless I have misunderstood the theologians whom I have read between the lines, this class includes all those who do not come under either of the preceding classes. The descent of the dove was let alone by the committee, and no attempt was made by them to interfere with it, or to introduce it, or any allusion to it, in the Epistle. It was otherwise, however, with the ascent of the dove, which had attracted the notice of a Pagan writer and been made fun of by him, and hence the removal of this incident from the Gospel was very desirable. As already explained, the removal was effected by the simple expedient of changing the word 'dove' into 'water,' and making a little variation in the sequence of the narrative. The committee saw the opportunity of covering the alteration made in the

---

[1] In the early decades of the present century a very great number of the clergy apparently ranked in this first class, as Dr Arnold of Rugby speaks of the prevalence of *peristeralotry* (Stanley's *Life of Arnold*, Letter XLII., to W. W. Hull, Esq.).

text of the Gospel by introducing no less than five verses into the fifth chapter of the Epistle, which now are the 6th,[1] 8th, 9th, 10th, and 11th verses. These verses, which Bishop Lightfoot called "the most perplexing passage in the Epistle," are unintelligible, as I understand Dr Alexander, the commentator of the Epistle, to say, without reference to the 'most perplexing incident' in the Gospel (xix. 34). I coincide with Bishop Lightfoot in regarding these two passages as 'perplexing,' and not less so even when taken together if a meaning is sought to be extracted from them. All the efforts of all the theologians (Dr Alexander included) during the last seventeen centuries to explain them have been unsuccessful. The true explanation is the one which I have been enabled to give, by Bishop Lightfoot's assistance. These two perplexing passages are simply pious nonsense, introduced into the sacred writings by the committee of the second century, for the purpose of concealing the change made in the original text of Cerinthus' gospel.[2]

The difficulty presented by the Valentinian æon Paraclete was overcome by an equally simple device. In the second chapter of the Epistle, verse 1, Jesus is called an advocate or *paraclete* with the Father; the committee, by the change of a simple particle in the passage of the Gospel where the æon is first introduced, succeeded in converting the Holy Ghost into *another* advocate or *paraclete*. The original of John xiv. 16 was, I conjecture, as follows: "And I will pray the Father, and he shall give you Paraclete, that he may abide with you for ever." The τὸν παράκλητον of the original was changed into ἄλλον παράκλητον, another paraclete or advocate. This simple change, and a touch here and there in other passages, apparently sufficed to convert the æon Paraclete into the Holy Ghost. But there was also the powerful aid derived from the constant teaching and preaching in the schools and

---

[1] The seventh verse was introduced a few centuries later, after the Athanasian controversy.

[2] Dr Lightfoot, late Bishop of Durham, and his namesake, Dr John Lightfoot, probably a kinsman, are the only two theologians to my knowledge who have declared their inability to explain these two passages in the Fourth Gospel and 1st John v. 6-11. I trust that, for the credit of the cloth, there have been more, though I have no knowledge of them.

churches to enforce the change inaugurated by the committee. I have already spoken of other minor devices adopted by the committee with success for assimilating the Gospel and Epistle, and thereby to spread and consolidate the opinion that the author of both of these writings was the same individual, the Apostle John.

In discussing the changes probably wrought in the original Fourth Gospel of Cerinthus by the revision committee of the second century, it is necessary to draw a time demarcation, so as to discriminate the committee's work from that of subsequent operators. For practical purposes the date of Irenæus' great work will give us a reasonable limitation of the committee's transactions. I will take the chronology approximately fixed by Bishop Lightfoot, viz., A.D. 190 or thereabouts,[1] as the date of Irenæus' great work. In fact, Irenæus' quotations of the Gospel and his statements regarding the Gospel will form the criterion of the committee's work.

The Fourth Gospel as it came up for revision by the committee had already in all probability implanted in it the additions made by the Valentinians and Ophites which I have already indicated. I believe that the second verse of the Prologue, "the same was in the beginning with God," was not introduced by these sectaries or by the committee (A.D. 166-168), because Theophilus (A.D. 168), who quotes the Prologue and attributes it to. John, omits the second verse. Hippolytus likewise omits the second verse in quoting the Prologue (*Heresy of Noetus*, xii.); he wrote in the first half or early part of the third century. Clement of Alexandria, who was a contemporary of Irenæus, quotes the first verse twice and the third verse nine times, but there is no trace of the second verse to be found in his voluminous writings. But we find Irenæus quoting the Prologue with the second verse included. A reasonable inference from these facts is that Irenæus put in the second verse because he felt the need of in some way throwing back the chronology of the word from the beginning of the Gospel to the beginning of the world, a need, as I have already pointed out (p. 4), Theophilus likewise

[1] Lightfoot's Essays on the work entitled *Supernatural Religion*, pp. 259-261.

felt. Irenæus, in his explication of the Valentinian theology (I. viii. 5), lets the cat out of the bag; he says this clause discloses the order of production. In the Gnostic theology of Cerinthus, the Spirit [or Word] was an emanation from the Supreme deity given off at the time of the promulgation of the Gospel, and Paraclete was an emanation subsequent in order of production to the Spirit [or Word]. This chronology of production did not suit the orthodox opinion that the Word and the Holy Ghost and God were identical, and from the beginning of time co-existent. Hence the introduction of the second verse into the Prologue was deemed necessary to establish the orthodox chronology. But even in this comparatively small interpolation, the latter by itself would hardly have been effective without the enforcement of the orthodox interpretation in the schools and churches.

The remarkable clause in the tenth verse of the Prologue, "and the world was made by him," was probably introduced by this committee. In what it implies, this clause is unique in the sacred writings, and in the whole body of Christian literature, so far as my knowledge extends. It means that the concrete Jesus, the son of Joseph the carpenter and of Mary the hairdresser, made the universe: a statement which is nowhere else made. As I have already pointed out, the Valentinians limited the creative operations of the Word within the area of the pleroma, or Gnostic heaven. This did not suit the orthodoxy of the time; but one wonders why ancient orthodoxy troubled itself so much with the heretical interpretation of the third verse of the Prologue. The reason I take to be that the Valentinian interpretation was very influential at the time, and that it was thought necessary to oppose it not merely by argumentation, which was of a kind by no means convincing, but by an actual introduction into the Gospel of words distinctly extending the action of the Word beyond the Gnostic celestial regions. Other Gnostic sects of considerable influence also denied the orthodox view. Hence the interpolation was deemed essential for the stability of the orthodox doctrine. Irenæus quotes the clause with great satisfaction in connection with his refutation of the Valentinian interpretation of the third verse of the

Prologue: and he complacently remarks that apostolic John himself by this clause removed the subject from controversy (*Ad Hær.*, III. xi. 2). Such a statement, in my judgment, clearly indicates that the revision committee (who, according to the Muratorian fragment, agreed to attribute their transactions to the Apostle John) were the authors of the clause, which was grievously needed to counteract the Valentinian interpretation of verse 3. The connection of the clause with the third verse being so intimate, it would have been wiser if the clause had been interpolated in the third verse thus: " All things and the world were made by him, and without him was nothing made." This suggestion is unfortunately proposed seventeen centuries too late.

I am grateful to Irenæus for the running table of contents he gives (II. xxii. 3) of the Fourth Gospel as it issued from the hands of the committee, at a time when it was perhaps twenty years in use in the schools and churches. From this authentic statement it is certain that the story of the conversion of water into wine (ch. ii. 1–11) was in the Gospel in the second century: it will be remembered that I attribute the authorship of this anecdote to the Ophites. After the marriage at Cana, Irenæus states that Jesus went up to the festival day of the Passover, on which occasion it was written, " For many believed in him, when they saw the signs which he did." I conclude from this that all the verses intervening between the story of the marriage at Cana and the visit to Jerusalem, *i.e.*, from verse 12 to verse 22, were not in the Revised Gospel. In Tatian's *Diatessaron* they appear at a later stage of the narrative. The story of the expulsion of the traders from the temple was thus absent in the Gospel in the second century, for it is too salient an incident to be overlooked by Irenæus. Eusebius' account of the origin of the Fourth Gospel was obviously founded on the circumstance of the occurrence in it of stories not found in the Synoptic Gospels. One is tempted to suspect that this story was wanting in the Fourth Gospel when Eusebius wrote.[1] The

---

[1] The existence of the passage, ii. 12-22, at this part of the Fourth Gospel is puzzling. None of the early Fathers refer to it as existing in the Gospel of John. Tatian in his *Diatessaron* (end of second century) relates

interview with Nicodemus is not alluded to; but it should be remembered that the object of Irenæus was to illustrate the number of passovers during Jesus' ministry; hence the omission of any incident not connected with the Passover is not necessarily proof of its absence from the text. We have, however, the testimony of Justin, who was an earlier writer than Irenæus, that the story of Nicodemus was known to him. Irenæus next alludes to the woman of Samaria, to show that Jesus had left Judæa, and he also refers to the cure of the centurion's son. Irenæus regarded the feast of the Jews in ch. v. 1 as the Passover, to observe which Jesus next proceeded to Jerusalem, and he indicates the cure of the paralytic man as wrought on this occasion. Jesus then withdrew to the other side of the Sea of Tiberias, where he wrought the miracle of feeding five thousand with five loaves and two small fishes, and twelve baskets of fragments remained. The walking on the sea is not mentioned by Irenæus, and also the discourse on the bread of God, and the declaration that Judas was to betray the Lord. That the discourse on the bread and the sacramental doctrine was in the Gospel is satisfactorily established by the numerous quotations from the discourse in the writings of Clement of Alexandria, a contemporary of Irenæus. The walking on the sea, however, is not mentioned by any contemporary writer as existing in this Gospel, nor is the miracle spoken of in Origen's *Commentary on the Fourth Gospel.* In the *Diatessaron* the account of the miracle is taken from Matthew, but a feeble attempt is made at the conclusion of the story to bring it up to date (xix. 11). No allusion is made to the incidents in connection with the feast of the tabernacles, to the story of the woman taken in adultery, nor to the discourse on the sheep and the sheepfold, nor to the attempted stoning of Jesus, and his escape and retirement beyond

the story of the driving at a later period, and so also the dialogue regarding the destruction of the temple in three days. This dialogue is referred to by Irenæus and Tertullian, but it cannot be ascertained whence they derived it, or from what part of the Gospel, the earlier or later chapters. I conclude, subject to correction, that the passage was not in the second chapter in Irenæus' copy. It might have been subsequently copied from the Valentinian recension of the Fourth Gospel (see Origen's *Commentary on John,* x. 14, 15, 19; and *ante,* p. 238).

Jordan, these incidents not being connected with a Passover. All these incidents, however, are referred to, or verses quoted, elsewhere in Irenæus' writings, and also in Clement's writings, and in the Clementine Homilies (John ix. 1–3, in xix. 22), as well as in Tatian's *Diatessaron*, with the exception of the anecdote of the woman taken in adultery, which is now excluded from our Revised Version. Irenæus next proceeds to state that after raising Lazarus from the dead, and finding that plots were raised against him by the Pharisees, Jesus retired to Ephraim, all these incidents being related in the Fourth Gospel; and thence, to quote the old Latin translation (*Ad Hær.*, II. xxii. 3): "*Et inde ante sex dies paschæ veniens in Bethaniam scribitur, et de Bethania ascendens in Hierosolymam et manducans pascha et sequenti die passus*"—it is written, coming six days before the passover into Bethany, and going up to Jerusalem from Bethany and eating the passover he suffered on the following day.

Neither in this passage nor elsewhere in his writings does Irenæus make any allusion to Mary anointing the feet of Jesus at Bethany. His contemporary, Clement of Alexandria, also makes no allusion to the incident, and, further, it appears clear to me that he knew nothing of this passage in the Fourth Gospel. In *Pædag.*, ii. 8, he refers to the corresponding anecdote, as related by Matthew (xxvi. 6–13) and Luke (vii. 36–50), of the woman with an alabaster box of ointment who anointed the feet of the Lord. By a process of theological reasoning, utterly incomprehensible to me, he comes to the conclusion that the anointing of Jesus' feet "prophesied the treason of Judas." In the *Diatessaron*, xxxix. 1–4, is a very remarkable mosaic passage made up of bits from the Fourth Gospel, and from the First and Second Gospels (Matt. xxvi. 6–13; Mark xiv. 3–9). In this passage, while the house in which the supper was served is said to be that of Simon the leper, as stated in the Synoptic Gospels, and not that of Lazarus, which is the most natural and obvious meaning in the Fourth Gospel, the chronology in the Fourth Gospel (six days before the passover) is retained to the exclusion of the chronology given in the Synoptic Gospels (two days before the passover). Herein lies the difficulty in the way of accepting the authority of the *Diatessaron* as it has come down to us: from a variety of indications it is apparent that the work had been very naturally written up to date from time to time in the early centuries. My conclusion is that the episode of Mary's anointing the Lord's feet at Bethany six days before the Passover did not exist in the Fourth Gospel in the second century. Our two reliable authorities, Irenæus and Clement, show no consciousness of the existence of the passage in their time. And in Origen's *Commentary on the Fourth Gospel* this episode is not mentioned.[1]

That there was a statement in the revised version of the Fourth Gospel in the second century of the eating of the passover by Jesus is made an historical certainty by Irenæus' clear announcement in the passage quoted above in Latin, that Jesus eat the passover and suffered on the following day. One cannot doubt this fact, as it is plain that Irenæus had the revised Gospel before him when he drew up the running table of contents. Surely there can be no longer any hesitation in admitting the fact that the Gospel had been grossly tampered with in the subsequent centuries, and the historical truth it contained perverted into falsehood. Reading over the references in Tertullian to the thirteenth chapter of the Fourth Gospel, it appears to me just possible that the deceitful change made in this passage was with regard to the time only, viz., that the preposition 'before' the feast of the passover was substituted for 'at' the feast of the passover. It appears to me that Tertullian perceived no discrepancy between the Synoptic account and that in the

---

[1] Origen's dealing with the ointment stories puzzles me. He nowhere makes the slightest allusion to Mary's performance, described in the Fourth Gospel, xi. 1-9; but in his *Commentary on Matthew* (Bk. xi. 9) he quotes verses 5 and 6 in connection with Judas' roguery, clearly taken from our Fourth Gospel. In his *Commentary on John* (Bk. i. 13) he describes the story as given in Matt. xxv. 6-13 and in Luke vii. 36-50, but he makes no allusion whatever to Mary's performance, and does not show the least consciousness of the story related in the Fourth Gospel. I think in course of time I might be able to find an explication of this puzzle: at present it weakens to a certain extent the statement made in the text above regarding the episode.

Fourth Gospel: a discrepancy very apparent in the latter as the text now stands. In the composition called *Adversus Judæos*, ch. xi., he speaks of the Jewish *Passover of the Lord* as identical with the Christian *Passion of Christ*, because the Jews slew Christ on the first day of unleavened bread; and he proceeds to remark that the day hastened to make the evening, or darkness, in the middle of the day, alluding to the darkness at the crucifixion. It is clear enough from this statement that Tertullian did not understand that Jesus was slain in the evening, but before midday of the first day of the Passover. The first day of the Jewish passover extended from the evening of the 14th, when the passover was eaten, to the evening of the 15th Nisan. According to Tertullian the crucifixion or passion took place before midday on the 15th Nisan.

I am unable to find in any of the surviving works of Clement of Alexandria or of Hippolytus, who were writers of this period, any reference to this passage (xiii. 1-3). The result of my investigations of this passage of the Fourth Gospel, wherein as the text has come down to us is a discrepancy with the Synoptics, is that there is no statement to be found in the surviving Christian literature of the second and third centuries that gives support to it, and in none of the writers of this period have I discovered any consciousness that such discrepancy existed in their times. In discoursing on the Paschal controversy of the second century, Eusebius does not mention any disputant who spoke of such discrepancy, nor does he himself declare that such a discrepancy existed. Had there been a variance between the Fourth and the Synoptic Gospels at this epoch, it is unlikely that Eusebius would have omitted to refer to it, nor that the disputants in the Paschal controversy would have been silent regarding it. The evidence constrains me to assert that in the Fourth Gospel, as it passed out of the hands of the revision committee of the second century, the statement existed, as Irenæus expressly intimates, that Jesus eat the passover, and the narrative showed that he suffered on the following day. At this period the passage under notice probably read as follows: "1. Now at the feast of the passover, when Jesus

R

knew that his hour was come that he should depart out of this world unto the Father, having loved his own which were in the world, he loved them unto the end. 2. And the passover being eaten, the devil having now put into the heart of Judas Iscariot, Simon's son, to betray him," etc.; or the phrase at the beginning of the second verse might have been, "the passover or paschal meal being ended." Hence there was no discrepancy on this subject between the Fourth Gospel and the Synoptics in the second century.

The only passages in ancient writings that appear to assert that a discrepancy as to the eating of the passover by our Lord existed in the second century between the Fourth and the Synoptic Gospels, are four quotations found in the *Chronicon Paschale*, a work of the seventh century, by an anonymous chronicler, an unknown or rare bird in the region of profane history, but common in that of early ecclesiastical history (*e.g.*, the authors of the Gospels and Acts). In this work four passages are quoted, two from a treatise *On the Paschal Festival* by Apollinaris, Bishop of Hierapolis in Asia Minor about A.D. 170, who, though repeatedly noticed by Eusebius in his history (Bk. iv. 26, 27; v. 5, 16, 19), is not represented by him as having taken part in the Paschal controversy. A translation of these two passages will be found on p. 239 of Bishop Lightfoot's Essays on *Supernatural Religion*, and also in the Ante-Nicene Christian Library, *Lactantius*, vol. ii.; second part, "Fragments of the Second and Third Centuries," p. 141. The other two quotations are said to be from treatises of Hippolytus, *Against all Heresies* and *On the Holy Supper*. There are objections to the authenticity of these four quotations; but I will waive these objections, inasmuch as competent scholars like Bishop Lightfoot, Dr Martineau, and Matthew Arnold accept the quotations as genuine. Hippolytus' treatise, *Against all Heresies*, though long lost, was discovered in the first half of this century, but the quotation from it in the *Chronicon Paschale* is not to be found in the recovered work. Matthew Arnold contends that the latter work cannot be pronounced with certainty to be the same as the *Refutation of all Heresies*, by Hippolytus. Translations of the two quotations from Hippolytus will be found in the Ante-Nicene Christian Library, *Hippolytus*, vol. ii. p. 94.

The first quotation from Apollinaris states that 'ignorant persons,' meaning thereby, it is presumed, all the bishops of the Churches of Asia Minor excepting himself, and including also such men as Irenæus, and perhaps also Clement of Alexandria, say that on the 14th Nisan our Lord eat the lamb with his disciples and suffered on the following day, and they affirm that Matthew represents it so, as they interpret him. "Thus their interpretation," to quote Bishop Lightfoot's translation, "is out of harmony with the law (ἀσύμφωνος νόμῳ), and on their showing the Gospels seem to be at variance with one another (στασιάζειν δοκεῖ κατ' αὐτοὺς τὰ εὐαγγέλια)." Bishop Lightfoot understands the passage to refer to "the difficulty of reconciling the chronology of the Paschal week as given by St John with the narratives of the Synoptic Evangelists"; and following the terms of his translation his inference may be taken as justifiable. But it seems to me that the translation of this great scholar is faulty, and not a correct rendering of the Greek original, which should be, the Gospels seem to disagree *with them*, or to rebel *against them*, i.e., the aforesaid 'ignorant persons.'[1] The passage is correctly translated by Dr Sinker, the present librarian of Trinity College, Cambridge, in the Ante-Nicene Christian Library. I submit that this quotation from Apollinaris, correctly translated, does not point to a discrepancy between the Gospels, which discrepancy did not exist in the second century, but rather to the unanimity of the Gospels on the subject of the eating of the passover by our Lord, which unanimity then existed, as all the evidence that I can gather, proves.

The second fragment from Apollinaris, quoted in the *Chronicon Paschale*, is said by Bishop Lightfoot to bear out the impression left by the first; but it clearly cannot do so, as the impression left on the great prelate's mind by the first

---

[1] The Greek words κατ' αὐτοὺς mean *against them*; κατ' ἀλλήλους mean *against one another*. Theologians, like other people, copy from each other. I fancy Bishop Lightfoot copied from Tischendorf, who copied from somebody else, and so on *ad infinitum*.

extract was obviously wrong, and the result, in its bearing upon the point I am discussing, of mistaken preconception, common to the learned bishop and all other theologians. The second fragment simply states the opinion of Apollinaris that "the 14th was the true passover of the Lord," an opinion that was repeated by Hippolytus as his own also in the two fragments from his works quoted in the anonymous chronicle aforesaid, and an opinion that is largely discoursed upon by Origen in his *Commentary on the Fourth Gospel* (Bk. x. 11–14). None of these writers, though touching on the incident in our Lord's history which I am discussing, impugn the individual accuracy of the Gospels, or refer to any disagreement between the latter on this subject. It is the interpretation of the story in the Gospels which the two former challenge: Apollinaris imputing 'ignorance,' Hippolytus 'error' to people who were not of their way of thinking. The latter writer in the fragment from his treatise on the Holy Supper speaks thus: "Now that neither in the first [Gospel?] nor in the last [Gospel?] there was any thing false is evident; for he who said of old, 'I will not any more eat the passover' [Luke xxii. 16], probably partook of supper before the passover. But the passover he did not eat, but he suffered; for it was not the time for him to eat." In Origen's rambling discourse, which extends over four somewhat lengthy chapters of his commentary on the subject of the passover, I find no statement that Jesus did not eat the last passover, which, according to him, was the second of his ministry; nor that there was any discrepancy on the subject between the Fourth and Synoptic Gospels. Origen deals with unusual boldness with the discrepancies between the Fourth and the Synoptic Gospels. The list of these discrepancies in the table of contents of Origen's *Commentary on the Fourth Gospel* is lengthy; but it is to be remarked that a discrepancy between the Synoptic narratives of the last paschal meal and the account in the Fourth Gospel is not included in the list, the obvious reason being that in Origen's age the discrepancy now found in the Fourth Gospel did not exist. In the passage from Hippolytus, quoted above, the writer bases the probability that a supper was eaten before the passover upon a text in Luke, which he certainly would not have done if the text of the Fourth Gospel was in his time such as we find it to be in ours; instead of a supposition, supported from Luke's Gospel, he should have had a certainty from xiii. 1 and 2 of the Fourth Gospel, as we now have it. I am unable to state when the impiously fraudulent change of this passage in the revised text of the second century was made, but it must be taken to be subsequent to the time of Eusebius, as neither this historian nor any writer prior to him appears to have had the least consciousness of the passage in the Fourth Gospel as we now have it, viz., that Jesus eat a supper, but not the passover itself, before he suffered.

The opinion, however, that Jesus did not eat the passover before he was crucified, but that he was himself the paschal lamb and suffered on the 14th Nisan, which originated in the latter half of the second century, gained strength as time advanced. It appears that, as a consequence of the growing strength of this opinion, sundry auxiliary passages gradually crept into the text of the revised version of the Fourth Gospel of the second century, and these passages I take to be the offspring of the Paschal controversy, which smouldered, I believe, through three or four centuries or longer before it was definitely settled that the Jewish passover should no longer be commemorated by the Christian communities. These subsidiary passages in support of the Paschal lamb doctrine are the following : ch. xviii. 28, the concluding clause only, " but that they might eat the passover"; xix. 14, "and it was the preparation of the passover"; xix. 31–33, " The Jews therefore, because it was the preparation, that the bodies should not remain upon the cross on the Sabbath day (for that Sabbath day was an high day), besought Pilate that their legs might be broken, and *that* they might be taken away." I shall first speak of the crurifragium or breaking of the legs, which, according to Lactantius (*Divine Institutes*, Bk. iv. 26), was the prevailing custom at crucifixions. I find no reference to this episode in contemporary writers before Origen, who speaks of it in his *Commentary on John* (Bk. x. 13), and quotes xix. 32 and 33 *verbatim*, in connection with the Jewish practice of not breaking a bone of the paschal lamb, according to the Mosaic ordinance (Ex. xii. 8), which he says John appears to have made use of in his Gospel, as applying to the transactions connected with the death of Jesus. Lactantius also, a contemporary of Eusebius, says, in connection with the usage at crucifixions, that the executioners considered it unnecessary to break Jesus' bones, but they only pierced his side. It is thus proven that the incident existed in the Fourth Gospel in the time of Eusebius (a contemporary of Lactantius), who, however, makes no reference to the passage, and what it implies, in his account of the Paschal controversy in his *Ecclesiastical History*. Taking into account Eusebius' silence and the silence of Irenæus, Clement of Alexandria, and Tertullian on this subject, I think it would be fair to consider it undecided whether this incident of the breaking of bones was in the revised Gospel of the second century, or was inserted after the time of Irenæus. I might further remark that none of these Fathers named above seem to have regarded the incident, assuming that they were aware of it, as a fulfilment of prophecy. Neither Irenæus nor Tertullian, who often refer to the fulfilment of the prophecies concerning Jesus, mention the *soi-disant* unbroken bone prophecy (Psalms, xxxiv. 20), which, I suspect, was a modern discovery, unknown to the ancients. Origen distinctly connects it with the Mosaic ordinance,[1] and Lactantius gives another reason, viz., that it was a special design of God that the body of Jesus should not be mutilated and thus be rendered unsuitable for rising again. It should be finally borne in mind that Justin was ignorant of the incident and that the Synoptic Gospels do not mention it. I should state a fact that has influenced my judgment on this point, that in the Ante-Nicene Christian Library, *Lactantius*, vol. ii., is a collection of fragments from ancient Christian writers. One of these, Melito, Bishop of the city of Attica, distinctly states that no bone of Jesus was broken on the cross (p. 127). The date of this bishop I am unable to ascertain, but the curious

---

[1] I suspect, for the reasons stated in the text, that the statement in the Fourth Gospel referred to the fulfilment of the Mosaic ordinance that no bone of the paschal lamb should be broken. The prophecy was, I think, discovered in 1857 (see *National Review* for that year, July, page 112). The subject needs further investigation (see *ante*, page 134).

information regarding Jesus given by him points to considerable antiquity. I think he might have been a contemporary of his namesake of Sardis, for both the Melitos have a curious opinion in common with regard to the alleged darkness in the middle of the day during the crucifixion, viz., that the luminaries 'and the elements' fled away because they could not endure the sight of the Lord hanging on the tree. Assuming that Melito of Attica flourished in the second half of the second century, he was likely to have been cognisant of the revised version of the Fourth Gospel. But there is no statement in the fragment that the bishop derived his information from the Fourth Gospel; and it is clear that his sources were other than the Fourth Gospel or Synoptics, for he gives some new information regarding Jesus. He says (unwittingly contradicting his curious opinion just quoted) that he was slain in the evening and buried at night—which none of the Gospels say. He further states that Jesus was put to death "in the midst of Jerusalem": that the cause of his death at the hands of the Jews was because he cured the lame, cleansed lepers, raised the dead, etc.; that Jesus was crucified naked;[1] all theological facts which were recorded in other gospels of the period, but not in those that are now canonical.

Regarding the other subsidiary passages, we must conclude that they were not in the revised version of the second century, simply because they are not compatible with the fact that Jesus eat the passover before he suffered, which Irenæus expressly says was narrated in the Fourth Gospel. The omission of the crurifragium can hardly be regarded as incompatible with the fact that Jesus eat the passover before he suffered, with which it had no physical relation, but only a doctrinal connection. Whatever statement had been previously made, as to the eating or non-eating of the passover by Jesus before he suffered, the crurifragium may be related as a mere incident in the proceedings, without inconsistency.

While the crurifragium is a neutral incident, as it were, the clause in verse xix. 31 describing it, viz., "for that Sabbath was

[1] Perhaps the good bishop only meant to say that Jesus had been divested of his usual garments, and was clothed only with the *subligaculum* or loin cloth, or with that trifling garment called a *lungootee* in the East.

an high day," is not, and undoubtedly implies that the coming Sabbath was the Passover, and this implication is confirmed by xix. 14, where it is definitely stated that " it was the preparation of the passover and about the sixth hour." The clause in xviii. 28 also distinctly implies that the passover was still due. I have not succeeded in discovering any trace of these three clauses in Christian writings till we come to the times of Eusebius, the end of the third and early part of the fourth century. The three clauses are cited in a long passage quoted in the *Chronicon Paschale*, the work of the seventh century already spoken of, from the writings of Peter, Bishop of Alexandria, who was a contemporary of Eusebius, and is referred to in his *Ecclesiastical History* in various places (ix. 6 ; vii. 32 ; viii. 13). A translation of the passage will be found in the Ante-Nicene Christian Library, *Methodius*, etc., p. 329. Peter quotes these three clauses *verbatim* as they are to be found in our Fourth Gospel, in support of the statement he puts forward that Jesus indeed eat the 'legal and shadowy Passover' on the 14th Nisan before his public ministry, but after that he did not eat the lamb, but suffered himself as the true lamb in the Paschal feast. What has struck me in Peter's argumentation is the singular fact that while he quotes these three subsidiary clauses in support of his view, he makes no reference whatever to ch. xiii. 1 and 2, where, as our text reads, he would have found the subject of his argumentation fully stated without mistake. I feel justified in inferring from this strange abstinence of Peter from making use of a recognised authority, viz., ch. xiii. 1 and 2, that the latter passage in his days was not the same as it is given in our present text: and yet it would be hard to think that Peter would have ventured on his argumentation if ch. xiii. 1 and 2 was in his days such as I have restored it on the competent authority of Irenæus, viz., that Jesus eat the passover before he suffered. The only clue out of this dilemma is the supposition that the text of ch. xiii. 1 and 2 had undergone some change in the interval which rendered the meaning doubtful, so that each person might take the view which best suited him, namely, that Jesus did eat, or did not eat, the passover—one of the triumphs of ecclesiastical craft. Mrs Lewis' valuable recovery of a suppressed copy of the Gospels, suppressed because, perhaps, not written up to date, supplies the missing link as it were, for the reading, in these Syriac Gospels, of xiii. 2, is "And there was a supper," an indefinite statement which might be understood either as the passover or an ordinary evening meal. Our present text is in reality indefinite, but, possibly owing to centuries of positive teaching, it is always understood to mean an ordinary supper. A puzzling statement made by Peter is that the fact of the eating of the passover by Jesus before he suffered is not related by the holy evangelists, nor has it been handed down by any of the blessed apostles. The only explanation of this positive statement that I can think of is, that Peter and Hippolytus and others put a special interpretation on the Synoptic narratives, the details of which interpretation have not survived to our times: and that Peter was unaware of, or disbelieved, the distinct statement of Polycrates and Irenæus that the Apostle John of Ephesus commemorated the passover because Jesus eat it.

Peter in the passage quoted points out an error in the Fourth Gospel in the hour of the day on which Jesus was convicted and executed. The Fourth Gospel says 'the sixth hour,' which Peter says was an error for 'the third hour': and he adds that the 'correct books' have it so, and also the autograph copy of the Gospel written by the Apostle John which was preserved to that day in the Church at Ephesus. As no other writer alludes to such a precious copy, the presumption is that on this point Bishop Peter pulled the long bow. Irenæus says (IV. xxxiii. 12) that the crucifixion took place from the sixth hour onwards. The Gospel according to Mark, however, mentions the third hour (xv. 25) as that on which the crucifixion took place, *i.e.*, at 9 A.M. of our time. This was about the time that Tertullian understood the crucifixion to have taken place (*Ad. Judæos*, xi.), *i.e.*, before midday. The possible error pointed out by Peter does not help his view that Jesus was the paschal lamb in all details: because the paschal lamb was slain in the evening (Ex. xii. 6, 18), perhaps the tenth hour, or 4 P.M., or perhaps at the twelfth hour, or 6 P.M. Had the crucifixion taken place at this late hour of the day, the burial must necessarily have been performed at night, on the Sabbath : a fact that neither canonical Gospels nor Christian authors state, with the single exception of Melito of Attica, the source of whose information was probably some sectarian gospel.

It appears then to be highly probable, if not certain, that the revised Gospel of the second century did not give support to the doctrine that Jesus was the Passover in all the details of the ceremonial. The Gospel was in the course of more than a century gradually warped into giving support to it. The central theological fact stated in xiii. 1 and 2 was not in the Gospel up to the days of Eusebius, *i.e.*, at the end of the third century and beginning of the fourth. The accessory theological facts, or some of them, appear to have been the first to be introduced into the Gospel, and to have gradually led on to the final change of the passage in xiii. 1, 2. At what period the episode of the anointing of Jesus' feet at Bethany by Mary was introduced into the text is not traceable : no mention of it is to be found in the Christian writers prior to Eusebius. That this episode was no new invention but a *réchauffé* of the anecdote related in Matthew xxvi. 6–13, is rendered clear from Mrs Lewis' Syriac Gospel (John xii. 1–7), where the connecting words and incident, 'an alabaster box' and the pouring of the ointment on the head of Jesus, both omitted in the Fourth Gospel as it has come down to us, will be found as put down in the Gospel according to Matthew. Eusebius' rule that the Fourth Gospel supplied the omissions of the Synoptics may, I think, with justice be applied to the exclusion of the ointment anecdote till after the time of Eusebius. It is obvious that Eusebius' rule was an inference from the fact that in his time the Fourth Gospel did not repeat the stories found in the Synoptics. The ointment story is found in Matthew, in Luke, and also in Mark (xiv. 3–9), and its presence in these Gospels implies that it was absent in the Fourth Gospel when Eusebius wrote. I have already stated (see *ante*, p. 131) the object for which this incident was introduced into the text, viz., to mark the day on which the paschal lamb was chosen. The purpose for which the anointing was made is stated in the Fourth Gospel as said by Jesus himself to have been " against the day of my burial" ; in Mark, "aforehand to anoint my body to the burial ; " in Matthew, " she did it for my burial." This reason being assigned for the anointing evidently implies that it was the custom to anoint the dead prior to burial in Jesus' times. Now I have failed to discover that the anointing of the dead was practised by the Jews. Bishop Westcott does not supply any information in his commentary. But it was a Pagan custom, and one practised by the Christians also in the second century perhaps, but certainly in the third century. Clement, in the passage already referred to (*Pæd.*, II. viii.), merely says, " For the dead are anointed," without saying whether the Pagan or Christian dead were anointed, or both ; but he cannot be understood to be referring to a Jewish practice. Minucius Felix distinctly states in the discussion with Cæcilius that the Christians, while avoiding the use of flowers, scents, etc., " reserve unguents for funeral rites " (*Oct.*, xii.). Tertullian also says the same (*On Idolatry*, ch. xi.). If I am right in these facts, it follows that the ointment story in the Gospels is an anachronism ; perhaps my inference should be restricted to Jesus' explanation of the purpose of the anointing ; and that either the story itself, with all its variations, or Jesus' explication, was an invention of the second or third century.

We have ample proof that the scene of the feet-washing existed in the revised Fourth Gospel of the second century. Irenæus refers to the incident (IV. xxii. 1), and Clement has a very characteristic passage regarding it. He says (*Pæd.*, ii. 3) : " The Lord cooked in a paltry vessel, and the unpretentious god and lord of all things placed his disciples reclining on the sward of the meadow, and girded with a towel, washed their feet, without bringing down from heaven a silver foot-bath." Clement again refers to the feet-washing in a subsequent chapter (viii.). Tertullian makes frequent allusions to it, and quotes (xiii. 10), viz., " He that is washed needeth not save to wash *his* feet, but is clean every whit," in a very extraordinary manner, so as to give ground to a strong doubt whether the colloquy between Jesus and Peter had not been trimmed subsequently to Tertullian's time. Tertullian knew Greek and had sufficient means to procure a Greek codex of the Gospels, and had no need to restrict himself to the old *Itala* codex which may have been corrupt. He thus quotes the address of Jesus to Peter: "*Qui semel lavit, non habet necesse rursum*," which is translated in the Ante-Nicene Christian Library (*Tert.*, vol. i. p. 245): "He who hath once bathed hath no necessity [to wash] a second time"; a sanitary precept which will not be accepted in our days, even though declared to have been an utterance of Jesus Christ.

There is no doubt in my mind that the story of Judas had been introduced into the sacred history in the second half of the second century. Paul, Peter, James, Jude, and the writers of the Hebrews and other epistles in the New Testament do not show any consciousness of a knowledge of the traitor Apostle and make no allusion to him: nor do other early writers, not even the loquacious Justin Martyr, mention him, though the latter knew well the orthodox biography of our Lord as we have received it, in almost every detail, with the exception of the Judas story, the crurifragium and a few others. The story of Judas was the offspring of prophecy, and hence it is marvellous that so great a prophecy-forager as Justin is silent about the prophecy which led to the introduction of Judas into the sacred biography. We first encounter Judas in the writings of Irenæus about the close of the second century, and this author certainly had the knowledge of a story of which there is no trace in the writings of his predecessors. That Judas was put into the revised Fourth Gospel we have to take on slight evidence. Irenæus' references to Judas are not numerous, and the only allusion to Judas as a character in the Fourth Gospel made by him is in Bk. II. xx. 5, where this author says Jesus called Judas 'the son of perdition,' an expression that is only found in ch. xvii. 12 of the Fourth Gospel. Clement of Alexandria had also a knowledge of the story of Judas, but all his facts were derived from the Synoptic Gospels. Hippolytus makes no mention of Judas in any of his surviving writings, and these are by no means inconsiderable in amount.[1] Tertullian, also, is rather

---

[1] Judas is only inferentially noticed by this author, in his account of the careers of the Apostles very briefly narrated (see "Hippolytus on

reticent on the subject of Judas. I can only discover five or six allusions to Judas in all his works. In the treatise, *Adversus Judæos*, xiv., the devil is called the instigator of Judas the traitor (*diabolus, auctor scilicet Judæ traditoris*). This possibly might indicate knowledge of two passages in the Fourth Gospel, in which the word διάβολος or devil is used in connection with Judas (vi. 70 and xiii. 2). In his work against Marcion he makes a bare allusion to the remorse of Judas, as related by Matthew (Bk. iv. 40). In the composition, *De præscriptione hæreticorum*, xxii., Tertullian gives fuller information: he speaks of John as the best-beloved (*dilectissimum*) disciple, leaning on Jesus' bosom, to whom he had foreshown the traitor Judas. In the treatise, *Adversus Praxeas*, xxiii., this heretic is said to have inculcated that Judas betrayed the Father. In Origen's writings we find clear traces of the presence of Judas in the Fourth Gospel. While in the work against Celsus all the facts about Judas are taken chiefly from the Synoptics; in his other works Origen quotes verses from the Fourth Gospel bearing on Judas, viz., that the devil had put into the heart of Judas to betray Jesus (xiii. 2), and Satan entered into him (xiii. 27), and he repeats these statements in his *Commentary on John* (Bk. x. 30) with the addition to the latter statement that Satan entered Judas after the sop; and the latter statement he repeats in his *Commentary on Matthew* (xiii. 8). The above evidence does not satisfy me that the whole passage in ch. xiii., from verse 18 to 30, was in the revised Fourth Gospel of the second century. I am confirmed in this scepticism by the fact that Origen quotes the wrong prophecy predicting the treachery of the traitor Apostle. The prophecy put into the mouth of Jesus in the Fourth Gospel (xiii. 18) is: "He that eateth bread with me hath lifted up his heel against me" (Ps. xli. 9). Origen quotes (Ps. cix. 1, 2), as words spoken by the mouth of Jesus (*Celsus*, ii. 20), "Hold not thy peace, O God of my praise; for the mouth of the wicked and the mouth of the deceitful are opened against me." Origen's quotation is applicable in only a very wide sense, and it is obvious he would have quoted the more specific prophecy as

the Twelve Apostles," Ante-Nicene Christian Library, *Hippolytus*, vol. ii. p. 131).

put into Jesus' mouth had he known it or seen it in the Fourth Gospel. The quotation, as we find it in the Gospel as it has come down to us, was a new find since the time of Origen, and was substituted in the place of the prophecy which he quoted. It is very plain to me, after my experience of quotations and adaptations of prophecies during my investigation, that all these alleged prophecies were consecutively discovered, the last discovery being made so late as 1857 (see page 262, footnote). I shall take an opportunity hereafter of announcing a prophecy of my discovery, which to my mind predicts clearly that the afflicted servant of Jehovah, *i.e.*, the Messiah, lived a prosperous and happy life after the severe persecutions he had undergone, and brought up a family ; and I shall give some evidence of the fulfilment of this prediction not less convincing than any alleged fulfilment of a prophecy in the sacred writings. In the *Apostolic Constitutions*, Bk. v. 14, in a mosaic passage made up of quotations from Matthew, Luke, and the Fourth Gospel, John the Apostle is represented as giving his reminiscences of the interesting scene of the last supper, which he says was the passover eaten on the fifth day of the week. It is a singular fact that the imaginary apostle omits all mention of the incident particularised in ch. xiii. 24 of the Fourth Gospel, viz., " Simon Peter therefore beckoned unto him, that he should ask who it should be of whom he spake." This omission at once raises reflections, which are not allayed by the historical facts brought forward by Bishops Lightfoot and Westcott, already quoted in this work (p. 196), from which I drew the conclusion that Peter beckoned to the back of John's head, and hence could not have attracted his attention. The imaginary Apostle in this passage, in spite of his 'incomparable modesty,' distinctly speaks of himself as more beloved than the rest, and further as lying on the Lord's bosom. The approximative date of the *Apostolic Constitutions* can be ascertained from the work itself in which this statement appears. In ch. xiii. Bk. v., the birthday of Jesus is directed to be celebrated on the 25th December : this indicates the date as one subsequent to the institution of the festival of Christmas, which was either the close of the fourth or the beginning of the fifth century. Irenæus says nothing of Jesus' preference for John, though he twice refers to this passage of the Fourth Gospel (Bk. III. i. 1, and IV. xx. 11), but only mentions the leaning on Jesus' bosom at supper. I do not think the rule of Eusebius should be applied to this episode, for although the Synoptics describe the same scene, even if the passage under notice did not exist in full in the revised Fourth Gospel of the second century, there were some additional circumstances not found in the Synoptic narratives which justify its exemption from the operation of the rule.

I do not think the cock story is entitled to exemption from Eusebius' rule, as there is no additional circumstance mentioned in the narrative of this episode which is not found in the Synoptic Gospels. There is no reference to this story in Irenæus, Clement, nor Hippolytus. Tertullian in his treatise against Marcion (iv. 41) refers to the denial of Peter in a passage the meaning of which is not clear, but he makes no mention of the cock. Origen, in his *Commentary on Matthew* (xii. 40), alludes with precision to Peter's denial thrice before the 'well known cock-crowing,' but his reference is to the narrative in Matthew, not in the Fourth Gospel. The latter supplies no omission in the story as related in the Synoptics, and in fact it omits the penitent weeping of Peter, which Dr Martineau considers was an express omission to prejudice Peter. From the above facts I think it justifiable to assert that the cock story did not exist in the revised version of the Fourth Gospel in the second century. It is probable that the story was an acquisition of the third century, and was introduced or received currency in orthodox Christian literature at that period. It strikes me as very singular that we find no allusion to the cock-crowing story in Christian writings before the time of Origen (died 230 A.D.).

The beautiful discourses of Jesus after the last supper, with all their interpolations, were, I think, in the revised Fourth Gospel of the second century pretty much as they are to be found in it at the present day. There are indications here and there of rhetorical amplifications and additions being subsequently made in certain passages, and of changes in the position of certain clauses and verses, but I have not discovered any material accretions that had been superadded. The interpolations attracted more attention and discussion than the really beautiful language and thought of the original. The interpolation detailing the conversation between Philip and Jesus, in ch. xiv. 7-14, appears to have been a foolish, wanton, and unnecessary innovation, changing the current view of the relation between God the Father and Jesus. That relation had hitherto been nebulous, vague, and metaphysical; there was no clearness or precision in it, men were satisfied by describing him as the Son of God and the only begotten of God, the divine Word of God, and so on. The interpolation upset all this, and introduced precision where there had been indefiniteness; a bright light in place of the dim religious light that prevailed before. Suddenly the announcement is made that Jesus and the Father are identical; he who has seen the one has seen the other. This interpolation was as unwise as a similar interpolation in ch. i. 10 (in which Jesus is represented as the maker of the world), and apparently there was no need for it, as no sect or heretic held any faulty opinion on the subject that called for a remedy. It appears to me that there must have been some influential members of the revision committee who were fanatical, defective in judgment, and even knavish, who were bent on introducing their personal views into the sacred writings, regardless of the prevailing opinion. There are quotations of this interpolation in the writings of Irenæus, Hippolytus, and Tertullian, which do not quite correspond with the text of the Gospel, and thus may fairly be considered as giving ground for the suspicion that the latter had been trimmed, in order to tone down the original meaning. It is quite fair, however, to conclude that the sentences omitted in the quotations were not considered absolutely relevant to the subject, and were hence omitted as unnecessary. It is interesting to compare the quotations with the text of the Gospel as we now have it.

FOURTH GOSPEL.	IRENÆUS.	HIPPOLYTUS.	TERTULLIAN.
xiv. 7. If ye had known me, ye should have known my Father also; and from henceforth ye know him, and have seen him. 8. Philip saith unto him, Lord, show us the Father, and it sufficeth us. 9. Jesus saith unto him, Have I been so long time with you, and yet hast thou not known me, Philip? he that hath seen me hath seen the Father; and how sayest thou *then*, Show us the Father? 10. Believest thou not that I am in the Father and the Father in me? The words that I speak unto you I speak not of myself; but the Father that dwelleth in me, he doeth the works. 11. Believe me that I *am* in the Father, and the Father in me; or else believe me for the very works' sake.	(9) Have I been so long time with you, and yet thou hast not known me, Philip? He that sees me, sees also the Father; how sayest thou then, Show us the Father? (11) For I am in the Father, and the Father in me; and (7) henceforth ye know him and have seen him. (The above is given as a continuous passage.) (Bk. III. xiii. 2.)	Philip inquired about the Father, saying, "Show us the Father and it sufficeth us," to whom the Lord made answer in these terms: " Have I been so long time with you, and yet hast thou not known me, Philip? He that hath seen me hath seen the Father. Believest thou not that I am in the Father, and the Father in me?" (*Noetus*, 7.)	Have I been so long time with you, and yet hast thou not known me, Philip? He that hath seen me hath seen the Father. If ye had known me, ye would have known the Father also. Believest thou not that I am in the Father and the Father in me? The words which I speak unto you are not mine, but the Father that dwelleth in me doeth the works. (*Praxeas*, xxiv.) I and my Father are one (John x. 30; *Pr.*, xx.).

I am of opinion that the revision committee of the second century intended to inculcate by this interpolation that Jesus and the Father were one and the same; that, to quote their language, he who saw the one saw the other also; that Jesus and God the Father were identical. I take it that Irenæus

S

understood the passage in this sense, as the context of the quotation given above clearly indicates. Immediately before the quotation he speaks of those who saw God after the resurrection ("*qui Deum viderunt post resurrectionem*"), repeating this expression twice with the intention of giving emphasis to it. It is impossible to believe that Irenæus meant anything else by this expression than that Jesus was the physical or concrete God, if I may, with reverence, so express myself, who was visible to men. Immediately after the quotation he remarks that in that passage the Lord declared that in himself the disciples knew and saw the Father (" *Quibus ergo Dominus testimonium dixit, quoniam et cognoverunt in ipso et viderunt Patrem*"). All this was said by Irenæus, not as exegesis of the passage quoted, but as a theological argument, which he doubtless considered clinching, in refutation of the statement of Marcion that Paul only knew the truth (" *Solum Paulum veritatem cognovisse*"). Having said that Peter and others, like Paul, saw the risen God after the resurrection, and that the Lord had declared that he who saw him, saw and knew the Father, Irenæus added the finishing stroke of the argument, "*Pater autem veritas*," but the Father is the truth; *ergo* Peter and others knew the truth as well as Paul, and hence the Marcionites were refuted and rolled in the dust. Irenæus' argument is far-fetched; and I cannot believe that Philip's interpellation was introduced by the committee to supply the means of refuting Marcion. I attribute the interpolation to the mischievous desire of a majority of the committee to give currency and authority to a pious fad, and I think they were influenced in their action by the same feeling which has since burdened ecclesiastical religion with other fads of Swiss and German theologians, enriched though they are with great learning, and enforced with considerable rhetorical and argumentative skill.

This fad of the revision committee, that Jesus and the Father were identical, received an amplification and development which the committee did not expect. In the last quarter of the second century, towards its end probably, a strong and troublesome sect arose called Patripassians, who held the strange doctrine, founded on the above passage of the Fourth Gospel, xiv. 7-11, that God the Father entered the womb of the Virgin Mary, was born as Jesus, lived on earth, and was crucified, died, was buried, and experienced the other phases of being according to the ecclesiastical faith. This interpolation introduced into the Fourth Gospel practically upset the view that hitherto prevailed, that God the Father and Jesus were not the same, but distinct beings; but, as ecclesiastical opinion gradually aggrandised the divine nature of Jesus, and finally culminated in attributing godhead to him, the only way of avoiding polytheism, and of maintaining the unity of God, was to coalesce the Father with Jesus and to make one individuality of the two. Doubtless there may have been a metaphysical conception of this union in the minds of the committee, which I confess my inability to grasp and express in words, and which in the same manner was beyond the competency of the Patripassians. The sect took rise in Asia Minor, but prominent members of it spread the doctrine to Rome and to other parts of the world. Tertullian wrote a refutation addressed to Praxeas, and Hippolytus another addressed to Noetus, both advanced Patripassians. These treatises are translated in the Ante-Nicene Christian Library, where the reader may perceive for himself the quality of the arguments employed against the sect. The Church got much more than it bargained for when it introduced Philip's interpellation and its response into the revised Fourth Gospel. The sect must have been very influential at the start, as probably three bishops of Rome, or popes, but certainly two, were members of it. These popes (Victor, Zephyrinus, and Callistus) were remarkable for violence of temper, folly and feebleness, and knavery respectively. The character of the last, Callistus, as given by Hippolytus, himself a bishop, is one to be pondered. After describing his disreputable career, which, however, culminated in his being elected Bishop of Rome, he abuses him roundly: calling him a senseless and knavish fellow, a blasphemer, one guilty of scandalous conduct, who gave a religious sanction to the sensual indulgences of unmarried females, and so on.[1]

---

[1] *Refutation of all Heresies*, Ante-Nicene Christian Library, ix. 6 and 7; Miller, ix. 11 and 12.

One is reminded of the account given by Lucian of Peregrinus Proteus, who attained a great reputation as a local Christian leader. Such men as Peregrinus and Callistus, clever rogues, were doubtless sufficiently numerous in the second century amongst Christians, and acquired influence amongst them. To such men I attribute the introduction into the sacred writings of much that is most objectionable in them.

It seems to me that theologians shirk the discussion of Philip's interpellation and its response. They say as little about it as they possibly can. Bishop Westcott's comments on these verses, 8–11, are very curt. The chief clause, " he that hath seen me hath seen the Father," he thus briefly comments upon : "hath seen not God in his absolute being (i. 18), but God revealed in this relation." What the expression " God revealed in this relation " means is not apparent. He refers to chaps. xii. 45 and xv. 24. Both these verses I have excised as interpolations; they being obviously put in to support this response to Philip: the latter verse (xv. 24) implies that not only the disciples or followers of Jesus, but even his enemies, had " both seen and hated both me [*i.e.*, Jesus] and my Father." Bishop Westcott adds the following separate short paragraph to the comment already quoted : " The words give for all time a definiteness to the object of religious faith; and it is impossible to mistake the claim which they express." I must confess my inability to understand the first clause; and as to the second, regarding mistaking the claim, I may perhaps refer to the troublesome sect of the Patripassians, supported by popes of Rome, and to the sects that emanated from them, and inquire, Did these sects 'mistake the claim,' and how then can it be consistent with history to speak of the impossibility of mistake?[1] The statement, " he that hath

[1] I can hardly think that Bishop Westcott would not regard the view taken of this passage, ch. xiv. 7–11, by Dr Arnold of Rugby as a mistake, viz., that it abrogated the second commandment. Dr Arnold says, "God has sanctioned one conceivable similitude of himself, when he declared himself in the person of Christ" : hence he concluded, "the second commandment is in the letter utterly done away with by the fact of the Incarnation" (Stanley's *Life of Arnold*, 7th ed., p. 244, Letter XLII. to

seen me hath seen the Father," is of so incredible a nature that some minds, as devout and learned as the commentator's, cannot take it in. Bishop Walsham How, in covert but transparent language, says that he cannot understand it, but devoutly hopes to be able to understand it in the next world! His exact words, in his remarks on this passage in his commentary on the Fourth Gospel, are the following: "The human mind as yet sees 'through a glass darkly' (1 Cor. xiii. 12), and the truths here revealed are heavenly mysteries. We profess not to measure and fathom them now. We hope some day to know even as we are known." I regret to repeat here the remark that I have often made elsewhere, that it is pitiable that the sad circumstances of their position constrain learned and amiable prelates of the Church to treat as divine utterances the base, and in this instance irreverent, interpolations of knaves and rogues, made in the dark age of the second century.

I am not satisfied that the incident related in ch. xix. 25-27, in which Jesus on the cross delivers his mother into the guardianship of the beloved disciple, existed in the revised Gospel in the second century. It is so strikingly pathetic, and so important in its bearings, that we would naturally expect it to be noticed by theological writers. Nevertheless it is not referred to by Irenæus, Clement, Hippolytus, and Tertullian, and we do not meet with it until we come to the third decade of the third century, in Origen's *Commentary on the Fourth Gospel*. In this work the incident is alluded to in the preface or preliminary remarks and not in the body of the *Commentary*, and it is not introduced as a quotation from the Fourth Gospel, nor is any reference made to the circumstances under which it occurred. The mere reception from Jesus of Mary to be his mother, and the saying of Jesus, "Woman, behold thy son," are brought in to aggrandise the value and importance of the Gospel and of the writer. Origen, in a spirit of exaggeration not habitual with him in speaking of

---

W. W. Hull, Esq.; see also Arnold's *Sermons*, vol. ii. p. 439 ff., and vol. iii. p. 40 ff.). I have not met with any other modern view of the passage. As I remark in the text, divines now shirk the passage, a reprehensible one in my humble judgment.

the *facts* in the sacred biography, says that the saying of Jesus amounted to the identifying of the beloved disciple to himself as if Jesus virtually said to his mother, " Lo, this is Jesus, whom thou didst bear." We hear no more of the incident till we come to the era when our various codices of the Gospels date, perhaps for a period of a hundred and fifty years or longer. There is no mention of the incident in the *Divine Institutes* of Lactantius, not even in the *Apostolic Constitutions*, although both these works give accounts of the crucifixion. I need hardly refer to the absence of the incident in the Synoptic Gospels, for the rule of Eusebius applies; but it is important to note that there are statements made in the Synoptics which are incompatible with the incident. In the Fourth Gospel four women are said to have been standing at the foot of the cross, viz., Mary the mother of Jesus and her sister, Mary the wife of Cleophas, and Mary Magdalene (xix. 25). In Matthew xxvii. 55 and 56, it is stated that many women, who had followed Jesus from Galilee, were at the crucifixion 'beholding afar off,' and of these are mentioned Mary Magdalene, Mary the mother of James and Joses, and the mother of Zebedee's children: Mary the mother of Jesus being omitted. In Mark xv. 40, of the women 'looking on afar off' are named Mary Magdalene, Mary the mother of James the Less and of Joses, and Salome. In Luke xxiii. 49 it is explicitly stated that 'all his acquaintance, and the women that followed him from Galilee, stood afar off, beholding" the crucifixion. With the exception of this incident, and a presumptive interpolation in Acts i. 14, Mary disappears from the evangelical narratives at the same time as her husband Joseph, and but for this incident and interpolation, the theological explanation of the disappearance of Joseph would apply to Mary, namely, that she had been removed by death. From the above considerations I am disposed to believe that Origen obtained his knowledge of the incident not from the Fourth Gospel, but from an apocryphal gospel. In his age the apocryphal gospels had not quite lost their authority, and they were even quoted as scripture by some contemporary writers. The apocryphal gospel of Nicodemus, or *Acta Pilati*, already referred to in this work, is the only one in which I find the story of Mary at the crucifixion. It is to be found in Tischendorf's second Greek form of the *Acts of Pilate*, and this may have been the source from which Origen obtained his information (see translation in Ante-Nicene Christian Library, *Apocryphal Gospels*, p. 159). This apocryphal gospel is quoted both by Justin and Tertullian, the latter a contemporary of Origen. I have further to remark that the apocryphal version of the incident is not so pathetic or simple as the version of the Fourth Gospel, in which skilled revision is apparent; but the latter, unfortunately, has imitated and repeated the unnatural and unfilial expression of 'woman,' which the apocryphal gospel does not employ. The interpolator of this incident manifestly considered himself bound to imitate the rude and unbecoming language put into the mouth of Jesus by the narrator of the miracle of Cana; whereas the apocryphal chronicler followed the usage of eastern people, and avoided the employment of an unfilial expression. For these reasons I am inclined to regard the apocryphal story as the original.

The exciting incident of the foot-race between Simon Peter and the disciple whom Jesus loved, described in ch. xx. 2-10, does not appear to have caused the least interest in the second and third centuries amongst the writers whose works have survived to our days. Irenæus, Clement, Hippolytus, Tertullian, Origen, Lactantius, and others are silent on the subject, so that a doubt is cast upon the existence of this passage in the revised version of the Fourth Gospel in the second century. The story is also inconsistent with the well-known modesty of the beloved disciple, a modesty usually characterised by theologians as 'incomparable.' The beloved disciple, in the course of the narrative, describes himself as the winner of the race in a marked manner, his words being "the other disciple did outrun Peter." Is it conceivable that the possessor of 'incomparable modesty' could have opposed the instinct of his nature by recording so insignificant a theological fact, the omission of which would not have rendered the Fourth Gospel a penny the worse?

Just the opposite remark is due to the passage (verse 17) in which the ascension of Jesus is spoken of, for, instead of creating no interest and no notice, it has been quoted by writer after writer. After the resurrection, Mary Magdalene encounters Jesus in the garden, and, on recognising him, after first having mistaken him for the gardener, Jesus says to her, "Touch me not; for I am not yet ascended to my Father: but go to my brethren, and say unto them, I ascend unto my Father, and your Father; and *to* my God, and your God." The passage was in the second century of immense theological importance, for it is one in which the Lord himself bears testimony to his ascension. I have already in a former part of this treatise spoken of some bearings of the ascension of Jesus (*ante*, p. 199); and this appears to be a proper place in which to speak of other aspects of the subject. The human and material body of Jesus was an embarrassment to second century theologians when the divinity of Jesus was inculcated and generally accepted. Prophecy gave material aid to the idea of the immaculate conception, and the obscurity of the early history of Jesus covered the miracle of his divine birth. Jesus came into the world as the offspring of the deity and a virgin, according to the orthodox theologian, and grew up to adult life, when he became known to his disciples. This view, if we are to give credit to Tertullian's representation, was rejected by Marcion, whose devout and valiant mind found comfort in believing that Jesus came down direct from heaven, a mature individual, with a weight of perhaps 150–200 pounds (for the Palestinian Jews were sturdy and robust folk), and first set foot upon earth at Capernaum, in the fifteenth year of the reign of Tiberius Cæsar, as set forth in the Third Gospel (ch. iii. 1, iv. 31). This religious view of the advent of the Redeemer (which is stated on the authority of Tertullian) was able to maintain its ground for upwards of four centuries amongst a powerful Christian sect, formidable to the Mother Church, from the numbers, piety, and talents of its members. I am unaware whether Marcion and his followers devoted any thought to the mundane and perhaps secondary subject of the clothing and shoeing of the descending divine being, a subject which it is obvious had no need to be considered by the Mother Church at the birth of the infant saviour. I am also unaware how Marcion and his followers accounted for the disappearance of Jesus from earth. It will be readily understood by all thinking persons that though the introduction of Jesus upon earth was rendered easy by the practical application of prophecy, the removal from earth of his solid human body was a serious embarrassment to the orthodox Church of the second century, as pointed out by Dr Martineau. The ordinary mode in which human beings made their way to a higher sphere was unworthy and unsuited to a divine personage; and prophecy further gave no support to this ordinary mode of exit as it did to the ordinary mode of entrance to this world. Prophecy, indeed, was not altogether silent on the subject, for David had ecstatically exclaimed, "The Lord said unto my Lord, Sit thou at my right hand" (Ps. cx. 1); but there prophecy halted and failed to give information as to the mode of transit of the Lord from earth to this sublime and lofty position. Wanting this great guide to important incidents in the biography of Jesus, of which the theologians of the second century had availed themselves in the chronological order in which suitable prophecies were discovered, the theologians of the Mother Church were thrown upon their own resources. I believe no chronicler or theologian, orthodox or otherwise, before the fourth century, possessed authoritative and authentic information that Jesus ascended bodily to heaven. I find no trace of it in the authentic Christian literature of the first hundred and fifty years of the Christian era. Neither Paul, nor Peter, nor James, nor the writers of the various epistles commonly attributed to Paul, show the least consciousness of the knowledge. It is manifest that in such a weighty matter as the ascent of a solid human body weighing 150–200 pounds, an express statement is necessary to intimate that the knowledge of such ascent was possessed. Such expressions as "at the right hand of God" (Rom. viii. 34), even when there is no suspicion of interpolation, are insufficient proof of such knowledge. Nor even are such expressions as "hath highly exalted him" (Phil. ii. 9), "ascended up on high" (Eph. iv. 8), "received up into glory" (1 Tim. iii. 16), "passed into the heavens" (Heb. iv. 14), "gone into heaven" (1 Pet. iii. 22), to be taken as indicating the possession of such knowledge. The ordinary reader has, no doubt, with the usual preconceptions of the modern Christian, always understood these expressions to mean the body ascension of Jesus. But from my point of view a more explicit statement is imperative, especially as I am unable to find anywhere a single explicit authoritative statement on the subject before the fourth century. There is no objection to these expressions above quoted being understood to mean that Jesus went up or ascended to heaven in the sense in which any pious person is said to go to heaven, or to be taken up to God, leaving his body behind. Indeed, there is proof that it is in this sense only that the writers employed the expressions, for there are passages in which similar expressions are employed of the saints; thus, in Eph. ii. 6, it is said God "hath raised *us* up together, and made *us* sit together in heavenly *places* in Christ Jesus," words which exactly correspond to, and must be taken to mean the same as, the words which precede them by a few lines, where the same writer speaks of the mighty power of God, "which he wrought in Christ, when he raised him from the dead, and set *him* at his own right hand in the heavenly *places*" (Eph. ii. 20). There are two passages in the New Testament, which, although they are in my judgment interpolations made in the interests of a grotesque dogma, will serve as illustrations of my contention, viz., Eph. iv. 9 and 1 Peter iii. 19 and 20. In these passages Jesus is represented during the interval between his death on the cross and his resurrection to have "descended first into the lower parts of the earth" (Eph.), and "went and preached unto the spirits in prison" (Peter). Modern theologians, or some of them, show a strong disinclination to accept these passages as the basis of the clause in the ecclesiastical code of faith that Jesus descended into hell, of which it is very probable a good many of them are ashamed.[1] I am

---

[1] The dogma of the descent of Jesus to hell during the interval between his death on the cross and his resurrection—a very difficult enterprise for the mind to realise—was supposed to be derived from an Old Testament prophecy by second century theologians. Justin Martyr and Irenæus quote the prophecy, but they seem undecided whether Jeremiah or Isaiah uttered it. Justin thus quotes it: "The Lord God remembered his dead people of Israel who lay in their graves; and he descended to preach to

unaware that any theologian, ancient or modern, inculcated the information that in this descent to the nether regions Jesus took his body with him. Speaking for myself, as a member of the Church of England who had been duly instructed and confirmed in the ecclesiastical faith, this item of instruction had never been taught me. If these two passages are to be understood as stating that Jesus descended into hell, leaving his body behind him, the other passages in the New Testament in which Jesus is spoken of as ascended to heaven must be understood in the same sense as leaving his body on earth, unless an explicit and authoritative statement to the contrary is made, and this explicit statement in every instance is wanting.

In the writings of the Fathers of the first half of the second century we find no explicit statement of the mode of ascension, though the ascension of Jesus is alluded to by most of them. Here I should give a warning with regard to the epistles of Ignatius ; in the longer Epistle to the Smyrnans, ch. iii., Acts i. 11 is quoted, showing that the writer knew of the bodily ascension ; but this information does not exist in the shorter recension. Both these readings are of doubtful authenticity, but the former is absolutely rejected. The ascension is alluded to in the Epistle to Barnabas, ch. xv., as having occurred on the 'eighth day' or Sunday, the same day

them his own salvation," and names Jeremiah (*Trypho*, ch. lxxii.). Irenæus quotes it repeatedly, with some changes of expression, thus : "And the holy Lord remembered his dead Israel, who had slept in the land of sepulture ; and he came down to preach his salvation to them, that he might save them" (*Adv. Her.*, iii. 4), and names Isaiah ; but in IV. xxii. 1 he names Jeremiah. Other passages in Irenæus are IV. xxxiii. 1 and 12 ; V. xxxi. 1. But alas, and alas ! this prophecy is not to be found in our Bible, nor in any Jewish Targum, nor any document known in these days. Its source was probably some sectarian gospel of the second century, now lost. The need for fresh supports of this dogma was urgent, and hence arose the interpolations quoted in the text of the Epistle to the Ephesians and of 1st Peter. This position of the dogma of the descent to hell must surely be known to the clergy ; but they abstain from communicating facts of this nature to the laity. A prophecy was discovered subsequently to support the dogma, viz., Psalms xvi. 8-10 (see Pearson on the Creed). Irenæus found a subsidiary prophecy (Ps. lxxxvi. 13), which is quite as good as Pearson's ; but the second century Father did not count upon it much, but preferred the not-to-be-found-in-our-Bible prophecy. Irenæus quotes the Ephesian interpolation (Bk. V. xxxi. 1).

on which Jesus rose from the dead, as is narrated in the Third Gospel. These two separate accounts of the early 'ascension' of Jesus give me the idea of early death after the resuscitation from the condition of collapse, rather than of bodily ascension. Justin Martyr is full of allusions to the ascension of Jesus both in his *Apology* and in his *Dialogue with Trypho*; but nowhere does he give any hint of the mode of ascension (*First Apology*, 21, 31, 42, 45, 46; *Trypho*, 38, 45, 108), which I think would not have been the case if this garrulous Father had the knowledge of a bodily ascension. I believe I am fully justified in concluding, from the absence of a specific statement to the contrary, that these early writers believed that the transfer of Jesus to heaven was performed in the ordinary way by somatic death. The Greek verb employed, which has been translated by the word 'ascend' by clerical translators, was almost invariably ἀνέρχομαι, which, as applied to human locomotion, did not imply the idea of *ascension* or *rising into the air*. Justin in all the passages uses this verb, and in one passage (*First Apology*, xlv.), ἀγαγεῖν or ἀναγεῖν, and only in one passage, in which Trypho the Jew is the interlocutor (ch. xxxviii.), is the verb ἀναβαίνω employed. The word ἀνέρχομαι ought not to be understood to imply anything more than *going up* to a place, just as we say 'going up to town' or 'going up to the 'varsity': just as in the converse sense κατέρχομαι implies only the meaning of 'going down to the country,' or the usual university phrase of 'going down'; not of descent down a pit or mine, for which the word καταβαίνω would be appropriate. I have already spoken of an obscure passage in the Epistles of Paul (2 Cor. v. 15-17), where he appears to account for the disappearance of Christ 'after the flesh,' in which there is no trace to be found of an ascension or floating up to heaven through the atmosphere. Paul openly declared his belief in the immortality of Jesus on earth: and so perhaps did Ignatius, as I have previously pointed out (see *ante*, p. 200). It is a strange coincidence that the latter writer, like Paul, was embarrassed by the disappearance of Jesus; for in the Ignatian Epistle to the Ephesians (ch. xix.) he speaks of 'three mysteries of the Shout,' or as Dr Lightfoot translates, 'three mysteries to be cried aloud,' τρία μυστήρια κραυγῆς, which he specifies to be (α) the virginity, (β) the pregnancy of Mary, and (γ) the death of the Lord. These three mysteries were so secret that they were "hidden from the prince of the world," *i.e.*, I suppose, the devil or Satan, being wrought "in the silence of God." The virginity and pregnancy of Mary were without doubt evangelical mysteries, but the 'death of the Lord' on the cross was no evangelical mystery, but was known to the devil and the public, and was openly and not secretly or silently wrought by God. The real mystery was the death of the Lord subsequent to the crucifixion and resurrection, of which nobody had given an account. Ignatius would not have spoken of the mysterious death of the Lord if he had known the story in Acts i. 9–11 of the bodily ascension of the latter to heaven. James, the reputed brother of Jesus, but more probably only a disciple, makes a direct allusion to the death of the Lord (v. 10, 11). Inculcating the duty of patience, he gives the prophets as examples of suffering affliction and patience, ultimately rewarded for endurance by a pitiful God; and mentions the 'patience of Job,' and 'the end of the Lord,' which latter he says 'you have seen.' The idea communicated to me by the language employed is that the Lord, after his heavy afflictions, ended his days happily, a consummation for which I doubt not all good men and women will rejoice. Eusebius in his *Ecclesiastical History*, iv. 3, speaks of the *Apology* of Quadratus (A.D. 123–125), and gives a quotation from it, in which the apologist speaks of people who had been healed and raised from the dead by the Lord; and of these people he says, "οὐδὲ ἐπιδημοῦντος μόνον τοῦ Σωτῆρος τοῦ Σωτῆρος, ἀλλὰ καὶ ἀπαλλαγέντος, ἦσαν ἐπὶ χρόνον ἱκανόν." Clerical translators have misunderstood and mistranslated this passage unconsciously under the influence of preconceived notions. In Bohn's Ecclesiastical Library (Rev. C. F. Crusé, A.M.) this passage is rendered: "they remained living a long time, not only while our Lord was on earth, but likewise when he had left the earth." Bishop Westcott translates: "not only while the Saviour sojourned on earth, but also after his departure for a considerable time" (*Canon of the New Testament*, 5th ed., pp. 84–86). These renderings are of a neutral nature, *i.e.*, they are compatible with the ideas of 'ascension' or of natural death. In the mind of the modern Christian reader the idea of 'ascension' would, from the very fact of his education and preconceived notions, be associated with the statement of the 'leaving' or 'departure' of the Lord; but such an association would never arise in the mind of a Turkish or Japanese reader, who was unacquainted with Christian mythology: but rather the idea of natural death. I submit it to the judgment of any Greek scholar, whether the latter was not the sense in which the writer Quadratus used the word ἀπαλλαγέντος. The Greek verb ἀπαλλάσσομαι does not imply 'ascension,' but it does mean 'departure from life or decease' in the passage above quoted and nothing else. Quadratus' meaning was that the people who had been healed and raised from the dead by our Lord remained living not only while our Lord was dwelling on earth, but also after his death. Quadratus had not the information of the bodily ascension of Jesus, invented later on as Christian knowledge extended.

A careful study of the surviving writings of Christian authors subsequent to Justin Martyr justifies me in making the statement that the ascension of Jesus, as a precise elevation of his body from earth to heaven, was not authentically known, and was not a dogma of the Church, before the fourth century. A palpable progress in Christian thought beyond the stage arrived at by theologians of the first half of the second century is noticeable in the Ante-Nicene writers. The expressions used more distinctly convey the idea of ascension than the words ordinarily employed by apostolic and sub-apostolic writers. The Greek verb ἀναβαίνω takes the place of ἀνέρχομαι, and the Latin word *ascendo* is in common use, as well as such expressions as assumption, taken up, carried up, etc. Tertullian, a bold thinker and speculator, uncompromisingly maintained that the earthly body of Jesus was transferred to heaven, in his argumentative treatise on the *Resurrection of the Flesh* (ch. li.). "*Cum illic adhuc sedeat Jesus ad dextram Patris; homo, etsi Deus; Adam novissimus, etsi Sermo primarius; caro et sanguis, etsi nostris puriora, idem tamen et substantia et forma qua ascendit, talis etiam descensurus, ut Angeli affirmant; agnoscendus scilicet eis qui illum convulnaverunt."* Jesus is sitting there now at the right hand of the Father; man although God; the last Adam although the primary Word; flesh and blood, although purer than ours, yet the same both in substance and form in which he ascended, such also as he will descend, as the angels affirm, so that he should be known to those who have wounded him. Tertullian had no authority in the sacred writings, the Gospels and Hebrew Scriptures, for any of these statements, except the first; they were statements peculiar to him, and they are not used by his contemporaries or successors till after the fourth century, when the dogma of the bodily ascension of Jesus was fully established. But, distinct and definite as are these affirmations of Tertullian, he stopped short of the mode of transfer of the body of Jesus from earth to heaven. On this point there was no authentic information in that early age, no prophecy having been yet discovered that could throw light upon the subject. Lactantius was the first to announce the prophecy, which indicated the mode of the bodily ascension of Jesus by the agency of a cloud. A writer who had made a substantial addition to Christian knowledge deserves an extended notice, which I shall epitomise from the preface written by William Fletcher, D.D., Headmaster of Queen Elizabeth's School, Wimborne, Dorset, to his translation of the writings of Lactantius in the Ante-Nicene Christian Library. This learned divine describes our author and theological discoverer as a teacher of rhetoric of great eminence, who was invited by the Emperor Diocletian to settle at Nicomedia, and to practise his profession of pleader at the imperial city, instead of in proconsular Africa. He, however, attained no success under royal patronage, from causes which are not stated, and fell into penury; and "it was probably at this period that he embraced the Christian faith, and we may perhaps be justified in supposing some connection between his poverty and his change of religion." With his religion he changed his profession, and devoted his talents to literary composition, chiefly dissertations on ecclesiastical subjects. The style of Lactantius was characterised by dignity, elegance, and clearness of expression, and gained for him the appellation of the Christian Cicero. His writings give evidence of varied and extensive erudition. But his claims as a theologian are open to question, and he has been charged (undeservedly) with a leaning to Manicheism. Notwithstanding this, however, he was of sufficient reputation to be invited to settle in Gaul, *c.* 315 A.D., by the Emperor Constantine, who intrusted him with the education of his son Crispus. His principal work was *The Divine Institutes*, and in this great composition he devoted a chapter to the elucidation of 'the three mysteries of the Shout,' as Ignatius styled the subjects of the virginity and child-bearing of Mary, and the ' departure of the Lord from earth.' To the discussion of these subjects he brought a mind richly stored with facts of natural science, chiefly of comparative physiology,[1] and overflowing with an exuberance of knowledge of prophecy. Lactantius obviously regarded the third mystery as outside the domain of natural science, as he does not apply to it the scientific knowledge which he brought to bear on the subject of the virginity and child-bearing of Mary. Lactantius quotes Daniel vii. 13 and 14: "I saw in a vision of the night, and,

[1] The impregnation of a virgin by the Spirit of God seemed to the scientific mind of Lactantius a very simple affair, like the falling of a stone from a height. Why should any one think it wonderful, he exclaims, since it is well known that certain animals are accustomed to conceive by the wind and the breeze? The learned translator corroborates Lactantius' remark by a quotation from Virgil, and the observation that "the theory of the impregnation of mares by the wind was general amongst the ancients." I may add, on the authority of Origen, that vultures propagate their species in a similar way; and, on the authority of the Rev. Charles Gore, M.A., in his Bampton Lectures for 1891, on "The Incarnation of the Son of God" (note 15, page 246), that 'virgin procreation' is an ordinary phenomenon for the naturalist, according to the late Professor Huxley. This subject, in itself simple, was rendered still more credible by prophecy, and Lactantius quotes Solomon, thus: "The womb of a virgin was strengthened and conceived; and a virgin was impregnated, and became a mother in great pity." The learned translator says in a footnote: "This passage does not occur in the writings of Solomon or in the Old Testament." Lactantius, however, also quotes the conventional prophecy.

Since writing the above, I have ascertained that Tertullian added to the store of scientific fact that the domestic hen was "able to bring forth by her own energy," and, further, that among vultures there are only females, which become parents alone (*Adv. Valentinianos*, ch. x.). Theologians eagerly avail themselves of the resources of natural science.

behold, one like the Son of man coming with the clouds of heaven, and he came even to the Ancient of days, and they brought him near before him. And there was given unto him a kingdom, and glory and dominion; and all people, tribes and languages shall serve him: and his dominion is everlasting, which shall never pass away, and his kingdom shall not be destroyed." From this prophetic revelation Lactantius drew the corollary that after the resurrection Jesus proceeded to the Father borne aloft on a cloud (*Divine Institutes* of Lactantius, iv. 12). This induction of Lactantius is the source of all subsequent Christian knowledge on the ascension of Christ. I desire to lay stress upon the importance of this fact. In none of the four Gospels is the information to be found that Jesus was borne aloft on a cloud. In Matthew there is no statement on the subject of the ascension, which is left undetermined. In Mark the narrative terminates at the resurrection; the conclusion from verse 9 of ch. xvi. is an addition made subsequently to the first quarter of the fourth century; the statement in verse 19 that "he was received up into heaven" is indefinite. In Luke xxiv. 51 and 52 is a vague statement, having an air of precision: "he was parted from them, and carried up into heaven. And they worshipped him." Unfortunately, these clauses are spurious, and were added subsequently to the first quarter of the fourth century. The Revised Version states in the margin that some ancient authorities omit them. Bishop Ellicott says of the first clause that it is wanting "in some of the best MSS.," and of the second that it is "absent from most of the best MSS." Bishop Westcott and his colleague, Dr Hort, admit the absence of these clauses from the MSS. which they specify; they call them 'Western Non-interpolations,' and say apologetically that "the ascension apparently did not lie within the proper scope of the Gospel, as seen in their genuine texts; its true place was at the head of the Acts of the Apostles,[1] as the preparation for the Day of Pentecost, and thus the beginning

---

[1] If the reader will refer to Acts i. 2, he will see that the writer distinctly says that his former treatise comprised the statement of the ascension, the additional information on the subject which he proceeds to set forth being supplemental to his former treatise.

of the history of the Church" (*The New Testament in the Original Greek. Notes on Select Readings*, p. 72). This apology is partially plausible; it may account for the absence of the ascension in the Gospels, but it cannot account for the absence of authoritative information regarding the ascension in Christian literature for three centuries, and the latter omission is as important and necessary to account for as the former. It is clear from this thoughtful defence of the omission in the Gospels of a theological fact in the sacred biography now held as orthodox, but not so held in the early centuries, that Bishop Westcott was unaware that the bodily ascension of Jesus in a cloud was without authority during the first three centuries of Christianity. There is not a trace of this authority in the Christian literature extant prior to Lactantius.

With all deference to Bishop Westcott and his learned and lamented colleague, I differ in opinion from them, for my own investigations constrain me to conclude that the subject of the ascension was left open and undecided in the Gospels from the dearth of authority, no prophecy having been discovered in the second half of the second century to be a guide to the nature of the ascension. It lay within the proper scope of the compilers of the Gospels to narrate the death or departure from earth of the subject of their biography. In all biographies written in ancient times, an account of the death of the subjects was included. The lives of Plutarch and Cornelius Nepos, of the Hebrew judges, kings, and prophets, were before the evangelists as models—in all these the deaths of their illustrious subjects are described whenever known. With their scanty materials the Gospels make a great show of embracing much. Two of them trace the genealogy of Jesus to David and Adam, with a pretentious precision only equalled by the Gaelic biographies which trace the descent of Irish heroes to Pharaoh, King of Egypt. In the same two Gospels the compilers are not content with commencing their narrative from the birth of their subject, as is the custom of writers, but they go back to his conception in the womb, having in this particular detail of biography but a single competitor in the history of literature.[1] With

[1] Smollett.

such pretensions as these in the beginning of their narratives, it is not right to declare that the evangelists conceived the nature of their vocation restrained them from recording the departure of the Lord from the scene of his earthly ministry.

I am of opinion that the account of the Ascension in Acts i. 9-11 was an addition introduced into the sacred text subsequent to the publication of the *Divine Institutes* of Lactantius in the first quarter of the fourth century. Previous to this period I can discover only two writers who seemingly quote the passage above indicated. Tertullian appears to refer to it in the passage I have already quoted from ch. li. of *De Resurrectione Carnis*, and again in ch. xxii. of the same treatise, thus, " *Quis cælo descendentem Jesum talem conspexit, qualem ascendentem Apostoli viderant, secundum Angelorum constitutum?*" Who has seen Jesus descending from heaven just as the Apostles *saw him* ascending, according to the agreement, or ordinance, or appointment of the angels? The sense of the word '*constitutum*' is indefinite from the absence of the context of the original passage referred to. A third seeming allusion is found in Tertullian's *Treatise on Baptism*, ch. xix., " . . . . *tunc in cælos recuperato eo. Angeli ad Apostolos dixerunt sic venturum quemadmodum et in cælos conscendit, utique in Pentecoste.*" " . . . . he being then received into the heavens. The angels said to the Apostles that he would come just as he also ascended to the heavens, of course at Pentecost." I am unable to persuade myself that these three allusions to the ascension were taken from Acts i. 9-11. One meets with the same puzzle here as in the quotation from the sacred writings found in Justin Martyr and the Apostolic Fathers; they bear a strong resemblance to, but they are not the same as, the reputed original. Tertullian speaks of Jesus descending the *same in substance and form*, which perhaps may be taken by some as an amplication of the words in the Acts translated 'this same Jesus,' but the word *same* has no corresponding word in the original Greek text; but the clear intention in the Acts is to show sameness not of substance, but of manner, οὕτως. In the three passages Tertullian speaks of angels, but there is no word of angels in the Acts, but of "two men in white apparel," who may perhaps be regarded as angels; but it is singular that Tertullian should not have specified the number, which is strictly limited in the Acts. If the passage in the Acts was the source of Tertullian's reference, the words '*Angelorum constitutum*' should have found the context needed for the proper sense of the latter word, but such explanatory context is not to be found. Nor is any light thrown upon the puzzling words 'of course at Pentecost.' What connection there is between the Ascension and Pentecost is not to be found in the narrative of the ascension in the Acts. Modern Christians, whose information is restricted to the four Gospels and the Acts, do not know that Jesus ascended or descended at Pentecost. Further, Tertullian speaks of the Apostles alone having witnessed the ascension, and of the angels having addressed the Apostles only—nothing is said of other people. In the Acts the 'two men in white apparel' address 'ye men of Galilee,' which, in my judgment, is not appropriate to the Apostles, who were not all from Galilee, but was meant for the followers generally who were present. It would indeed be an odd way of addressing a select limited body like the Apostles. Tertullian adds a remark, which is not to be found in the Acts, viz., that the object of Jesus in descending in the same substance and form in which he ascended, was that he may be recognised and identified by his aggressors. All these discrepancies and difficulties constrain me to conclude that the narrative in the Acts was not the story to which Tertullian was indebted. But the family likeness between these passages induces me to think that the same source supplied Tertullian and the writer of the narrative of the ascension in the Acts; and that source was probably some Apocryphal Gospel in which the story of the ascension was in the formative stage, and contained much more theological information regarding the angels, the Apostles and disciples, and something new about Pentecost, which was not thought prudent to introduce into the account in the Acts.

It was this Apocryphal Gospel that was probably utilised by the pseudo-Ignatius in the long recension of the Epistle to the Smyrnæans, ch. iii., for he also makes the statement that the object of Jesus in descending at the end of the world with the same body was that he may be seen and recognised by those who pierced him. Acts i. 11 is accurately quoted according to the Syriac MS., translated in the Ante-Nicene Christian Library, but the source is said to be 'the Oracles,' a form of expression common in the first century, and perhaps in the early years of the second century, employed to be in keeping with the assumed character, but inapplicable to the Acts, because not used after the second half of the second century in referring to the sacred writings, but may be appropriate to an Apocryphal Gospel.

The reader will have remarked, in the course of this treatise, the power of prophecy over the minds of Christians during the first and second centuries. To Paul, every great incident in the life of Jesus was according to the Scriptures; and according to Justin Martyr, a great prophecy-monger, Jesus hardly moved a step that had not been foretold by the Hebrew prophets. But here we have a remarkable incident, the return of the Redeemer to heaven in the bosom of a cloud, related in a sacred Scripture without any intimation that this sublime movement had been predicted by the prophets of old. This omission *per se* stamps the narrative as of a late day, *i.e.*, subsequent to the second century, when the Acts of the Apostles were published, and as an after accretion to this work. The three verses, 9–11, of the first chapter of the Acts are parenthetical. Their presence adds to the theological information, and their absence decreases the theological information, to be derived from the chapter; but the continuity of the narrative is not interfered with either by their presence or absence. Their absence will merely leave the aggregate of evangelical information in much the same condition in which it was at the conclusion of the Gospel narratives of Matthew and Luke, where the story stops abruptly after the final address of Jesus, and no further information regarding his future doings is given. As the Acts and Gospels were simultaneous, or nearly simultaneous, in publication in the second half of the second century, the presumption certainly is in favour of the amount of theological information on the evangelical history being pretty much on a par in both. The additional information regarding Jesus, contained in the first chapter of the Acts really consists of two parenthetical passages, one a parenthetical clause in verse 3, "being seen of them forty days," and the other verses 9–11; both passages may be justifiably regarded as subsequent interpolations. Irenæus did not know of the Saviour's sojourn on earth of forty days after the resurrection (*Ad Her.*, Bk. v. xxxi. 2). Of these two interpolations, verse 3 was prior to verses 9–11. I also suspect that the larger passage is a double interpolation, that is to say, that it consists of probably two distinct interpolations made at different periods, viz., the clause, "and a cloud received him out of their sight,"[1] being subsequent to the rest of the passage, and derived from a different source. This clause was, I think, derived from Lactantius, who founded it on the prophecy of Daniel, while the rest of the passage was derived from an Apocryphal Gospel that has not survived to our days. The omission of the prophecy is most remarkable in the Acts, in which book very considerable importance is attached to prophecy, and possibly may be due partly to the cause already suggested, viz., that the addition was made at a later period, when less importance was attached to prophecy, and partly, perhaps, to an opinion that the prophecy quoted by Lactantius was not quite satisfactory and not quite appropriate. I have been much struck by the repudiation in silence of the prophecy in Daniel vii. 13, 14, by Bishop Pearson in his chapters on the clause, "He ascended into heaven," for one can hardly imagine that so learned a prelate was unacquainted with the value placed upon it by an eminent Father like Lactantius, with regard to the ascension. I think I may venture to say that the ascension by the agency of a cloud is the only theological fact in the biography of Jesus which Pearson has not supported and strengthened by the citation of a special prophecy. His peculiar manner of quoting Luke xxiv. 50 and 51, and Acts i. 9 and 10, is

---

[1] In Tertullian's *Apologeticus*, 21, the words '*circumfusa nube*,' encompassed in a cloud, occur in the account of the ascension. As these words, or any mention of a cloud, are not found in his bold arguments in *De Resurrectione Carnis*, and other treatises, they may have been a gloss; or Tertullian obtained the fact from an apocryphal source.

most noticeable, the two passages being interlaced the one into the other, a mode of citation unique in Anglican theology.

To an ordinary untheologically educated man it will not seem *outré* to conclude that Jesus left the earth in the way natural and usual to humanity. "That which hath been is that which shall be; and that which hath been done is that which shall be done; and there is no new thing under the sun," saith Ecclesiastes, or the Preacher, i. 9. It is not possible to come to any other conclusion after due consideration of the facts that I have brought together. There is no evidence in the Christian writings of the first century that there existed in the minds of the saints or sons of God any conception of the bodily ascension of Jesus, that is, of the elevation of his body into the atmosphere. There may possibly have been an idea of that sort, but in a form thoroughly indefinite and vague, that originated and prevailed in the first half of the second century, deducible only from certain words employed by Christian writers of that period. This vague and indefinite idea assumed some definiteness in the second half of the second century, and the body of Jesus was perhaps understood to have been transferred in its solidity to heaven, possibly through the atmosphere, though so very definite a medium of transfer was not explicitly formulated. It was not till the fourth century that the mode of transfer, by means of a cloud, was authoritatively enunciated to Christendom in the Acts. Had the ascension of Jesus in the bosom of a cloud been a physical fact it would certainly have been known to Christians in the first century, and been alluded to as a physical fact in their writings. The absence of the least trace of such knowledge in the first century, and the gradual growth, perceptible to the historian, of the idea of a physical ascension during three centuries, constrains me to conclude that the ascension of Jesus was not a physical but a theological fact, or conception or article of faith. The ecclesiastical creeds must be understood to declare belief in theological facts, conceptions, or articles of faith; and the attempt to convert theological into physical facts would be an obvious mistake. The theological fact of the bodily ascension of Jesus must be regarded as the equivalent, in the department of theology, of the legal fact or postulate that 'the king can do no wrong,' which is considered the necessary theoretical basis of a political system, though, judging from actual experience, such legal fact is not equivalent to historical fact.

There is a remarkable want of unanimity regarding the duration of the interval between the resurrection and the somatic death or theological ascension of Jesus, to be noticed in the first three centuries. I can gather no explicit statement on this subject from the surviving Christian writings of the first century; but an inferential period can, I think, be made out, of which I shall speak hereafter. From the writings of the second century we ascertain that the Ophites, or snake-worshipping Gnostic Christians, believed that Jesus tarried eighteen months on earth after the resurrection before he was received up into heaven, and sat down at the right hand of his father, Ialdaboth (Irenæus, *Ad Her.*, I. xxx. 14). In the Gnostic gospel, *Pistis Sophia*, believed to have been written by Valentinus, is a distinct statement that after Jesus had risen from the dead "he passed eleven years speaking with his disciples," but the final limit of his residence on earth is not stated (Bk. I. 1). This testimony, it should be observed, is that of sectaries, and it precedes orthodox information on the subject. I regard Irenæus as the first who has given us information from orthodox sources, which in his case should be regarded as the four Gospels, or other sacred writings. Irenæus distinctly says that Jesus was taken up when he rose from the dead, "*post triduum resurgens assumtus est*" (Bk. V. xxxi. 2), which may be understood to mean that the resurrection and ascension took place three days after the crucifixion. In none of the sacred writings, as they have come down to us, is such a statement to be found, except the Third Gospel (ch. xxiv. 51), in which the narrative is clear that the ascension took place on the same day as the resurrection. But Bishop Westcott and his learned colleague, and all Biblical scholars, concur in regarding this passage in the Third Gospel as a late addition, or, as they are pleased to call it, a 'Western non-interpolation'; so that the inference is justifiable that Irenæus derived his information (if he did not invent it himself) from some lost Apocryphal Gospel, which possessed authority in the second century. The next writer, who speaks on this subject is Origen in his *Treatise against Celsus*, ii. 63, and he distinctly quotes from the Acts that Jesus, "being seen during forty days," expounded to his disciples "the things pertaining to the kingdom of God" (Acts i. 3). The above account displays considerable divergence of knowledge on a subject about which there ought to have been no difference: and one feels surprise that the Christian Church should have taken more than two centuries to have made up its mind, not about a theological fact on which any doctrine depended, but upon a pure historical or physical fact, with which nothing in a theological sense was associated. In my judgment, the duration of Jesus' stay on earth is not settled on the authority of an interpolated clause in the Acts; because Irenæus distinctly states, on the authority of the very best evidence available, that Jesus lived to old age, whereas, according to the Gospels and Acts, his residence on earth was only up to his thirty-first or at most thirty-third or thirty-fourth year of age, for he began his ministry about thirty years of age (Luke iii. 23): a period of life which cannot in any sense be regarded as old age. Speaking of the age of Jesus, Irenæus says as follows:—"*A quadrigesimo autem et quinquagesimo anno declinat jam in ætatem seniorem, quam habens Dominus noster docebat, sicut evangelium et omnes seniores testantur, qui in Asia apud Joannem discipulum Domini convenerunt, id ipsum tradidisse eis Joannem. Permansit autem cum eis usque ad Trajani tempora. Quidam autem eorum non solum Joannem, sed et alios apostolos viderunt, et hæc eadem ab ipsis audierunt et testantur de hujus-modi relatione*" (*Ad Her.*, II. xxii. 5). But from the fortieth and fiftieth year a man begins to incline to old age, which possessing our Lord gave instruction, as the gospel and all the elders, who were in Asia with John, testify and agree that John had delivered this to them. And he remained with them up to the times of Trajan. But some of these saw not only John but other apostles also, and they heard the same things from them, and testify of a statement of this kind. A few lines earlier in the same chapter Irenæus speaks of Jesus having passed through every stage of life—infancy, childhood, youth, and old age. The above statement is not opposed to the Gospels, because they do not embrace the story of the entire life of Jesus, and do not go beyond the crucifixion and resurrection. Irenæus, unable to resist the force of the evidence of unquestionably credible witnesses, tries hard to establish that Jesus was an old man when he suffered on the cross, quotes in support of the statement John viii. 56 and 57, and argues that the Valentinians were wrong in assigning one passover to the ministry of Jesus, but that there must have been more, and that they were out in their reckoning to the extent of twenty years. Irenæus here appears to imply that the Valentinians arranged the Gospel story, on which point I am disposed to agree with him, associating other sects with the Valentinians, as joint participators in the sacred work. In reading this chapter in Irenæus on the age of Jesus, the mind is filled with vague suspicions that the Asian Church in the second half of the second century was striving to elongate the interval between the beginning of the ministry of Jesus and the crucifixion, in order to reconcile the Gospel story with what was known to the elders at Ephesus to be the real age of Jesus. The subject is obscure, and deserves closer investigation than I feel capable of giving it. There cannot be a doubt in anybody's mind that Irenæus believed the elders when they asserted that John and other Apostles declared that Jesus had attained old age on earth, and that his estimate of the number of passovers related in the Fourth Gospel was stimulated by the fact. Archbishop Ussher has actually thrown back the date of Jesus' birth to four years before he was born, according to the modern system of chronology. Nobody to my knowledge has yet ventured to throw back the birth of Jesus twenty years, as a task less hopeless than the attempt to prove the ministry of Jesus to have extended over twenty years. The date of the crucifixion is historically fixed to the period during which Pilate was procurator of Judæa, *i.e.*, between A.D. 26, when he was appointed, and A.D. 36, when he was deprived of his office, and cannot be tampered with. It would be a forlorn task to throw back the date of the birth of Jesus, for the problem of the number of years to be added is now insoluble.

Irenæus indicates twenty years (*Ad Her.*, II. xxii. 6) at a venture, according to his conception of what constitutes old age, but no reliance can be placed on his conjecture. As a practical measure it is unadvisable to make any change in the present system of chronology, for the additional number of years necessary to complete the actual term of Jesus' sojourn on earth could well be added to his life after the crucifixion, which has a fixed historical date, without doing violence to chronology or theology. Christians of the first century expressed no concern regarding the duration of the life of Jesus after the resurrection. Christians of the second century were content with the knowledge that Jesus ascended on the same day that he rose from the dead. Christians of the third century were divided between the view that prevailed in the second century and a new view, probably started by an Apocryphal Gospel, and thence introduced into the Acts, that he was 'seen for forty days,' which does not imply that Jesus did not remain on earth longer, though in concealment, and not seen.

I have already spoken of Paul's belief (see *ante*, p. 70), when he wrote the Epistle to the Romans, that Jesus was immortal on earth, a fact that is by no means incredible, as a similar belief prevailed amongst primitive Christians in respect of the Apostle John (see John xxi. 23).[1] Paul had been undeceived when he wrote the Second Epistle to the Corinthians, just as the Christians were undeceived when John died at the close of the first century. Jesus then, according to Paul, was alive on earth when he wrote the Epistle to the Romans (see Rom. vi. 9–10), but was deceased when he wrote the Second Epistle to the Corinthians (see 2 Cor. v. 14–16). It is impossible to fix the exact year in which these epistles were written, but the date is put down tentatively as A.D. 57 or 58. The internal evidence of the verses quoted gives priority of date to the Epistle to the Romans over the Second Epistle to the Corinthians, contrary to the prevailing chronology, which gives

---

[1] Tertullian relates that Menander, the pupil and successor of Simon Magus, a contemporary of Paul, gave out that all who partook of his baptism became immortal and incorruptible (*De Anima*, l.). This belief of Paul's was not singular.

precedence to the latter.[1] The latter conclusion, however, is founded on Rom. xv. 24-28, compared with 2 Cor. viii.-ix., in connection with the great collection that was made, throughout the Churches of Macedonia and Achaia, for the needy Church at Jerusalem. But as the genuineness of chaps. xv. and xvi. of the Epistle to the Romans is open to doubt, the current chronology is not reliable, and must yield to the strong evidence of the verses I have quoted from these two epistles regarding Jesus being immortal on earth from the earlier epistle, and then being known no more on earth from the later epistle. Fifty-seven years may thus be taken as the probable duration of the life of Jesus. If James, the Bishop of Jerusalem spoken of by Josephus, be the author of the Canonical Epistle, he had the opportunity of being aware of the third mystery of the Shout, for he suffered martyrdom about A.D. 62 or 63, and was in a position to know of the personal circumstances of the great founder of Christianity (see James v. 11).

The life of the resuscitated victim of a judicial execution was necessarily passed in concealment and obscurity. But if prophecy be of any avail to illumine the darkness of the declining years of the risen Lord, the beautiful poem of the Hebrew seer should give us an insight into the subsequent history of Jesus. The servant of Jehovah, the prophet Isaiah announced, was despised and rejected of men; a man of sorrows, and acquainted with grief: and as one from whom men hide their face he was despised, and we esteemed him not. Surely he hath borne our griefs, and carried our sorrows: yet we did esteem him stricken, smitten of God, and afflicted. But he was wounded for our transgressions, he was bruised for our iniquities: the chastisement of our peace was upon him; and with his stripes we are healed. . . . . He was oppressed, yet he humbled himself and opened not his mouth; as a lamb that is led to the slaughter and as a sheep that before her shearers is dumb; yea, he opened not his mouth. By oppression and judgment he was taken away; and his life who shall recount? for he was cut off out of the

---

[1] In the *Canon of the New Testament* the Epistle to the Romans has priority over the Epistles to the Corinthians.

land of the living: for the transgression of my people was he stricken. And they made his grave with the wicked, and with the rich in his death; although he had done no violence, neither was any deceit in his mouth (Isa. liii. 3-9).

But the Lord is very pitiful and of tender mercy, and we count them happy which endure (James v. 11).

Yet it pleased the Lord to bruise him; he hath put him to grief: when his soul shall make an offering for sin, he shall see *his* seed, he shall prolong his days, and the pleasure of the Lord shall prosper in his hand. He shall see of the travail of his soul, and shall be satisfied: by his knowledge shall my righteous servant make many righteous: and he shall bear their iniquities. Therefore will I divide him a portion with the great, and he shall divide the spoil with the strong; because he poured out his soul unto death, and was numbered with the transgressors: yet he bare the sin of many, and made intercession for the transgressors (Isa. liii. 10-12).

There is not a word about ascension in the declaration of the Hebrew prophet regarding the reward of the righteous servant of Jehovah, after his faithful devotion wrought in affliction and suffering nigh unto death; but he speaks of domestic life, marriage and children, of prolonged days and peaceful prosperity. History provides a faint adumbration of such a tranquil 'end of the Lord' as the Hebrew prophet portrayed and James saw (James v. 11).

Eusebius, in his *Ecclesiastical History*, iii. 19, states that when the Roman Emperor Domitian had issued orders that the descendants of David should be slain, according to an ancient tradition, some heretics informed on the descendants of Judas, the brother of Jesus. He quotes the following story, apparently *verbatim*, from Hegesippus, who flourished in the second half of the second century, but whose work is now lost: "There were yet surviving of the family of our Lord the grandsons of Judas, called his brother according to the flesh, who were informed against as being of the family of David. The Evocatus brought them to the Emperor Domitian; for he, like Herod, feared the advent of Christ. And he questioned them, if they were from David, and they confessed. Then he inquired of them, what property they have, or what wealth they possess. Both answered that they had only nine thousand denarii, half belonging to each of them. And they said that they had this not in silver, but in the value of only thirty-nine *plethra* of land, from which they raised their taxes and supported themselves by labour. And then they showed their hands, as evidence of their labour, the hardness of their body, and the callosities existing upon their hands, impressed by their continual labour. Being asked about Christ and his kingdom, what nature it was, when and where it will appear, they replied that it was not worldly nor of the earth, but heavenly and angelic, that it will be at the end of time, when coming in glory he will judge the living and the dead, and will render to every one according to his work. Thereupon Domitian passed no condemnation upon them, but contemptuously regarded them as simple folk, and set them free, and put a stop by decree to the persecution against the church. Being released, they became heads of churches, as being both martyrs and of the family of the Lord; and when peace was restored, they continued in life up to the time of Trajan."

The above interesting narrative should be scrutinised, as all ecclesiastical histories ought to be: the result of such scrutiny is sometimes a surprise. An examination into the chronology of the story of Herod and his ruthless decree shortly after the birth of Jesus, recounted in Matt. ii. 16, resulted in the alarming discovery that Herod had died four years before. A Hibernian theologian was, however, equal to the occasion, and bravely put back the birthday of Jesus to four years before he was born; and the earth has continued to revolve on its axis comfortably.[1] What strikes one at the

[1] Another vigorous Hibernian divine postponed an eclipse of the sun, which fell upon a cloudy and rainy day, to the first fine day following. Archbishop Ussher's chronological discovery has no effect upon the date of the birth of Jesus, but it simply discredits the fable of the slaughter of little children by Herod. The archbishop's device of putting back the date of the birth of Jesus is equivalent to the ingenious device of the Hibernian architect for increasing the height of a room by digging up and lowering the floor. Professor Ramsay has recently produced reasons for dating the taxing spoken of in Luke ii. 1-3 B.C. 6, and suggests that the birth of Jesus should hence be thrown back six years. If these reasons are substantial, they would imply that the preposterous story of Joseph dragging a

beginning is the singular nature of the decree said to have been issued by Domitian to slay the descendants of David, a Jewish kinglet or sheikh, who had reigned a thousand years before, and whose minute kingdom had been already annihilated, its chief town razed to the ground, and its people dispersed. There are no means of verifying the statement from the writings of contemporaries, for such a decree is not mentioned by any other historian, nor can it be compared with the original, which is now lost. The only resource in the circumstances is to see whether the statement harmonises and tallies with the rest of the narrative. In the two chapters preceding chaps. xvii. and xviii. of Bk. III., Eusebius speaks of the persecution against Christians raised by Domitian, and he records the fact that the niece of one of the Roman consuls was, for professing Christ, punished by transportation to Pontia. In the examination of the two alleged descendants of Judas, the emperor appeared to take little or no interest in the fact of the descent of the two prisoners from David, but displayed very deep interest in Christ and his kingdom ; and Hegesippus further makes the statement that Domitian was alarmed at the coming advent of Christ. The examination of the accused gives one the impression that the fact of their being Christians of some importance was more in the emperor's mind than their descent from David. The impression is strengthened by the result of the examination : for the emperor released the prisoners, and forthwith commanded a cessation of the persecution against Christians. This remarkable termination of the proceedings rather indicates that the accused were brought up before the emperor as important Christians, against whom a general persecution had been ordered. Had the emperor by decree ordered the execution of the descendants of David, there appears on the face of the story no reason why two obscure descendants, discovered probably in Syria or Palestine or somewhere in the east, should not have been summarily executed by the local gover-

young woman, who was not his wife, on the eve of her confinement, from Nazareth to Bethlehem, through a rough country infested with robbers, was a fabrication. This is the common-sense view to be taken of the effect of Professor Ramsay's laborious investigation.

nor, in obedience to the imperial decree, instead of being sent to the emperor at Rome. The historian Hegesippus himself in the quotation makes no direct reference to such a decree. The emperor, in releasing the two prisoners after their confession that they were descendants of David, stultified his own decree. I suspect that there was no such decree issued by Domitian. Tertullian and Lactantius refer to Domitian, but they both speak only of his persecution of Christians, and say nothing of his decree against the descendants of David. The suspicion arising in the mind, that there was no such imperial decree, gains strength when it is further remarked that the report of the decree is attributed by Eusebius to an ancient tradition, and not to Hegesippus. Can the statement have been made by the later historian to ward off some discredit or dishonour to the Church? Could the earlier historian have made some statement that implicated the credit and honour of the Church and required a corrective? The knowledge that the Jews gave no support to the descent of Jesus (or of Joseph and Mary) from David, and that the leading events in the life of Jesus were not quite settled, or perhaps not generally accepted, at the early date of Hegesippus, gives ground for the surmise that Hegesippus may have recorded some fact that was unpalatable and needed suppression. Can it be possible that the two men brought before the Roman emperor were not the grandsons of Judas, but the sons or grandsons of Jesus? The ascension in a cloud was unknown to Hegesippus, and he might well have innocently recorded the fact that Jesus left descendants without being aware that he was uttering a gross heresy. The alteration of his history could be effected by Eusebius with impunity and without compunction; we have already seen that the latter had deliberately falsified a public document—the letter of the Church of Smyrna on the martyrdom of Polycarp. Hegesippus was a small chronicler and an obscure one, as few writers of antiquity have named him. I know of only two—Eusebius and Jerome. Hence the absence of risk of discovery of an alteration in his text, which no one would deny being the correction of a heresy.

I am disposed to side with Isaiah that the righteous

servant of Jehovah left posterity. The prophet, however, spoke no prophecy: he drew a natural and probable word-picture, in very beautiful language, of the career of a righteous and zealous servant of Jehovah dealing with a fanatical people who had gone astray. After undergoing persecution and infliction which nearly cost him his life, the servant of Jehovah retired to Syria, probably to the neighbourhood of Damascus, where he was last seen by Paul. (Compare Gal. i. 12, 16, 17 with Acts ix. 26 and 27.) If the estate of thirty-nine *plethra*, equivalent to thirty-three acres, had descended to his children from Jesus, the latter had attained a very respectable position by his industry, assisted, perhaps, by gifts from his followers. The owner of so much land would be a person of some little consequence in our days in an English village: but in an eastern country he would be regarded as one of the head-men of the village. Thus in the matter of social position the prophecy of Isaiah regarding the righteous servant of Jehovah may be regarded as fulfilled. The peaceful conclusion to the life of Jesus, after the crucifixion, which I have endeavoured to construct out of the scanty and obscure historical materials available, appears to my judgment to be more probable, more suitable to the character and public career of Jesus, and more in harmony with the feelings of his real sympathisers, than the mythical and impossible canonical journey into the cold regions of the upper atmosphere mounted on a cloud.

To return to our text (ch. xx. 17), where Jesus, on being recognised by Mary Magdalene, tells her not to touch him; the reason assigned appears to be so great a mistake that the presumption is inevitable that the passage was put in by the revision committee without due consideration. About eight days after this interview Jesus permits Thomas freely to handle him (verses 26 and 27), although he had not yet ascended to his Father, which was the reason assigned by Jesus for the prohibition to Mary. A natural and probable reason is very readily found from ordinary experience of the conduct of people who have sustained severe injuries. Jesus deprecated the seizure of his hands, because they were tender from the wounds inflicted by the nails; and his whole body doubtless was sore from the scourging inflicted, and the buffeting and general rough usage to which he had been subjected. Eight days after, the acute suffering had much abated, and permitted the gentle handling to which Thomas was invited. It would seem from these anecdotes that the feet of Jesus had not been nailed to the cross. He was never incapacitated from the use of his legs, which would not have been the case if his feet had been penetrated by nails.

The next passage that comes up for remark is xx. 21-23. I have very serious doubt whether this passage existed in the revised Gospel of the second century. Verse 21 is not referred to by any writer of the second or third century; verse 22 is not quoted by any writer earlier than Origen,[1] and verse 23 not by any before Cyprian. The same remark made respecting the introduction of the previous passage into the Gospel is applicable to this passage also, namely, that it was interpolated without due consideration, especially to verse 22. For Jesus to impart the Holy Ghost to his disciples was *primâ facie* a flat contradiction to his solemn declaration, repeatedly made in xiv. 16, 26, xvi. 7, 13, that it was necessary that he should first go away, before the Father will send Paraclete, which, according to the orthodox theology, was the same as the Holy Spirit. This verse, contrary to the previous declarations, asserts that Jesus himself, not the Father, imparted the Holy Ghost, and before he departed. Such evidence, however, as is available, discloses the fact that these verses were not in the revised version of the second century. Irenæus, Clement of Alexandria, and Tertullian do not quote them. It may be permissible to assert that the former two writers had not occasion or opportunity to quote them, as their surviving dissertations did not discuss subjects which required or called

---

[1] In the Ante-Nicene Christian Library (*Irenæus*, vol. ii. p. 182) is an alleged fragment (numbered lii.) of Irenæus, in which is a statement that Christ "breathed the Holy Spirit into his disciples." I have no means of ascertaining the genuineness of this fragment. The style does not seem to me to indicate Irenæus as the author. It is not included in Stieren's collection of the fragments of Irenæus. The Ante-Nicene Christian Library has another fragment, containing a similar statement, numbered xxi., which is found in Stieren's collection, numbered xxi., but is excluded from Harvey's collection, because regarded by him as spurious.

for the quotation of these verses. But such a remark is not applicable to Tertullian, who in his treatise *De Pudicitia* discusses the subject of the remission of sins and the power of the Church to remit sins. He quotes and discusses Matt. xvi. 18, 19, in which Peter is declared by Jesus to be the rock on which he will build his Church, and to whom the power was given to bind and loose. Tertullian explains this power to mean the abrogation of such portions of the Jewish Law which Christians had abandoned, and the validating or binding of those which were reserved. While he admits the power of the Church of the Spirit, a metaphysical body, to forgive sins, he in express terms denies the power of a Church consisting of a number of bishops to do so. The forgiveness of sins, he emphatically states, is the right of the Lord not of the servant, the right of God not of the priest[1] (*De Pudicitia*, xxi.). Throughout this discussion of the subject of the remission of sins, which covers several chapters, Tertullian does not quote, and shows no consciousness whatever of, the existence of verse 23 of the twentieth chapter of the Fourth Gospel : "Whose soever sins ye remit, they are remitted unto them ; and whose soever *sins* ye retain they are retained." The only reasonable conclusion that I can form to account for this omission on the part of Tertullian is that this verse was not in the Fourth Gospel in his time. I am confirmed in this conclusion by the remarkable manner in which Origen deals with the passage. Origen, in his *Commentary on Matthew*, goes over the same subject of forgiveness of sins, but in a very diffident spirit ; and I am not sure that it is practicable to say to what conclusion Origen had come with regard to the power of the clergy to forgive sins (*Com. on Matt.*, xii. 11–14, xiii. 31). The question was manifestly at this time in course of discussion : the texts in Matthew (xvi. 18, 19, and xviii. 18) were *en evidence*, but not xx. 23 of the Fourth Gospel. The remarkable way in which Origen quotes this

---

[1] Besides the fact that Irenæus does not refer to this passage of the Fourth Gospel, it is impossible to believe that he was cognisant of it when he argues from the power of Christ to forgive sins (Matt. ix. 6) that he was necessarily divine : for " no man," he says, " can forgive sins but God alone " (Bk. v. xvii. 3).

passage of the Fourth Gospel raises, in fact invokes, suspicion : a text which would definitely settle the point at issue was indicated, but not quoted. I give here the translation of the passage from the Ante-Nicene Library (Bk. xii. 11, p. 456 of the additional volume). "But if this promise, 'I will give unto thee the keys of the kingdom of heaven,' be common to the others, how shall not all the things previously spoken of, and the things which are subjoined as having been addressed to Peter, be common to them ? For in this place these words seem to be addressed as to Peter only, 'Whatsoever thou shalt bind on earth shall be bound in heaven'; but in the Gospel of John the Saviour having given the Holy Spirit unto the disciples by breathing upon them, said, ' Receive ye the Holy Spirit,'" etc. Why should the very words which would have clinched the decision be indicated but not quoted? and they are not quoted elsewhere in any of Origen's voluminous writings which have survived to our days. But when the third century had further advanced beyond the period of activity of Tertullian and Origen, when we come to study the writings of Cyprian, Bishop of Carthage, when the second half of the third century was attained, this passage (John xx. 21–23) ceases to be occult. Cyprian repeatedly quotes the passage in full in almost the exact terms in which we find it in our Fourth Gospel : "As the Father hath sent me, even so send I you. And when he had said this, he breathed on them, and saith unto them, Receive ye the Holy Ghost : whose soever sins ye remit they are remitted unto them ; and whose soever sins ye retain, they are retained" (the Epistles of Cyprian, lxxii. 7, lxxiv. 16 ; *On the Unity of the Church*, iv.). The facts are these : at the beginning of the first half of the third century, Tertullian, writing on the subject of remission of sins, is unaware of the existence of verse 23 of the twentieth chapter of the Fourth Gospel, and utters a sentiment which is directly antagonistic to the sense of this verse. Cyprian, writing fifty years after Tertullian, in the beginning of the second half of the third century, quotes the verse repeatedly and without any hesitation. Both these writers were denizens of proconsular Africa. Origen, intermediate between the two, dwelling in Ægypt or

Syria, seems to know the verse, but he merely quotes the words preceding, but does not quote the verse itself, although it was apposite to the subject he was discussing, and was, in fact, urgently called for. From these facts it is justifiable to draw the conclusion that the passage was interpolated in the first half of the third century. I have not been able to ascertain, from the perusal of the Christian writings of the first three centuries, what means existed and what precautions were taken to preserve the integrity of writings attributed to the Apostles and to apostolic men. That there was an organised system of alteration of the sacred writings, and of making additions to them, by an authority which was capable of enforcing its behests, is, however, a reasonable inference from the many facts already brought forward. In regard to the passage under discussion, we find Tertullian to have been absolutely unacquainted with it. Origen manifestly knew the passage, but he hesitated and stopped short of quoting it. Cyprian quotes the passage without hesitation, and with a consciousness that it was universally received as the authorised sacred text.

It is impossible, on the assumption that Paraclete and the Holy Ghost are the same, to reconcile the solemn and affectionate assurance of Jesus, repeatedly uttered, that he must first depart before Paraclete could come from the Father, with the statement that Jesus breathed the Holy Ghost upon the disciples within a week after the resurrection, and before he departed to the Father. Yet amiable, learned, and respected prelates of the Church find themselves placed in the painful and pitiable position of being obliged to effect such reconciliation. Bishop Westcott is fully sensible of the difficulty, but believes that he has got over it by a grammatical distinction. This eminent prelate is a consummate Greek scholar, of whose attainments an ancient English university is proud; but we can hardly prevail upon ourselves to regard the rude Hebrew peasants, to whom the Gospels are ascribed, to have employed the Greek article with the nicety that Bishop Westcott's distinction demands. According to the learned bishop, τὸ πνεῦμα ἅγιον is the Holy Ghost or Paraclete, but πνεῦμα ἅγιον, without the article τὸ, means 'a gift of the Holy Ghost.' In ch. xx. 22, the article is not employed, and hence

Bishop Westcott argues, if I understand him rightly, that Jesus' alleged speech, "Receive ye the Holy Ghost," means "Receive ye a gift of the Holy Ghost," or "Receive ye the power of the new life from the Person of the Risen Christ"; or, as he again changes the expression in the same passage, "the Holy Spirit as dwelling in him." If it be permissible, without irreverence, to change this sacred subject, *cæteris paribus*, to a profane one, and to convert the expressions, "Receive ye the Holy Ghost," with and without the article, into more familiar conceptions, requiring little intellectuality, such as "Receive ye Ten Pounds" and "Receive ye a cheque or gift of Ten Pounds," it will be readily perceived that whatever may be the change of expressions, the solid meaning at the bottom of all such expressions, however much they may be varied, is the same: provided always, and this is a fair condition, that the changes are limited to the form, and do not extend to the substance. The expressions may be varied to "Receive ye the purchasing Power of the sum indicated by this Cheque upon my Balance in the Bank," or "Receive ye ten pounds from the Pocket on the right side of my Person": but the inherent meaning is the same. It is an absolute necessity that no change of the substance be made while the form of expression is varied, for if such change of substance be covertly introduced, in the hands of a skilled master of language, the gift of ten pounds may ultimately dwindle down to the gift of a sixpenny piece. If Bishop Westcott intended to convey the meaning that the expression 'Holy Ghost' without the article, in this passage, was not the Holy Ghost familiar to Christians, and which theologians teach is the same as Paraclete, he ought to say so in open and definite terms. After carefully reading over his comments on John xx. 22, '*the Holy Ghost*,' I find that Bishop Westcott does not say so in express terms, though he says a great deal. His endeavour is rather to show that the expression 'Holy Ghost' without the article in the text means something else than the meaning which the ordinary reader would put upon it: but as I have pointed out, his endeavour is a failure.[1] If

---

[1] In colloquial English the article is used or not used indifferently. The boys in a public school as often speak of the headmaster as doctor as The

Bishop Westcott means anything else, I must express my regret that I am unable to understand him : his profundity is beyond my mental grasp.

Bishop Ellicott is also an accomplished Greek scholar ; but he does not consider the absence of the Greek article τὸ as worth any notice at all, and makes no reference to it in his comments on this passage. He tells us that the words "Receive ye the Holy Ghost" do not mean "a promise of the future gift of the Holy Ghost," or the "promised advent of the Paraclete"; but he vexatiously abstains from saying whether the Holy Ghost in the text is or is not the Holy Ghost or Paraclete. He says the meaning is that Jesus 'gave a sign,' 'his act was sacramental,' and so on; and it is clear that the venerable bishop is simply evading the point, and doing so without much cleverness.

Bishop Walsham How, in his *Commentary on the Fourth Gospel*, does not evade this crucial point, if I understand him rightly. Speaking on the text, "Receive ye the Holy Ghost," he says that "this gift is but a sort of earnest of further and fuller gifts to come"; and that the disciples' "full power as Apostles were to be bestowed at Pentecost." By these words I understand that in Bishop How's mind the Holy Ghost was divisible into portions, and that an earnest of a small portion of the Holy Ghost was given on this occasion, and that the remainder and larger portion was to be given at Pentecost. This meaning is not to be derived either from Bishop Westcott's or from Bishop Ellicott's comments on the passage. But how the presentation of the Holy Ghost (which is presumably the same as Paraclete), even in a limited degree, by Jesus himself to the disciples within a week after the resurrection and before his final departure to the Father, is to be reconciled with the impressive assurances of Jesus that he must first return to the Father before the latter will send Paraclete (or the Holy Ghost), Bishop Walsham How does not attempt to say.[1]

doctor : and household servants of their employers, as master or mistress, as The master or The mistress. The grammarian who would seriously try to make a difference between the two forms of expression would simply raise a smile.

[1] One is almost driven to think that Bishop Walsham How's explanation implies that he considered that there was no conflict between the alleged fact and the statement. Just as a young woman pleaded in exculpation of the

The interpretation of verse 22 given by each bishop differs from that rendered by his episcopal brother, and it is not possible that such interpretations could be seriously accepted by any man who is studying the subject in downright earnestness. The learned bishops wasted their erudition and ingenuity in finding each a plausible exegesis, in fact in weaving sophistical webs unworthy of their talents and unbecoming to their high station. It would be a benefit to society if the lay reviews would occasionally apply the lash of sound satirical criticism to theological writings in the wholesome style in which Sydney Smith in the *Edinburgh Review* once castigated the sanctimonious ineptitudes of Methodist missionaries. Such criticism, or the fear of it, would help greatly to clear out of commentaries and volumes of sermons many cargoes of pious rubbish, covered over with ',draperies of sanctity,' as Dr Martineau says. The talent and erudition of Bishops Westcott and Ellicott would have found their proper field in the investigation of the authenticity of the passage under discussion, which *primâ facie* is a flat contradiction of the assurances of Jesus regarding the sending of the Holy Ghost or Paraclete by the Father after his own return to the Father. None could be found in the whole bench of bishops more competent to do for this passage that which Bishop Westcott did for John i. 3 and 4. His additional note on these verses is a triumph of learning and research; although it failed to impress upon the revision committee of 1881 the duty of reintroducing the original text. Doubtless the learned commentators compared the received text of this passage (John xx. 21-23) with the ancient codices of the New Testament; but these latter date not earlier than the fourth century or later. There were two centuries of progressive corruption of the Church preceding, during which long period it was necessary to ascertain that the sacred text had not been tampered with. The standard followed by the bishops is the text of the fourth century, whereas it ought to be that of the second century, to which date means exist for detecting falsifications in some

fault of having an illegitimate child, that "it was a very little one; if it was bigger it would be different."

passages. In omitting to perform this necessary retrospection of the passage under discussion, the commentators failed in their duty to the Anglican Church, to Christian society, and to Jesus, whom they receive not only as an illustrious man but as God. When they undertook to write commentaries, a function to which their great abilities peculiarly fitted them, they accepted and were justly expected to fulfil all the obligations involved. The neglect of this obvious duty has landed them in a pitiable position; they are obliged to accept the wording of the passage, but to change the plain meaning of the words employed. "Receive ye the Holy Ghost" is forced to mean something else than the words imply, and the sentences, "whose soever sins ye remit, they are remitted unto them; *and* whose soever *sins* ye retain, they are retained," also are made to mean something else than the ordinary reader would naturally understand from the words. The Roman Church understands the words to mean that Jesus gave the power of forgiving sins to the Apostles, and through them to the clergy. This is the sense in which the passage was accepted in the third century by Origen perhaps, and by Cyprian, who were the first expounders of the passage. I have already quoted Origen's words on the subject, and have drawn attention to his singular trick of pointing to the passage, but not quoting it. Cyprian is very precise and clear, and there is no shuffling of phrases with him. He says the prerogative of forgiving sins was given by Jesus to the *Apostles*; hence he concludes that only those who are set over the Church are allowed to baptise and to give remission of sins (Ep. lxxii. to Jubaianus, ch. 7). In another passage of a letter addressed to him by a Bishop of Cæsarea the statement is repeated that the power of remitting sins was given by Jesus to the *Apostles*, and to the Churches which they set up, and to the bishops who succeeded them (Ep. lxxiv. (Firmilian) ch. 16). In his *Treatise on the Unity of the Church*, after quoting the passage in Matt. xvi. 18, 19, regarding Peter being the rock on which the Church is built, Cyprian quotes the passage under discussion (John xx. 21-23), and remarks that the rest of the *Apostles* were the same as Peter, and were endowed with the same honour and power. The Roman

Church claims this power to the present day as appertaining to her clergy. The Anglican Church rightly protests against the claim, and does not consider that her own clergy is invested with the power. The premier living bishop of the Anglican Church, which position may courteously and justly be assigned to Bishop Westcott, founds the protest partly on grammar and partly on a finical interpretation of the passage of Scripture which gives the power of forgiving sins to the Apostles and through them to the clergy. Bishop Westcott says "the pronouns in this case are unemphatic"; the main thought in the passage is the reality of the power of absolution, not the " particular organisation through which the power is administered "; and taking advantage of the use of the word 'disciples' in the narrative, he says "that there is nothing in the context, as has been seen, to show that the gift was confined to any particular group (as the Apostles) among the whole company present," and comes to the conclusion that the power of forgiving sins "must be regarded properly as the commission of the Christian society, and not as that of the Christian ministry (Matt. v. 13, 14)" (these verses are part of the Sermon on the Mount; in them Jesus tells his disciples that they are the salt of the earth and the light of the world). The candid reader in perusing the passage will assuredly decide that the Roman Church has the most ancient and the correct interpretation of the passage. The Anglican Church, however, has instinctively the feeling that the passage is false and antagonistic to the spirit and character of Jesus; and whatever may be the shifty and thriftless arguments of her bishops, the foundation of the protest of the Anglican Church against the divine prerogative claimed by the Romish priests, is that human nature cannot endure the thought that a worm of the earth, who may be a drunken and immoral priest, is commissioned by God to forgive the sins of another worm, who may be morally superior to the priest. Investigation into the origin of the passage (John xx. 21–23) gives ample support to the truth of this natural human feeling against the passage.

The perusal of the Christian literature of the second and third centuries is a sorrowful task to the earnest investigator, when he perceives in it the steady increase of superstition and corruption in the Christian Church, its rapid approximation to heathenism, and the gradual extinction or perversion of the spirit, temper, and conduct inculcated by Jesus upon his disciples. Far from being the evolution of good, the development of the Christian Church may be broadly described as the evolution of evil; the only merit that I can perceive that retrieved the progressive vitiation of the Christian Church is that the moral precepts of Jesus, though not practically in operation, or only partially so, were not obliterated or cancelled in the sacred writings, and were theoretically approved and inculcated by the Fathers.[1] I am incompetent, and it forms no part of my plan in this work, to describe the general history of the Christian society at this period, but it is a necessity in connection with the examination of the passage, xx. 21-23, to indicate the state of morals prevalent amongst Christians at the end of the second century and the first half of the third century. The sins spoken of in the passage were not such as are taken cognisance of by the civil magistrate, because for their remission the authority of the Apostles and their successors was of no avail. These sins were such as were outside the sphere of the civil magistrate, or which only indirectly came within judicial cognisance. The relations between the sexes provided the chief sins, if not the only ones, which the passage alluded to covered. Thus a delineation of the state of sexual morality amongst the Christians of this period will afford a clue, and in my judgment a most satisfactory clue, to the origin of this passage in the Fourth Gospel. In the writings of Clement of Alexandria, of Tertullian, and of Hippolytus, we obtain a painful insight into the sad state of morality prevalent amongst the members of the Christian Church in

---

[1] The history of the rise and progress of the Christian religion in the early centuries is yet to be written. The subject has been hitherto almost entirely treated by ecclesiastics, and they have sadly misrepresented it. The spirit of Eusebius prevails amongst ecclesiastical historians, to cancel or put out of sight everything discreditable and dishonourable to the Church. Whatever good has been accomplished by ecclesiastical Christianity has been on the moral side; on the religious side, only evil was perpetrated.

three great centres of civilisation—in Alexandria in Ægypt, in Carthage in proconsular Africa, and in Rome.

The interesting work of Clement of Alexandria, called *The Pedagogue*, or *Instructor*, gives us a clear insight into the manners and customs of the Alexandrian Christians at the close of the second century. Unless specifically stated otherwise by the author, I take the descriptions of manners and conduct to apply to the Christians. For instance, where Clement says of the Persian royal family that they practised promiscuous intercourse with sisters, mothers, wives, and courtesans innumerable, like wild boars, such a description does not apply to the Christians (I. vii. § 55). But wherever he does not specially limit his description to certain nations, or generally to the Pagans, I feel justified in applying them to the Christians. Thus, his general remarks on extravagancies and excesses in eating and drinking, dressing, bathing, etc., are applicable to the Christians as well as to the heathen. He himself so applies them: for instance, in his account of the luxurious *agapæ* (II. i. § 4), of the wretches staggering home after a drinking bout (II. ii. §§ 25 and 26). In our own days we find Christians, of all classes and nationalities, indulging in vicious excesses of many kinds. Clement draws many scenes of vice, misconduct, and indecorum, with the object of deterring people from indulging in debasing, iniquitous, and immoral practices. The vivid picture of drunken men, staggering home with crowns round their necks like wine jars, spewing wine upon each other in the name of good fellowship, with dry and withered faces, pale and livid, is accompanied with wholesome remarks on the subject of drunkenness. He is very minute in his account of the foibles in dress and conduct of women. He remarks on the manner of drinking of women out of alabastra with long and narrow necks, throwing back their heads, and baring their necks indecently. Frequent spitting, violent clearing of the throat, and wiping the nose, are objected to as improper at entertainments. The avoidance of the use of crowns and ointments was enjoined, for no stronger reason assigned than that they are unnecessary and impel to pleasure and indulgences on the approach of night: but the real reason, I should say, was because crowns and ointment were especially employed by Pagans. The dyeing of clothes was deprecated, because colours were of no use against cold, and reproach in manners sprang from it. The colours most in fashion were the dye of Sardis, which is not defined, olive, green, rose, scarlet, and ten thousand other dyes. The colour most desired by the women was purple; everything, says Clement, is made of purple. White garments, he says, are the most suitable for Christians, and this colour, it may be accepted, was the prevalent colour amongst good Christians. Flowered garments he considered most objectionable, fit only for Bacchic rites; but he could not have foreseen that in the nineteenth century they would be much worn by Christian women. The dresses of the rich were costly: a single dress may cost 10,000 talents, or over £240,000, which Clement thought too much to clothe the bodies of ladies who, if sold, would not fetch a thousand Attic drachms, or £40. The follies of fashion appear to be perennial; long trailing robes were then, as in these days, worn by women of fashion, the garment sweeping the surface dirt of the ground like a broom. Shoes were also used as means of display: golden ornaments were fastened on them, and gold-plated and jewelled meretricious devices, such as amorous embraces, were depicted upon sandals. Clement would only sanction the use of white shoes to women, but on a journey a greased shoe was to be permitted. The use of shoes was permissible because it was unseemly for the foot to be shown naked, and besides, woman was a tender thing easily hurt. Jewellery was much used by women. Precious stones of all kinds were fastened to chains and set in necklaces, and the pearl was very highly prized. Golden chains were much in vogue fastened round the body. Aristophanes' list of female ornaments is quoted. The ears of women were bored for ear-rings and ear-drops. All these ornaments were in Clement's judgment superfluities; modesty and chastity were, in his opinion, collars and necklaces and the chains that God forges. The love of finery Clement regarded as a greater vice than the love of dainties and wine. The effeminacy of the men is minutely described.

Clement represents licentiousness as diffused over the

cities and become law. Luxury has changed all things, he says, it has brought dishonour upon man. A luxurious *empressement* seeks all things, attempts all things, constrains all things, confounds nature. Men play the part of women and women of men, contrary to nature; women who are married marry women (γαμούμεναι τε καὶ γαμοῦσαι γυναῖκες[1]); no path of licentiousness is untrodden; promiscuous intercourse is declared a public institution, and luxury is domesticated. O, pitiable spectacle! unspeakable conduct! (*Pæd.*, III. iii. § 21).

The public baths were open promiscuously to men and women, and both sexes publicly bathed naked. Women who had not become utterly destitute of modesty shut out strangers; but bathed apart with their own servants, stripped naked before their men-slaves, and were rubbed by the latter.[2]

Women are enjoined to go to church entirely covered, so that they may not be gazed upon. She will not fall, Clement says, who puts before her eyes modesty and her veil; nor will she invite another to fall by uncovering her face.

Throughout this treatise, it is to be remarked that Clement draws his models of morality and conduct from the Pagan writers, poets, and philosophers; he appears to be unaware of Christian sources beyond the Word. He held up to admiration the images of Virtue and Vice delineated by the Ceian sophist (II. xi. § 110), and of the model maiden described by Zeno the Cittiæan. For the seemliness of veiling, besides the wish of the Word that it was becoming for women to pray veiled, he refers to the wife of Æneas,

---

[1] The Ante-Nicene Christian Library translates: "Women are at once wives and husbands." This was obviously a form of vice that has become extinct. It was perhaps the same that Tertullian obscurely indicates as prevalent in Carthage: *Aspice lupas popularium libidinum nundinas, ipsasque quoque fictrices* (*De Pallio*, iv.). "Behold the prostitutes, emporia of the people's lusts, and the *fictrices*," which I do not know how to translate. The Ante-Nicene Christian Library translates, "female self-abusers with their sex."

[2] See *Apostolic Constitutions*, i. 9, on the subject of Christian women bathing naked with men.

who, even in the terror of the flight from burning Troy, remained veiled.

I do not find that Clement of Alexandria had any admiration of celibacy, or perceived any special virtue in virginity ; he says nothing whatever regarding the celibacy of the clergy. He was an encourager of legitimate marriage, and has expressed no sentiment on the subject of marriage or celibacy that can be regarded as open to objection. He did not consider second marriages as illegitimate. In spite of the general profligacy of manners, in which the Christians of Alexandria participated, Clement's views on the relations of the sexes are sound. The subject of the celibacy of the Christian clergy was obviously not mooted at the close of the second century.

Tertullian has written no treatise similar to Clement's *Pedagogue*, in which information regarding the prevalent manners and customs of the people of proconsular Africa is concentrated within a small compass. But remarks are scattered through his voluminous writings from which a general idea can be gathered of the condition of sexual morality in that region of the Roman empire. Sexual vice appears to have been less rampant in Carthage than at Alexandria, though plentiful enough, and of much the same variety and genus as was observed in the Ægyptian capital. Not only are there evidences in Tertullian of corruption of ritual, and closer approximations to Paganism in doctrine, but there is clear proof of the establishment of an institution, started originally, without doubt, from pure religious motives, but which proved pernicious to a degree, namely, the institution of virginity. The dominance of mistaken notions regarding the moral excellence of the preservation of virginity led to undue accumulations of unmarried young men and women in the Christian Church. These virgins, male and female, seem to have been organised bodies, more especially the females, of an obscure and indefinite sort, regarding which precise information is wanting. With regard to the females, poverty seems to have been one incentive to entrance into the body of virgins, for Tertullian distinctly states that the brotherhood readily undertook the maintenance of virgins.

The evils that resulted from this unnatural institution led Tertullian to cogitate a remedy, which he concluded he had found in inculcating the veiling of the virgins in the churches. To this subject he has devoted one of his most interesting treatises. The opinion expressed by a female member of the Church, who is not named by Tertullian, when the institution was first mooted, namely, that it was not the grace of God nor the merits of individual virgins that was pleasing, but their numbers only, should have taught Tertullian the true remedy. I shall give a translation of our theologian's account of Christian virgins under the care of the Church, not only as a sample of the state of sexual morality in the beginning of the third century, but also as an example of the evils resulting from ecclesiastical attempts to suppress, rather than to guide, the natural impulses of humanity :—

When this question, How shall we allure other virgins to this work? was first asked, they report a saying by a lady: truly, if they were plenty of them, they will make us happy, and not the grace of God or the merits of each. Do virgins adorn the Church and commend it to God, or the Church virgins? She has confessed that glory is the motive. But where glory is, there is solicitation; where solicitation is, there is a coming together; where there is a coming together, there is longing; where longing is, there is frailty. Deservedly, therefore, while they do not cover their head that they may be solicited for the sake of glory, they are compelled to cover their bellies by the ruin resulting from frailty. For emulation (or the desire to excel others), not religion, is their motive; sometimes it is that god, their belly, for the brotherhood readily undertake the support of virgins. But not only are they ruined, but they drag after them a long rope of sins. For put forward in the middle of the church, elated by the publicity given to their goodness, and laden by the brethren with every honour and function of kindness, so long as they do not conceal when any sin is committed, they meditate as much naughtiness as the honour they enjoyed (*i.e.*, the naughtiness they meditate was in proportion to the attentions they received).[1] If an uncovered head is the mark of

[1] "*Prolatæ enim in medium, et publicato bono suo elatæ, et a fratribus*

virginity, then if any virgin should fall from the grace of virginity, that she be not betrayed, she continues with uncovered head: and now goes about in a costume foreign to her, *i.e.*, one which virginity claims for itself: nevertheless she continues in the costume, then entirely alien to her, lest in fact she should be betrayed by a change. Conscious now of an undoubted womanhood, they dare to approach God with the head bare. But the jealous God and Lord, who said, There is nothing hidden which shall not be revealed, brings forth most of them to the public view. For they will not confess until they are betrayed by the cries of the infants themselves. But the more numerous they are, will you not have them suspected of so many more crimes? I will say, though I would rather not, that a virgin who does not fear to become a woman, once become so, it is hard for her to act the lie before God. How much will she not dare regarding her womb in order that her maternity be not discovered? God knows how many infants he has perfected and brought safely to birth, though a long while fought against by their mothers. For virgins of this sort always conceive very easily, have the happiest deliveries, and children very like their fathers. A forced and unwilling virginity incurs these crimes (*De Pudicitia*, xiv.).

The remedy for this state of things, in Tertullian's judgment, was that the virgins should be veiled in the churches, where, in fact, he considered the mischief was brewed.[1] He

omni honore et caritatis operatione cumulatæ, dum non latent ubi quid admissum est, tantum dedecoris cogitant, quantum honoris habuerunt." The passage is rendered as follows, rather unintelligibly, in the Ante-Nicene Christian Library: " For, after being brought forth into the midst [of the church], and elated by the public appropriation of their property, and laden by the brethren with every honour and charitable bounty, so long as they do not fall—when any sin has been committed, they meditate a deed as disgraceful as the honour was high which they had. [It is this.]"

[1] The Pagans of the period were worse than the Christians, according to Tertullian, who says in *Apologeticus*, ch. xv.: "All know that adulteries are arranged in the temples, that enticement is carried on amongst the altars, that in the very tabernacles of the temple-wardens and priests, under the same head-bands, mitres and purple robes, while incense is burning, lust is gratified sometimes."

sternly demanded the reason why the virgins were unveiled in church, while they veiled themselves in the streets in the presence of the heathen? Was it to please God or the brethren? (ch. xiii.). He makes the remarkable statement, which one does not know how to understand: "I will praise their vigour, if they should sell anything of virginity to heathens."[1] They fear strangers, let them stand in fear of the brethren also. He objects to their being specially distinguished by the removal of the veil in church, by which they were gazed at, and their 'glory' magnified before the brethren, while the he-virgins had no mark of distinction by which they also may be singled out and glorified. Whether by way of joke, in which these austere Fathers occasionally indulged in their grim way, he claims for the latter some distinctive marks—either the feathers of the Garamantes, or else the fillets of the barbarians, or the golden cicadas or grasshoppers worn by the Athenians, or the curls of Germans, or the tattooing of the Britons; or, the most satirical stroke of all, let the opposite course be pursued, and the he-virgins be veiled and concealed in the churches.[2] He proceeds gravely to argue that if the Holy Ghost had granted the privilege of unveiling in church to the maidens, he was sure he would have granted some such concession as he indicated to the he-virgins, to whom the preservation of virginity was a greater struggle. But as the Holy Ghost had conceded nothing to the male, he was much more unlikely to have granted any privilege to the female.

Tertullian's views on marriage and celibacy were austere. Second marriage, after the death of the husband or wife, was condemned by him, both in the laity and the clergy; he considered it fornication or adultery. Like Clement, Tertullian seeks his models from the heathen. Priesthood, he says, is a function of widowhood, or of celibate men and women among the heathen nations. It is unlawful for the

[1] "*Laudabo vigorem, si aliquid et apud ethnicos virginitatis nundinarint*" (*De Virginibus Velandis*, xiii.).

[2] "*Debebunt etiam et ipsi aliqua sibi insignia defendere, aut pennas Garamantum, aut strophulos Barbarorum, aut cicadas Atheniensium, aut cirros Germanorum, aut stigmata Britonum: aut ex diverso fiat, capite velati in Ecclesia lateant*" (*De Virg. Cel.*, x.).

king of heathendom, the Pontifex Maximus, to marry a second time (*Ad Uxorem*, i. 7). Monogamy (by which he meant single marriage in contradistinction to re-marriage), he says, is held in the highest honour amongst the heathen. The flamen and his wife must be but once married. The fact that the chief pontiff can only marry once is a glory to Monogamy (*Exhortations to Chastity*, xiii.). He refers to numbers of Gentile women who, devoted to the memory of beloved husbands, abstain from re-marriage; to the vestal virgins who tended the sacred fire at Rome; to the virgin chosen by lot for the service of Achæan Juno in Ægium; to the unmarried priestesses at Delphi, and the widow priestesses of African Ceres (*Ad Uxor.*, i. 6). Tertullian was born and educated a Pagan, and he obviously retained his heathen predilections when he was converted to Christianity. He was the first to apply to the Christian clergy the technical expressions employed by the Pagans to the officiating ministers in the temples—*sacerdos* or priest, *antistes, pontifex maximus*, and *sacerdotium*, priesthood. He was also the first who regarded the Eucharist as a sacrifice, and it is from his writings that we obtain the first glimpses of prayers or offerings for the dead and of the sign of the cross (*De Corona*, iii.).

We must conclude that the sexual morality prevalent amongst the Christians in Rome at this period was not much different from what we have seen it to have been in Alexandria and Carthage. We have no special history or description to refer to, but we must draw our conclusions from the narratives of the disputes that raged at this period between successive bishops of Rome and other bishops and dignitaries of the Christian Church. I have already, with reference to the colloquy between Philip and Jesus, had occasion to speak of three bishops of Rome—Victor, Zephyrinus, and Callistus. The first had been removed by death, but we have still to do with the two latter prelates. Zephyrinus was a feeble and incapable man, but his adviser and instigator was the crafty and vicious Callistus, who is represented by Hippolytus to be a man of unscrupulous character. This charlatan, as Hippolytus calls him, established a school of theology at Rome, in which he gave instruction and inculcated his obnoxious views. Hippolytus ascribes to him the distinction of inventing the system of sanctioning sensual indulgence by assuming the power of forgiving sins. By indiscriminately offering pardon to moral transgressions he rendered himself popular amongst a profligate Christian community, and his school was rapidly filled to overflowing. Some of the opinions he propounded would not in our days be condemned as objectionable, viz., that bishops, priests, and deacons, who had been twice and thrice married, or being already in orders should get married, should retain their position among the clergy. But there were other offences of a heinous sort, to which also he showed indulgence. He propounded the opinion that if a bishop be guilty of any sin, even a sin unto death (1 John v. 16), he ought not to be deposed. The vicious indulgence which the indiscriminate forgiveness of sins generated amongst men was likewise extended to women. Christian women of rank, who were without husbands, and did not wish to marry beneath their condition, were permitted to take one of their house-slaves or freedmen, and to regard him as a husband. The passage in Miller's edition of the *Refutation of Heresies*, by Hippolytus, is corrupt, but the above is the only probable sense that can be obtained from it.[1] Dean Milman thinks the deaconesses of the Church of Rome availed themselves of the liberty of re-marriage, but it is not improbable that they also permitted to themselves the indulgence of unmarried companions, in common with the male clergy. These vicious

---

[1] The Ante-Nicene Christian Library translates as follows: "For even also he permitted females, if they were unwedded, and burned with passion at an age at all events unbecoming, or if they were not disposed to overturn their own dignity through a legal marriage, that they might have whomsoever they would choose as a bed-fellow, whether a slave or free, and that [a woman], though not legally married, might consider such [a companion] as a husband" (see Milman's *Latin Christianity*, Bk. I. ch. i.). The deaconesses were a female order of clergy, performing duties towards women similar to those rendered to men by the deacons. Anointing the body with oil or chrism was in the second century, and subsequent to it, a part of the rite of baptism; and this rite therefore required the services of deaconesses in the baptism of women, as infant baptism was then unknown.

practices naturally led to further crimes for the purpose of concealing and destroying the fruit of such unbecoming connections (*Hippolytus*, ix. 12).

The bishops of Rome had now begun to claim the right of controlling the Churches of Christendom, and we know of the attitude assumed by the imperious Victor on the question of the Paschal controversy (see *ante*, p. 132, ff.), who was on the point of excommunicating all the Churches of Asia (Eusebius, *Eccl. Hist.*, v. 24). One fruit of this controversy was obviously the insertion of an interpolation into the Gospel of Matthew (xvi. 18 and 19): "And I say unto thee, That thou art Peter, and upon this rock I will build my church; and the gates of hell shall not prevail against it. And I will give unto thee the keys of the kingdom of heaven: and whatsoever thou shalt bind on earth shall be bound in heaven: and whatsoever thou shalt loose on earth shall be loosed in heaven." The predominance claimed by Victor was unsupported by Scriptural authority, and hence the above interpolation was made to supply the necessary sanction. The success of this proceeding gave encouragement to Victor's successor, Zephyrinus, to do the same, backed up and instigated as he was by a strong and unscrupulous ecclesiastic of immense theological and social influence and popularity in Rome—Callistus. We have seen that Tertullian was aware of and acknowledged the passage in Matthew (ch. xvi. 18, 19), which he probably found in the Gospel at the time of his conversion to Christianity. He, however, turned the edge of the passage by asserting what was in all probability only the publicly avowed object of the interpolation, that it merely gave the power of declaring how much of the Jewish law was binding on Christians, and how much was abolished. There is no trace of any consciousness on his part of the passage in the Fourth Gospel (xx. 23) granting to the Apostles, and through them to the clergy, the power of remission of sins. On the contrary, we find him strenuously objecting to a decree issued by the Pontifex Maximus, or bishop of bishops, whom I take to be Zephyrinus, Bishop of Rome, to this effect: "I remit to such as have repented the sins both of adultery and fornication" (*De*

Pudicitia, i.). Whether the sins of adultery and fornication be taken as meaning only second marriages, or the full and absolutely unjustifiable offences ordinarily known under these names (and I believe the latter were practically included), Tertullian objected to the pretension of the Bishop of Rome to grant remission. To him remission was the same as indulgence, which without doubt the practice really was. In fact, as I understand it, the Bishop of Rome granted indulgence in fornication and adultery, not only to the clergy, but to the laity. This was the beginning of the system of flagrant immorality which culminated in the sixteenth century, and was the main cause of the Protestant Reformation. What were the conditions under which Zephyrinus granted indulgence to adultery and fornication is not stated by any writer. But Hippolytus in two passages distinctly asserts that Zephyrinus was open to persuasion by proffered gain (Bk. IX. 7), was covetous and accessible to bribes (Bk. IX. 11). It is a credit to the Christian community of the third century that it possessed amongst its members men like Hippolytus and Tertullian, and there were doubtless many more, who raised a righteous opposition to the pretension and action of two such rogues and knaves as Zephyrinus and Callistus,[1] bishops of Rome.

Such, then, was the foul source from which sprang the passage in the Fourth Gospel (xx. 21-23), in which the Scriptural sanction required by Zephyrinus and Callistus for their nefarious practices was falsely obtained and attributed to our Lord: "Then said Jesus unto them again, Peace be unto you: as my Father hath sent me so send I you. And when he had said this, he breathed on *them*, and saith unto them, Receive ye the Holy Ghost: whose soever sins ye remit, they are remitted unto them; and whose soever *sins* ye retain, they are retained." It will be remarked that this passage may be deleted without the meaning of the immediate context being in any sense disturbed, and its removal will take away the palpable contradiction to the assurances of Jesus that Paraclete

---

[1] Rabelais' opinion of the character of Pope Callistus may be inferred from the vile occupation which he assigns to him in hell (Works, *Pantagruel*, Bk. II. 30).

(or the Holy Spirit) will be sent after his own departure to the Father.

I trust I have succeeded in clearly setting forth the circumstances under which this crafty interpolation was introduced into the Scriptures, and the evidence that it was not in the revised version of the second century, but put in by the authority of the Pope Zephyrinus and his knavish colleague, Callistus. I am, however, sensible that this investigation would have been more thoroughly and effectively carried out by Bishops Westcott and Ellicott, and hence I deeply regret that these learned prelates had not bethought themselves of examining the authenticity of the passage prior to the fourth century. I even fear that, notwithstanding the strength of the case, the Christian clergy will perversely use their undoubted talent and learning to explain away the circumstances and facts recorded by Clement of Alexandria, Tertullian, and Hippolytus, and to maintain that the unprincipled manœuvre of two episcopal rogues and knaves in the third century is an inspired account by the beloved disciple of the actual deed and words of the great Master.

I am satisfied that the story of Thomas' disbelief, narrated in ch. xx. 24–29, existed in the revised version of the second century, as both Irenæus and Clement of Alexandria make allusions to it, and the latter quotes verse 29. The description of Thomas as 'one of the twelve' has struck me as worthy of notice. It corresponds to Paul's expression that Jesus was seen, after the resurrection, 'of the twelve' (1 Cor. xv. 5). Now, in Matt. xxvii. 3–10, is an account of Judas' remorse and of his suicide before the crucifixion; and this diminution in the number of the disciples is at once marked by the expression 'the eleven disciples' in Matt. xxviii. 16. That the evangelist of the Fourth Gospel, in writing of a circumstance that occurred after the resurrection, should not note the diminution in the number of the disciples, appears to my mind to indicate that he was not aware, like Paul, of such diminution. I have retained this anecdote of the disbelief of Thomas in the original Gospel of Cerinthus, who, I believe, knew nothing of the story of Judas, which was entirely an invention of the second century.

Verse 31 of the twentieth chapter I take to be the conclusion of the original Gospel of Christ put forth by Cerinthus. Chapter xxi. is a postscript, which he had nothing to do with, and the various incidents related in it had no concern with his object in writing the Gospel. This final chapter has the look of a collection of anecdotes taken from various gospels or story-books current in the second half of the second century. If any object or purpose was kept in view in selecting them, I should say it was the aggrandisement of Peter, and the correction of the popular error regarding the immortality of the Apostle John. Verse 24 is, I believe, the only reason which exists for connecting the beloved disciple with the authorship of the Gospel; 'these things' being regarded as including the whole Gospel; and they identify the writer, Bishop Ellicott says, as the author of the Gospel, though Bishop Westcott says the words may be limited to the narrative of ch. xxi. The chapter was obviously added by the revision committee of the second century.

CHAPTER IX.

THE DISHONOURABLE CONDUCT OF BISHOP IRENÆUS.

THE lapse of over eighteen centuries since the forgery of the Fourth Gospel was perpetrated has effectually prevented the discovery of the actual perpetrators. The names of the members of the revision committee of the second century at Ephesus cannot now be ascertained: all traces of them have been obliterated. If the destruction of Christian literature during the persecutions of Decius and Diocletian had not taken place, some information, direct or indirect, may have survived to assist in the discovery; but under the actual circumstances I have not been able to find any clue to the identity of these individuals. It must be admitted, however, that the fact being that the Fourth Gospel, a pre-eminent work in Christian literature, was a modification of the writing of Cerinthus, which latter, as the Gospel of Christ, was actually read in some of the Churches of Asia Minor, many, if not all, the bishops and Fathers of the second half of the second century must be presumed to have been aware of that fact. Amongst these eminent members of the ancient Christian communities stands the renowned Bishop of Lyons, Irenæus, who, I am convinced, was cognisant of the greatest and most influential Christian religious forgery that has ever been perpetrated.

The clue to the discovery of this supreme forgery was furnished by the account of the martyrdom of Polycarp, as already set forth in this treatise (see *ante*, p. 47, ff.). The escape of the dove from the body of the martyred saint is the counterpart of the return flight of the dove of Cerinthus from the body of the crucified Lord, the martyrdom being expressly said to be according to the 'pattern of the Gospel of Christ.' In no gospel known to history was such a pattern exhibited except in the Gospel of Cerinthus; and for this knowledge we are primarily indebted to Irenæus (*Ad Hær.*, I. xxvi.), and his testimony is confirmed by Hippolytus (*Ref.*, vii. 33; x. 21; Miller, corresponding passages in the Ante-Nicene Christian Library, *Hipp.*, vii. 21, and x. 17). Now, Irenæus was a contemporary and pupil of Polycarp, and in his youth and early manhood a resident of Smyrna, where 'the Gospel of Christ,' containing the pattern, was known and read. In the absence of evidence to the contrary, we must conclude that Irenæus, who received his religious education from Polycarp, was acquainted with the 'Gospel of Christ' and the pattern, and as his familiarity with the doctrines of the Gnostics and of Cerinthus was considerable, it is not possible to believe that he was ignorant of the authorship of the pattern and of the gospel containing it. There is, further, direct evidence that Irenæus was acquainted with the account of the martyrdom of Polycarp, in which the escape of the dove is mentioned as effected in accordance with the 'pattern of the Gospel of Christ.' In the Pionian copy the history of the transmission of the account of the martyrdom is stated, and I should add that Bishop Lightfoot does not question the authenticity of the statement. The record runs: "This account Gaius copied from the papers of Irenæus, a disciple of Polycarp. The same also lived with Irenæus." The messenger who conveyed the letter of the Church of Smyrna to the Church at Philomelium was one Marcianus ($\delta\iota\grave{a}$ $\tau o\hat{v}$ $\dot{a}\delta\epsilon\lambda\phi o\hat{v}$ $M\alpha\rho\kappa\iota\alpha\nu o\hat{v}$). Seeing that Irenæus and his family were inhabitants of Smyrna contemporary with Polycarp, it is not improbable that the messenger was the brother of Irenæus, to whom ($M\alpha\rho\kappa\iota\alpha\nu\hat{\omega}$ $\tau o\check{v}\nu o\mu\alpha$) Eusebius says Irenæus dedicated one of his books (*Eccl. Hist.*, v. 26).

It would be an impertinence to assert that Bishop Lightfoot had a concealed motive in his endeavour to demonstrate that the incident of the dove in the martyrdom of Polycarp was a later interpolation, while he is in favour of the genuineness of the rest of the account. The complete document, as we now possess it, including the dove incident, is derived from a *Life of Polycarp*, which purports to have been written by a Pionius, who was martyred under Decius (A.D. 250), but which was really, the bishop maintains, the work of a forger of the fifth century. These facts are not disputed, and they are fair grounds to generate suspicion, for in those corrupt centuries the Christian religious orders lived, and delighted in living, in an atmosphere of fraud, falsehood, and forgery, usually excused by theologians as pious. That the dove story is not found in the quotation of the whole passage made by Eusebius confirmed his suspicion. The incident itself is of a ridiculous nature, and of course there can be no doubt of its falsity. All these are natural reasons for the belief that the dove story in the martyrdom was an interpolation, and they influenced the bishop's judgment, just as they have done the minds of other men. But there are other and more persuasive reasons for accepting the dove story as authentic, that is, that it existed in the original letter of the Church of Smyrna to the Church of Philomelium. I have already set forth some reasons for maintaining the genuineness of the incident, notwithstanding its omission in the *Ecclesiastical History* of Eusebius (see *ante*, p. 49), and others now suggest themselves. By denying the existence in the original of the dove story Bishop Lightfoot practically contradicts himself, for where would be "the parallel to the incident recorded in St John's account of the crucifixion," which the bishop says is 'obvious'? If, in the sentence "there came forth a dove and a quantity of blood," the words 'a dove and' be cut out, there would be no parallel to the account of the crucifixion in the Fourth Gospel. Then the question would arise why the pious brethren of the Church of Smyrna, seeing that they strove to make a parallel, should have omitted to mention 'water,' supposing that word to have been in the original Gospel, so very easy to do, and appropriate besides, as they say that the fire was extinguished by the flow of blood, a result that could have been told with magnificent exaggeration if they had added to the blood a great cataract of water. Munchausen and Rabelais obtain grand effects from the flow of water. If it be contended that the Smyrnæan letter really contained the word 'water,' which the pseudo-Pionius changed to 'a dove,' there would arise the difficulty to explain what reason could have induced Eusebius to omit the word in his *Ecclesiastical History*.

In support of his charge of interpolation against the pseudo-Pionius, Bishop Lightfoot brings forward some facts damnatory to the moral character of the former. In the Pionian *Life*, and in his note to the *History of the Transmission of the Account of the Martyrdom of Polycarp*, there are unscrupulous references made to ancient documents which have no existence. Further, this individual was before all things an incorrigible miracle-monger. "Among other miracles," says the bishop, "he relates that on the eve of Polycarp's appointment to the episcopate a dove hovered round his head." All these charges may be readily admitted without cross-examination, seeing that so many pious Christians, even Christians occupying eminent positions, such as bishops in the Church, were guilty of similar offences, which were common pious sins in the second and subsequent centuries in the Christian communities. Having thus fully developed the bad character of pseudo-Pionius, Bishop Lightfoot proceeds to draw his conclusion that the two doves—the one at the inauguration of the saint's episcopate, and the other at his martyrdom—were 'caged and let fly by the same hand.' It would almost seem that the learned bishop attributes originality of invention to his forger, as if the latter was the creator of this poetical conceit of the dove. But we know that he was simply an imitator. So far from the first miracle of the hovering of the dove at the inauguration leading on to the second miracle of the flight of the dove at the martyrdom of Polycarp, it appears to me that the fact was the reverse, viz., that the escape flight of the dove at the martyrdom suggested to the scribe the entrance flight at the inauguration. Seeing that the brethren of the Church of Smyrna alleged the exit of the dove at the martyrdom, the author considered himself justified in alleging the entrance at the inauguration; for naturally the dove could not escape from the body of the martyr if it had not previously effected an entrance.

It will hardly be conceded that the pseudo-Pionius was the inventor of the dove incident, and the question arises, where did he obtain the idea? He was not the first who put it to use, for Prudentius, the Latin Christian poet, who flourished in the latter half of the fourth century and beginning of the fifth, had used it before him. Jacobson, in his edition of the *Apostolic Fathers* (footnote to ch. xvi., " De Martyr. Polyc."), quotes the following verses of Prudentius from the hymn in praise of the virgin Eulalia:—

> "Emicat inde columba repens,
> Martyris os nive candidior
> Visa relinquere et astra sequi.
> Spiritus hic erat Eulaliæ
> Lacteolus, celer, innocuus."

Then suddenly a dove, whiter than snow, springs forth, and was seen to leave the mouth of the martyr and to follow the stars. This was the spirit of Eulalia, milk-white, swift, and innocent.

There can be no doubt that the evangelical dove was the creation of Cerinthus. It was unlikely to have been employed by Christian poets and writers, in connection with the deaths of saints and martyrs, from the Gnostic and heretical writings of Cerinthus, if it had not previously been consecrated and employed by the Church, as had been done in the Churches of Smyrna, Philomelium, and the neighbourhood of these places. Though the Church had subsequently abolished the escape of the dove at the crucifixion, retaining as a sacred truth the entrance of the dove at the baptism, there remained an undercurrent of literary appreciation which cherished and preserved the former beautiful poetical conception. The adverse verdict of the Church was unable to annihilate this phantasy of Gnostic genius: "*les idées ne meurent pas.*"

The gist of these remarks is that Bishop Lightfoot points out certain parallels of statements in the account of the martyrdom of Polycarp and the Fourth Gospel, and draws hence the conclusion that the Fourth Gospel was recognised in the Church early in the second century. Of these parallels, all but one are forced and strained, and may even be said to be no parallels at all. The exceptional parallel is clear and obvious, and it is sufficient of itself to establish Bishop Lightfoot's contention. Having thus proved his point and vanquished his opponent, the bishop, after an interval of several years,[1] proceeds to destroy his own proof by maintaining that it was an interpolation. If the dove incident in the account of the martyrdom be deleted as a forgery, the balance of the text will contain no parallel to be found in the Fourth Gospel.

Throughout his great work on heresies Irenæus displays a considerable interest in the Fourth Gospel, and makes much use of it in his controversies against the Gnostics. With the exception of a single quotation by Theophilus (c. A.D. 168) his quotations from, and references to, the Gospel are the earliest extant. He was probably the first who introduced Paraclete into general Christian literature, as mention of it is made in the letter of the Church of Lyons, describing the great persecution under Marcus Aurelius and Verus (c. 177), of which letter he is considered to be the author, being at the time a presbyter at Lyons, and a man of literary talent. I think it will be admitted, though definite proof is not available, that the revised Fourth Gospel was brought over to Europe from Asia Minor, and was recognised and accepted by the Western Churches under his auspices, assisted, perhaps, by Clement of Alexandria. Under these circumstances, his concealment of the fact that he was aware that the Fourth Gospel was a modification of the Gospel of Cerinthus, will be regarded in our days as conduct of considerable moral turpitude.

And a similar opinion would have been pronounced upon it by Pagan society in the second century: for the practice, very common amongst Christian communities of the second and subsequent centuries, of plagiarism, forgery, attribution of writings to a false author—usually a man of repute—with the design of deceiving, interpolation and falsification of sacred documents, and similar literary offences, were not in vogue amongst the Pagans. The public opinion of the Pagans regarding such offences was pretty much what it is amongst civilised communities of the present day.

---

[1] The chapter on Papias in the Essays on *Supernatural Religion* was published in October 1875, and the remarks on the martyrdom of Polycarp were published in 1891. The charge of interpolation was an afterthought.

Christian public opinion of the second and subsequent centuries did not, however, regard these delinquencies as seriously reprehensible. We are obliged to come to this conclusion on account of the wide prevalence and intensity of this perversity amongst even the leaders of the Church. In perusing Christian documents it is essential that a preliminary inquiry be instituted as to their authenticity and freedom from falsification before their subject-matter can be considered. Even their authorship must be investigated, although an honoured and revered name is frequently attacked. The result of my investigation of the Fourth Gospel is an example in point: it is a serious question whether the Gospel of Luke is not an amplification of the Gospel of Marcion: the Gospels of Matthew and Mark possess very little of the writings of these eminent individuals: the Acts of the Apostles were written by God knows who, but are complacently attributed to Luke, said to be a companion of Paul, by the Church. The genuine Epistles of Paul contain obvious falsifications and additions in various parts: and the Church, ostensibly under the 'guidance of the Spirit of Truth,' has fathered upon him several epistles written by other authors, all of them living in the second century. The anonymous Epistle of John is assigned to the Apostle of that name, after being deceitfully tampered with: and the same revered authorship is bestowed upon the lunatical writing known as the Revelations, which had also been doctored. The Second Epistle of Clement was attributed to the same author as the First Epistle, although there is a difference of about half a century, or thereabouts, in their dates of publication. The Epistles of Ignatius have been so foully used that, like the beggar's cloak, the original pieces cannot be discovered without difficulty or freedom from doubt. Of pure plagiarism some examples have already been mentioned; the Gospel of John was an appropriation of the writings of Cerinthus, the Gospel of Luke is seriously suspected of being a transcript, with additions, of a sectarian gospel, used by Marcion; the Epistle of Barnabas has chapters which are copied from the *Didache*, or teaching of the Apostles. Bishop Lightfoot expresses his belief that very considerable parts of the fifth book of Irenæus are borrowed, without acknowledgment, from the works of Papias (Essays on *Supernatural Religion*, vi., " Papias," p. 202).

Bishop Lightfoot defends the plagiarism imputed by him to Irenæus. "Literary property," he says, "was not an idea recognised by early Christian writers. They were too much absorbed in their subject to concern themselves with their obligations to others, or with the obligations of others to them. Plagiarism was not a crime where they had literary things in common" (Essays on *Supernatural Religion*, vi. p. 202). This was a view neither expressed nor silently acted upon by Pagan contemporary writers. But Irenæus' offence and conduct in connection with the Fourth Gospel cannot be so easily extenuated. The appropriation bodily of the Gospel of Cerinthus, after alteration and addition, the declaration that the modified gospel was the composition of the Apostle John, and a work inspired by the Holy Ghost, a divinity, was dishonest and dishonourable conduct in Christian public opinion in the second century, if Christian principle is to be considered of any force in that age. Christian principle was unfortunately very weak amongst the Christian communities of the second and subsequent centuries. An educated man of good social position, a bishop and chief in a religious society professing a pure morality, availing himself of his literary and religious eminence to approve and recommend to the members of his community a gospel which he knew to be a forgery, is an object without parallel in profane history. Irenæus was a product of the ecclesiasticism of the second century ; it will be difficult to find his match outside the limits of the history of ecclesiasticism. It will be wrong and unjust, however, to attribute the development and fostering of ecclesiastical knaves and rogues to the moral system of Jesus.

In the fierce and unrestricted competition in the second century of the various Christian or pseudo-Christian sects for followers, upon whose numbers and wealth depended the prosperity and power of the leaders, the principles of conduct inculcated by Jesus were suffocated and displaced by the base motives which prevailed at that age, and which, alas! still prevail in the prosecution of commercial pursuits. Each sect strove for the suppression of its rivals, and was not scrupulous about the means employed to achieve that object. The Valentinians had appropriated early in the century a gospel which was of literary and doctrinal merit, and which doubtless contributed to the success and affluence which that sect enjoyed. This gospel had been in use in Asia Minor from an early date in obscure Churches, but had manifestly been unknown in orthodox circles in Rome. The Valentinian gospel, the original of which was the Cerinthian, was seized upon, and some trimming being accomplished, was introduced to the orthodox Churches of Europe as the work of the Apostle John; all this very probably being the suggestion of Irenæus, and certainly known to him, who was an Asiatic ecclesiastic employed in Europe. The orthodox sect thus came into possession of a spiritual gospel in common with the Valentinians, and its claims to public patronage were at least equalised with those of the Valentinians, or rather made better. It would have been treacherous and base for Irenæus to betray the secret, and doubtless dangerous to his prospects or even life. The counterpart of honour exists amongst knaves in very great force, and a breach of it is heavily punished. The above explanation of the conduct of Irenæus is the view which I have formed from the conceptions of the morality, in these matters, of the Christian clergy and writers of the second and third centuries, derived from the perusal of their own works. The early Fathers debased the Christianity or moral system of Jesus to the condition of a commercial institution, and they barely made the effort to conceal their design. The natural desire for personal advancement was not concealed under the later refinement of *Nolo episcopari* (I do not wish to be a bishop), overcome by the prayers and entreaties of the faithful, and the persuasion of the Holy Ghost. Mental struggles and spiritual workings, and prayers for heavenly guidance, such as those which distress the mind and soul of the modern rector or vicar, holding a living of £500, when offered a living of £900, before he tearfully accepts the latter, were unknown to the presbyters of the second century. I have found no trace of them. The later refinement of solicitude for souls is absent

Y

in early patristic literature. The Fathers of the Church in the second and third centuries were powerfully actuated by the desire to smash their sectarian rivals, regardless of the fate of their souls, and to gather in their followers (who provided 10 per cent.), and they made no concealment of this desire under elegant phrases or pretences. It is my conclusion that the second century Fathers and ecclesiastics, as the result of the fierce competition between them and the Gnostic and other sects, debased Christianity to the condition of a commercial institution; and this character the organised Christian Churches have maintained ever since. For such degradation the moral system of Jesus is not responsible; but its sweetness and innate power still prevail to restrain the degraded religious system within bounds endurable by men.

CHAPTER X.

THE ORIGIN OF THE DOCTRINE OF THE TRINITY.

I BELIEVE that the origin of the doctrine of the Trinity is to be sought in Cerinthus's writing, the original of the Fourth Gospel, and in the hinterland of his writing, the mysterious region in which the singular and incomprehensible theology of the Christian Gnostics flourished.

In the genuine Christian writings of the first century, the four epistles of Paul being taken as the nucleus and standard of the Christian literature of that early period, there are no traces of a belief in a triple Godhead. Paul did not regard Jesus as a god and object of worship, but as an extraordinary man, declared to be the Son of God by the resurrection from the dead, as a suitable subject for love, veneration, and obedience (Rom. i. 4). Nowhere is he spoken of as 'God the Son,' a phrase which was exceedingly common in subsequent centuries, but simply as the Lord Jesus. In all social relations Jesus was looked upon as a man, and nothing more, by the early Christians. Even shortly after his withdrawal from public life, his followers formed factions, taking as leaders prominent men in the Christian communities, among whom Christ appeared as one of several (1 Cor. ii. 12). This could not be possible if Christ was regarded as God by the Christians of that period. The Holy Spirit, in the same manner, is never alluded to as God, and is never named God the Holy Ghost. The Christians of the first century recognised one God only, who was known and alluded to as God, or our Father, or the Father. The name God was never applied to another being (Rom. i. 7, 9, 10, 16, 17, 18, 19, 21,

23, 24, 25, 26, 28, 30, 32; ii. 2, 3, 4, 11, 13, 16, 17, 23, 24, etc., etc.). Our Father (Rom. i. 7; 1 Cor. i. 3; 2 Cor. i. 2, 3; Gal. i. 4). The Father (Rom. vi. 4; 1 Cor. viii. 6; xv. 24; Gal. i. 1, 3).

In the second century, when corruption had infiltrated the Christian communities, we find adoration and worship given to several gods. Honest Justin, writing in the middle of the second century, distinctly states that the Christians of his day, the members of the orthodox communities, 'worshipped and adored' God the Father, the Son, a host of good angels, and the prophetic Spirit (*First Apology*, vi.). These divine beings were not all of equal potency; as the Son is declared to be the "first power after God the Father" (*First Apology*, xxxii.), and it is to be remarked that in the order of mention the Holy Spirit followed the good angels. Athenagoras, writing a few years after Justin, A.D. 177, and subsequently to the publication of the revised Fourth Gospel, distinctly states that the Christians of his time acknowledged "God the Father, God the Son, and the Holy Spirit": he appears to have hesitated to have written God the Holy Spirit. He defines the Holy Spirit to be "an effluence of God, flowing from him, and returning back again like a beam of the sun" (Ante-Nicene Christian Library, *Athenagoras*, ch. x.). He continues to remark that the divine nature was not limited to the above three beings; but that the Christians recognised a multitude of "angels and ministers," who were distributed by God and his Logos over the world, "to occupy themselves about the elements." The belief in angels was very ancient, was widespread amongst the Jews, and prevailed amongst Christians of the first century; but they were not objects of worship to the Jews. The belief ran into worship amongst Christians in the second century, and was prohibited in Colossians ii. 18, and Revelations xix. 10, which were publications of the earlier part of the second century. Neither Irenæus nor Clement of Alexandria, nor any of the Ante-Nicene Fathers, speak of the angels as objects of worship. Irenæus and Clement recognised the divinity of Jesus; but I can discover no clear expression of a belief in the divinity of the Holy Ghost, as God and an object of worship or adoration, in the writings of these Fathers.

The formulation of the doctrine of the Trinity, as we now have it, is found in Tertullian's treatise, *Adversus Praxean*; and in it occurs the first appearance of the technical expression 'Unity in Trinity' in Christian literature (*c*. 220). Praxeas was a Patripassian, a sect that took its origin from the exact interpretation of the interpellation of Philip and Jesus' reply to it (John xiv. 8–11) (see *ante*, p. 274), in which is the clear statement of the identity of the Father and Son, *i.e.*, of God the Father and Jesus. This sect took no note of the Holy Ghost: as Tertullian expresses it, Praxeas put Paraclete to flight (*Ad. Prax.*, i., "*Paracletum fugavit*"). The appearance of this sect compelled the theologians of the day to put their vague ideas regarding the Godhead of Jesus and other divine objects into definite shape. It was clear that as the ideas on these subjects stood, the theoretical objects of worship and adoration were numerous, and hence the orthodox Christians of the day were, theoretically at least, polytheists, and hence Pagans. To Tertullian, a lawyer, is due the renown of having reconciled the conflicting conditions of the recognition and adoration of several divine beings with the worship of one God. He put forth the doctrine of 'Unity in Trinity,' retaining as divine personages, to whom worship was due, the Father, Son, and Holy Ghost, and dropping the good angels.

In refuting Praxeas' contention that the Father and the Son must be the same person, or otherwise it would not be possible to believe in one God, Tertullian says the Patripassian heresy "considers itself to possess the pure truth, since it thinks that one only God is not otherwise to be believed in than if one should say that the Father, Son, and Holy Spirit[1] are self-same, as if even so one may not be all, while all are from one, namely, by unity of substance; nevertheless the sacrament of the æconomy (*æconomiæ sacramentum*) is preserved, which disposes unity in trinity, placing in a line the three, Father, Son, and Holy Spirit. But three not in rank but in grade; not in substance but in form; not in power

[1] Tertullian here makes a mistake, because the Patripassians took no notice of the Holy Spirit, just as Tertullian himself dropped the good angels.

but in aspect; but of one substance and of one rank and of one power, because it is of one God, of whom we reckoned these grades and forms and aspects. But how they [*i.e.*, the three] suffer number without division our treatise as it proceeds will demonstrate."[1]

So far Tertullian was thoroughly original. I am unaware that any one before him had conceived the paradox of 'unity in trinity.' It is sad and painful to remark that the dogma was a lawyer's justification of an unjustifiable, unchristian, and reprehensible course of conduct—the recognition and worship of a plurality of gods. A modern counterpart of the dogma may be said to be the legal justification of the unjustifiable, immoral, and hateful operations of simony in the Churches of Rome and England, and, indeed, in all Churches, which justification or legislation is in fact a public declaration that ecclesiastical Christianity is practically a commercial institution.

While Tertullian was original in the enunciation of the dogma of the Trinity, he ceased to be so in the arguments that he brought forward in support of the doctrine. To explain the physically impossible condition of how the Trinity was susceptible of number without division, he had recourse to the theory of 'emanations' brought forward by the Gnostics. He himself acknowledges his obligation, though in an ungracious manner (ch. viii.). Valentinus and other Gnostics named their emanations from the Deity æons; but Tertullian carefully abstains from applying this appellation to the Son and Holy Spirit, although he plainly implies that the latter were of the same nature as the æons. The

[1] ". . . . hæc [hæresis], quæ se existimat meram veritatem possidere, dum unicum Deum non alias putat credendum, quam si ipsum eumdemque et Patrem et Filium, et Spiritum sanctum dicat: quasi non sic quoque unus sit omnia, dum ex uno omnia, per substantiæ scilicet unitatem; et nihilominus custodiatur œconomiæ sacramentum, quæ unitatem in trinitatem disponit, tres dirigens, Patrem, et Filium, et Spiritum sanctum. Tres autem non statu, sed gradu; nec substantia sed forma; nec potestate, sed specie; unius autem substantiæ, et unius status, et unius potestatis; quia unus Deus, ex quo et gradus isti et formæ et species, in nomine Patris et Filii et Spiritus sancti deputantur. Quomodo autem numerum sine divisione patiuntur, procedentes retractatus demonstrabunt" (*Adversus Praxean*, ch. ii.).

difference between the Gnostic and the Christian emanations is stated to be the following: "Valentinus probolas suas discernit et separat ab auctore: et ita longe ab eo ponit, ut Æon patrem nesciat. Denique desiderat nosse, nec potest; imo et pene devoratur et dissolvitur in reliquam substantiam. Apud nos autem solus Filius Patrem novit, et sinum Patris ipse exposuit, et omnia apud Patrem audivit et vidit; et quæ mandatus est a Patre, ea et loquitur." Valentinus divides and separates his emanations from their author: and places them so far away from him, that an æon does not know the Father. It indeed longs to know him, but cannot; in fact it is almost swallowed up and dissolved into the rest of matter. But amongst us the Son alone knows the Father, and has himself displayed the bosom of the Father, and has heard and seen all things with the Father; and what things he has been commanded by the Father, these he speaks. The theology of Valentinus is not here correctly represented, for Valentinus' æons dwell in the Pleroma or divine region: but one of them only departed outside the Pleroma (Tertullian, *Adv. Val.*, chaps. xiv., xv.). The point, however, is that Tertullian, the author of the doctrine of the Trinity, declares that God the Son is an emanation (an æon, though he does not use the word) from God the Father. "Hæc erit probola veritatis, custos unitatis, qua prolatum dicimus Filium a Patre, sed non separatum." This will be the emanation of the truth, the guardian of the unity, whereby we declare that the Son is an emanation from the Father, but not separated. The Holy Spirit is not noticed in this argumentation, and throughout the treatise the argumentation has reference to God the Father and God the Son, while the God the Holy Spirit is left out. Tertullian proceeds to state that God put forth the Son as a root puts forth the tree, and a spring the river, and the sun the ray, for these are (*"probolæ earum substantiarum"*) emanations of the substances from which they proceed (ch. viii.). Tertullian has no hesitation to say that the tree is the son of the root, the river of the spring, and the ray of the sun; because every origin or source is a parent, and everything which emanates from an origin or source is an offspring. Much more is the Word of God, who has actually received the name of Son. But yet the tree is not separate from the root, nor the river from its spring, nor the ray from the sun, just as the Word is not separate from God. "Nec dubitaverim Filium dicere, et radicis fruticem, et fontis fluvium, et solis radium ; quia omnis origo parens est : et omne quod ex origine profertur, progenies est : multo magis sermo Dei, qui etiam proprie nomen Filii accepit ; nec frutex tamen a radice, nec fluvius a fonte, nec radius a sole discernitur, sicut nec a Deo sermo." Tertullian proceeds to say that following the form of these examples, he confesses that God and his Word, the Father and his Son, are two. For the root and the tree are two things, but joined. The spring and the river are two kinds, but undivided. The sun and the ray are two forms, but coherent. Everything which proceeds from something else must necessarily be second to that from which it proceeds, without being on that account separated. But where there is a second, there are two ; and where there is a third, there are three. Now the Spirit is third from God and the Son, just as the fruit from a tree is third from the root. The brook from a river is third from the spring. And the apex of the ray is third from the sun. Nothing, however, is different from the matrix, from which it derives its own properties. "Igitur secundum horum exemplorum formam, profiteor me duos dicere, Deum et Sermonem ejus, Patrem et Filium ipsius. Nam et radix et frutex duæ res sunt, sed conjunctæ. Et fons et flumen duæ species sunt, sed indivisæ. Et sol et radius duæ formæ sunt, sed cohærentes. Omne quod prodit ex aliquo, secundum sit ejus necesse est de quo prodit, non ideo tamen est separatum. Secundus autem ubi est, duo sunt ; et tertius ubi est, tres sunt. Tertius enim est spiritus a Deo et Filio, sicut tertius a radice fructus ex frutice. Et tertius a fonte, rivus ex flumine. Et tertius a sole, apex ex radio. Nihil tamen a matrice alienatur, a qua proprietas suas ducit" (*Adv. Pr.*, viii.).

Tertullian's argument for the antiquity or eternity of the Son or Logos is the following : "Ante omnia Deus erat solus, ipse sibi et mundus et locus et omnia. Solus autem, quia nihil aliud extrinsecus præter illum. Cæterum, ne tunc quidem solus ; habebat enim secum, quam habebat in semetipso, rationem suam scilicet. Rationalis etiam Deus, et ratio in ipso prius; et ita, ab ipso omnia. Quæ ratio, sensus ipsius est. Hanc Græci λόγον dicunt, quo vocabulo etiam sermonem appellamus. Ideoque jam in usu nostrorum, per simplicitatem interpretationis, Sermonem dicere in primordio apud Deum fuisse. . . . . Nam etsi Deus nondum Sermonem suum miserat, proinde eum cum ipsa et in ipsa ratione intra semetipsum habebat, tacite cogitando et disponendo secum, quæ per sermonem erat dicturus" (*Adv. Prax.*, v.). For before all things God was alone, himself for himself, world and space and all things. But alone, because there was extrinsically nothing else except himself. But not even then was he alone; for he had with him that which he had in himself, namely, his own reason. For God is rational, and reason was previously in him; and so all things from himself. Which reason was the sense of himself. This the Greeks call λόγος, by which term also we designate the Word. And so it is now in the practice of our people, from the simplicity of the interpretation, to say that the Word was in the beginning with God. . . . . For although God had not yet sent his Word, all the same he had him with himself and in his reason within himself, when he silently meditated and arranged with himself, what he was subsequently to declare through the Word. This argumentation of Tertullian, an improvement on the primitive conception of Theophilus (see *ante*, p. 4, footnote) that the Word existed in the beginning in the bowels or stomach of God, has not been improved upon in subsequent centuries, and has been silently accepted by theologians and the Churches as an exhaustive and convincing explication of the eternity of the Word, or second person of the Trinity, God the Son. I am unaware that any orthodox theologian has controverted Tertullian's views. The argumentation of the African lawyer and theologian has indeed not been repeated in subsequent centuries, but the fruit of his argumentative ingenuity, the doctrine of the Trinity in Unity, is universally accepted by the Churches.

Tertullian's argumentation on the eternity of the Word, if applied to any other subject but one of divinity, would hardly be considered convincing. For instance, if applied to the subject of solitary confinement, and the assertion be made that the prisoner shut up alone in a cell is nevertheless not solitary, but has his reason to keep him company, not to speak of his five senses, which he retains in his possession, and the society of his hands and feet and the rest of his body —such an argument would be regarded as simply whimsical.

Tertullian, ás already said, does not give much attention to God the Holy Spirit, and does not devote a special argument to demonstrate the antiquity or eternity of the third person of the Trinity. But he incidentally furnishes a proof of the eternity of the Holy Spirit. He quotes the Elohistic passage in Genesis i. 26, "And God said, Let us make man in our image," and inquires, Why does a being who is 'one and single' (*unicus et singularis*) speak in the plural? His explanation is, Because he was himself Father, Son, and Spirit, thus representing himself as plural. This argument maintains its ground to the present day, and I have heard a preacher in a village church (Anglican) expound it complacently to a congregation of English peasants, in proof of the doctrine of the Trinity. As any stick will suffice to beat a dog with, any pious assertion will convince the orthodox and confirm the faith of the faithful. The eternity of the Holy Ghost has hence never been disputed in the Church. An intelligent person is apt, however, to inquire why the plurality of the expression, 'let us make,' should be limited to three without special proof of the fact. The Hebrew word Elohim, rendered θεός in the Septuagint and God in our Authorised Version, means the gods, an indefinite number of them.

In speaking of the emanations (or æons) proceeding from the supreme Deity, Tertullian markedly avoids reference to Cerinthus's theology, but limits himself to the religious speculations of Valentinus. There may have been design in this exclusion of the views of the earlier Gnostic; for the distinction which the Christian lawyer and theologian draws between the Valentinian æons and his own emanations (or æons) does not apply to the Cerinthian æon. The latter is in fact identical with the Tertullian emanations, and includes the special conditions which Tertullian asserts constitutes their peculiarity. The Christian emanation, the Son, says Tertullian, is not divided from the Father, but has knowledge of him, and has himself displayed the bosom of the Father. This statement corresponds with the accounts given by Irenæus and Hippolytus of the Cerinthian æon, Christ, and is confirmed by the statements and addresses to be found in the Cerinthian Gospel. Irenæus says of the doctrine of Cerinthus regarding Jesus, that Christ descended upon him in the form of a dove from that power, which is above all, that then he announced the unknown Father, and perfected his virtues: "descendisse in eum ab ea principalitate, quæ est super omnia, Christum figura columbæ; et tunc annuntiasse incognitum Patrem et virtutes perfecisse" (*Iren.*, I. xxvi. 1, Stieren). Hippolytus repeats the statement, "that Christ descended upon him in the form of a dove from that supreme power which is above all things. And then he preached the unknown Father, and perfected his powers or faculties; but towards the end Christ departed from Christ (Jesus), and that Jesus suffered and rose again, but Christ had been without suffering, being of the Father": "κατελθεῖν εἰς αὐτὸν τὸν τῆς ὑπὲρ τὰ ὅλα αὐθεντίας, τὸν Χριστὸν, ἐν εἴδει περιστερᾶς. Καὶ τότε κηρῦξαι τὸν [ἄ]γνωστὸν πατέρα, καὶ δυνάμεις ἐπιτελέσαι, πρὸς δὲ τῷ τέλει, ἀποστῆναι τὸν Χριστὸν ἀπὸ τοῦ Χριστοῦ, καὶ τὸν Ἰησουν πεπονθέναι καὶ ἐγηγέρθαι, τὸν δὲ Χριστὸν ἀπαθῆ διαμεμενηκέναι πατρικον ὑπάρχοντα" (*Refutatio Hæresium*, vii. 33, Miller). [I have added the particle ἄ to the word γνωστὸν, a clear omission in the manuscript (see Bk. X. 21)]. (See also Ante-Nicene Christian Library, *Hipp.*, vii. 21.) It is worthy of remark, in connection with the distinction between the Christian and Gnostic emanations (or æons) drawn by Tertullian, that this Father gives a very meagre account of the doctrine of Cerinthus, and entirely omits to state that Cerinthus inculcated that after the descent of the æon Christ upon Jesus, the latter preached the unknown Father.

After what has been said of the æons of Cerinthus and Valentinus in the earlier part of this treatise, the verisimilitude of the second and third persons of the Trinity with the æons Christ and Paraclete will seem remarkable. The apparent design of Tertullian, the founder of the doctrine of the Unity in Trinity, to suppress the theology of Cerinthus and to disparage the theology of Valentinus, will confirm the conclusion that the three persons of the Trinity in Unity are the counterparts of the supreme God and the Gnostic æons, Christ and Paraclete.

CHAPTER XI.

CONCLUDING REMARKS. DECADENCE OF ECCLESIASTICAL
CHRISTIANITY. SUBSTITUTION OF A MORAL SYSTEM.

THE decadence of ecclesiastical Christianity is a fact patent to the ordinary observer. It is not necessary to search it out, but it lies plainly manifested on the surface of history and society, and can be viewed without special effort by the casual spectator. The immense political power of the pope has disappeared, and even the temporal power in the papal principality has been overthrown. Nations that stood in awe of the political might of ecclesiastical Christianity, now scarcely regard it as worthy of a thought. The one remnant of the possession of political power by ecclesiastics is to be found in the presence of prelates, comparatively few in number, in the Upper Houses of Parliament in several European countries, a position, however, which is doomed, and will not last long. The political influence of ecclesiasticism is still, however, very powerful, and suffices to seriously embarrass strong governments and to retard the progress of civilisation. Laws enacted in past centuries, in the interests of ecclesiasticism and for the maintenance and support of its power over the people, have been repealed, or have fallen into desuetude, a result brought about by the spontaneous action of the judicial authorities in sympathy with the feeling of the people. Severe punitory laws, under which such men as the Rev. Dr Momerie, Rev. Mr Voysey, Rev. Dr Martineau, the most learned of English divines and the *doyen* of English theology, may be imprisoned and sentenced to hard labour, remain as dead letters in the Statute Book, which they disgrace by their ecclesiastical presence. Any attempt to revive these hateful and unrepealed ecclesiastical laws will meet with the combined and skilled opposition of the judicial authorities and the people. The people are even prepared to offer physical resistance to ecclesiastical Christianity when offensively aggressive, as was seen in the revolt in some districts and parishes against Church rates and tithes. Modern legislatures are markedly chary in dealing with subjects favourable to the pretensions of ecclesiasticism. Ecclesiastical doctrines, of great magnitude and antiquity, such as transubstantiation and its later congener the real presence, the Trinity, eternal damnation, etc., are openly opposed and condemned, in some instances even by ecclesiastics themselves in the pulpits. There is a strong undercurrent throughout Christendom, but of less force in religious England, of distrust and disbelief in the whole scheme of ecclesiastical Christianity. Men of great acquirements in all departments of science and knowledge, whose names are landmarks of human progress, have openly expressed their disapproval and rejection of ecclesiasticism. Great educational institutions, like our Universities of Cambridge and Oxford, and numerous others on the Continent, which were for centuries occupied with ecclesiastical studies and pursuits, and almost nothing else, have now been diverted, in some measure, to the cultivation of sciences which have no affinity to ecclesiasticism, but are intrinsically hostile to it. This change has been effected by the progressing mind of the people, in direct revolt against ecclesiasticism and its beneficed supporters.

The decadence of ecclesiastical Christianity is not less apparent in the diminution of its power over the minds of men than in the decline of its capacity for collecting money. The papal granaries for the storing and accumulation of treasure, which in former centuries were overflowing with wealth, are now announced by the newspapers to be very insufficiently filled. The revenue of the pope for the past year is declared to have fallen below half a million sterling: and the pope is reported to have made an appeal to Christendom for more pence. In the face of an enormously increased population and wealth, this is an extraordinary proof of the decline of financial prosperity, the main object and pursuit of ecclesiasticism, as it was the cause and mainspring of its origin in the second century. In our own country there has been a steady decline in the results of the financial operations of the Church, apparent in the course of the present century. In all ages of the Church the bishops have enjoyed the greatest share in the dividend arising from the financial transactions of ecclesiastical Christianity. The varying phases of the financial position of bishops may hence be fairly taken as indicating the rise and fall of the ecclesiastical empire. In the initial years of this century our bishops are represented to have been princes in wealth, real occupiers of thrones, who maintained regal style in their palaces and equipages. What their incomes were is unknown : but there cannot be a doubt that the English bishops were enormously rich. It is said by a popular writer in 1832 that it was believed that "the clergymen of the Church of England and Ireland receive, in the year, more money than the clergy of all the rest of the Christian world put together."[1] The Bishop of Durham was considered to have an annual income of £70,000, the Bishop of Winchester a little less, and so on: but these massive incomes were far underrated. The real figures will never be known, as ecclesiastical secrecy is impenetrable. The popular writer already quoted states the annual average income of the episcopal bench in his day (1832) to have been, for two archbishops, £26,465 each ; and for twenty-four bishops, £10,174 each (p. 58). These enormous official incomes did not include the great sums received as renewal fines on leases falling in, nor the multiform smaller streams of money that flowed from what may be vulgarly called 'pickings.' Turning to *Whitaker's Almanac* for 1898, I find the salary of the Archbishop of Canterbury set down as £15,000,[2] of the Arch-

[1] The extraordinary *Black Book : an Exposition of Abuses in Church and State, Courts of Law, etc.* (p. 5), London, 1832. Purchasable for a few shillings from any second-hand bookseller.

[2] The enormous disproportion between the salary of the Archbishop of Canterbury and the salaries of other great State officials is very marked. The salary of the archbishop is a very great advance upon the salaries of the Lord High Chancellor of England, £10,000 ; of the Prime Minister,

bishop of York, £10,000; of the Bishop of London, £10,000; of the Bishop of Durham, £7000; of Winchester, £6500; and gradually diminishing sums to £3000 for the Bishops of Bristol, Truro, and Wakefield, and then a great fall to £1600 for the Bishop of Sodor and Man. Thus in the short space of a few years the financial prosperity of the Church of England had considerably depreciated. The decline of ecclesiastical Christianity is still more marked in Ireland. The writer already quoted gives the yearly incomes, as they were stated to be, of the bishops in 1832 in detail (p. 173), and thus I am able to construct, with the help of *Whitaker*, the following comparative statement of episcopal incomes in Ireland in 1832 and 1898:—

		1832.	1898.
Archbishop of Armagh		£15,080	£2,500
" of Dublin		No return.	2,500
Bishop of Meath		£5,815	1,500
"	Limerick	2,915	3,015
"	Cashel	3,500	1,175
"	Clogher	9,000	1,273
"	Tuam	5,548	1,493
"	Down	...	1,800
"	Cork	3,000	1,700
"	'Derry	10,000	2,000
"	Killaloe	4,600	1,500
"	Kilmore	...	1,200
"	Ossory	3,000	1,535
"	Raphoe	5,379	...
"	Leighlin and Ferns	5,000	...
"	Dromore	4,863	...
"	Waterford	5,000	...
"	Cloyne	2,000	...

In canny Scotland, where economy piously prevails, the salaries of bishops vary from £914 (Edinburgh) to £638 (Argyll) (*Whitaker*, p. 245, 1898).

The monetary nourishment of ecclesiastical Christianity having thus manifestly been reduced from springs that in

£5000; of the First Lord of the Admiralty, £4500; of the Commander-in-Chief of the Army, £4500. While the great State departments controlled by the lesser paid officials are each of them subjects of national pride, the department controlled by the extravagantly paid officials is in a state of anarchy and discord, a national scandal and discredit, full of traitors to Protestantism, whose pay they receive.

former centuries provided abundant streams, ecclesiastical enterprise has tapped fresh sources. The sale of indulgences, or religious grants for license in vice, while it added immensely to the wealth of the Church, eventually led to a revulsion of popular feeling, which dealt a severe blow to the vitality of ecclesiasticism, and was the main cause of the decadence we are now considering. But religious and pious commerce of that description is not suited to the temper of our age. The sale of the Gospel, or 'the traffic in Christ,' an expression for which I am indebted to Bishop Lightfoot, is the expedient which modern ecclesiastical ingenuity has substituted for the sale of indulgences, as not repulsive to the popular mind. It possesses the alluring recommendation of combining the dissemination of the knowledge of the Gospel with the collection of handsome subsidies from wide areas of Christian society spread over the world. The monopoly of the sale of Bibles is the joint possession of the Universities of Cambridge and Oxford,[1] institutions maintained chiefly for ecclesiastical requirements: and the object of the grant of the monopoly was the pecuniary gain resulting from the sale of Bibles. The ramifications of the commerce in Christ are very numerous, but I can only refer to one, the pious sale of sermons. These passionate expositions of the Word were at one time the most valuable wares in the booksellers' shops: their sale exceeded that of all other descriptions of books put together. The gain from their sale was immense, the prices varying from half-a-crown to thirty shillings for each volume or set of volumes of the exposition of the Word.[2] This is the modern ecclesiastical illustration of the Great Teacher's command to preach the Gospel without money and without price. This source of gain to ecclesiastical Christianity is gradually becoming less productive; and the newspapers announced last year that the sale of novels has exceeded the sale of

---

[1] The University of Dublin and the Queen's Printers also, I believe, are included in the monopoly.

[2] The sinews of war during the great Tractarian controversy in the first half and middle of the present century were in the main derived from the sale of sermons and religious works. Cardinal Newman made a fortune from the sale of his sermons and religious publications.

sermons.[1] The 'traffic in Christ' is not limited to the written and printed Word, but it extends to the spoken Word. A considerable body of unbeneficed clergy, the *colones* of the ecclesiastical army, hire themselves out to preach the Gospel at a retail price of a guinea the sermon : no guinea, no sermon.[2] The Romish priest sells masses, the Protestant priest or minister sells sermons, as the cobbler sells his shoes. The latest development of ecclesiastical enterprise for the collection of money is the institution of bazaars, not for the sale of Bibles and sermons, but of certain articles of merchandise, the proceeds being devoted to ecclesiastical purposes. Women have in all ages been the prey and tool of the priest : and they have been of immense service in the promulgation and maintenance of ecclesiasticism. The natural attractions of the female have been utilised by the priest for the purposes of gain in all ages, from the days of the priests of Mylitta to the days of the priests of Mary and of her divine son. Ladies of rank and of personal beauty and charm are utilised at ecclesiastical bazaars in the only way that public opinion will now permit, in effecting the sale and enhancing the price of articles of merchandise useless to the purchaser. The practice of palmistry and the telling of fortunes by engaging dames and attractive belles are not despised as lucrative modes of obtaining money for the purposes of ecclesiastical Christianity. The above remarks apply only to the modes of collecting money adopted by the highest and purest form of ecclesiastical Christianity, the Church of England. In the degraded sinks of Romish Christianity to be found in foreign lands, in South

---

[1] The clergy have discovered that sermons are becoming less productive of gain, and they are now giving their attention and talents to the composition of novels. Their first attempts were a combination of sermon and novel ; but the novel pure and simple has been latterly produced.

[2] These ecclesiastical gentlemen are known to the populace as *guinea-pigs*. The poverty of these unfortunate gentlemen, and of a great many of the inferior beneficed clergy, is actually utilised in a manner indicated by the anonymous writer of the *Black Book* : " It is supposed that the Church looks upon the poverty of some of her members as sturdy beggars look upon their sores, considering them a valuable adjunct for exciting an ill-judged compassion for the whole body, and securing impunity for idleness and over-feeding" (p. 66).

America, India, etc., baser methods are pursued, of which I shall only mention raffles for the relief of souls from purgatory.

The evidences of the decline of ecclesiastical Christianity are perceived in the falling-off of attendance at the churches. The sacred building is one that the majority of men avoid to enter, and speak of in sarcasm. If one could venture to imitate the definitions of Samuel Johnson, the lexicographer, a church may be defined as a place of congregation for women, for the mutual exhibition and admiration of their dresses and bonnets. The clergy complain that the churches are insufficient in number, and cannot seat a quarter of the population: on which plea they claim donations for the building and endowment of new churches. But they are unable to fill the existing churches with the quarter of the population for whom seats are available. There are millions upon millions who do not take the communion, but decline it: a miserable remnant, consisting in large part of old maids, and decayed women and men, comprise the communicants of the Church of England, according to my experience. In Roman Catholic populations the sacrament is more numerously received, but chiefly as a conventional ceremonial required by custom or complaisance. These are prominent signs of decadence, similar to those that Pliny remarked of Paganism, that the temples were deserted and the rites neglected. It is my deliberate conclusion, formed after a life's intercourse amongst Christians, among whom I am numbered, that the overwhelming majority of the members of Christian society are only nominal adherents of the various Churches whose names they bear. The fact is patent and lies manifest on the surface, and ought to be recognised candidly and honestly. Young men who enter the ministry are no better than their fellows, and are actuated by the same motives as the latter in choosing professions or other occupations. The ministry of the Church is merely a profession, like the law, medicine, engineering, or the blacksmiths' or carpenters' trade, taken up with the object of gaining a livelihood thereby, and nothing else. The very fact that the ministry of the Church is a means of gaining a livelihood is indisputable proof of the firm establishment of the 'traffic in

Christ,' the felicitous expression of Bishop Lightfoot. Like all other professions and occupations, the Church is a great commercial institution for obtaining money: and in spite of its progressing decadence ecclesiastical Christianity is the most successful financial enterprise in the world.[1] When it ceases to pay, its extinction will follow: the natural sequence, according to all experience, observed in other commercial undertakings. Great commercial institutions, which have existed through a century or two, and have weathered the storms of adverse times, like a great bank, are slow in falling into decay and in ceasing to exist. The fate of ecclesiastical Christianity will be similar. It will probably survive two or three centuries more, and then be superseded by some religious or perhaps moral system of a higher order. The decadence of ecclesiastical Christianity at the present time offers strong points of similarity to that of Paganism in the days of Pliny at the beginning of the second century. As Paganism was practically superseded by Christianity two centuries after, that period may approximately be taken as the probable remaining duration of ecclesiastical Christianity. Hostile forces have heretofore operated slowly and insidiously, but in these times of great mental activity and rapid material action they may acquire overwhelming impetus in a shorter period; while the unmanageable weight of the supernatural element in ecclesiastical Christianity will, as the years go on, more and more embarrass its power of resistance. All attempts of reformation and revision have heretofore failed, and have only helped to expedite its gradual and steady decline. The greatest mainstay of ecclesiastical Christianity appears to me to be the depth and extension of its roots in the mercenary interests of the community.

The craft of ecclesiasticism has provided a very effective means for maintaining the duration of its teaching, and hence of its existence, by preventing the propaganda of hostile views. Prohibitions and penalties directed against the pro-

---

[1] We have heard of colossal fortunes having been created by men who began life with the sale of old bottles or a basket of eggs; but ecclesiastical Christianity began its financial career with *nothing* but the wits of the 10 per cent. apostles and prophets at the beginning of the second century.

mulgation of the latter by the press or by public addresses have either been withdrawn or fallen obsolete. But one prohibition still remains in force, perhaps because it operates in disguise. The public mind is convinced, and rightly so, that worship should not be interrupted; but worship ceases when teaching or preaching begins, and no interruption is offered to worship when the preacher is interrupted in a polite manner or followed by another speaker. The practice is admissible and very common at all public gatherings where addresses are delivered; it is permissible in the churches, where it is not unusual, amongst Methodists and others, for a succession of preachers to address the audience. The attempt of a layman, however, to address the audience in a church is by ecclesiastically-instigated law punished by magistrates as 'brawling.' Let us imagine a case. It is unnecessary to have recourse to living personages, for the mighty and respected dead may with greater advantage and point for my purpose be recalled to life. Let us imagine a preacher expounding in a church, after the prayers and ceremonial worship have been got over, a historical passage in Scripture, in which the history has been manifestly falsified; or descanting on the wonderful incident of the standing still of the sun at the command of Joshua; or rendering plain to the audience the passages in Scripture (John xix. 34 and 1 John v. 6-8) which the most learned Anglican bishop of the century (Bishop Lightfoot) declared were puzzling to him and inexplicable. Let us further imagine that Gibbon stood up and attempted calmly to correct the false history; that Sir Isaac Newton arose and explained that the sun was normally stationary; and that Huxley declared the *raison d'être* of the puzzling Johannine passages as unravelled in this work. Let us further imagine that the respect of the audience for the last three speakers induced them to retain their seats and listen to them. It is, however, in the power of the preacher and his disciples to create disorder so as to prevent the hearing, and then to institute a prosecution; and the magistrate, upon the evidence, will be compelled under the existing law to convict Gibbon, Sir Isaac Newton, and Huxley of 'brawling.' The repeal or desuetude of this law is desirable. The classes in society who attend churches are those who are difficult to reach for the purposes of enlightenment except in the churches. The congregations of churches may be roughly classified as follows: The main body of church-goers are novel readers and readers of millinery and costume literature, a class who outnumber sermon-readers, according to bookselling statistics. Next to them in numbers come sermon-readers and readers of culinary literature. The overwhelming majority of these two classes are women. A third class consists of readers of price currents, prospectuses of new companies, financial and commercial journals, and literature of this business character. To these men church-going, and even, I am given to understand, the reception of the sacrament, is a part of business, and they are valuable members of the churches. The last class, a minor one as to numbers, consists of people who do not come under the above categories. The readers of the vast sporting literature that has sprung up in the last quarter of the century are not conspicuous in churches as a separate class. It is most difficult to reach the first three classes, who have no knowledge of the forgeries, errors, false history, and ineptitudes from which ecclesiasticism has derived its chief nourishment and maintenance. The churches themselves are the only places in which they can be reached and undeceived. The law unjustly has lent itself to deprive these classes of enlightenment.

The separation of the State from the Anglican Church will probably attain consummation in the near future. A collateral consequence will be the separation of the Anglican Church from the great profession of Law, whose interests are in some measure coincident with those of the Anglican Church, and whose influence is powerfully exerted in its favour. The separation of the State from the Anglican Church will not complete the sum of its duty. There should follow a separation from ecclesiastical Christianity. It is the deliberate conclusion of modern society, arrived at after centuries of persecution and slaughter of innocent men and women, who were good and useful subjects, that the State should abstain from interference with religious opinions. The adoption by the State of any one set of religious opinions inevitably leads to injustice to those sections of the people who adopt other sets of religious opinion. The only course open to the State that is consistent with perfect impartiality to all classes of its citizens is absolute abstention from the adoption of any religious opinions. The whole function and *raison d'être* of the State is concerned with the happiness and prosperity of living people in the present world, but is not concerned with the destinies of dead men in the next world, which is the function exclusively of religion. The State ought to be as indifferent to religion as a firm of engineers, the Inns of Court, or the Colleges of Surgeons. The greatest function of the State is the inculcation of morality, and this duty is fulfilled when its citizens are brought up in good manners. The unanimity of its citizens on the subject of good manners or morality is practicable; but all human experience in the past proves that unanimity in religious opinion is impossible and unattainable on earth.

A secondary but useful function of the State is the protection of its citizens from the wasteful expenditure or loss of their wealth. The laws against imposition and the obtaining of money by false pretences, against swindling and quackery, give expression to its sense of the importance of this duty. There are circumstances which remove from some of the offences above mentioned what lawyers consider to be criminality, or which render it unadvisable to inflict criminal penalties. But the State nevertheless displays its disapprobation in these circumstances by withdrawing its countenance and support. The practice of quackery affords the readiest illustration of these remarks. It is disapproved by the State, and it is considered advisable simply to let it alone, but no assistance is afforded to it. By an ingenious arrangement of the law the uneducated and unaccredited practitioners of medicine or surgery cannot legally claim remuneration for their services, though no serious obstacle is placed to their pursuing their practices, provided no damage results to their victims, who are at liberty to give remuneration at their pleasure. The financial prosperity of a class of men who were formerly social pests, who acquired considerable wealth, have thus been reduced to insignificance. If it be the duty of the State to renounce religion, a subject on which unanimity is impossible, and the truth of which is not verifiable, it becomes incumbent on it to cease to recognise religion amongst its citizens. Religion should be outside the sphere of the Law, and all matters connected with religious operations, as all operations connected with quackery, should be deprived of the assistance of the Law. All financial obligations undertaken in the interests of religion should be purely voluntary and outside the jurisdiction of the Law, in the same manner as all financial obligations in the interests of quackery or in the interests of private immorality are now denied the support of the Law. The contract of a religious society with a missionary to preach the Gospel in consideration of a salary—a scandal to Christianity and a shameful and odious excrescence of our civilisation—should be a dead letter in a court of law. The withdrawal of religious financial transactions from within the jurisdiction of the Law may have the advantage of rendering religion pure and undefiled, to the desirable degree of invisibility to the human eye, and of confining it to the hearts of men—its proper sphere.

It may have the effect of checking and restraining the present waste of the produce of industry on ecclesiastical Christianity, which is of no practical use in this world, and the benefits it confers upon dead men in the next world do not come within the range of political and judicial economy. The expenditure of society in this country on religious subjects, the incomes of the clergy of all denominations, the theological universities, colleges, and schools, the Church establishments of servants, the cost of maintaining and restoring existing churches and erecting new ones, the cost of sermons and theological literature, and the thousand and one other objects which clerical ingenuity is constantly devising for raising money, may be roughly estimated at £30,000,000 sterling per annum. This is an enormous annual expenditure to be incurred by society for the teaching and promulgating of the simple proposition—Jesus Christ was born of a virgin, rose from the dead, and ascended to heaven on a cloud—which forms the foundation of ecclesiastical Christianity. This is the basis and plea for extracting from English society an annual sum of £30,000,000 sterling.

This proposition has the look on the surface of an ordinary mundane statement, and, if historical, ought to be capable of investigation, and to have its truth verified. Thirty-three learned gentlemen, of the first official rank in the kingdom, and a very considerable number of learned men of the clerical profession are prepared to face death in maintaining it to be truth. But there are also, on the other hand, a considerable number of eminent men in the past and now living who regard it as fiction. Amongst these are numbered the greatest historian of modern days, Gibbon, and other eminent historians, Buckle, Froude, etc., and a multitude of other men, eminent in science, law, literature, politics, and in all branches of human knowledge and activity. Amongst them are to be found some of the greatest leaders of modern thought. The deliberate conclusion of these eminent men, arrived at after patient research and reflection, ought to be sufficient to justify a national inquiry into the truth of ecclesiastical Christianity, on which the nation annually incurs an expenditure of £30,000,000. Religion has been made the subject of inquiry by a people now rising into importance amongst the nations of the world. The enlightened Japanese nation has made investigations on various subjects of national importance amongst civilised nations, and as the result of such investigations they have introduced into their own country a system of administration—political, military, naval, educational, judicial, medical, postal, etc.—on the lines of European civilisation. The Japanese commissioners have also investigated ecclesiastical Christianity as it is displayed in Europe and America; and it is a matter of great significance that they have deliberately reported to their Government that the Christian religion is not worthy of adoption, for the reason that it has no influence on the morality of the people.[1] The

[1] This may mean that it is ineffective to suppress rogues, or that it generates rogues, or both. The facts that I have set forth in this work justify the Japanese view. Ecclesiastical Christianity appears to have generated in modern days an obliquity of the moral sense amounting to a peculiar form of mental aberration. A reference to history (see, for instance, Froude's *Oxford Lectures on the Council of Trent*) will show that in pre-Reformation times there was no mental aberration, but knavery and roguery, pure and simple, in popes and bishops. In our days mental

Government has lately submitted the question of the usefulness of vaccination to a Royal Commission, on the ground of aberration is noticeable. I find it impossible to reconcile the statements, mode of thinking, and conduct of theologians, men of undoubted honour, of the highest probity, and held in esteem, with sanity of mind. I have great respect for the piety, the learning, and ability of Bishop Westcott, but I regret to say that the following statement, deliberately made by him, has startled me : " Christianity is essentially miraculous. This is a postulate of Biblical criticism, and it follows that miraculous circumstances are exactly in the same position in the Gospel-history as natural circumstances in common history. If the postulate be granted, the conclusion is inevitable ; if it be denied, argument is impossible. No external evidence can produce faith" (Introduction to the *Study of the Gospels*, viii. ; *Difficulties of the Gospels*, p. 404, eighth edition). This is as if a mathematician should announce that it has pleased God, in his infinite and inscrutable wisdom, to change the multiplication table, and that in all mathematical calculations must henceforth be recognised the postulates that $2 \times 2 = 5$, $3 \times 3 = 10$, and so forth, and argument is no good. Theologians and mathematicians of this order are examples of a form of mental aberration. The revision committee of 1881 consisted of theologians of the highest personal character, whose learning and probity are universally acknowledged ; they undertook to alter the translation of the New Testament made in 1611, 'consistently with faithfulness.' Was it consistent with faithfulness to retain the word '*given*' in John vii. 39, which is not in the original Greek ; to change the expression '*which is* the Holy Ghost' into '*even* the Holy Spirit' (John xiv. 26), neither of the words in italics being in the original Greek? The tendency and design of these departures from faithfulness were to amalgamate and render into the same the Gnostic spirit Paraclete and the Jewish spirit the Holy Ghost. Was it consistent with faithfulness to retain the translation 'minister' instead of substituting 'deacon,' the correct rendering of the original Greek διάκονος, in Ephesians iii. 7 and Colossians i. 23, 25? The tendency and design of this departure from faithfulness were to convert Paul the deacon, a writer of the second century, into Paul the apostle, a writer of the first century (see p. 102). Surely these deliberate and well-considered falsifications of translation, the intent of which is self-evident, are perversions of the moral sense dependent on some subtle form of mental aberration in theologians, whose personal probity is beyond question. Another erratic theologian, Rev. George Salmon, D.D., F.R.S., Regius Professor of Divinity, Dublin, says : "In my judgment, a critic who cannot divest himself of the anti-supernaturalist feelings of the nineteenth century is not one who can enter into the mind of the second century, and is incompetent to judge what arguments a writer of that date would have been likely to use" (Historical introduction to the *Study of the Books of the New Testament*, vi.; *Justin Martyr*, p. 79, second edition). I have endeavoured to enter into the mind of the men of the second century, upon the facts of their lives, not troubling about arguments. I find the nameless stipendiary apostles and prophets who fabricated the supernatural stories of ecclesias-

the opposition offered to it by the lower classes. I am personally unaware of any eminent person who has opposed vaccination as a useless operation, which may be followed by danger to health and life. The large numbers of persons of considerable eminence and of many thousands of educated men who oppose ecclesiastical Christianity, on the ground of its falseness, ought to suffice to justify the grant of a Royal Commission to investigate its truth or falsehood.

The withdrawal of the State and of the action of the Law from ecclesiastical Christianity will not imply a reflection upon the latter, or upon the many excellent and honourable men who belong to its ministry, and it should not be understood to operate to their detriment. The purpose and object of such withdrawal will be simply to confine the functions of the State and of the Law to such action as experience has proved to be appropriate and likely to be most conducive to the happiness and prosperity of the people living under their jurisdiction. It is not reasonable that the State or the Law should exercise any authority or engage in any action connected with the destinies of dead men, who have gone to another world which is outside their jurisdiction and understood to be under higher, divine, and more supremely powerful control. The withdrawal is only from the religious interests of dead men, and every concern connected with them, but the legal rights of living men will still be enjoyed by the members of the ecclesiastical churches and of their ministry.

tical Christianity to be knaves and rogues pure and simple. Aristides and Justin Martyr and others were honest and upright, like Lightfoot, Westcott, and others of our times, but blinded in their minds. Irenæus I find to have been a rogue and knave, the primeval type of rogue-bishop, whose equal in knavery I have not yet found outside ecclesiastical history (see ch. ix.). Moral perversity prevails to a larger extent amongst the Anglican clergy than in any other liberal profession. The Anglican clergy, who, taking Protestant pay, render Papist service, have been justly characterised as dishonourable men in the House of Commons. There is no background of mental aberration to fall back upon in their case. These Anglican clergy appear to think that moral perversity consists in drunkenness and illicit intercourse with females, and almost nothing else. The military and naval conception of 'conduct unbecoming an officer and a gentleman' does not prevail amongst the Anglican clergy, nor the medical conception of 'unprofessional conduct.'

Their right to worship God in their own way, and to provide for their destinies in the next world, will be strictly respected; they will be protected by the State and the Law from molestation and interference in the exercise of this right, so long as they conform to the laws and requirements of the State. They will retain all the rights and privileges of citizens, with which they ought to be satisfied, in common with their fellow-citizens who differ from them in religious opinion. The greater freedom which they will enjoy, and the probable purification from mercenary and other motives foreign to their future interests in the next world, are distinct advantages which may follow from the withdrawal of the State and of the Law from participation with their religious pursuits. At present Law interferes but little with the dissenting Churches, which are hence much purer in their internal administration and discipline than the Church of England, in which prevails much Law, which is the cause of the general prevalence and even legalisation of simony, and of a condition of indiscipline and scandal amounting to anarchy. The withdrawal of the State and of Law, so far from being a reflection, is a practical admission that religion is not mundane, but is so superior in its nature and so divine as to be above and beyond State and Law.

It would be a mistake to imagine that because ecclesiastical Christianity is founded on error and fallacy, due to the knavery and roguery of its progenitors in the second century, that the men and women who profess it and honestly believe in it, or even merely assent to it, are unworthy of esteem and of honourable credit. If we look back upon the history of the past, and reflect upon our estimate of living men of other faiths in the present day, we shall find examples of the highest virtues in men and women whose religious beliefs are regarded by us as manifestly erroneous and even degrading. The religious belief of a civilised man does not appear to have any appreciable influence upon his conduct or morality. The moral behaviour of a Parsee, Mahomedan, Buddhist, Hindoo (and of these religions we have numerous living examples in our Indian dominions) is as good as that of persons professing ecclesiastical Christianity, and as worthy of esteem and credit,

Civilisation furnishes an efficient antidote, though slow in its operation, to whatever may be socially or politically pernicious in religious belief.[1] We are perfectly conscious of the probity, kindness, and good feeling of the millions of men and women who accept ecclesiastical Christianity. The discovery, approaching completion, that the latter is founded on knavery and roguery, does not bring dishonour on those who profess it as a legacy from their forefathers, or on persuasion, but rather calls for sympathy and commiseration on their behalf. No persons are more deserving of being dealt with with tenderness and consideration than the thousands of good men, possessed of ability, education, and personal worth, who, giving up other careers, have committed their lives to the Christian ministry as a profession and means of livelihood.

I do not think that ecclesiastical Christianity has any moral or scientific right to its name. The legal right is unquestionable. A pebble of granite, weighing a couple of ounces, on the margin of a muddy stream, may in the course of centuries acquire an accretion of mud adhering to its surface so as to increase its collective bulk and weight to a ton. The whole mass, however hard and solid it may have become, cannot accurately be described or named as granite from its nucleus: any compound name that may be applied to it, as alluvial granite, can only be regarded as a makeshift for the purpose of distinction. The whole mass, weighing a ton, cannot however be in any sense granite, and to indicate it correctly a new name must be invented. In a similar vein

[1] Lord Roberts, late Commander-in-Chief of the army in India, gives the following account of an educated Hindoo: "The late Maharajah of Travancore was an unusually enlightened native. He spoke and wrote English fluently; his appearance was distinguished, and his manners those of a well-bred, courteous English gentleman of the old school. His speech on proposing the Queen's health was a model of fine feeling and fine expression, and yet this man was steeped in superstition. His Highness sat, slightly retired from the table, between my wife and myself while dinner was going on; he partook of no food or wine, but his close contact with us (he led my wife in to dinner and took her out on his arm) necessitated his undergoing a severe course of purification at the hands of the Brahmins as soon as the entertainment was over; he dared do nothing without the sanction of the priests, and he spent enormous sums in propitiating them" (*Forty Years in India*, by Lord Roberts, vol. ii. pp. 387-88).

of reasoning, the nucleus *Christianity*, as it existed in the first century, has in the course of subsequent centuries acquired a huge incrustation of foreign matter: and the ponderous collective mass thereby formed cannot accurately be said to be Christianity, and the compound name *Ecclesiastical Christianity* is merely a makeshift. It will be reasonable and convenient to devise a new name. The peculiar quality of ecclesiastical Christianity, its very essence, is belief or faith, and the statement of its constitution is called the creed. There are two creeds, which supersede all others, and each other also I believe, and begin with the word *credo*, or I believe. The word *credo* may be conveniently employed as the basis of a new name, Credonism, for ecclesiastical Christianity, and Credonists for its followers. The terms *Christianity* and *Christians* will then be reserved for the moral system of Jesus and his followers, to which and to whom it was originally applied in the first century; and *credonism* and *credonists* for the religious system and its followers, which in subsequent centuries incrusted and covered over and gave unmanageable ponderosity to the Christianity of Jesus and his followers.

The moral system of Jesus, or Christianity, pure and simple, is by no means extinct. It exists broadcast over the country, but it has not been organised. The primitive plans adopted by Jesus and his immediate followers carried Christianity through a century, but it was swallowed up in the next century by Credonism and its ministry. A revival of early Christianity, based upon what can be ascertained of the teaching of Jesus, is desirable. Jesus' system of morality, I think, required a personal practice of the precepts of morality, by each individual, independent of his fellows. It further postulated a belief in God, but it did not go beyond that. Good people, who care for morality, usually have that belief; but there are some good people, who also care for morality, who dispense with the belief.[1] A religious

[1] I think it would be advisable not to make a belief in God a condition for admission to the Society. Though we in England, of all ranks of society, undoubtedly believe in God (I have met in the course of my life with only a single Englishman who disbelieved in God), we must not be

sanction is not essential. The precepts of morality are the offspring of human experience, and are as independent of a religious sanction as the precepts of law, or of hygiene. A religious sanction is no more necessary for doing a kind act than for cooking a good dinner. Those who think that a religious sanction is needful have it to their hands, and should not press their personal necessity upon their fellows. It is desirable to keep religion apart from morality, to avoid the catastrophe that overtook Christianity, or the moral system of Jesus, in the second century, when it was overwhelmed by a religious intermixture or credonism. The natural guides of morality are reason and conscience, which all men possess, and not religion, which all men do not possess,[1] and all are not unanimous upon. There are precepts of morality which are of permanent force in all ages and in all conditions of being and in all circumstances; there are others which are variable. Morality must be in agreement with the facts of life, and all extremes are undesirable.

The dangers incurred by the mistakes of the primitive Christian society should be avoided. Attempts to introduce religion into morality should be deprecated and avoided. Everything beyond common sense or reason should be avoided, and speculation seldom resorted to. The great danger of corruption should be guarded against, especially of a mercenary corruption. The officials of the Society should not be paid. The agents of propaganda should be voluntary, and all contributions should be private and the names of contributors unpublished. All other transactions, however, should be public, and all books of accounts open to any member who desires to inspect them.

blind to the fact that there are millions of good and kindly people in France and Germany, the Social Democrats, who are avowed atheists. These good people ought not to be excluded from the sphere of wholesome moral influence on account of their disbelief.

[1] I make this statement on the ground that the influential and increasing body of select men, who are known in society as Agnostics, are without a religion, and are content with morality and the simple belief in God. The tens of millions of nominal Christians, or rather Credonists, may also be considered as without a religion, but having the simple belief in God : these also are content with morality.

Such a Society of Christians for the practice of personal morality should be open to the whole human family, without regard to variances of religious belief, with which it should be utterly disconnected. The religious beliefs of its members should be as indifferent to the Society, and be regarded in the same light, as the form of their garments or the colour of their skins. Religion in any form should be excluded from the discussions, or lectures, or addresses at the meetings of the members. Systems of religion, as forms of human thought and activity, are of course legitimate subjects for discussion. Prayers at the assemblies should be avoided. Jesus, the great founder of Christianity, did not object to prayer, according to the only authority, the Synoptic Gospels, that we possess ; but, apart from the suspicion under which these unreliable histories lie, they do not relate that he intruded prayers upon public assemblies. The great gatherings of the people to hear his discourses were without prayers. Jesus inculcated that prayer should be private and personal (Matt. vi. 5–13), and never public and general. Public prayer was characterised by Jesus as hypocritical and Pharisaic, and all men who have watched and reflected upon the manifestations of Credonism or ecclesiastical Christianity will concur with him. The bishop or other beneficed clergyman who prays in public in the sight of men offends, in my judgment, against the teaching of Jesus in two cardinal points—in praying in public, and in taking a salary for so doing. Collective prayer, or prayer for other people, such as a whole congregation, never entered the mind of Jesus, and formed no part of his teaching. Prayer is a religious function, and does not come within the sphere of morality, and should be strictly avoided in assemblies of the Society. Members who are so minded can pray in private in their own homes, or in their churches or mosques, or elsewhere.

The officials of the Society, amongst whom executive and menial servants are not included, should be unpaid. Agents for propaganda should receive no money, but be assisted in kind by passes for free passages by railway or steamer, etc., and the usage of hospitality and kindness. No gifts should be permitted to individuals. There should be no opening or opportunity offered for the mercenary interests of individuals to be promoted. Mercenary disinterestedness should be a marked and indispensable feature in the conduct of officials and members who are engaged in the inculcation of personal morality.

In existing society I can call to mind only one social function, in the discharge of which mercenary disinterestedness is theoretically inculcated and very largely carried out in practice. The reproduction of the species is a most important social function; and in the practice of it mercenary disinterestedness is, in the present state of society, more abundantly apparent than in any other social function. Since the abolition of slavery this function, amongst nations which forbid slavery, has ceased to be a subject of merchandise having a price amongst one half of the nations, the male portion, while it has very largely diminished amongst the other half, the female portion, and is in a fair way of being extinguished amongst them also. No man in these days (amongst nations which prohibit slavery) can earn a living, or in any way make a profit, from the function; from the highest to the lowest and most depraved, the same sentiment of abhorrence prevails. It was not always so: it was a trade of limited extent in England a century or two ago, and it was practised in British territory before the abolition of slavery (see Miss Schreiner's works).

Religion, or the worship of God, is represented to be the highest of all social functions. Mercenary disinterestedness is inculcated in the discharge of religious duties, but practically it is invisible. Credonism, or ecclesiastical Christianity, is in fact the most successful mercenary undertaking known in history. In the Church of England the most pious saint, provided he possesses suitable talents, has the best chance of obtaining the most valuable bishopric or deanery. In other Churches the same practice prevails: the most sainted person, who is endowed with eloquence and good abilities, has the best chance of winning the largest income.

The practice and inculcation of personal morality, which, in my judgment, is second in importance to the human family to the function of maintaining the race, ought to be, like the latter, free from mercenary interest. We have the example of the maintenance of the moral system of Jesus for a century, practically without a mercenary taint. With our greater enlightenment, with the more vivid sense of personal duty which centuries of civilisation have created, and the greater wealth prevalent in society, practically absolute freedom from mercenary taint is within our reach. I should recommend the organisation of a modern Club in which the officials, the chairman or president, and the managing committee, are voluntary, but only the executive, *i.e.*, the secretary, clerks, and menials, are paid. The organisation of any of the Churches is objectionable for imitation, because it is arranged on the mercenary principle throughout. The modern club system appears to me more suitable than any of the Church systems now prevailing. The Society for the practice of personal morality will thus provide its members with agreeable places of resort, in no way different in principle from the present clubs which are scattered all over the world. In fact the only difference, if a difference is perceptible, will, perhaps, be a mitigation or relaxation of the strict exclusiveness now observed in the admission of members, a relaxation which will be the less discerned, and will altogether disappear, as the principles and tendency of the Society accomplish their legitimate effect. The tendency of the inculcation and practice of good manners, in the full significance of the term, will be the making of gentlemen in the correct understanding of that good old English word. Manners make the gentleman, not wealth nor social position, nor accomplishments, nor the colour of the skin. The tendency and ultimate aim of the Society is the formation of gentlemen and gentlewomen in the high sense of these words, who will be fit for the society of each other, whatever may be the disparity between individuals in wealth or social position, or occupation and business of life. It will be outside the object of the Society to endeavour to equalise its members, in all points, by theoretically suppressing the real facts of life, the variances of social station, of wealth, or mental qualities or cultivation. It is the sole and only aim of the Society to equalise men and women in manners or morality, to equalise them in moral, and hence honourable, thought, feeling, behaviour, and conduct of life, and to attain this object association with each other is essential, so that the less advanced may profit from the proficiency and example of the more advanced. Practical common sense will indicate that the clubs must be adapted to the means and social position of its members. It would be foolish to expect that the same style of club will suit the rich and the poor. It will be the function and interest of the Society to erect these clubs in the style suited to the means and position of their members, and to conduct them as to cost so as to meet the resources of the latter. The clubs must be in all respects adapted to the means of the members who frequent them. The maintenance of the clubs will devolve on its own members, and poor clubs must necessarily be assisted by the Society. The principles of morality will equally animate all the clubs, they will be all affiliated, and members of one club may even ultimately be members of others or of all, if it be found, after experience, that the privilege is advantageous for furthering the objects of the Society.

A written code of morality will be indispensable. The construction of such a code will secure uniformity of thought and conduct on the subject of morality. The form of the code should, I think, be epigrammatic whenever practicable, the precepts being expressed in clear and concise language, capable of being easily committed to memory. There should be no dependence and necessary harmony of the precepts of morality with religion, law, philosophy, or even science. Regarding religion, I have already emphasised and deprecated any association between it and morality. Religion, or what passes for such, as all history proves, is above reason, above experience, above common sense, above science, above law, and above everything else. Any connection with religion will be the introduction of an element which will necessarily and surely lead to discord, disunion, and disruption. Religion is the private concern of members, like their businesses, professions, and trades, and should not be obtruded into the code of morality. The religion professed by the members is their own personal chattel and not common property. Mahomedans, Hindoos, Buddhists, etc., are as desirable members of the Society as Roman Catholics, Anglicans, Baptists, Mormons, and the other two or three hundred divisions of credonists or ecclesiastical Christians. No particle of religion should be introduced into the code, so that the emotions, feelings, beliefs, and susceptibilities of any person, or of any considerable number of persons, should be offended, and their joining the Society, to which the religious element may be the only objection, be thereby prevented. Proselytism, or change of religion, or religious beliefs, is no part of the object of the Society, and should be scrupulously eschewed. Members of the Society should not be pledged either to proselytise or to abstain from proselytising. The subject should be neutral and indifferent, and not recognisable in any form by the Society, but absolutely prohibited within the sphere of its operations.

Equally with religion the Law should not be taken as a guide or pattern for the construction of the moral code, and should equally be eschewed. The Law is uncertain in its language, and can be interpreted in various ways. It recognises religion, and hence its ordinances will often be opposed to the object and aim of the Society. The Law varies in different nationalities, and may be grounded on principles which are not moral. As in the case of religion, each member should keep his Law to himself, and not obtrude it upon his fellow members. It should, however, be a moral duty, recognised by the Society, that the Law of the land should be obeyed. As an illustration of the reason for rejecting the Law as a guide of morality, I may point to the Law or Laws regulating the relations of the sexes. The Law of England, formed under sacerdotal direction, recognises marriage and marriage only, which is a religious ceremonial, involving the payment of fees to priests, which they appropriate to their own purposes; or a secular function, performed by a secular officer, paid by the State, and the marriage fees are part of the public revenue. All children born out of wedlock are outcasts, banned as bastards, deprived of all legal claims to the protection of fathers (except a small weekly payment), and of inheritance of the property of either fathers or mothers, or of their ancestors. The punishment of innocent children for the transgression or omission of parents, sanctioned by Credonism or ecclesiastical Christianity, and enforced by the Law, is *primâ facie* immoral and cruel. In the famous Breadalbane case, in which the descendant of a couple who were formally not married was recognised by the House of Lords as the legitimate heir to an earldom, on the ground that *conduct* was the essential of marriage, true morality is vindicated. The Law prohibits marriage in certain degrees of blood-relationship, and of what is technically called affinity, defined by priests, beginning with grandfathers and grandmothers, and ending with a wife's sister's daughter and a husband's sister's son. Many of these degrees of relationship and affinity are purely arbitrary, and not objectionable in practical life as impediments to marriage. They are erroneously stated in Anglican prayer-books to be prohibited in the Scriptures—they are not. The real purpose of these extensive prohibitions was to serve as sources of revenue to the Romish clergy, who were empowered or rather assumed the right to grant dispensations from them, which means that the prohibitions can be withdrawn on the payment of money to priests. The prohibitions are hence practically inoperative in countries professing Roman Catholicism. The whole body of Protestant Christendom, with the exception of priest-ridden England, has now risen in revolt against the prohibition of marriage with a deceased wife's sister. Not only has England maintained an undesirable prohibition at the behest of priests, but it has broken international law and offended intercolonial courtesy and amenity by refusing to recognise such marriages when they are contracted in other countries and colonies where they are legal. Such prohibitions, where they extend beyond reasonable limits, are immoral, and productive of fictitious immorality, and can form the basis of no precept in the moral code.

The only precept that morality could formulate on the relations between the sexes is fidelity or conduct. Whether monogamy or polygamy be permitted by the Law, there is no moral offence committed by individuals in polygamous countries who obey the moral law of fidelity. The subject of divorce is attended with more difficulty. There is no sadder incident in human life than the separation of husband and wife to whom children have been born. A partial and one-sided antidote against divorce is polygamy, but that is a medicine that will not be taken by western nations. Divorce, however, is so completely in the hands of the Law, that the necessity for a moral precept on the subject is hardly needed in practice. The facts of life should, however, never be forgotten in morality. There are misfortune and evil in divorce, but no immorality, when unavoidable. On the contrary, the continued forced union of a couple who have come to detest each other, or one of whom may be insane, or a prisoner in penal servitude for a long term or for life, or otherwise unfit and incapacitated for conjugal life, is one that is *primâ facie* not conducive to morality. The English Law on the subject of divorce, instigated as it is by all that is most unreasonable and undesirable in ecclesiasticism, is in my judgment cruel and immoral. The Law, I believe, is habitually unheeded, and people who are prevented from availing themselves of a legal divorce dispense with the Law; but they do not thereby commit a breach of morality. The union of Mr George Henry Lewis and George Elliott (Miss Marion Evans), during the lifetime of the insane wife of the former, was moral, but I regret to say legally and ecclesiastically improper. The English Law on the subjects of marriage and divorce is constructed on an ecclesiastical rule of thumb, and cannot be taken as a guide to morality.

Similarly it would be advisable to avoid moral speculations, as manifested in the various schools of moral philosophy.

I think it will be advisable to inculcate as high a standard of morality as is conceivable to be practicable for the civilised races, and to lower the standard for the less civilised and more backward races of the human family. The same standard of morality for all would be impracticable and unreasonable. The highly civilised Frenchman, Englishman, American, or German could understand and appreciate an elevated standard of morality, and could make efforts to reach it. The less civilised races, such as many in India,

Burmah, Siam, and China, would neither understand, appreciate, nor be capable of making the effort to attain a similar standard. The barbarous but amiable races inhabiting the Pacific islands and the continent of America would still less be possessed of the ability to understand, appreciate, and attain the standard of morality which the former races can reach. The facts of life must be recognised, the degree of civilisation and the physical conditions of inferior races must be fully taken into consideration in constructing codes of morality for them, and the standard of morality be lowered and adapted to their intelligence and power of appreciation. As they progress in civilisation, and attain greater intelligence, the standard of morality will spontaneously and without seeming effort elevate itself, and gradually in the course of time approximate the standard attainable by more advanced races. There is now a vast amount of knowledge regarding these inferior races accumulated in the accounts of travels of men and women who are not missionaries, and who are not blinded by the foolish, though well-meant, aims and objects of religious societies. With the assistance of persons who have resided amongst these inferior races, suitable codes of morality may be constructed for them.

The names of the Society and of its officials should be carefully considered. Some title that will clear the Society from any suspicion of a religious character should be selected. "The Society for the Practice of Morality," or "The Ethical Society," would not be unsuitable; but perhaps some other name, less like a label of contents, would be preferable. To adopt a nomenclature already in use by the various Churches would be utterly foolish, as it will give rise to the erroneous suspicion that there is a connection between the Society and Credonism or ecclesiastical Christianity. The names of officials now in use in clubs are perhaps the best that can be adopted, especially as the club system is the most suitable for carrying out the objects of the Society. The agents of propaganda may be styled lecturers.

I should not advocate any essential difference between the clubs of the Society and those already in existence, which are taken as models for imitation. The clubs, besides being agreeable resorts, in which newspapers, magazines, and books may be read, should also supply food and refreshment on payment. If funds permit, the clubs for poorer members should be provided with large halls for lectures, concerts and dancing, etc. As the richer clubs are provided with conveniences for personal cleanliness, the poorer should be likewise supplied with lavatories and baths on a larger scale, for the poor are more in need of them. A few acres of land for lawns, gardens, cricket, tennis, football, nine-pins, and other outdoor amusements would be very desirable adjuncts to the poorer clubs. All these appliances and adjuncts to the clubs are humanising, and have a wholesome tendency to improve morality. All clubs, however, should, as far as is practicable, even poor clubs, be self-supporting. The financial success of individual clubs is an important element for thoughtful consideration.

As religion is inadmissible into the clubs, there can be no observance of Sundays and saint-days as holidays. The ordinary work and proceedings of the clubs should not be interrupted on account of such holidays. I think the feeling is gaining strength that these holidays are national nuisances. They entail upon society a loss of fifty-five days' work of the whole nation (fifty-two Sundays, and three holy days—Good Friday, Easter Day, and Christmas), or nearly two months out of the twelve in the year, or one-sixth of the year. Apart from the religious factor in these holidays, waste of time and loss of combined work can hardly be considered moral or necessary. Their purpose is purely religious, and the invariable complement of concrete religion mercenary. The restrictions, exceedingly vexatious, placed by the Law, in obedience to priests, upon the business, occupations, and amusements of the people on Sundays, are designed to drive people into the churches, and to compel them to read the works of ecclesiastics on religious subjects. Collections of money made in churches and the sales of Bibles and sermons are thereby increased. This design is now being gradually defeated, and when ecclesiastics feel convinced that money can no longer be obtained by the enforced observance of Sundays and saint days, their holy fervour in support of the Lord's day will die away, and be directed to some other saintly and more prolific measure, if it be possible to discover such. The facts of life, however, cannot be overlooked. As people have become accustomed to have one day, in every seven, in which they do no useful work, the expectation must be satisfied. The paid employés of the Society may be allowed one day of idleness in every seven; but, as the ordinary work of the club ought not to be interrupted on Sunday, the employés may take each a day in turns, not all together on the same day, so that the absence of one or a few will hardly be felt. So that if there be seven employés each may have one day in his turn, the ordinary work being carried on by the remaining six. The members may please themselves whether they avail themselves of the advantages of the club or not on Sunday. No law so far as I know, will be infringed if the ordinary work of the club be carried on on Sundays. Lectures, concerts, dancing, or any other function carried on on week days can be freely accomplished on Sundays without a breach of the Law. Continental Christian nations are in advance of us in Sunday non-observance: and hence they are less drunken than the English. It is stated that large numbers of English workmen regularly spend a great part of their weekly wages, paid on Saturday evening, in drinking on Sunday, so that they are unfit for work on Monday. This pernicious and immoral practice would perhaps be corrected if Sunday was not observed as a holiday, but each workman obtained any one day in seven in turns with his fellow-workmen. Two months of combined work would thus be saved to the nation every year, and the produce of industry be thereby increased, while one day of rest in every week will still be secured to the labourers. An alternative may be the substitution of a two months' holiday, with working pay, every year for workmen. This simple and sensible plan will be opposed by ecclesiastics, not on its demerits, but because it will interfere with church-going, the pastime chiefly of frivolous and religious women.

The questions of the qualifications necessary for admission to the Society and of the mode of admission are worthy of consideration. The only qualification, in my judgment, should be the appreciation of morality and the desire to practise it personally, without regard to the conduct of others. There should be no money-payment for admission. The advantages of the clubs should be open freely to the enjoyment of all who value morality, and desire to see it established and spread. The question of exclusion should be carefully considered. As it is a matter of vital importance that no particle of religion be introduced into the Society, the admission of the clergy and ministers of religion demands attention. These gentlemen form a mixed body, including many who are learned, wise, broad-minded, well-informed, energetic, eloquent, persuasive, and who possess other valuable qualities, and many more who are superficially educated, narrow-minded, with few ideas unassociated with theology, fanatical, morally perverse, and with remarkable powers for mischief-making. And there are those who are strange combinations of both classes of qualities. The question is whether these gentlemen should be excluded at all, or whether they should be excluded partially, or in the lump. The question is vital, as a mistake will be attended with serious consequences—discord, the perversion of the aim and purpose of the Society, disunion, and disruption. The maintenance of the Society and of its object, unalloyed morality, should be the leading consideration in the discussion of this question. The safest course, in my judgment, is the absolute exclusion of all persons whose profession, or means of livelihood, is religion or of a religious character. The clerical profession is, at this moment, subjected to absolute exclusion from several districts of activity. In our own country it is strictly excluded from the House of Commons, and it is denied admission to the Inns of Court, and a clergyman's intrusion is unwelcome in many departments of business. No clergyman is admitted into the Educational Department of the Government of India; and the same exclusion is largely practised in the Board Schools of England, and practically exists in the Educational System of the Government of France, and is likely to become statutory. These are results of experience, which may be taken as a safe guide, that the clerical profession is not to be trusted, and should be excluded from the Society. An

Irenæus, Newman, or Pusey introduced into the Society might lead to its distraction, and even destruction.

It might be desirable, however, to make exceptions, and to avoid a too rigid exclusion. As the profession of cleric is practically for life, clergymen who have abandoned clerical functions for two years or thereabouts, and have neither desire nor intention to resume them, may be declared admissible. Also clergymen of unexceptional character, of the correctness of whose moral sense there is no doubt, men of broad minds, unfanatical, not saintly, and not too enamoured of concrete religion, may perhaps be admitted into the Society, if they pass the ordeal of a ballot. All clerical costume, as savouring of religion, should be prohibited within the precincts of the clubs. This rule, rigidly enforced, will probably act as a deterrent to the great majority of the clerical profession. The cardinal and bishop will be as unwilling to lay aside his purple robes, or the apron and knee-breeches, the dean and archdeacon the latter garment, and the inferior clergy the white necktie and clerical raiment, as the Gascon of romance to part with his moustache, or the Chinaman with his tail. The tonsure will be contraband. These rules will apply not merely to the clergymen of the two or three hundred sections of credonism, but to the priests of all religions throughout the world. Any costume of garments, or style of wearing the hair or shaving the head and eyebrows, or marks on the forehead or other parts of the body, or any other distinctive peculiarity, assumed by the priests of any religion, should be prohibited within the precincts of the clubs. This rule cannot be brought to bear upon the exclusion of the Brahminical thread, or of the sacred thread of the Parsees, or of any other distinction adopted by castes, or races, or members of a religion, which are worn by the whole body of a people, including those who discharge sacerdotal functions as well as those who do not.

The mode of admission should be easy and simple. The introduction and recommendation of any two members should be accepted as sufficient for the admission of a candidate. The principle of honour should be greatly relied upon, and the honour and integrity of the introducers should be accepted as a guarantee that they are satisfied that the candidate will not bring discredit on the Society. An additional safeguard, if considered necessary, may be the approval of the president and committee of the club, or of the whole club, the name and address of the candidate being screened for a week. The number of members admitted to any one club should be limited, according to the capabilities of the club buildings.

The clubs of the Society are intended for both sexes; but there will be no departure from the objects and aims of the Society if some of the clubs be reserved for one sex alone, if considered desirable by the members to have them so at their own cost. But in the poorer clubs it will be better to have both sexes united in the clubs. The separation of the sexes is morally undesirable, as the presence of both sexes is conducive to decorum, good order, and good behaviour. The admission of women to the Society should be on the same lines as that of men, and their privileges on the same equality. Unmarried women, married women, and women without their husbands should not be denied admission. The wives of the clergy of all denominations, and of the ministry of all religions, should be excluded like their husbands, and for the same reason. Exceptions, however, may be made, and admission permitted by ballot, as in the case of clergymen. Women belonging to, or actively connected with, religious associations in an official capacity, like sisters of mercy, nuns, and suchlike, should be rigidly excluded. All offices in the Society should be open to competent and eligible women: they should not be excluded from the presidency, council, or the committees, or from the functions of propaganda. Men and women should be on a perfect equality as members of the Society, and encouraged to be of equal service for the purposes of the Society.

Misbehaviour and moral irregularities are necessarily to be expected, and must be dealt with. It is desirable, however, that the punishments should be of an exceedingly mild nature. For petty acts of misconduct, or of non-compliance with rules, small pecuniary fines or simple censure may suffice. More serious offences against morality or conduct of life should be visited with public censure or screening, with suspension from the privileges of the clubs for shorter or longer periods, extending from a few weeks to two years, or with expulsion from the clubs and the Society. Members convicted by the magistrates or courts of serious offences should be liable to suspension for longer periods, or be expelled both from the clubs and the Society. Punishments should not be inflicted in a vindictive spirit, and transgressors who have been suspended from the club for a longer or shorter term should, if so desired by them, be readmitted with full privileges. The action of the Society should be always conciliatory, forgiving, full of grace and amenity. The fault of individuals who have undergone their period of suspension should be forgotten and never thrown into their teeth. Expulsion should not be for life, but for fixed limited terms of years, so as to encourage reformation of conduct.

Members should be careful of the credit and good repute of the Society, and should notice the misconduct of fellow-members. Oversight of breaches of morality is undesirable, and members should honourably remonstrate with their fellows on perceiving irregularities of conduct. Persistence in immoral conduct of any description should be brought to the notice of the committees of clubs to be dealt with by them. Minor breaches of morality may be summarily punished by club committees by short terms of suspension of a few weeks, but not exceeding two months; when more severe punishment is called for for graver breaches, a meeting of the members should be convened for confirming or modifying the punishment recommended by the committee. Suspension should be limited to the club, but expulsion should include dismissal from the Society.

It is desirable that the Society should be national, each nation having a Society of its own, and framing a code of morality and conduct of life suitable to the temper and mind of the nation. The work of the Society should be carried on by a president and council, consisting of as many members as may be needed for the work. The services of all must be voluntarily rendered: actual travelling expenses (third class if by rail) and hotel expenses at a moderate rate being paid, if asked for, out of the funds of the Society. The treasurer may be unpaid, but the secretary, clerks, and similar officials must necessarily be paid. The primary duty of the president and council will be the framing of a code of morality, adding to or, if necessary, modifying it from time to time, subject to the confirmation of the body of the members. The entire financial work of the Society should be in the hands of the president and council, assisted by a paid or honorary treasurer and paid body of clerks; as well as the whole executive work of the Society, assisted by a secretary and clerks, who should be paid. The president and council should be the recipient of all contributions made for the general purposes of the Society. The inculcation of the precepts of morality should be effected chiefly by means of voluntary lecturers, selected and approved by the president and council. These lecturers may either be selected at the scene of their labours, or deputed by the president and council, in which latter case their travelling expenses (third class if by rail) and moderate hotel charges, if local hospitality be not available, may be paid when asked for. All gifts to lecturers to be strictly prohibited, and any acceptance of gifts by lecturers is to be regarded as a serious breach of morality, to be dealt with by long suspension or expulsion from the Society and the clubs to which they belong. When a sufficient number of members can be got together in a locality a club should be established. The buildings necessary may be either erected or rented, according to the circumstances of the members, by a president and committee, to be appointed in any way approved by the members. All legal responsibilities should be accepted by the president and committee, supported and guaranteed by the individual members on the limited liability principle. No considerable outlay should be entered upon in which the members are unwilling to take a share of responsibility. The cost of maintaining the club should be borne by the members, either by monthly or annual subscriptions, or by donations at their pleasure. In no case should a member be excluded for the reason that he is unable to pay a fixed sum. The poverty of one member should be compensated by the competence or wealth of another. It will be a breach of morality for a member competent to pay to withhold his or her due contribution to the common cost. It will be a natural expectation that members of pretty nearly equal social station and means should combine to form a club, but the social station or the means of an individual should not be regarded as an element in the qualification for membership. A person of good social station, but of small means, should not be excluded from membership, nor a person of inferior social station, but of good means, shut out from membership of a club in the vicinity of which he resides. Means or social station do not enter into the question of qualification. Good feeling and common sense should guide a member in selecting his club. The cost of running a club should not exceed the average means of its members. Rich clubs should avoid luxury, the taste for which cannot be regarded as a moral quality. Substantial comfort, not much exceeding the average comfort enjoyed by the members in their own homes, should be the point aimed at. In the poor clubs the standard of comfort will necessarily be lower, but should nevertheless be substantial, and exceeding the comfort enjoyed by the members in their homes. The number of members in a club should be adapted to the capabilities of the building; if enlargement of the premises be not practicable or a larger building not available, a second club should be started for the accommodation of the excess members. Though it is very desirable that every member of the Society and his family should attach themselves to a club, even if only nominally, it is not essential that a member of the Society should be also a member of any club. It will be necessary that the poor clubs be assisted by the funds of the Society. The probable annual cost of maintaining a club (apart from the cost of furniture, etc.) of a thousand members amongst the poor of an ordinary town may be estimated at between £400 and £500, of which more than a moiety may perhaps be contributed by small donations and subscriptions from its members, and a further amount be collected from the sale of food and refreshments. An average contribution of sixpence a month, less from some and more from others, according to the means of individuals, will fetch £300 per annum. If the sales of food and refreshment be assumed to fetch an average profit of a halfpenny a week from each member, the annual profit from this source will amount to £108. The deficiency of £92 per annum will have to be met by a grant from the general funds of the Society. I am afraid that there exists in English society a stratum of poor to whom the payment of sixpence a month, or three halfpence a week, may be too great a strain on their resources. To these unfortunates the gift of a club may perhaps be unsuitable, and it must be left to benevolent ingenuity to devise a means by which they may be brought within the pale of moral influence. It may, perhaps, be found practicable to distribute them, in part at least, among the poor clubs as guests or free members, the additional cost being defrayed by the Society. It will, perhaps, be advisable to have a special class of voluntary officials, of both sexes, in the poor clubs, to supervise the members, and to instruct them when necessary in the various simple modes of personal behaviour adopted by good society, and to enforce cleanliness of person and clothing. These officials should be carefully selected, and should carry out this important duty in a gentle, courteous, and kindly spirit. They may be called stewards, and may wear a rosette to indicate their official position. These officials will, of course, be unnecessary in the richer and self-supporting clubs. In no point can the members of the Society confer a greater benefit upon their fellow-members than by personal association and intermixture. It would be certainly preposterous to advocate a general affiliation of the clubs in the sense that the members of one club have the right of *entrée* to all other clubs. There may, however, be inaugurated a system of permanent invitation of a limited number. The poorer clubs will marvellously benefit by association on equal terms with the members of both sexes of the clubs of the more fortunate classes who have had the benefit of greater culture. If the poorer clubs be moderately comfortable, and their members be well behaved and clean in their persons and clothing, their clubs may be attractive or convenient as occasional resorts to the members of the higher clubs. The only existing institution that I am aware of in which all classes of society may meet on an equality, and in which they actually do meet and promiscuously intermingle (not as in the churches in distinct groups), is the reading-room attached to the Free Libraries. The quiet and unassuming people who are frequently seen in these rooms reading side by side with laundresses, charwomen, postmen, and stable boys, are ladies and gentlemen moving in good local society, some of them even of world-wide eminence. It is not urged that dukes and duchesses should frequent the poorer clubs, but it is highly desirable that the members of the middle-class clubs should as much as is practicable resort to the former. They should sit, read, converse, smoke, partake of food and refreshments, and mingle with the poorer members on terms of perfect equality, without any pretensions to superiority on the one side, or any resentful consciousness of inferiority on the other side. Association of this nature of cultivated people with people of less or of no culture is a moral education to the latter, without any appreciable deterioration being suffered by the former. Such valuable association, in my judgment, is practicable, and can be brought about by the observance of moral and physical cleanliness in the poor clubs, and by the provision of a reasonable amount of comfort. The absence of bad language and of unconventional behaviour, of uncleanliness of person and clothing, will assuredly remove the main obstacles to the association of the middle with the lower class. With regard to the use of our public conveyances there is now no difference between the two classes. People who not many years ago objected to use omnibuses now use them freely. The railway companies, by their gradation of first, second, and third classes of passengers, obviously intended to adapt their carriages to the three classes of society, which were more or less disinclined for each other's company. I am unaware that the first-class passenger traffic has materially increased, while the third class has enormously increased, with a considerable diminution of the second-class passenger traffic, to the extent that on some lines the second-class carriage has totally disappeared, and the companies are seriously considering the question of the abolition of this class on all lines. The apparent reason is that second-class passengers, who were solely of the middle class, are content with the reasonable comfort of third-class carriages and do not object to the company in them. People of the middle class, who at one time found association with the lower class unpleasant, do not now find the company of the latter disagreeable. The fact is that the lower class in England has made considerable progress in the moral virtues of personal cleanliness and behaviour, and have closely approximated to the moral standard of the middle class. It is a common thing to see in the same third-class carriage gentlemen and ladies of good social position, officers of rank in the army and navy, or members of the various learned professions, artisans, domestic servants, and others of the lower classes. I have travelled with my family in the same third-class compartment with a colonial bishop, a market gardener and his wife and daughter, and the company in no way gave the least cause of offence to each other. Heterogeneous mixtures of the various ranks of middle and lower-class society are now the rule and usage in the third-class passenger traffic on railways. What has been done in approximating the middle and lower classes by railway travelling, can assuredly be done to a much more effective and useful extent by the clubs of the Society.

The moral approximation of the upper and middle classes of society has already been effected, and there is no marked disparity to be noticed in a moral point of view between them. The distinction between them lies in rank and wealth. Knaves and rogues exist in both classes, and their number indicates the importance of a deeper inculcation of the precepts of morality. It would be impossible for these delinquents to attain maturity in their malpractices if the medium in which they flourish, the persons about them and within their reach, and whom they make use of as tools, were more imbued with moral principle. These knaves, who are in our days chiefly of the commercial middle class, receive material and advantageous aid from their own and the upper class of society. A wider and deeper reception of moral precepts would extinguish or very greatly reduce their number and the magnitude of their depredations. Perhaps the greatest blotch on our civilisation is the vast amount of dishonesty prevalent among the commercial sections of the middle class, aided and abetted by members of the upper classes. It would be desirable if the crown, which, at its pleasure, bestows rank, would exercise its undoubted right to withdraw rank, when it is disgraced by the aiding and abetting of dishonesty, whether the offence be of a nature cognisable by the criminal law or not.

Perhaps the only opposition to the institution of clubs, as here advocated, would proceed from the clergy of all denominations and the publicans, and from the supporters of both, and for the same reason. The clergy and the publicans, however much they may disguise their hostility by plausible considerations, would oppose these clubs, because they may interfere with church-going, mass-going, and public-house-going. The people, they will imagine, will prefer going to their clubs rather than to the churches and public-houses. As the churches and public-houses are now managed, this danger to their custom will probably be a real one. But the danger may be averted by an improvement in the administration of churches and public-houses. If the clergy would devote more attention to their sermons, adopt more practical and useful subjects for their discourses than the virginity of the mother of Jesus, the resurrection of the dead and ascension on a cloud, the miracles of Jesus and of his disciples, the remission of sins, the efficacy of baptism and prayer, the power and influence of the Holy Ghost, the importance of faith and such like—subjects which interest only those who are theologically-minded, but which are all beneath the average intelligence of the mass of the people of the present day, and of which the intelligent laity are sick ; if the clergy will study and work up useful subjects of a moral nature, such as the value of honesty, of truthfulness, cleanliness, hospitality, benevolence, the evils of gambling, swindling, cheating, betting, the duties and responsibilities of wealth and labour, etc., texts for which abound in the Scriptures, especially in the parables : if they would treat these subjects in the style of the modern lecturer or essayist, they need not fear the competition of the clubs. On the contrary, the members of the clubs will fill the churches. But the delivery of such addresses will require a body of clergy far better educated than those that now occupy the pulpits. I do not think the clergy, on the whole, compare well with the other learned professions : their education is deficient in breadth and comprehensiveness. In the same way, the publicans may overcome the competition of the clubs, by introducing refinement and moral tone in their establishments. The poor man will reasonably and naturally prefer to resort to a place where he can obtain food and refreshment, without increased cost, amidst comfortable surroundings and in a good moral atmosphere.

I do not think that there could be any reasonable objection to the establishment, in connection with the Society, of special clubs, in which, while the inculcation and practice of morality in all the relations of life is predominant, other special and useful aims and objects may be consentaneously carried out. In such clubs the principle of exclusion must necessarily come into play with or without the exclusion of women. A body of lawyers, of medical men, of merchants, of scientists, of authors, of tradesmen, of plumbers, of carpenters, of costermongers, of publicans, or of other classes may combine and form a club, limited to their own body, in association with the Society. A liberal extension of this principle may include clubs formed for the propagation of certain political principles and the attainment of certain political objects. The gain to the community will be considerable if politics could be brought within the pale of morality, and if individual politicians be primarily subject to a moral rule, and their projects be examined from a moral point of view. It does not follow that of two or more rival political views and aims one or other must be necessarily immoral: diverse political objects may be mutually hostile and incompatible, but not necessarily immoral. The morality of the political recognition and maintenance of concrete religion, in its various forms, may perhaps, in the present stage of civilisation, be regarded as a neutral subject. The practice of concrete religion is a matter of mental atavism, an inheritance left by countless generations of ancestors, and will need time for its extinction. Its continuance has been due solely to priestcraft, which traded with it to make a profit. The belief in witchcraft, a cognate instance of mental atavism, is now extinct amongst civilised nations, and limited only to uncivilised nations, and to those few individuals of civilised nations who have intellectually lagged in the rear. Concrete religion, moreover, in political thought is merely a system, like free trade, graduated taxation, and such like, and is dealt with as a system, apart from doctrines or beliefs. In this sense concrete religion, or any form of it, whether Credonism, Mahomedanism, Buddhism, etc., in the purely political view, may legitimately be regarded as admissible, as an object that may be politically supported without a breach of the rule regarding the exclusion of religion. The political view of religion, as a system or systems of human activity and thought, apart from the beliefs, dogmas, practices, etc., in detail, which should be absolutely excluded, may legitimately be admitted in discussions in all the clubs of the Society.

The premises of the clubs, I think, should be made available for political meetings. In the poorer clubs, those for the lower middle and lower classes, the large halls, which I have advocated as useful adjuncts for lectures, concerts, dancing, etc., should be open for political meetings of all shades of opinion, on the understanding that courtesy and good behaviour are expected from all who attend. Workmen's meetings for the discussion of matters connected with their trades may also be advantageously held in these halls. The convenience to the general public afforded by the existence of these halls will assuredly be appreciated : propriety of speech and conduct will be generated, and moral influence be widely spread.

Besides the framing of the code of morality and the transaction of the general work of the Society, the president and council should appoint from their own body two influential committees : one for watching, and, if possible, guiding, legislation in all departments in which morality is involved; and the other for watching the action of the courts of law in all matters which have a bearing on the morality of the people. There is much in our legislation that is of an immoral tendency and which even generates immorality. It should never be forgotten that our representative system introduces into Parliament men of whose personal morality nothing is known, and men who are suspected or known to be personally immoral. Immorality is not limited to sexual irregularities, but implies immorality of all descriptions, even political and financial immorality. Many knaves and rogues, of great ability, and more dangerous to morality from the talents that they possessed, have been members of Parliament. The greatest financial rogue of the century, Jabez Balfour, was an M.P. It is very doubtful whether the preponderance of votes in legislatures is always on the side of morality. The grosser forms of immorality are indeed absent in the decrees of modern legislatures, but the subtler forms, barely masked from detection, are unfortunately largely prevalent. The predominant legislative immorality, the one most marked and very prejudicial to the national moral sense, is inequality of taxation. Absolutely heavier taxes are levied upon the rich than upon the less rich, upon one class than upon another, and taxation is lightened upon one class by being increased upon another. The principle of equal justice to all, of proportionally equal contribution by all, according to their means, to the public needs, is violated, the moral sense of the people is thereby perverted, and the principle of plunder is authoritatively promulgated, and weakens or displaces the principle of honesty in the public mind. When the legislature, the highest physical and moral force in the realm, adopts the principle of plunder, the common man finds in it a plea and justification and encouragement for the adoption of the same principle in his own conduct. As the legislature compels the richer man to pay absolutely more than the less rich for the same governmental services, the common man finds in this conduct a justification for demanding more for his own services from the rich man than from the less rich ; and further, for demanding more for the same article of merchandise from the rich man than from the less rich. The element of force, which the legislature possesses and exercises when needed, is wanting to the common man, but its place is supplied by deceit, falsehood, refusal of service or of sale, and by other immoral contrivances by which dishonesty gains its own ends. The circle of immorality is ever widening. Barely a year passes in which the legislature does not enact a law in which the underlying design is the taking from one class of the people a larger proportion of taxation in order to lighten the taxation upon another class. This immoral legislation is justified as political benevolence and justice, but those who see below the surface regard it as political corruption and bribery. A good example of this form of legislative immorality is the "Agricultural Rates Act, 1896." The object of this Act is said to be to relieve "the occupier of agricultural land" of half the rate in the pound payable in respect of buildings. The object of the devisers of this Act would have been attained and have been better understood by the people if the Law, instead of the periphrasis "occupier of agricultural land," had employed the intelligible English word 'farmer.' That would have been an honest exposition of the mind of the politicians who devised the Act, but it would have had the objection of too clearly indicating that the object was to benefit the farmer class, and the farmer class only. There are hundreds of thousands of occupiers of 'agricultural land,' as defined in the Act, viz., " any land used as arable, meadow, or pasture ground only," but who are not farmers, but retired tradesmen, officers of the army and navy, and such like, who, preferring to pass the remnants of their lives in the country, have taken a few acres of land around their residences which they use as agricultural land only. This large class of not wealthy men, but of men with a modest competence, are totally excluded from the benefit of this Law, because, it appears to me, that the executive intrusted with the levying of rates, *i.e.*, the Guardians of the Poor, exert all their ingenuity to bring the land occupied under one or other of the exceptions under which "land occupied together with a house" is set down as a park, gardens, or pleasure grounds, and is excluded from the half rate. The assessment committees follow not the Law, but the intentions of the politicians who enacted the Law, since farmers also occupy land together with a house. The singular result is that side by side, two holdings occupied by a farmer and a gentleman, but worked exactly in the same manner and with the same object, viz., profit to eke out a scanty income, the former is charged with the half rate and the latter with the full rate. Surely such a result is reversive of all sense of justice and of equal dealing between man and man. The law is even dragged into the region of burlesque by the anomaly that when the land is occupied by a gentleman residing in a house, it is non-agricultural, but when the same land is underlet to a farmer it becomes agricultural ; when it reverts again to the gentleman it becomes non-agricultural. This is as if a horse owned by a gentleman becomes a cow when hired to a farmer, and reverts to a horse when it comes back to the gentleman. Orchards,.

turnip-plots, cabbage gardens, gooseberry beds, meadows, occupied by a gentleman residing in a house, are metamorphosed into parks, gardens, and pleasure grounds for the sole purpose of excluding the occupier from the benefit of an Act which politicians devised for the advantage of a special class whose votes were desired. It has even been asserted that allotments to labourers have been rated as non-agricultural, on the plea that the land so occupied was part of a gentleman's land; neither gentleman nor labourer being understood to be admissible to the benefit of the Act, but only farmers. The decision of the Guardians of the Poor, through the assessment committees, is final. There is practically no appeal to the aggrieved ratepayer. According to the Law, the latter may appeal to the assessment committees themselves. The Guardians of the Poor transact their business generally in public, and they give facilities to the local press to report their transactions, their altercations and 'speeches'; but they hear appeals against the rates of their own fixing with closed doors. Appeals to the Justices are also allowed by the Law; but, apart from the facts that the Courts of Quarter Session largely consist of Guardians of the Poor, and that the 'justice' they dispense is not highly estimated by the public, the heavy expense of these appeals, exceeding the sums in dispute often by thirty or fortyfold and more, is prohibitory. The Guardians of the Poor are an autocratic, rapacious, and arrogant body, and the assessment of rates should not be in their hands.[1] The Agricultural Rates Act will do no good. The

[1] The collection of taxes, historically known to be a heart-hardening and rapacious vocation, should not be combined with the function of the care of the poor; they are incompatible and antagonistic offices. The Guardians of the Poor are rapacious as tax-gatherers, and basely economical towards the poor. They are harsh and hard towards their officials, especially towards their medical officers, to whom they assign a degraded official position and humiliating pay. For the poor they have erected bastilles of despair, and contrived a condition of existence which may justly be described as the last survival of slavery or serfdom on English soil. The sentiment created thereby in the minds and hearts of the honourable poor is that it is an ineffaceable disgrace to accept the degrading 'relief' afforded by the Guardians of the Poor. They have been known to prefer to undergo the acutest privations, and even in some instances to suffer death from cold and starvation. It is providential, however, that the administration of the Poor Law was not intrusted to the clergy. Wild beasts show their nature

landlords will raise their rents, or cease to make remissions of rent, and will withdraw various indulgences, so that the farmers will not benefit. The retired tradesmen, officers, and others now residing in the country will probably resent the exclusion of their holdings from the benefit of the Act, and migrate to the towns: house property in the country will depreciate in value, and the rates will suffer from their departure; many labourers will lose employment. If the Act be renewed, these evils will be aggravated, and many pleasant country residences will be untenanted and probably fall into ruins. If the occupiers of the numerous small holdings which have been metamorphosed into parks, gardens, and pleasure grounds by rapacious Guardians of the Poor to please politicians, refuse to make returns to the Agricultural Department of their live stock of foals, cattle, sheep, and pigs; of their stacks of hay, their orchards, and pasture lands, for the reason that their land has been declared to be non-agricultural, the agricultural statistics of the country will exhibit an awkward decline of the national prosperity.

The legislation on subjects of education is markedly obnoxious to the charge of public immorality. A few centuries ago benevolent men and women in various ranks

when they see blood, and the clergy when they see gold. The historical avarice and self-seeking of the clergy would have created out of the Poor Law a select body of clerical sub-almoners, aspirants to bishoprics and deaneries, with large salaries and vested interests, who would piously distribute fractions of farthings to the poor. Such has been the destination of the tithes and offerings to the Church, which in the vicissitudes of the ages have settled down in the pockets of bishops and clergy, while the poor have only such sums as were invested in trustees; and many even of these slender endowments have vanished, the records say not where or how. The English Poor Law, had it been administered by noble and generous minds, would in the nineteenth century have developed a beneficent system of honourable provision for the unfortunate, incapable, and aged poor. There is a sorrowful contrast between the institutions for the sane poor, created and administered by the sordid and base minds of Guardians of the Poor, and the institutions for the insane poor, organised and administered by the nobler minds of physicians. The Board of Guardians of the Poor is an ancient body, an antique stinkpot, which no reformer has ventured to meddle with. It is not surprising that no Continental nation has shown the least disposition to imitate the most faulty of English institutions, which utterly misrepresents and perverts the kindness and generosity of the English people.

of life, kings and queens, members of the aristocracy, prelates, merchants, grocers, and others springing from the labouring classes originally, left property to be employed for the education of the children of the poor. The deeds and wills of these kind and generous donors are still extant and ought to be legally binding. By a singular perversion of the moral sense of the legislature these gifts of benevolent donors, designed especially for the education of the children of the poor, have been practically embezzled, misappropriated, and diverted to the purpose of the education of the sons of the rich, of the sons of cabinet ministers, members of Parliament, prelates, lord mayors of London, of the aristocracy, and merchants and others of the wealthy classes. In this diversion of the funds left for the education of poor children to the education of the sons of the rich, the clergy of the Church of England, foremost amongst them being the magnificent and influential gentleman who enjoys the great salary of £15,000 per annum, were largely, if not mainly, instrumental. May it not be remembered against them in the day of disendowment! This unrighteous work should be undone. The property left for the education of the poor should be restored to its proper and just purpose. The great public schools should be reopened to the poor, for whom they were intended. The Parliamentary Committee should labour for the repeal of an iniquitous Act of Parliament, which despoiled the poor of a great boon and benefit bequeathed to them and to them alone, but now almost absolutely diverted from them and presented to the rich. The Public Schools Act of 1868 is a most shameful and odious example of the moral degeneration of the legislature in the present century, acting on the instigation of a self-seeking clericalism. It should be remembered that the head and assistant masters of these public schools were formerly exclusively and still are chiefly derived from the clergy of the Church of England, and that they make great gains from the board and lodging of the sons of rich men. The public schools are used by the clergy as stepping-stones to bishoprics and deaneries. It is a sad feature in the history of public schools, in the curriculum of which religion and theology form a great part, and religious services are even burdensome, that shameful accounts of immorality have emanated from them. The public schools make no charge on parents for the inculcation of morality, a branch of instruction which they either neglect or perhaps are understood to provide free. The Scotch schools once charged 3d. a week for teaching 'manners,' and that small modicum of moral instruction was valuable.

It is a fair question for discussion whether the principle of compulsion is a correct and useful one to introduce into national education. Compulsion is of value to prevent evil, but it is of no use to produce good. The principle has been tried in connection with religious belief, and has been found by sad experience to be grievously defective. It has also been tried partially in medical subjects, but has been totally abandoned as utterly mischievous. The enforcement, under penalties, of the practice of vaccination by law will be found in the future, as it has been found in the past, to be ineffective. If the public mind be convinced of the value of vaccination, no compulsory law is necessary. In the same way, if the public mind be convinced of the value of education, legal compulsion is unnecessary. In the lowermost grades of society, in which the people are barely supplied with the means of animal existence, the enforcement of education by penalty borders on cruelty: to so marked an extent that magistrates refuse to inflict the penalty. Education ought not to need the services of the police constable and the magistrate; these minister to the suppression of evil, not to the direct production of good. The policeman and magistrate are of no use in the inculcation of morality; but they are of inestimable service in the prevention of immorality. They are of no use in the cause of education, and the recourse to their services brings discredit on the latter. Universal education is a most desirable object to attain, but the means of attaining it should be rendered easy, alluring, and attractive. Schools should be established wherever parents are disposed to make use of them, and attendance should be free from compulsion, and non-attendance without police supervision and penalty. In the existing stage of civilisation all classes are desirous of educating their children, but the difficulties arising from poverty and privation practically debar large numbers of the poor from availing themselves of the means of education at present open to them. Special provision should be made to meet the necessities of this unfortunate class, but compulsion should not be resorted to. Assistance in kind, such as clothing and daily meals at school for the children, is far more effective for attaining the desired object; while punishment of the poverty-stricken parents for non-attendance of the children is a grave form of cruelty.

Elementary schools should be of a quality, with regard to the capacity of the buildings, the nature of the furniture, the tone and qualifications of the teachers, to suit a very wide area of the population. They should be of a character to satisfy at least the middle classes of society, as well as the lower classes. The upper classes and the more prosperous members of the middle classes will neither desire nor expect the statutory schools to be suitable for their children. Very large numbers of the middle classes, on the other hand, will be glad to avail themselves of the elementary schools, if the quality of the instruction, the character and social position of the teachers, and the general tone of the school be such as they deem desirable for their children. An overwhelming number of the middle classes at present contribute to the elementary education of other people's children, while they are not relieved from the burden of providing elementary education for their own children. This great evil and injustice ought to be remedied on the lines indicated. A very desirable national advantage will be gained by the association in early life of the children of the lower and middle classes. The former will assuredly derive considerable moral benefit by mixing with children who have the advantage of dwelling habitually in a higher moral and social atmosphere; while the latter, except, perhaps, at the initiation of the system here advocated, will not suffer appreciable deterioration. The benefit to the poor children will be analogous to the benefit derived from the association in the public schools and universities of boys and young men of the middle and upper classes. The system will tend to the ultimate removal of the moral differences between the various classes of society—a very valuable result for the happiness of the people.

The question of religious education has much exercised the public mind, and the clergy, Anglican and Roman, have been the most active and zealous partisans of religious education in elementary schools. By religious education the clergy, and perhaps also the public, do not mean education or instruction in religion alone, but a combination of religious and secular education. The plea of the clergy for the special inculcation of religious knowledge in the elementary schools is that the parents possess the right of having their children educated in their own religion. The assertion of the right does not, however, carry on its face the proof of its existence. I am personally unacquainted with any Law which has directly conferred the right upon the parents, upon one of them, or upon both. In cases of differences of religion, the usage requires that the boys be brought up in the religion of the father and the girls of the mother; but the father has the legal power of overruling the usage, and of bringing up the children of both sexes in his own religion, or any other religion, or in no religion at all, at his pleasure. In the case of illegitimacy the mother has the legal power of bringing up her natural offspring in her own religion, or another religion, or in none. In cases of divorce the judge is invested with the power of intrusting the care of the children to one or other parent, or of dividing them between the two parents, at his discretion; but he is not authorised by the Law, and carefully abstains from giving any order regarding the religious education of the children. There is no right unless expressly or indirectly conferred by the Law. So obvious a duty as providing suitable medical attendance for young children and sick persons has been declared by the judges, in recent prosecutions of individuals of the religious sects known as 'peculiar people' and 'medical scientists,' to be not a legal right, because not expressly conferred by statute, and the withholding of it constitutes no breach of the Law. The Law gives no right to parents to have their children educated in their own religion. The Law, now perhaps absolutely obsolete, though unrepealed, enforces the observance of religious services, attendance at church, taking the sacraments, Sunday observance, and the like; and for religious services the Law expressly decrees that they be performed by the clergy alone. Similarly, wherever the Law touches upon religious instruction, though these statutes are also practically obsolete, it expressly directs, or indirectly implies, that such instruction be imparted by the clergy alone. The history and tradition of the Christian Church in all ages, since its organisation in the latter half of the second century, prove that religious instruction was an important part of the normal duty of the clergy. Up to a recent period it was the practice of the clergy to teach children the catechism and the Bible; and the instruction in the doctrines of the Church to candidates for confirmation was given by the clergy. In the days when religion was regarded as of pre-eminent importance, and the primary article of all education, the clergy alone constituted the teaching profession. They conducted every educational establishment, because the teaching of religion was their especial function, and religion could not be divorced from education. The clergy claimed and enjoyed the right of being the sole teachers of religion, and as education was considered inseparable from religion, they practically monopolised the whole teaching profession. We have still surviving amongst us the vestiges of this monopoly in the fact of the masters and heads of colleges at our universities and the headmasters of public schools being, with very rare exceptions, clergymen of the Church of England.

In our days is to be seen the noteworthy fact of the clergy departing from the traditions and practice of the Church in the past by, in a very large measure, relieving themselves of the duty of teaching religion, and of transferring that duty, in a very large measure, to the laity. I find myself unable to explain this singular phenomenon on any of the principles of what may be called Church or religious economy. The duty of teaching religion is a most important part of the office of the clergy, second only to the duty of maintaining the facts of religion, or theology. This duty of teaching religion the Church has reserved to herself for ages past, and all manner of canonical, statutory, and social enactments have been constructed to secure to its members solely the privilege of discharging the function. While Church principles afford no explanation of the singular fact that the clergy are casting off one of the most important duties of their sacred calling, while still clinging tenaciously to the tertiary duty or right of performing the mechanical services of religion, the ordinary and profane principles of political or commercial economy supplies a lucid explanation. I have already stated the fact that in all the greater public educational establishments, the universities, the public schools, and similar establishments, the clergy maintain their position as teachers of religion : and I now contrast this fact with the striking circumstance that in the elementary schools the clergy, while maintaining the supreme importance of religious instruction, do not teach religion. The duty of teaching religion in elementary schools has been relegated to lay teachers, male and female. These two remarkable contra-distinct facts, though not explicable on Church principles, are easily explicable on profane principles. In the greater educational establishments the pecuniary profit of teaching religion is considerable, while the pecuniary profit of teaching religion in elementary schools is *nil.* The teaching of religion, like every other commercial transaction, has followed the economical rule of self-interest. The alleged command of the Great Master to the 'eleven Apostles,' and to their successors in modern days, "Go ye therefore, and teach all nations" (Matt. xxviii. 19), must be interpreted in our times as implying that the successors of the Apostles are authorised to get other people to teach religion instead of themselves, the other people being employés on a small salary, of the Government, or of societies. It is well known that a large proportion of the teachers, male and female, in the elementary schools, of all descriptions, undertake the task of teaching religion not from choice but from compulsion, and from the necessities of their position. I have not the least doubt in my own mind that if the teaching of religion in the elementary schools was substantially lucrative, the clergy would claim the monopoly of it as a right due to their sacred calling, and would in any case continue to secure for themselves a very large slice of the emoluments. The anomaly of lay men and women being employed as teachers of religion, instead of the clergy, has not attracted public attention, from the circumstance that the practice has been gradually and insidiously introduced. The fact is, moreover, highly significant in the present day, when there is stated to exist a large body of superfluous Anglican clergy, amounting in number to some thousands, who maintain a precarious existence from the performance of odd jobs of religious service, which laymen are legally disqualified from performing.

The present dual system of elementary schools is not one that recommends itself on its own merits. In the quality of the instruction which the schools impart they are pretty much on an equality. The characteristics of the two classes of schools, however, is an ignoble jealousy of each other, and internecine discord and strife, which cunning politicians find to their advantage to encourage and foment. There are Church or voluntary schools and Board schools. The former are older institutions than the latter, which only recently came into being, when the Government awakened to the duty of educating the people. In the prior period, before the education of the people was regarded as a public duty of the Government, certain benevolent societies sprung up, in association with the Church, which in a partial manner endeavoured to educate the children of the poor. All honour is due to these societies and to the clergy for their laudable exertions in educating poor children. When the Government, however, became alive to the importance of educating the people, and instituted legislation to carry out the measure systematically, it appears to me that it was the patriotic duty and obligation of the societies and of the clergy to have retired and to have left the field to the Government: and to have placed at the disposal of the Government the plant that they had already set up for the purpose of the education of the poor. I am unable to perceive how the contrary conduct, which was actually pursued by the societies and the clergy, in opposition and rivalry to the Government, is morally justifiable, and how it is consistent with the duty and obedience of good citizens. To the clergy was due entirely this unpatriotic antagonism to the Government: to them alone the hostility to the measures of the Government can be ultimately traced: and the deep underlying motive of the clergy in their opposition was the fixed purpose of casting off their own shoulders of the duty of teaching religion to the poor, and of transferring it to lay teachers.

The statesmen who propounded the scheme of national elementary education, the officials to whom the execution of the scheme was intrusted, were not irreligious men; the teachers employed were persons of respectability, of fair acquirements, and good moral character. The clergy, nevertheless, found their consciences justified them in condemning the Board school system as 'godless,' and in the pulpit, on the platform, and in social intercourse pouring out vials of evangelical vituperation upon the 'godless' Board schools. I believe the final impression in the public mind, created by the repeated commotions on the question of religious education started by the clergy and their followers, is that the clergy are an unpatriotic, rebellious, mischievous, and troublesome body of men.

The opposition offered to the legislative system of elementary education by the Roman clergy was actuated by motives of a different character. Their demand was, I believe, that special elementary schools, conducted by priests and teachers of the Roman faith, should be provided for the children of their community. The demand was one that could not be entertained by a Protestant nation. A coalition, however, between the Anglican and Roman clergy, not remarkable under the circumstances, but singular between bodies historically hostile, has succeeded in prevailing upon politicians to confer upon the Church or voluntary schools, Anglican and Roman, a considerable annual grant of public money. The education of the Roman Catholic community is a subject of great embarrassment to English statesmen. The Roman clergy prohibit the members of their Church from resorting to educational institutions in which the whole staff are not members of their faith, and the whole tone and character of the teaching is not Catholic. The Roman Catholic laity are prohibited by their clergy from resorting, not only to Board schools but to public schools and the universities, and to the various private and public establishments for higher education scattered over the country, and even, I am told, to the colleges for professional education in which the conditions they deem essential do not exist. The power of the Roman clergy over their laity lies in the strength of the superstition which they have succeeded in establishing —a superstition apparently more unmanageable than the superstition prevalent amongst Hindoos, Mahomedans, or the people of any other religion. The sacraments are regarded as essential to salvation in the next world, and it is in the power of the priest to withhold the sacraments at his pleasure, and thus to consign any member of the Catholic Church to eternal damnation. The threat of withholding the sacraments, it is said, is sufficient to deter parents from sending their sons and daughters to any educational establishment under ban. The Catholic clergy should bear in mind that a threat of that nature is a breach of the law against intimidation, and that religious toleration is incompatible with disobedience to the law, though they may enjoy impunity in the absence of prosecutor or witnesses. It is surprising to be told that the gentlemen of the Roman Catholic faith who enter professions, the training for which is undergone in non-Catholic colleges, do so in revolt against the priests of their religion. In Ireland, it is said, that the influence of the priests is very largely used to prevent the Catholic youth of both sexes from receiving the general and professional education from the universities and colleges existing in the country, which are not under the influence of Roman priests.

The above, I believe, are the chief embarrassments that lie in the way of statesmen in their endeavours to educate the people. On the Anglican side there exists an aggressive eagerness to engage in the religious and secular education of the rich, combined with a strong disposition to shirk the duty of teaching religion to the poor, and of transferring the task to the laity. On the Roman side there is a strong and inflexible indisposition to accept education which is imparted under Protestant influences. These are the facts of life in connection with national education which statesmen have to deal with. The legislative measures proposed to meet these perplexing difficulties should be closely scanned by the Parliamentary Committee of the Society. The education of the people is a matter of great importance to morality; for the mental growth and intelligence of the people regulate the standard of morality: and all educational measures are necessarily appropriate subjects for the consideration of the committee.

It appears to me that it is consistent with the trend of modern opinion that the entire system of education, elementary and secondary, theological and professional, should be under the control, direct or indirect, of the Government. All schools, colleges, and universities for both sexes should be enrolled, and Government officials, or specially authorised individuals, should inspect the buildings, the sanitary arrangements, the furniture, bedding, the kitchen and dining appliances, the playgrounds, the class and lecture rooms, dormitories, rooms for hats and cloaks, etc. All educational establishments should be licensed or chartered, and the Government should retain the right of withholding a licence in order to avoid an undue accumulation of schools where they are unnecessary. No encouragement should be given to sectarian schools, when good schools in sufficient number and generally accessible already exist in the neighbourhood. In like manner the teaching profession, including all grades of teachers of both sexes, should be enrolled. Two classes should be recognised, viz., teachers of religion and teachers of secular subjects, and these two classes of teachers should be distinct and separate, like the barristers and solicitors in the legal profession. The teachers of religion should consist solely of clergy of all sects in holy orders: the teachers of secular subjects should belong to the laity. The two classes may be interchangeable, on the single condition that the clergy on entering the other class should abandon holy orders, while the laity on joining the other class must take holy orders. Each class should be strictly limited to their respective functions: the one class to teach religion alone, the other class to teach secular subjects alone. No teacher of secular subjects must in any way be connected with a religious order, or in any way possess a sacerdotal or quasi-sacerdotal character, such as friar, monk, deaconess, nun, sister of mercy, or such like. On acquiring any connection of this character the teacher should be struck off the rolls.

The teachers of secular subjects may be of any religion, and no religious test should be imposed upon them; but their moral character in every respect, and in all the relations of life, should be strictly maintained.

In all educational establishments for secular subjects no religious instruction should be imparted; and in like manner in institutions for religious or theological instruction no secular subject, not connected directly or indirectly with theology, should form part of the curriculum of studies. Under this exception the study of ancient and modern languages will be admissible in theological institutions and may be taught by religious teachers. But no other secular subject should be permissible, except by the special permission of Government, and on the condition that such subjects be taught by laymen. No religious services of any description should be permitted in the secular schools and institutions. No churches, chapels, oratories, or other buildings for divine worship should be erected in connection with them. Under exceptional circumstances, and until a reasonable time has elapsed for the creation of suitable arrangements, religious instruction may be imparted in secular institutions in secluded class-rooms by the various religious teachers of the inmates. The ordinary and most suitable buildings for religious instruction are the churches. There is hardly anything more conspicuous amongst a thrifty and busy nation than the ecclesiastical thriftlessness and waste displayed in the little use made of the numerous churches which fill the towns and are thickly scattered over the country. These fine structures, varying in size and pretensions from the magnificent cathedral to the modest dissenting chapel, lie idle and useless for six days in the week: these are commodious and appropriate schools for the religious instruction of children. All the appliances necessary for imparting religious instruction exist in the churches, or if any more be needed they can be readily supplied. Desks and ink-bottles and such like are not needed, for all secular instruction in which these articles are required will be imparted in the secular schools. No more appropriate buildings or plant are needed than already exist in the churches. It is the legal and moral duty of every beneficed clergyman of the Church of England to give religious instruction to the children of his parishioners, and the moral duty of every clergyman of every denomination to do the same, without further remuneration than the emoluments of his office. Appropriate work will thus be supplied to occupy the leisure of the clergy, which is at present the idlest professional class in the community. Two afternoons in the week ought, I think, to be regarded as sufficient to provide a suitable amount of religious instruction to children, the Sunday School being no longer necessary. The weekly day of rest is more needed by the child than the adult. Sunday should be a day of absolute mental rest to the child. In parishes in which the children are numerous and beyond the capabilities of a single teacher, the services of the curates and of all clergy in the neighbourhood should be requisitioned and rendered free. By such conduct the clergy will give an example of duty performed and of pecuniary self-denial practised which will bring them more substantial respect from the community than the superficial estimation which they now derive from their wealth, their possession of an obsolete erudition, and their sacerdotal piety, some forms of which latter attribute are discounted by public disgust and disapproval.

A powerful lever for breaking up the dual system of Church or voluntary schools and Board schools, and of unifying the elementary system, to the great advantage of education, of the easy working of the elementary system, and of public tranquillity, will be the legislative discontinuance of the present practice of supplying grants-in-aid from imperial taxation, and of throwing the cost of elementary schools, when not voluntary, on the rates or local taxation. The existing system is practically a playing into the hands of the Anglican and Roman clergy, and is the outcome of a coalition or compromise between political parties and the clergy. The entire expenditure incurred by the Government in grants-in-aid, as well as the cost of the Board schools, now levied on the rates, should be defrayed from general or imperial taxation. So long as a Board school is more expensive to the inhabitants of a parish than a Church school, the latter is apt to be chosen. Herein lies the secret of an apparent preference by the people of the Church school over the Board school; a secret well known to the clergy, and made use of when occasion arises for an expression of choice by the people. The fact, however, that, in spite of the greater cost to the inhabitants of a locality of Board schools, so many of the latter have been established, is a strong proof of the real preference of the people for Board schools. It is chiefly, if not solely, in poor localities, such as sparsely-populated country parishes, that the Church schools find a footing, apparently from choice, but really a choice necessitated by the poverty of the people; while in large towns, where poverty is less prevalent, Board schools flourish in greater numbers. Elementary education being made compulsory, and a fixed standard being decreed by the legislature, it is incumbent on the Government to equalise the cost throughout the country. It is inequitable that a poor locality should be harder pressed than a rich locality in order to comply with the law. It ought to be the part of Government to render obedience to the law as easy in the poor as in the rich quarter. This can only be done by the cost of the Board schools being entirely defrayed from imperial taxation. The present system of supporting Board schools from the rates imposes a heavier burden upon a poor locality than on a rich one, and hence practically forces the poor locality to shape its selection according to its poverty rather than its wish and desire. It is a playing into the hands of the clergy, and it is the outcome of the great political influence, detrimental and retarding to the progress of civilisation, still possessed by the clergy. The just and natural system of defraying the cost of compulsory elementary education from the national exchequer will lead eventually to the extinction of the Church schools, institutions which maintain their existence from the unpatriotic and rebellious spirit of the clergy and their followers, which society has not yet acquired the power to disregard or suppress.

A few words are necessary on the advantage claimed for Church schools in villages and rural districts, from the fact that such schools can always command the attention and supervision of an educated man, the rector or vicar, whereas a Board school cannot count upon more than the services of imperfectly educated farmers in the work of governance and supervision. There can be no doubt that the clerical profession provides the rural districts with some men of great ability and attainments and of personal worth, whose services in the work of elementary education are valuable; but there is also the countervailing fact that most country clergymen are not men of this description. The cream of the clerical as of other professions goes to the towns. It is not the fact that there do not exist in the villages men who are as fit as clergymen to govern and supervise elementary schools. There is a very large sprinkling of medical men in the villages, and the education and attainments and personal worth of these gentlemen are equal to, if they be not greater, than those of the clergy. The advance made by the medical profession in recent years both in public estimation and in the personal qualities which deserve it, is patent to all. Medical education at present surpasses in breadth and solidity the relatively trifling education which the great body of the clergy obtain; and the ordinary village practitioner is fully the equal, and often is the intellectual superior, of the ordinary village incumbent. The cure of bodies at present is less lucrative than the cure of souls, but the tide may change. There are always resident in the country a large body of educated gentlemen, landowners, professional men of various sorts, retired officers of the army and navy, and even amongst the farmers there are many who are intellectually fully competent to govern an elementary school; these are the men who manage the affairs of the county. They do not now come forward in educational work, probably and assuredly because they fear unpleasant collision with the Anglican clergy, amongst whom are men of pugnacious and aggressive qualities, self-asserting and jealous of their rights and privileges, and supposed to be provided with a reserve stock of evangelical vituperation and private slander. There is, further, slowly springing up in the country a new growth of intellectual force, generated by the higher education of women, which will eventually double the available talent for the education of the people in the rural districts.

In the measures above proposed for the advancement of education, in which religion is not set aside, the maxims of religious toleration are scrupulously respected. No favour or antagonism is displayed towards any religious denomination;

all sects are impartially dealt with with equal justice. Every system of religious belief is left free to develop itself, apart from interference with secular education, which, on its side, is protected from sectarian interference. The great obstacle to the dissemination of secular education I take to be the mutual jealousy and internecine discord and strife of sectaries amongst themselves. One sect is unwilling to accept education which is imparted in institutions in which the general influence and spirit of another sect predominate. This is a very natural feeling: a Roman Catholic is unwilling to send his children to a school, college, or university in which Protestant influences prevail, and may undermine the religious principles of the children: and a Protestant on his part is equally averse to sending his children for education to Roman Catholic institutions for the same reason. It is, therefore, the part of common-sense legislation to conciliate and assure these sectaries by removing sectarian spirit and influence from all institutions in which secular education is imparted. The only means available to the State to effect this desirable neutrality of secular educational institutions is to withdraw all religious teaching, worship, and services from these institutions, and to restrict the governing and teaching staff to lay men and women exclusively, who may be of any religion or of none at all, but whose moral conduct and character, in all the relations of life, must be unimpeachable.

This plain, consistent, and universally just scheme of unsectarian secular education is one, however, that will be difficult to realise in practice, and will be fiercely opposed by the Anglican and Roman clergy, who on this point seem of one mind, as they are on other points. The dissenting clergy, I believe, are more patriotic, more philanthropic, and hence less rebellious against measures that the progress of civilisation spontaneously gives rise to, at least in their present state of being; if they possessed the power of the Anglican clergy in England, the Presbyterian in Scotland, or of the Roman clergy in Ireland, they would naturally be of the same mind as their brethren of the more powerful Churches. The Anglican clergy are in actual possession of the universities, colleges, and schools, and the efforts they will put forth to retain the education, secular as well as religious, of the rich in their own hands will require a prolonged and persistent struggle to overcome. The Roman clergy are exerting all their authority and influence to establish educational institutions in which their spirit and influence will be dominant. I think it will be wise and expedient to curtail the power of the clergy by restrictive measures which do not involve religious intolerance. The extension of the franchise has, I believe, very largely increased the power of the clergy, as it has of unscrupulous politicians. Some useful measures for restricting the unfair operations of politicians have been passed with considerable success and public advantage, but I am unaware that any precautions have been yet taken to check the undue influence of the clergy. The prevalence of the practice of withholding the sacraments amongst the Roman clergy is a subject of popular belief; but there are no means of verifying the accusation, which is denied. A charge of this nature is not urged against the Anglican clergy; but they are accused of practices which, under the cover of religious ministration to the wants of the poor, combined with a pious distribution of eatables, drinkables, and wearables, and of small gifts of money, have the ultimate effect of gathering a considerable harvest of preservative votes. The increased activity of the religious ladies, who are known as district visitors, if not the origin of their organisation, has been consentaneous with the extension of the franchise, and all ecclesiastical agitations and ferments that have sprung up in recent years have been accompanied by an acceleration of the exertions of the Anglican clergy, with the aid of district visitors, in pious ministrations to the poor. Very large sums of money were collected by the Anglican clergy to fight the question of the Disestablishment of the Church of Wales, but no public account has been rendered to Churchmen, so far as I know, of the manner of expenditure of these sums. Peers are precluded from taking part in elections; and I think a legislative measure to prohibit clergymen of all denominations from taking part in elections for any public office, or in canvassing for votes, directly, indirectly, or mediately, without, however, depriving them personally of the right of voting, will have a good effect in restraining clerical electioneering malpractices, if they exist, and of relieving the public mind of prevailing suspicions of the undue influence secretly exercised by the clergy over the electorate by surreptitious breaches of the penal laws under the guise of religion. It is a sad reflection that the whole tenor of ecclesiastical history, from its inception in the second century up to the present day, has deeply fixed in the mind of society the sentiment that sordid motive and base conduct are inseparable from the ecclesiastical office and character, notwithstanding the existence of noble individual exceptions, and has generated the persistent suspicion that occult moral depravity, apart from sexual viciousness, is prevalent in the ecclesiastical profession to a far greater extent than in other liberal professions, such as the law, engineering, medicine, and the profession of arms, military and naval. The insidious attempt of the Anglican clergy, or of a considerable portion of them, to betray the Church of England, whose pay they are receiving, into the hands of the Church of Rome—a traitorous proceeding, persisted in for over half a century—has not elevated the clerical character in the minds of the thinking public.

The indifference to religious belief in the serious affairs of life, which is the basis of the scheme for the separation of religious from secular education which I here advocate, is very marked in the conduct of the nation. With the exception of the sovereign, whose religious belief must be the same as that of the Church of England by Law established, and of the clergy of the Church of England, in no walk of life, apart from those connected with religious societies and institutions, is the religion of an individual a matter of serious or of any concern. The Premier and the Cabinet, the highest body of public officials in the land, may be of any religion or of none at all. The Premier has been a Jew, of the Hebrew faith, and the members of the Cabinet have been of the Church of England, of the Church of Rome, of the Church of Scotland, dissenters, and one has been a Quaker and another an Agnostic. The members of the House of Lords and of the House of Commons have been and are of all kinds of faith prevalent in Europe, and even of none at all; two, if not more, members have professed eastern faiths, which western nations have always held in distaste. The highest offices in the great State departments of the law, the navy, the army, the civil service, the governorships of our colonies and dependencies, which are in magnitude equal to empires, are given to men from considerations connected with their personal abilities and merits and moral character, without concern about their theological beliefs. In our eastern dependencies — India, Ceylon, etc.—Mahomedans, Hindoos, and others of oriental faiths, but of personal moral and intellectual worth, are admitted into the local legislatures and to some great State offices. Hindoos and Mahomedans have filled the high position of judges in our courts, and have even been appointed to the exalted post of Lord Chief-Justice of Calcutta. If men of oriental faiths in our dependencies are excluded from the higher positions of civil administration and of military command, this is not done from theological considerations, but for political reasons, which will probably abate in their force as time goes on. The same principle of indifference to religious belief is observed in all the lower walks of life, in all the liberal professions, save and except the clerical, in all the various establishments of commerce, of manufacture, and in all the numerous branches of industry. Men and women are freely admitted and employed on their personal merits and qualifications and moral character, without concern regarding their religious beliefs. With such a contrast of universal indifference to special religious beliefs in the serious affairs of life, the amalgamation of religious and secular education in our schools, colleges, and universities is a grave anomaly and most serious evil, besides being an unnecessary and superfluous addition to the preparation of youth for the actual business of life. The pernicious results arising from such amalgamation are less apparent in England and Scotland, from the happy circumstance that the great mass of the people in both countries are of one religion, Anglican in one and Presbyterian in the other, but Protestant in both, the ruling power being Protestant. The numbers of persons of the Roman and other faiths in these two countries are insignificant, and politically of little or no account. In Ireland, however, in which the ruling power is Protestant, and the population of the Roman faith vastly exceeds the Protestant population, the evil of mixed religious and secular education has been disastrous to the progress and well-being of the people. The unwise prejudice of the ruling power and the self-interest of the Anglican clergy and laity determined that the great educational establishments should be Protestant. The self-interest of the Roman clergy, and the natural preference of the Catholic laity for their own religion, determined that these Protestant educational establishments should not be resorted to by their youth. The poverty of the Catholic clergy and population rendered the establishment of Catholic institutions in sufficient numbers an impossibility. The consequence is that the Catholic youth are largely deprived of the means of education, and great educational institutions established by the Government are half empty. This great national evil would have been avoided had the British Government adopted in Ireland the educational policy which it adopted in India with marked success. This great dependency is a hundred times larger than Ireland, and several hundred times more densely populated. The people consist of vast nations, covering wide territories, and differing from each other in national character, in religion, in personal habits and customs, and further differing in all these great features from their rulers. In the scheme for educating this vast population of diverse religions, the main religions being Hindoo, Mahomedan, and Sikh, the Government adopted the simple, righteous, and just principle of separating religious from secular education. The teaching of religion being left without hindrance to the religious teachers, secular education pure and simple formed solely the subject of the attention of the Government. The institutions for secular education were conducted by a staff of solely lay teachers, whose religion was a matter of indifference. From the circumstances of the case, the professors and masters of the Government universities, colleges, and schools are Europeans and Christians, but they are very largely being reinforced and displaced by educated natives of diverse religions—Hindoos and Mahomedans and others. These great neutral institutions for secular education are scattered over India, but, unlike the Irish Protestant institutions, they are thronged with native students of all the multifarious religions flourishing in the country. No churches, chapels, oratories, temples, mosques, or pagodas are erected in connection with the Indian universities, colleges, and schools under the auspices of the Government; no clergyman or priest is associated with them in the work of education; no prayers or religious services are heard or performed within their precincts. The native youth of all religions who are educated in these institutions are diligent, industrious, docile, assiduous in attendance, of good conduct and moral character. No scandal of the nature which has been reported from time to time as prevailing in public schools and colleges in this country, conducted by Anglican and Roman clergymen, has been known in connection with secular educational institutions in India exclusively conducted by laymen of personal worth and moral character, whose religious belief is their own private concern, and is not inquired into.[1]

The experience derived from the educational policy of the Government of India ought to be utilised in Ireland. A

[1] Since writing this passage I have seen a report of the speech of Lord Curzon, the new Governor-General of India, made as Chancellor of the University of Calcutta, on February 11, 1899. Some remarks in the speech are of great value, as displaying the important moral effect of secular education. "I say to myself, therefore, in the first place, is it possible, is it likely, that we have been for years teaching hundreds and thousands of young men, even if the immediate object be the passing of an examination or the winning of a degree, a literature which contains invaluable lessons for character and for life, and science which is founded upon the reverent contemplation of nature and her truths, without leaving a permanent impress upon the moral as well as the intellectual being of many who have passed through this course? I then proceed to ask the able officials by whom I am surrounded, and whose trained assistance makes the labour of the Viceroy relaxation rather than toil, whether they have observed any reflection of this beneficent influence in the quality and character of the young men who entered the ranks of what is now known as the provincial service, and when I hear from them almost without dissent that there has been a marked upward trend in the honesty, the integrity, and the capacity of native officials in those departments of Government, then I decline altogether to dissociate cause from effect. I say that knowledge has not been altogether starved by her children, grave as the defects of our system may be, and room though there may be for reform. I refuse to join in a wholesale condemnation which is as extravagant as it is unjust."

system of secular education should be legalised, religious education being dealt with apart and on a separate plane. The institutions for secular education should be distinct from those for religious education, and the teachers of religion should be distinct from the teachers of secular subjects. All priests and clergymen of any sect holding office in secular institutions should be replaced by laymen, whose religious opinions should be a matter of indifference. Religious services of every description should be prohibited in the secular educational institutions. An absolute secularisation of the schools, colleges, and universities will assuredly effect a change in the present condition of education in Ireland. The anxiety of parents lest the religious principles of their sons and daughters be tampered with and undermined will be allayed; and the natural parental desire to advance by education the prosperity and happiness of their offspring in the present world will not be chilled by the solicitude that their prospects of salvation in the next world will be endangered. The religious education of the people should be left without restriction or restraint absolutely in the hands of the Roman and other clergy. Any feeling of opposition on the side of the Irish people to the separation of religious from secular education will be appeased and disarmed, if the same educational policy be carried out, as it ought to be, in England and Scotland.

It will not be good statesmanship to encourage or to comply with the demand of the Irish Roman priesthood for educational institutions of composite character, conducted by Roman priests and pervaded throughout by Roman influences, to which students of all religious denominations will be admissible. This will be an imitation and perpetuation of the vicious educational system prevailing in England and Scotland, in which Roman will be substituted for Protestant tone and influence in educational institutions. It will be a retrograde step, opposed to the appreciable trend of modern public opinion, and if adopted will certainly leave to posterity a legacy of considerable moral embarrassment. If deliberately granted to Irish Roman Catholicism, there will certainly arise a difficulty hereafter, when the Catholic faith extends in England and Scotland, in resisting a similar demand in these two countries. And if yielded to Roman Catholicism, why should it not be equally conceded hereafter to other faiths which may spring up and spread in the coming century? At the close of the last century no human foresight could have anticipated the remarkable resuscitation in the present century of Catholicism in England, the treachery of the Anglican clergy, the establishment of a papal hierarchy, and the partition of the country into papal dioceses, and the grant of public money for Catholic schools, and hence for the propagation and maintenance of the Catholic faith in England. In less than seventy years a new and strange religion, Mormonism, has sprung up in America, and developed into a powerful sect, which has already acquired a secure footing and appreciable political power. The extraordinary sect of 'Christian scientists' appears to have planted itself in England, and may spread, and before the close of the next century may attain a magnitude which may justify the presumption to demand a university and colleges conducted on Christian scientist principles, and pervaded by its tone and influences, which will be open to students of all denominations.[1] Mahomedanism has also established itself in England, and there exist at London and Liverpool small congregations of English Mahomedans who have built themselves mosques for worship. We hear of Mahomedan missions being equipped in Constantinople and Hyderabad for the conversion of England to Mahomedanism, in the same sanguine spirit of hopefulness that prayers are offered in Catholic countries for the conversion of England to the Roman faith. I believe there is more real danger to be apprehended from Mahomedanism than from the miserable sects that spawn from ecclesiastical Christianity. It is a religion which has a great history. Our historians assert that European civilisation has been deeply indebted to it. A few centuries ago it had displaced Christianity in Spain, and bid fair to have overrun Europe. It is capable of being presented in an attractive form to the European mind. It is more reasonable and logical than ecclesiastical Christianity; it inculcates the worship of one merciful and beneficent God,

---

[1] Mrs Besant is agitating for a Theosophic university, to be conducted solely under Theosophic influences, but to be open to all.

and does not admit the least approach to idolatry. It accepts revelation, but beyond that has no dealing with supernaturalism. It is free from virgin conception, resurrection from the dead, ascension to heaven, from an incomprehensible trinity, and from miracles of all and every description: its worship is simple, without ritual and without priests: its sacred writings are genuine, have been carefully safeguarded, and are free from fraudulent interpolations and alterations. It has no forged writings falsely put forward as sacred. In all these points it has the advantage over ecclesiastical Christianity. Its doctrines are intelligible, and some of them identical with those of Christianity, though put into a different form. Its founder is a prophet, a man only, without supernatural qualities, but with all the feelings, thoughts, and emotions of a man: he enjoyed the society of women, and made no hypocritical, unmanly, and inhuman pretension that such society was sinful and irreligious. In this point the especial superiority of Mahomedanism is remarkable. Celibacy is not enjoined, but condemned. The wife is given a definite, stable, and honourable status, with which the position of the Christian woman compares badly. There is not in Mahomedanism the multifarious, indefinite, and uncertain position, shaded off in various tints of dishonour, which an ungrateful religion, which is much indebted to her for its propagation and maintenance, provides for the Christian woman. There is nothing in Mahomedanism to equal in social depravity and dishonour, and private womanly suffering, the following list of the various sorts of Christian wives:—1. The legal and canonical wife. 2. The legal but uncanonical wife. 3. The canonical but illegal wife. 4. The left-hand or Morganatic wife. 5. The castaway or judicially separated wife. 6. The illegal and uncanonical wife, recognised by her social circle. 7. The doubtful wife, about whom Her Majesty's judges cannot agree whether she is a wife or not. And finally, 8. The locally legal but uncanonical wife, *i.e.*, wife in the colonies and in all Christendom, but no wife in England.[1] Should

---

[1] In France and Italy ecclesiastical marriages are not recognised by the law, civil marriage alone being legal. In France it is penal for priests to perform the marriage ceremony before the civil marriage has been

a serious conflict ever arise between Mahomedanism and ecclesiastical Christianity, the manifest superiority of the position assigned to women by the former religion will have its normal effect upon the European mind. This superiority is also marked in the greater fairness of Mahomedanism in the rights over her own property given to the wife; but this subject has recently received the attention of Christian legislatures, and is now undergoing equitable revision. In no point is the weakness of ecclesiastical religion more marked as against the strength of Mahomedanism than in the position assigned to the Christian wife, and in none is the necessity more urgent for an international agreement between Christian nations to determine a stable, definite, and unimpeachable meaning, recognisable and intelligible throughout Christendom, to the honourable position of wife. The institution of polygamy is generally regarded as a serious and repulsive blemish in Mahomedanism; but reflection will show that it is not altogether to be condemned. Moslem missionaries will exert

accomplished; in Italy this is not so. The results are that in France a portion of the population are content with the civil marriage alone, and dispense with the canonical: in Italy, however, the vulgar people prefer canonical marriage and dispense with the legal, so that a considerable portion of the married people, markedly the peasantry, are legally unmarried. No. 6 is illustrated by the union of Mr Lewis and George Elliott, and there are others. No. 8 is the wife married to the husband of her deceased sister. An Australian or Canadian wife of this description, who is recognised as a wife throughout the world, ceases to enjoy that honourable position when she lands on the soil of England. This scandal is the final expression of the mind of the highest and purest form of ecclesiastical Christianity, the Church of England, and it emphatically indicates that the influence of the priest is still predominant in England. For there can be no question that the Anglican priesthood, represented by the bishops in the House of Lords, are the sole supporters of this hateful law. The mind of the Queen on the subject is well known, for Her Majesty was desirous that one of the royal princesses should contract a marriage of this description. The mind of the House of Commons has been repeatedly expressed by large majorities rendered with acclamation. Being an ecclesiastical question (falsely, however, so considered) the bishops gave expression to the mind of the House of Lords. It is a case of *Episcopi Anglicani contra mundum*; and the Anglican bishops have hitherto defied the public opinion of the nation and of the whole of Christendom: a very marked proof of the power of the priest in England, exercised in this instance for the degradation of the honourable position of a wife.

their ingenuity to modify it to the European taste. Polygamy is not compulsory in Mahomedanism, and is strictly limited to four wives. It is not forced upon the faithful; and in point of fact, I am told, the liberty is rarely indulged in, so that broadly Mahomedans in actual practice are monogamists like Christians. Moslem missionaries may be presumed to be capable of the same tricks as their Christian analogues, and they may interpret Mahomedan polygamy to mean monogamy restricted to four successive marriages after the death or divorce of previous wives—an interpretation which will remove European repugnance, and may even gain European approval, for there exist many good people who regard numerous successive marriages as bad taste and form, and condemn the six successive marriages of Henry VIII. as downright wickedness. Further, Moslem missionaries may represent that ecclesiastical Christianity is not opposed to polygamy: that in the New Testament there is no precept condemning polygamy, which was prevalent amongst Jews and other eastern nations, in whose midst the Christian religion originated. That the early Christians adopted whatever custom regarding marriage that existed amongst the peoples, and as polygamy was then common, the Christians were not prohibited from adopting it. That there is inferential proof that early Christian bishops were polygamists, and if bishops, therefore the Christian communities likewise. The chief reference to the subject to be found in the New Testament is the precept in 1 Timothy iii. 2, a bishop must be "the husband of one wife," a clear proof that bishops with more than one wife existed in the second century. If a serious writer in our days should write "a bishop should drink one glass of port at dinner," the conclusion is absolutely just that the practice by bishops of drinking several glasses prevails, and is disapproved by the writer. In Titus i. 6 the existence of polygamy amongst Christians is even more strongly expressed. The practice of monogamy was enforced on Christianity by Roman law and custom; and the same could be done on Mahomedanism by English law without in any way infringing the integrity of the religion; and zealous Moslem missionaries may thus conscientiously enjoin the practice of monogamy on their European converts. On the other hand, they will not be slow to point out that a restricted system of polygamy has some social advantages, and that in the various afflictions to which human life is subject, it is a far better resource than divorce. All the relations of marriage may be nullified by unperceived and unforeseen circumstances, for which neither party can be blamed, and which involve no guilt and do not abate natural tenderness. For these misfortunes divorce is a harsh and even cruel remedy, while limited polygamy supplies a softened, congenial, and honourable relief. The immorality and unspeakable baseness to which Christian popes, cardinals, archbishops, and bishops are compelled to resort to in order to nullify the unfruitful marriages of royal personages will be avoided. Such historical outrages on honourable and virtuous women of high rank as were perpetrated on Catherine of Aragon, Queen of England, and Josephine, Empress of France, would have been unnecessary had a restricted polygamy replaced the harsh and cruel and inflexible system of divorce justified by hypocritical, unmanly, and false pleas. The charge that Mahomedanism recognises concubinage is only a Christian slander, and as unjust as would be the accusation that Christianity recognises and encourages public prostitution. Concubinage is a social custom permitted by public opinion amongst Moslems, but is no institution of the Mahomedan religion : in the same sense that prostitution, though extensively and universally prevalent amongst Christian nations to a far greater extent than concubinage exists amongst Moslem nations, is not an institution of the Christian religion. The harem is an appendage of the household of the Moslem sovereign, of the noble and rich, and indicates rank and wealth in the same way as great retinues of servants, fantastically dressed, indicate rank and social position in Christian countries, but it has no religious significance. The seclusion of women, in like manner, is only a social custom or usage from which Christian nations are not quite free, as is witnessed in the establishment of nunneries, the separation of the sexes in schools and colleges, and in the various restrictions which etiquette imposes upon our womenkind. The veiling of women, which, however, is limited to the upper classes, bears the same relation to Mahomedanism that low-necked dresses have to Christianity. All such misconceptions and misrepresentations will be speedily removed by earnest and zealous Moslem missionaries, lecturers, and writers. Most Europeans coincide with Professor Max Müller's view of the superiority and greater attractiveness of the Mahomedan paradise over the Christian heaven; and there is nothing in the Mahomedan hell, which is only a conventional idea, to compare with the horrors of Christian eternal damnation.

In the mouths of fiery orators, such as Mahomedanism can produce, the merits of an historic and reasonable religion, set forth in fluent English, may be brought home to many in these islands, so that in half or three-quarters of a century the number of converts may attain a magnitude which no statesman can despise or pass over. In the face of the concession of universities, colleges, and schools to Protestants, to Roman Catholics, perhaps also to Christian scientists, it would be barely possible to deny a similar concession to English Mahomedans of educational institutions conducted under Mahomedan influences, to which students of all denominations will doubtless be cordially welcome. In the face of such possible, and by no means improbable, embarrassment that might arise in the course of the coming new century, it would be unadvisable artificially to propagate in Ireland the principle on which our English educational establishments have been spontaneously founded in the natural march of events. It would be judicious and reasonable, on the other hand, to anticipate the result towards which public opinion throughout the civilised world is slowly but steadily progressing, viz., to secularise the existing Protestant educational institutions in Ireland, and to remove from them all ecclesiastical influences of every description.

Such appear to me to be the appropriate subjects to which the Parliamentary Committee of the Society can profitably give its attention in the interest of morality. To these may be added the endeavour to secure a good moral tone in the *personnel* of the Houses of Legislation. The members of the Houses of Lords and Commons should be not only men of talent, varied acquirements, and experience, but also of virtue, of moral character unimpeachable in all the relations of life. The extraordinary growth of dishonest company promoting of late years, since the Companies Acts were passed, leads to the not unreasonable presumption that it is the outcome of recent legislation, or that the latter has at the least afforded facilities which dishonest men utilised for their own purposes. A further great object of the Parliamentary Committee will be to seek the repeal of ecclesiastical laws, apart from those for regulating ecclesiastical bodies, and to prevent the enactment of fresh ones. It will also be its endeavour to sever the connection of the State with all forms of religion, and to seek to obtain the non-recognition of religion by the State. All past history, prior and subsequent to the establishment of ecclesiastical Christianity, clearly indicates the injustice, inconvenience, and danger to subjects of the State adopting, propagating, or enforcing any one system of religious belief. The safest course, one demanded by the security and well-being of the people, is for the State to leave religion severely alone. It is not a subject for the State to handle, but is peculiarly appropriate to be left to its own development or decay in the hands of philosophers and thinkers. What may be called the police regulation of the *professors* of any system of religion is, however, a clear duty of Government. The necessity of maintaining public order demands the regulation of religious bodies, associations, or societies, or, as they are called, Churches, as of secular associations. The regulation of religious associations is as necessary as the regulation of legal, medical, and similar associations or professions in the interests of public order. Such regulations should be restricted to the personal or professional conduct of the professors or followers of any system of religion, and should not meddle with the doctrines, ceremonies, practices, or form of worship so far as these are consistent with public morality and public policy. The various Churches or religious associations should be regulated like the professions, such as the medical profession. The State exercises what may be called a police control over the members of the medical profession, while it does not meddle with the principles of medical science and the measures for the alleviation and cure of bodily aliments, which it leaves to scientific investigators and thinkers. The control exercised by the State over the Church of England is in excess of its duty, inasmuch as the State identifies itself with the Church, and further, regulates its doctrines and ritual, while it yields practically unbridled license to the clergy. The Church of England was established by law at a period when the conditions and sentiments of society were different from what they are now : it has not changed in due proportion to the changes in the circumstances and sentiments of society, and is hence an effete and archaic institution. There is a marked deficiency of control over the members of the clergy, to such a gross and scandalous extent, that the Prime Minister of England, in a public speech, declared the Church of England to be in a state of anarchy. The State organisation of the Church of Scotland (Established) and of the Church of Ireland (Established) is more in accord with the views here advocated: the State does not identify itself with either Church, nor meddles with doctrine and worship, while it indirectly or mediately exercises a limited control over the clergy. No State control of any description is exercised over other religious bodies or Churches. With regard to the Protestant Churches, always excluding the Church of England, there is not at present any urgency or need for specific State control. The clergy of these Churches limit their activity to the practice and inculcation of religion, and in no way interfere with public tranquillity. It is otherwise, however, with the Church of England and the Church of Rome. Both these Churches are turbulent and rebellious ; they do not limit their activities to the discharge of their religious functions, but intrude their religious interference into secular spheres alien to their religious character and office. The interference of the Anglican and Roman clergy with matters foreign to their sacred calling is such as would not be tolerated if imitated by other professional bodies. If the legal and medical professions, for example, should act as the clergy are understood or suspected to act, society would be placed in a very difficult position. What would result from the refusal of barristers and solicitors, surgeons and physicians to render their services to individuals unless the latter vote or act in a particular way indicated? What would be thought if a surgeon and all surgeons should refuse to set a fracture of the leg unless the sufferer solemnly agrees to regulate his public action according to the surgeon's direction? The analogue of this is what the clergy of these two rebellious and arrogant Churches are understood or suspected to do: and the perplexity is that they act thus, or are said to, in a secret and surreptitious manner, under cover and protection of the forms of religion, which the people regard as sacred. There is a serious defect in the moral sense prevalent amongst these clergy.[1] The remedy for this state of things is less difficult to be found against the Anglican than the Roman clergy. There can be no question that the present unspeakable confusion and absence of discipline among the Anglican clergy urgently calls for reform. It is simple folly to attempt to tinker an utterly unmanageable, worn out, and archaic constitution such as that of the Church of England. Its abolition and reconstitution is urgently called for by common sense. It should be reorganised on the simple and just principles that modern experience has found to be the best for the public good, that finally adopted by the Government for the army and navy and for the civil and military establishments in India. This system is essentially the same as that adopted by the Roman and dissenting Churches. The whole body of the beneficed clergy should be divided into grades—archbishops, bishops, and chaplains of various classes: the two former being administrative and the latter executive. The

---

[1] The following recommendations are taken from a private letter, dated 8 York Place, 3rd May 1867, from H. E. Manning, Catholic Archbishop of Westminster, to Monsignor Talbot, Private Chamberlain of Pius IX., Pope of Rome :—

" 5. That we ought to lay on our clergy the OBLIGATION to *hinder* our youth going to the universities by all means in their power.

" 6. That we pray the Holy See to enjoin us to act in this sense.

" If the Holy See will speak clearly and strongly, as above, we shall carry it through.

" A prohibition of the clergy must come first. *They* have not yet done their duty in dissuading the laity. Some have even advised them to send their sons to Oxford.

" With this we can begin ; and my belief is that it will suffice.

" But we must act at once, for the *evil is spreading*" (*Life of Cardinal Manning*, by Edmund Sheridan Purcell, vol. ii. p. 301).

archbishops and bishops should possess full power to maintain discipline amongst the clergy, to appoint them to parishes, and to remove them from parish to parish, on promotion, or exchange, or otherwise at their discretion. The executive clergy at present on the establishment should be equitably divided into classes, and all future admissions should be by competition,[1] after a medical examination for physical fitness, patronage being abolished. Promotion from one class to another should go by length of service. The pay of the administrative and executive clergy should be regulated on the equitable system adopted by the Government in its great departments of work. The Archbishop of Canterbury may be generously assigned a salary equivalent to that of the Prime Minister, £5000, and the Archbishop of York that of the First Lord of the Admiralty and of the Commander-in-Chief of the Army, £4500. The bishops' services may be appraised at the value of those of the junior ministers and of admirals and generals, £2000. The executive classes of the clergy may be assigned graduated salaries, beginning at £150, and rising from class to class eventually to £1500. In addition to the above salaries a suitable residence should be provided for each individual, or in lieu house-money on a graduated scale. Provision should also be made for aged clergymen, and for those who may be disabled from accident or disease, by the allotment of graduated pensions. A fund should also be created, partly by grant and partly by graduated contributions, made compulsory, from all classes of the clergy, for

---

[1] The theological subjects for examination should be left to the discretion of the bishops; but I should suggest that the Government should require candidates for admission on the establishment to show some proficiency in one natural science. The scope of theological education is narrow, and the quality of mind it produces is rather thin, even when individuals are possessed of considerable natural talent. The clergy do not think on the same plane as the laity. The study of natural science would fatten and invigorate the theological mind and bring it up to the sturdiness of the lay mind. I do not possess the honour of a personal acquaintance with Dr Westcott, the learned and esteemed Bishop of Durham, but I have studied his theological writings. I venture to draw the inference that he is unacquainted with any branch of natural science, from the extraordinary declaration that he has made on the subject of miracles (see page 362, footnote).

pensions for widows and children, for daughters for life or until marriage, and for sons to the age of twenty-one. The above scale of pay and pensions is ample in these days to secure for the Church men of high talents and attainments, equal to any who enter secular professions. To check the arrogance, pretensions, and caprices of the clergy, from which the laity now suffer so severely, all ecclesiastical buildings, from cathedrals downwards, all bishops' palaces and parsonages, all churchyards, all church furniture should be retained as national property, and kept in repair and renewed by Government. The charge of these buildings should be in the hands of laymen, appointed by Government generally, but in parishes elected by the parishioners. The curators and churchwardens, who may be of any religious denomination, should be in exclusive charge of Government property of this description, and should have the power to employ such property for any useful and appropriate purpose not inconsistent with the sacred character of the buildings. The cathedrals and churches may be appropriately employed on week days, when they lie idle, for schools for religious instruction by the clergy, for lectures on scientific and literary subjects by laymen, for concerts for the performance of the higher class of music, and similar purposes at the discretion of the responsible officers. The churchyards should be available for the interment of deceased residents of the parish, of any and every denomination, the religious ceremony, if any be desired by the friends of the deceased, being performed by laymen or clergymen of any denomination, provided always that the proceedings at funerals be conducted in a sober, serious, and reasonable manner. The furniture, and all questions regarding increase, change, or diminution of it, should be in the power of the laity, represented by the curators and churchwardens, subject to the supreme control of the Government. While the pay of the clergy will be in the hands of Government, and the appointment and control of the clergy, the doctrines, ceremonial, and ritual in the hands of the episcopacy, the ecclesiastical buildings and furniture will be in the hands of the laity, represented by the curators and churchwardens, subject to the supreme control of the Government. This is the only contrivance of organisation available for giving effect to the opinion of the parishioners under the reconstitution of the Church proposed. The curators and churchwardens, being elected by the parishioners, *i.e.*, all the residents of the parish of every denomination, are the representatives of the laity. When the latter are dissatisfied with the doctrines inculcated by the chaplains, or with their ritual, practices, or general conduct, their representatives are the natural medium for communicating their complaints to the bishop of the diocese, who will decide on the questions submitted at his discretion, or refer them for the decision of the archbishop of the province. The decision of the bishop and archbishop will, of course, be binding on the chaplain, who, if recusant, can be removed from the parish and appointed to another, or be recommended to the Government for dismissal. But if the laity are dissatisfied with the episcopal decision, they should have the power, through their representatives, on obtaining a majority of three-fourths of their body, of inhibiting the chaplain from the performance of the services in the church, pending the final decision of the Government, to whom the question should now be referred. The order of the Government should be final and binding upon both the laity and clergy. If the Government, however, think fit not to interfere for twelve months, the parish should be struck off the establishment, and one chaplain taken off the ecclesiastical department. An arrangement of this sort will give a natural, reasonable, and pacific vent to the local parochial sentiment, and will effectually prevent the scandal of the clergy forcing their own personal religious views and practices on an unwilling community. It will also offer a rational solution of the difficult position, which the Government has been hitherto unable to cope with, in which an Anglican church and clergyman are maintained in a parish in which the overwhelming majority of the parishioners are dissenters as in Wales and in some counties of England, or Roman Catholics as in most parishes in Ireland. It is understood that all previous ecclesiastical laws have been repealed, and that hence laymen will be under no legal disqualification to perform the services in the church during the inhibition of the chaplain. On ceasing to be on the establishment of the

Church of England, the church, churchyard, and parsonage will remain, as the property of Government, under charge of the churchwardens, who will be empowered to employ them according to the sense of the majority of the parishioners, the church for the performance of the religious service of the predominating or of any denomination, on ordinary commercial conditions, the parsonage as a residence for the minister or priest, or got rid of by sale; but the churchyard to continue to be a place of free interment for all denominations. While a natural method is thus made available for the diminution of the establishment of the Church of England by lopping off parishes and chaplains where the people do not want them, there should also be facility for increasing the establishment by the addition of new parishes with churches and clergy where the people want them. This could be done when the people in a locality are prepared to provide a church, parsonage, and perhaps also a churchyard, of a character acceptable to the Government, and also to pay Government the capitalised sum representing an income of say £500 per annum. The church may then be put upon the establishment and an additional chaplain taken on the departmental list.

Admission into the ecclesiastical establishment of the Church of England should be by competition, after the physical fitness of the candidates had been duly certified by an appointed medical officer; no deacon to be eligible for admission. Promotion from class to class should be regulated by length of actual service, all periods of absence exceeding six months being deducted. The members of these classes should be called chaplains, and be graded from one to six. The next higher grades may be called rectors and vicars: the bishop of the diocese should have the right to veto the promotion of a first-class chaplain at his discretion, so as to insure the admission into the ranks of rector and vicar of thoroughly approved men. Rectors and vicars should be mainly employed in assisting the archbishops and bishops, as assistant or suffragan bishops,[1]

---

[1] The heaviest portion of the duties of a bishop is, I believe, the discharge of the function of confirmation, in which the bishop's part is the laying on of hands. If it be possible to consecrate a bishop for a limited

for which those selected must be duly consecrated, as archdeacons, assessors, and similar positions. Bishops should be chosen by the rectors and vicars from their own number, and the archbishops by the bishops from themselves, the choice made in each case to be approved by the sovereign, as head of the State and Church. The pay of the clergy may be arranged as follows, according to grade and length of service :—

50 Rectors at £1500	£75,000
100 Vicars at £1200	120,000
300 First-Class Chaplains at £900 (promotion by vacancy)	270,000
£100 in addition, when promotion is vetoed	10,000
500 Second-Class Chaplains at £700 (promotion by vacancy)	350,000
1000 Third-Class Chaplains at £500 (five years for promotion)	500,000
5000 Fourth-Class Chaplains at £350 (five ,, ,,)	1,750,000
5000 Fifth-Class Chaplains at £300 (three ,, ,,)	1,500,000
2200 Sixth-Class Chaplains at £150 (three ,, ,,)	330,000
	£4,905,000
2 Archbishops £9,500	
33 Bishops at £2000 66,000	
	75,500
	£4,980,500

£7,000,000 being taken as the annual income of the Church of England, and it is probably more and will be very greatly increased when agricultural depression passes off, a round sum of £5,000,000 per annum will represent the cost of the working clergy. The balance of £2,000,000 per annum will cover the cost of provision for aged and disabled clergy, widows, and children, for the renovation and reparation of churches and of the residences of the clergy, for office establishments for the archbishops and bishops, and for the additions that it will be necessary to make to the offices of the

purpose and for a few years, the necessary number of junior chaplains may be so consecrated for the function of laying on of hands in the rite of confirmation. The time and energies of the diocesan may thus be relieved of what practically is an onerous mechanical burden ; and the necessity of employing for this purpose the older, more accomplished, and valuable clergy will be avoided. Age is not essential to the office of bishop, for Timothy was a boy-bishop.

Chancellor of the Exchequer and the Secretary of State to whom the Premier assigns the supreme control of the Ecclesiastical Department. The clergy should be retired at the age of sixty, the bishops at the age of sixty-five, and archbishops when they feel themselves unequal to their duties from infirmity, or at the discretion of the Government.

By the above disposition of the revenues of the Church there will be at present little or no balance, the entire revenues being wholly, or almost wholly, laid out upon the clergy, upon ecclesiastical edifices, and for the necessary expenses of administration. In course of time, however, as agricultural depression passes off, as it assuredly will, considerable yearly surpluses will accrue. These surpluses, not being needed for the necessities of the Church, which have been amply provided for, will be available for the benefit of the poor. There cannot be a doubt that the enormous wealth that the Church has accumulated has been derived from gifts that were designed by the donors not merely for the maintenance of religious services and of clergy, but also for the relief and sustentation of the poor. It will be quite in agreement with the wishes of the pious donors that some portion of their gifts to the Church should be employed for the benefit of the poor. The Government, therefore, will be morally justified in employing the yearly surpluses, beyond the needs of the clergy, for the support of institutions designed for the relief of poverty and the calamities to which it is liable. To no more righteous purpose could the surplus revenues of the Church be applied than to the support of hospitals and to the institution of a provision for the help of the aged, incapable, and disabled poor, and similar objects limited to the poor. It is not improbable that in a few years these surpluses will amount to the respectable sum of a few millions. To the employment of the surplus revenues of the Church for the benefit of the poor the clergy cannot decently apply the expression of 'plunder,' which comes so readily to their mouths, but which, in plain truth, is the only expression appropriate to their way of dealing in the past with the enormous funds intrusted to their keeping by our generous and benevolent ancestors, partly if not mainly on behalf of the poor. Past history proves very clearly that the clergy are untrustworthy trustees of funds for the benefit of the poor.

Such reconstruction of the Church as I have proposed will necessitate the removal of the bishops from the House of Lords and the withdrawal from them of all pretensions to nobility and the title of Lord. The proper mode of addressing them in letters and conversation should be Sir or Reverend Sir. There is no serious objection to an archbishop taking the prefix of Most Reverend, and a bishop that of Right Reverend. All other grades of clergy should be prohibited from assuming any other prefix than that of Reverend.[1] The cruel and unreasonable disparity in the incomes of the clergy now existing will be replaced by an equitable system of emolument, which will bring comfort and respect to every rank. No longer will a few scores of men enjoy thousands, quintaines and decaines of thousands and

---

[1] It is a strange circumstance that while British citizens are prohibited from accepting titles and decorations from foreign potentates, the clergy of the Catholic Church sport titles, very grandiloquent and imposing, obtained from a foreign potentate, though now without territory. The titles employed are Lord Archbishop, Cardinal, Lord Bishop, Monsignor, Eminence, Princes of the Church, and so on. This circumstance is the more remarkable, as the Roman clergy aim at acquiring political power, which, indeed, they practically possess in Ireland. The Salvation Army sports the titles of General, Colonel, Major, and so on; but this body does not seek political power. If the Roman clergy sport grandiloquent titles, which bring them social elevation and distinction which they would not otherwise acquire, why should not the great trades unions do the same? The plain titles John Smith, Chairman; Peter Jones, Secretary, bring no social consideration. But the assumption of grandiloquent titles, such as the Right Honourable Lord President John Smith; the Right Honourable Provost Peter Jones, and similar titles to other officials, would in time bring considerable social influence to the leaders of the trades unions, and introduce them into good society. Complimentary forms of address, such as Lord, Excellency, Honourable, and so on, should be habitually employed, just as the Catholic clergy address each other as Lord, Eminence, Grace, etc. The dissenting Churches have failed to obtain for their clergy, who possess considerable talent and personal worth, the same social status which the Roman Church, by this worldly device of grandiloquent titles, has succeeded in obtaining for its clergy, consisting of men inferior in talent and education. Dr James Martineau, the late Dr Dale, and numerous others of the dissenting clergy, are superior men to the Lord Archbishops and Lord Bishops, Cardinals, Monsignors and others of the Catholic clergy who receive more social consideration.

more of income, while thousands of good men are in receipt of incomes which mean privation and loss of self-respect. *Whitaker* says that in half of the 14,000 parishes in England the income of the incumbent is less than £130 a year: many of these unfortunate gentlemen have grown aged in the service of the Church. The defect in the moral sense of the clergy is as obvious in this unfair and immoral distribution of the ample revenues of the Church as in other matters. The dignitaries of the Church think their moral duty fulfilled by begging for assistance from the laity for the poorer clergy! Under the system here recommended, the clergy will be relieved from the demands of 'diocesan vultures' for firstfruits, repairs, fees, etc.: they will pay rates and taxes on the same terms as other citizens. The diversion of the funds of the Church to the legal profession will cease. The Army and Navy, the Civil Service, the various dissenting Churches, the Church of Scotland and of Ireland, and the Roman Catholic Church dispense with the services of the legal profession, and the reconstructed Church of England can do the same. The appointments of the Church being no longer obtainable by patronage, but by competition and personal merit, the great canker of simony, which has demoralised the Church, will be practically abolished. The motive for collecting preservative votes will cease to operate, for nothing is to be gained by votes. The activity of the clergy will be directed to the duties of their calling, the main portion of these being the religious instruction of adults and of children. The Houses of Parliament will be relieved from the discussion of ecclesiastical subjects, and have more time to devote to the affairs of the empire; and public tranquillity will be undisturbed by periodic ecclesiastical commotions. If religious instruction be of value, society will gain by the greater attention that the clergy will devote to this work under the more efficient superintendence that the bishops will be able to exercise. The Church of England will become docile and pacific, instead of being turbulent, factious, arrogant, and rebellious as heretofore. All political disabilities on clergymen should be removed, with the single exception that they should be prohibited, under penalties, from taking part in any form, directly, indirectly, or mediately, in elections, or in canvassing for votes for public offices, in which legislation is involved. They should be prohibited from taking part in any form in elections for members of Parliament, County Councils, or any other public body having the power of framing bye-laws, and from offering themselves for election, or from being elected. They should not, however, be disfranchised, and should retain their right of citizenship. This single political disability will not, however, be confined to clergy of the Church of England, on or not on the establishment, but will embrace all clergy or ordained ministers of every religion. This measure of restriction is required by public policy. Throughout history the clergy of every religion have proved themselves unfit guardians of the commonweal: with a few brilliant exceptions, they have exerted their authority, when intrusted with power, to further, less the public good than the aggrandisement of religion, and of their particular form of religion. The unmistakable trend of public opinion throughout the civilised world is towards the exclusion of religion from legislation, and the withdrawal of legislative power from the hands of the ministers of religion. The historic discredit of the clergy in this field of activity justifies their exclusion from participation in it in the future. Society has the right to protect itself from appreciated evil.

The curbing of the Roman clergy is a matter of greater difficulty. It is impracticable to establish the Roman Church on the lines of the Anglican Church, except the limited number of clergy employed by Government for the benefit of its servants, civil or military. But the measures of public policy advocated with respect to the Protestant clergy can be justly applied to them. The enrolment of the Catholic clergy as teachers of religion, and the limiting of their functions to the services and inculcation of religion, will withdraw them from meddling with the secular education of the people. Their churches will afford suitable accommodation for the religious instruction of children, but they cannot expect to obtain facilities for propagating and maintaining their religion from Protestant rulers, except as a favour. The restriction regarding participation in elections for public offices will be binding upon them. The alleged malpractice of the threat of with-

holding or of actually withholding the rites of religion, with
the view of influencing thereby the votes of Catholic electors,
is a breach of the law directed against criminal intimidation,
and whenever discovered should be brought before the magistrates by the public prosecutor or private complainants. The
efforts of the Parliamentary Committee should be vigorously
exerted to effect the abolition of auricular confession, not only
in the United Kingdom and Ireland, but also throughout the
British dominions all over the world. This should be done
as a great measure required for the maintenance of public
morality and public policy. The practice of auricular confession taints the minds and morals of the young, youths and
girls, and exposes the minds and morals of adults, men and
women, the electors to public offices, to undue priestly influence, and invades the privacy of domestic life. Auricular
confession is no essential part of Catholic Christianity, for it
was not practised by Vatican authority before the thirteenth
century; and even if it be regarded as essential, this would be
of no avail against its direct effect in corrupting the morals of
the young and old. It is the right and duty of civilised
governments to suppress any institution or practice which
militates against public morality. The suppression by the
British Government in India of the practice of Suttee, or the
burning of widows, an institution of the Brahminical religion,
a practice that was of much older date than auricular confession, and extended over a longer period of time, has obtained
the approval of all civilised nations, and eventually of the
very adherents of Brahminism, who originally opposed it as
an interference with their religion. Suttee was current in
India from the days of the Macedonian invasion to the early
part of the nineteenth century (1829), when it was summarily
suppressed by the British. It was enjoined in the *Institutions
of Manu*, the Brahminical law-giver. Auricular confession in
the Roman Catholic religion cannot claim similar authority or
antiquity. It should be suppressed as slavery was suppressed
throughout British territory. A simple act of a few sections
declaring auricular confession, being a means of immorality,
to be a criminal offence, and attaching penalties to its practice,
would be sufficient. Both parties engaged, the priest and

penitent, should be equally liable to the penalties: in the case of young persons below eighteen years of age, both parents to be also liable. A priest who is convicted of breaking the law three times to be deported from British territory, and not allowed to return for ten years. Special means should be adopted for insuring the widest publicity being given to the law, which should be delayed in its operation for one year after enactment. Endeavours might be made to obtain international prohibition of the practice amongst all Christian nations. I do not anticipate any serious opposition to the law when enacted. Similar excrescences to religions, not being essentials, have been suppressed by governments with insignificant resistance made by the people. There was not much serious opposition made to the suppression of Suttee in India, and recently the Government of the United States has successfully repressed the practice of polygamy amongst Mormons. Governmental restrictions have not been confined to objectionable religious practices alone. The practice of plundering graveyards, unavoidably resorted to formerly by the medical profession, has been suppressed by legitimate facilities being afforded for procuring subjects for scientific investigation and the education of students. The practice of vivisection has been greatly restricted, even though, unfortunately, it is absolutely necessary for the progress of physiological and therapeutic science. With the safeguards proposed, the Roman religion and clergy may be left undisturbed to follow their own development or decay in the march of civilisation.[1]

The function of the second committee will be to keep a watch over the operations of the courts of law. The most thoughtful and judicious legislation may be frustrated or perverted by the maladministration of the laws. Our judges are men of great legal learning and experience, and of unimpeachable probity, but they err not unfrequently from the

---

[1] It would perhaps be advisable to advocate Government supervision and inspection of nunneries, to avoid the historic evils to which these institutions are liable when left under the sole control of priests. The question of the expulsion of Jesuits from British territory should also perhaps be gravely considered.

fault of passive obedience to the law and a blind adherence to precedents or previous decisions of courts. Our advanced civilisation neither expects nor desires passive obedience in those who are intrusted with great offices of authority, and there are occasions when passive obedience practically approaches to a crime. Reflection and due consideration of personal duty are equally incumbent on those intrusted with authority and on those who are to render obedience to authority. Without such reflection and such consideration of personal duty on both sides there is no safety for the maintenance of the great principles of public security and order. A general intrusted with the command of an army in a distant region, and who fully understands and is pledged to carry out a certain great object, is bound by his personal sense of duty to disregard such orders or instructions which he may receive from a distant government or superior which manifestly are detrimental to the accomplishment of the object to which he is committed. An order or instructions may be given by a superior authority under mistake or without a full comprehension of local circumstances; and it would be an error, a manifestation of incompetency, and it may approximate to a crime, for such order or instructions to be passively obeyed. Not many years ago a magnificent and costly ship of war was sunk and another seriously damaged, hundreds of valuable lives of trained and skilled officers and bluejackets and considerable treasure were lost, from passive obedience rendered to a manifestly erroneous order issued by an officer in high command during peaceful manœuvres. The personal responsibility of obedience is as great as the personal responsibility of command, and there are occasions in human life in which the former may be the more onerous and important. Men placed in exalted positions must accept the responsibility of disobedience, when the latter is called for, by their sense of personal duty. Our English judges, of whose unimpeachable integrity we as a nation are proud, are unfettered in the exercise of their august functions. They form the only class of public servants in whom the confidence of society is almost unbounded. They are free from and are deemed above the base restraints imposed upon other officials, and they have proved themselves worthy of the trust placed in them by society. Our judges, honourably freed from restraints by the appreciation of society of their importance and usefulness and the trust placed in their honour, integrity, and sense of duty, are liberated from the considerations that generate and foster passive obedience in all other classes of public officials. Passive obedience to the law or to judicial precedents is incompatible with the position and the conditions under which our judges act. The great duty of our judges, under the circumstances of their position, is less the administration of law than the greater function of the administration of justice. Where the law, in the conscience and judgment of the judge, is not the counterpart of justice, the judge is justified in subordinating the law to justice. He would not be justified in subverting or changing the law, thereby making the law himself; but he is justified in declining to enforce an unjust law or one which in any special case before him operates unjustly, and the thinking portion of society will support him in so doing. This exercise of a duty inherent in the office of our judges, who, as public officials, are endowed with extraordinary privileges, giving them immunity for all acts judicially performed, is one that the Society should markedly encourage in the interests of morality. The power inherent in our judges to refuse the enforcement of a law, in general or in special applications, which would involve the doing of injustice, is the only constitutional antidote we possess to correct unjust, and hence immoral or defective, legislation. The sublime spectacle is yet to be seen of an English judge refusing to enforce a law or the application of a law in a particular case, which, in his judgment and conscience, is unjust and immoral.

Illustrations of these remarks are afforded by the judicial administration of the Companies Acts and the law of contract. The former deal with companies generally, and they make no classification of companies. The judges, under the influence of passive obedience and a blind adherence to precedents, administer these Acts in the lump, and they also make no distinction of companies. All companies are dealt with by them uniformly under the Companies Acts. But, as a matter of fact to which society is painfully sensible, there are two classes of companies, namely, swindling companies and honest companies. It was a defect of the law that the distinction was not made, and it was the passive obedience of the judges to the law which deterred them from correcting the defect. It was the judicial duty of the judges, in spite of the defect of the law, to make a distinction between companies, and to deal with honest companies under the Companies Acts, and to judge the swindling companies under the ordinary criminal laws. Theologians teach that God deals equally in this world with the just and unjust, that he sends the rain impartially to both, but society does not expect the law and our judges to follow the sublime example. Society expects a difference to be made in legislative and judicial conduct between the swindler and the honest man. The distinction between the swindling and honest company is not so obscure or indefinite that it is not readily perceptible. There was not a swindling company that has come before the judges under the Companies Acts in which the latter were not perfectly sensible of the fraudulent character of the transactions and business carried on by the swindlers. Yet they have dealt with these dishonest transactions and business as if they were honest and legitimate, and placed over them the protecting shield of the Law. The contracts between the managing directors of swindling companies and their shareholders regarding payments for shares are regarded as equally legitimate as those made between the directors and shareholders of honest companies. It sometimes happens that a swindling company goes into liquidation before the shares have been fully paid up; the balance is judicially exacted from shareholders. The company is known to the judges to have been fraudulent from the beginning, and that the directors had fraudulently effected allotments, knowing that they were thereby obtaining money for a fraudulent business, and that the money so obtained would be fraudulently employed. But these strong facts have no influence upon the judges. The shareholder's money is taken on the strength of the contracts made with swindlers; what has already been paid is retained, and what has not been paid is demanded on the decision of the judges by the official liquidator. Nothing can convert a swindling transaction into an honest one, not even a voluntary liquidation. Fraud is fraud, and nothing can convert it into honesty, except perhaps a judge's decision. Surely such a decision, though given by judges following precedent, is immoral, and sinks the Law and the judges to the unpleasant position of being allies and auxiliaries of the swindler. The thousands of innocent shareholders who have been deceived into making contracts for shares with swindling company directors have been plundered of their money, partly by the swindlers and partly by the Law as administered by judges. If the Companies Acts had not been enacted, the unfortunate shareholder would lose the money already paid, but he would save that portion of the price of the swindler's shares which was unpaid. Under the Companies Acts and the judges' decisions this portion is also swept up and added to the swindler's plunder. If the Companies Acts had been administered in the sense which, in my judgment, justice and morality required, they would be limited in their operation to the winding up of the affairs of honest companies, while swindling companies would naturally and justly fall within the jurisdiction of the police magistrate. Swindling companies, from their inherent nature, come within the province of the criminal laws. The police magistrate, unless he also be under the weird influence of passive obedience and precedents, would deal in a different spirit with the share contracts and allotments made by swindling directors with their victims. The police magistrate is not known to deal with the stores of a receiver of stolen property on the same terms as with the goods of an honest man. To the mind and in the hands of the police magistrate the contracts made with their victims by swindling directors would be devices of the swindler to effect his fraudulent purposes. He would not regard them as honest contracts, as the judges unquestionably do, to be enforced by the law, but invalid and of no force, being inherently fraudulent. The money of which the shareholders were swindled and cheated would be restored to them (excepting the shareholders who were in collusion with the swindler), if it was possible to do so; the money comprising the unpaid instalments for shares which the swindler had failed to gather up from his hurry to escape the grip of the constable, or other cause, will not be gathered up and added to the stores of the receiver of stolen money by officials acting on judicial authority. When the police magistrate had weeded out the elements of fraud and dishonesty, then the balance of the affairs of the swindling companies would become appropriate subjects to be dealt with under the Companies Acts. The Lord Chief-Justice of England has been recently addressing the great commercial and financial chieftains of the city of London on the subject of the immorality of swindling companies, and he remarked with compassion on the losses of shareholders and the distress thereby brought to many homes in our country. The Lord Chancellor of England has been similarly inculcating morality in financial undertakings in another great city. But both these great judicial officials failed to speak of the unconscious part taken by high personages of their own distinguished order in contributing to and widening and deepening the loss and distress occasioned to innocent shareholders by swindling companies. If the view that I have taken of the erroneous action of the judges in the administration of the Companies Acts be sound and correct, it would be an honourable thing for the judges, of their own accord, and from their own means, to compensate the defrauded shareholders for such portion of their losses for which the judges are responsible, or the nation should do so. The responsibility for the maladministration of the Companies Acts rests solely upon our judges, for, in the absence of juries, the bar has brought before the judges the view of the subject here advocated, but the judges were blinded by precedents, and, while commiserating the unfortunate shareholders, heroically legalised their spoliation.

The large share attributable to the judges in the encouragement and fostering of swindling companies becomes apparent when we consider that it is the money of the shareholders which the managing directors desire, and fraudulently work for. The money of the shareholders is the booty with which they acquire financial credit and social status, with which they dispense a splendid hospitality, purchase the names and services of the servile portion of the aristocracy, obtain intro-

ductions into high society, political clubs, and Parliament, gain
over the powerful influence of the Christian religion by the
building and decoration of churches, by costly gifts to the
sanctuary and charities to the poor, and with which they
make large settlements on their wives as an assurance against
the day of calamity. It is the money of the shareholders
which is unquestionably the object of desire of the managing
directors, and to obtain it they do not care for the risk of
imprisonment for a year or two for minor peccadilloes. Yet
by a singular fatuity the judges let them keep this money,
the very booty which they desire, and to obtain which they
concoct swindles: not only the money which they have themselves gathered, but also the money which they had not the
opportunity of gathering, which the judges chivalrously gather
in for them on their behalf. The ministers of justice secure
to the unprincipled plunderers the booty which they have
plundered, as well as that which they intended to plunder.
That plunderers so helped, so provided with efficient allies
and auxiliaries, should abound and multiply is a natural
consequence.

That the extraordinary multiplication and development
of swindling companies is due in great part to the peculiar
mode of administering the Companies Acts adopted by our
judges seems a reasonable conclusion in my judgment. There
is another group of social pests, largely increased lately, which
have been generated and developed solely by our judges. If
our judges be abolished, I believe extortionate money-lenders
would cease to exist. Our judges are essential to their being
—the very spark of life to them. Here also our judges have
erred from passive obedience to the law and blind adherence
to judicial precedents. The law demands that a contract
should be enforced, and our judges accordingly blindly enforce the law, regardless of consequences to justice and
morality. Contracts for interest at 60 and 90 per cent. and
even at the incredible rate of 3000 per cent., as recently
declared by a responsible cabinet minister in the House of
Lords, are enforced by our judges under the law. The
Roman fortitude of our judges in enforcing the law of contract in the interests of money-lenders was satirised in vain

by Shakspeare in the drama of the *Merchant of Venice*: our judges have remained inflexible on the point up to the present day. It is further singular that while maintaining heroic obduracy in the enforcement of the law of contract with money-lenders, our judges set the law aside in the instance of contracts with women for immoral purposes, and also of contracts with matrimonial agents. These are the only instances, as far as my knowledge goes, in which our judges have been known to exercise the power inherent in their office of not enforcing the law, when doing so, in their judgment, is contrary to public morality and policy. There is no express provision in the law which authorises such non-enforcement: and why a similar non-enforcement of the law is not practised in the instance of extortionate money-lenders is a mystery to me. Here, I think, is a proper field for the endeavours of the committee, by public protestations and rousing public opinion on the subject, to infuse or pump (if I may be pardoned the use of this expressive word) some moral *geist* into our judges, and waken them up to a full and beneficial use of a valuable power inherent in their office, which they allow to lie dormant to the detriment of the public good. The very doubtful contract or promise of marriage, which our judges deem themselves bound to enforce, is another contract which would be honoured in the breach, or perhaps in the breech, for it should be kicked out of our courts. These actions debase the female mind. No woman who respects herself or her sex would deliberately ask for compensation in money for her love troubles; and for a judge or jury to gauge in money one of the finest of human emotions is to create amongst the people a degraded notion of our human nature. In point of fact neither judge nor jury would tolerate a corresponding action brought by a man. No woman of the better classes has been known in this country to have recourse to an action of this nature: and in foreign countries such actions are absolutely unknown. The only compensation which judge and jury could give is sympathy; for neither the law, nor arithmetic, nor mathematics, nor judge, nor jury could reasonably form an equation between human feeling and any sum of money. Further, the breach of the contract or promise of marriage is a veritable gain to the woman, for it saves her from a union with a man who would neglect her as a wife. These actions are demoralising, and should be brought within the purview of the committee. There are other forms of contract, which the judicial notions of the 'sanctity of contract' entertained by our judges induces them to enforce, to the depravation of public morality, and the hardening of the mind of the people, rendering it impervious to the growth of feelings of honour, morality, fair play, and fair dealing. Our judges make a tenant continue to pay rent for a house burnt down, or blown down by a tempest, or knocked down by an earthquake, or destroyed by an explosion, or an inundation, or in any other way, unless each and every one of these accidents be specially named and exempted in the lease. The injustice and cruelty of the conduct of our judges in these cases is accentuated by the circumstances usually attendant on these calamities, for the goods of the tenant are also destroyed, he may sustain loss of limb or other damage, or some of his family may be killed or seriously injured: on the top of all this affliction comes the cruel, unjust, and inhuman decision of the judge that he must continue to pay rent for a house that is a mass of cinders or a pile of *debris*, and no longer habitable. How the judges reconcile their decisions in such cases with the dictates of conscience passes my comprehension, not being a judge myself. The omission of clauses of exemption does not justify them. The agreement to pay rent is founded on the agreement to provide a house: the rent is paid for the house; the house is provided for the rent. The landlord contracts to provide a house, and the tenant contracts to pay rent. The rent and house go together: the contract is broken when either rent or house fails. When the landlord is unable to provide a house the tenant ought to cease to pay rent. To compel the tenant to pay rent and not to compel the landlord to provide a house is, in my judgment, one-sided, and a gross perversion of justice. It is compelling the tenant to pay money for which he obtains no consideration. It is plundering the tenant for the benefit of the landlord. This is a vestige of the thought of the seventeenth century, when the landlord was invested with the attributes of divinity. Our judges blindly follow judicial precedents. No gentleman of the present day will expect his tenant to continue to pay rent when the house is destroyed, notwithstanding his knowledge that the judges will enforce payment if certain exempting clauses have been omitted through ignorance, or want of foresight, on the part of the tenant. That men who are not entitled to the honourable name of gentlemen would and do exact the payment of rent when the house is destroyed, is an immoral result due to the extraordinary views held by judges regarding the sanctity of contract.

There are other forms of contract in which the rigidity of the judicial view entails injustice, cruelty, and hardship, and hence its operation is pernicious and immoral. Such are contracts which cover a great period of time. When the contracts were formed there were one set of circumstances, when they come to be performed there are circumstances of a widely different nature. Such, for instance, are the contracts entered into by governments with their servants. I give as an example the contracts made by the Government of India with their servants on the subject of pensions, at a period when the rupee was of the value of two shillings. A public servant was offered a pension of say 5000 rupees after a long term of service, such pension at the time being equivalent to £500. The fall in the exchange has since very seriously reduced this amount, in some years to £250 or £260, a sum very inadequate for the maintenance of a retired public servant who had been accustomed all his life to a good salary, and for the education of his family. The fall was from a condition of modest competency to a condition of strait and penury. Not one of these unfortunate gentlemen, so cruelly reduced in circumstances, ventured to appeal to the law courts and the judges. Knowing the rigidity of construction of the law of contracts, they would as soon appeal for relief to a log of wood or a stuffed hippopotamus in a museum. Nevertheless, they were proper subjects for the judges to consider and to relieve, if our judges would have the moral *geist* to exercise the power inherent in their high office. To the credit of the Indian Government, who thus set an honourable example of high morality, the Government of its own accord undid the injustice of the contract, in which, from want of foresight, the relative value of the rupee and pound sterling was omitted to be noted. There are commercial contracts in which, from ignorance and want of foresight, precautionary clauses have been omitted, the rigid execution of which by our judges, acting under the influence of passive obedience to the law and precedents, is a positive injustice. Japanese commercial custom seems to my mind to be more just and honourable in these matters of contract than European judicial rule; the enforcement of a contract strictly legal and just in its terms at the time of agreement, but rendered unjust and inequitable in the lapse of time and in the march of events, is considered dishonourable, and the offender, though supported by a court of law, is placed under commercial ban as an unfit person to have commercial dealings with. No gentleman in the conduct of his private affairs would act as our judges do in the enforcement of contracts. The judicial administration of the law of contracts is, in instances such as those I have mentioned, simply immoral, and exercises an immoral influence on the minds and character of the people.

If the views above set forth are just and reasonable, the efforts of the committee to effect a change in judicial opinion and practice will assuredly be ultimately successful. Our judges and judicial administration are not of the same nature as theologians and theology. The latter are unchangeable: the theological nonsense and historical fabrications of the second century, with perhaps some refinements and reservations, are essentially the same in the nineteenth century: change will involve extinction both of theologians and theology. But it is not so with our judges: they are amenable to reason and are capable of improvement. Even in our century remarkable changes in judicial opinion and practice have been observed. The law of slavery in England is the same in the present day as it was in the beginning of the century: it has not been repealed or in any way modified: in fact, there exists no law on the subject in England. But in the early years of the century our judges were the supporters, I believe the only supporters, of slavery in England. They were weaned from their support of slavery, not by the enactment of a special law but by the representations of Granville Sharp, a simple solicitor. During the terror and panic that followed the French Revolution, the ministry instigated the judges to a sharp and severe administration of the penal laws: so energetic became the judges that many innocent gentlemen, who printed or expressed their thoughts on political institutions, were tried for treason and executed or sent into transportation. Had John Stuart Mill, Carlyle, or even Leckie, lived in those days, they might have been deported by the judges to spend the evening of their lives amidst the gum-trees of Botany Bay. The judges were restrained in this mad career by juries, the palladium of common sense. Within the remembrance of many now living the judges were accustomed, under the influence of their judicial view of the nature of insanity, to execute and imprison insane men and women for murder and murderous attempts. The advanced knowledge of the various forms of insanity acquired by medical men who had devoted their lives and opportunities to the investigation of mental disease was ignored by the judges and resisted for a season. In this instance, also, the ultimate conversion of the judges from their former judicial opinion, and their acceptation of scientific opinion, and the consequent change of judicial practice which followed, was effected by the intervention of juries. The above instances of the regeneration of judicial opinion and practice, effected without adding to the statute-book, already encumbered with useless, pernicious, and supererogatory laws, afford encouragement that the moral *geist* of judges may be advanced by reasonable representations. Something must always be conceded to the *aliquid humani* of judges: if the older judges prove impassable, the next generation of judges will be sensible that the exercise of the power, inherent in their high office, for modifying and restraining the application of a rigid law, is called for by every principle of honour, good feeling, morality, and justice.

A subject that should obtain the attention of the committee is the not infrequent cruel ignoring by judges of the maternal instinct in their adjudication in connection with the custody of children.

It is a sad fact that our civil courts of law have been in no small measure captured by swindlers, usurers, and others of that nefarious class. The amiable moral weaknesses of our judges, their foolish scruples on points of law and procedure, their very anxiety to avoid the doing of injustice, are scientifically studied by clever scoundrels, and made practical use of in the execution of their dishonest transactions. Our civil courts are, perhaps, as much used by rogues and knaves as tools for carrying on their nefarious practices as by honest folk to obtain redress of wrongs and justice. The threat of going to court is often sufficient to procure submission to unjust claims made by dishonest tradesmen. There is a general sense of want of confidence, or positive distrust, entertained by society regarding our civil courts, of which the common phrase of 'the uncertainty of the law' is the expression. In the sense above indicated, the action of the civil courts, being decidedly in favour of immorality, is a proper field for the oversight of an influential committee of the Society. The civil courts of law should cease to be a greater terror to honest folk than to knaves and rogues.[1] The enormous expense incurred in civil litigation ought to be done away with. The legal profession has a strong personal

[1] Until our judges in the civil courts cease to administer the law according to judicial rules and precedents, but not according to the interests of morality on a moral basis, honest folk should abstain from appearing in them to contest the dishonest claims sometimes made by tradesmen. It would be better to pay the dishonest claim, and thus avoid both giving a public triumph to dishonesty, and at the same time incurring the additional expense of costs, and then to cease all dealings with the dishonest claimant, and to relate the circumstances to friends. The practice of the French *Juges de paix* in deciding dishonest claims made by tradesmen is morally superior to that of our own judges in similar cases. The public press satisfactorily supervises the criminal courts, in which we do not find honest folk punished and knaves rewarded, but the civil courts are sadly neglected. *Punch*, however, is an honourable exception, and does occasionally direct attention to the immorality of the decisions of the civil courts. In an admirable cartoon in the number for 22nd March 1899, the Lord Chancellor, who holds, as second century theologians would say, all our judges in his belly or bowels,' is represented saying to 'Bookie,' "Bet away, dear boy, we're with you!"

interest in the existence of swindling companies and usurers, from whom it realises profitable employment. No swindling company experiences the least difficulty in obtaining the services of members of the legal professions on its staff.

A third committee may be advantageously formed for the function of observing and watching the progress of morality amongst the people, and reporting annually on the condition and progress of morality amongst the various classes of society. This committee should be in communication with the presidents and committees of the clubs, who should supply information on the subject.

The funds of the Society will consist in the main of contributions, donations, and legacies from persons who approve of the objects and aims of the Society. Material aid may also, I think, be obtained from the clubs themselves. It is not intended that these clubs be formed on an eleemosynary principle, but on the co-operative principle. The grants to the poorer clubs are not to be regarded as free gifts, but as grants or loans, liable to be returned when the prosperity of the clubs is established. It is my belief that all the clubs, even the poorest, will ultimately be in a position to repay all grants made to them by the Society. If there be maintained a proper and reasonable proportion between the comforts provided by a club and the means of its members, and economical management practised, the result is likely to be an annual balance in favour of the club. These annual balances, accumulated from year to year, will, in the course of ten, fifteen, twenty, or thirty years, repay to the Society all the expenditure incurred for the erection of buildings, the purchase of furniture, and the grants-in-aid during the early years of the club. It will be desirable that all clubs (even the poor clubs after they have repaid the cost of building, purchase of furniture, and have returned the early grants-in-aid) be required to contribute towards the general purposes of the Society a portion of the surplus funds, or balances, at the end of the operations of the year: the amount to be fixed at their pleasure, but not to be below 10 per cent. A third source of revenue may be found in the publication of a weekly journal, in which the transactions of the Society and of the committees may be published, and in which good practical articles or essays on moral subjects should appear. The journal may be supplied post free to all members of the Society who contribute at least 10s. 6d. or 12s. per annum towards the general funds. A certain number of copies, two or three, should be supplied free to all the clubs for the reading-rooms. For the poorer clubs, an edition on cheaper paper should be issued, to be sold at the clubs for a penny, or even, if possible, for a halfpenny to members only. The editor and sub-editor of the journal, who will necessarily be literary men, may, if they desire it and are dependent on their literary labours for their livelihood, be paid, as well as the printers and others employed. All literary contributions to the journal should, however, be unpaid, in accordance with the rule that the inculcation of morality must not be made a means of gain similar to the 'traffic in Christ.' It would be very desirable if this rule be made a fundamental principle to be accepted by all members of the Society. Writers on purely moral subjects should not take to themselves the profits obtained by the sale of their works. After the cost of publishing, and a certain reasonable sum for the literary labour bestowed on the work when the author is dependent for his livelihood, or part of it, on his literary labour are deducted, the balance should be contributed to the general funds of the Society, as a matter of honour. The president and council may, however, on a general consideration of the circumstances of the individual writers, on their representation, restore a portion of such balances, retaining 10 per cent. or more at their discretion. The annual reports of the committee on the moral progress of the nation should be published separately in book or pamphlet form. These reports, as the years go on and the Society extends, will be of immense value as historical works, and as the interest they will excite is likely to be considerable their sale will fetch in a welcome subsidy to the funds of the Society. They may be sold to members of the clubs at a small profit above the cost of production, and to the general public at the market rates.

The education of children as it is now carried on is defective from the want of moral instruction. This subject is, however, largely in the hands of Parliament, and will fall within the scope of the labours of the Parliamentary Committee. The examples set by parents and adults will be, perhaps, the best practical education in morality to children, though special instruction by short lessons at home and at school will have much value.

The heaviest work of the president and council of the Society will be the formation and organisation of the clubs. The want of funds at the start will necessitate a commencement on a small scale. Probably the initiation of the Society may be the formation of a small club in some obscure country town or village, and the gradual appearance of other clubs on the same plan in other obscure places may work up eventually to the formation of a great Society. If, on the other hand, the scheme here advocated be largely approved by the community a great Society may at once be inaugurated, and sufficient funds be collected to commence with. The aid of the Society will be specially needed for clubs of the lower middle and lower classes. It may be advisable that the buildings for these clubs should be provided before the members are enrolled. The main characteristics of these buildings should be the loftiness and spaciousness of the public rooms, while architectural beauty should not be overlooked. Each building should have the following apartments, all spacious and lofty: a library and reading-room, a smoking-room, a *salle-à-manger*, several large lounge rooms, a billiard-room for several tables, a large cloak-room for men, fitted up with several hundreds of pegs, all numbered, for hats and garments, and a similar room for women; as many retiring rooms as space will admit; a very large and spacious hall to accommodate 700 or 800 people, with an elevated stage at one end for theatricals, concerts, lectures, dancing, etc.; a bar-room; a large kitchen, an office room, linen and store rooms, etc. One of the lounge rooms should especially be reserved for old people, and should be the only one provided with one or two fireplaces for burning coals during severe weather, in addition to hot-water pipes. The entire building should be warmed in winter with hot-water pipes, as the most economical system, doing away with a multiplicity of fireplaces and chimneys, decreasing the risk of fire, and maintaining an equable temperature throughout. Each club with a thousand members should be provided with ten bath-rooms, with hot and cold water, for men, and the same number for women, and, if possible, a swimming bath for each sex; also with lavatories for each sex on every floor for washing hands. Simple but durable building materials should be used, and all ostentatious and costly decoration postponed till the club can have it at its own cost when the original outlay on the building has been refunded to the Society. The lighting may be by gas, or electricity, or oil, according to circumstances, and the cooking by gas or coals. The furniture should be simple, but strong and fairly comfortable, the standard of comfort for the poorer clubs being that maintained in omnibuses, tramcars, and third-class railway carriages. The buildings may be estimated to cost, according to size and style, between £2500 and £4000, and the furniture from £500 to £1000, second-hand furniture, sound and durable, being always available. If a quarter million can be diverted from the annual waste, as I think, of £30,000,000 sterling on ecclesiastical Christianity, the Society will be in a position, after deducting £10,000 for general purposes and grants-in-aid, to build and equip between fifty and sixty clubs annually for the lower middle and lower classes. As these clubs are all to be constructed and conducted on the co-operative and not on the eleemosynary system, all expenditure incurred for the building and equipment of the clubs, and the grants-in-aid in their early years of struggle, are expected to be returned to the Society. In half a century the Society will have been able to build, equip, and start more than four thousand of these clubs in the kingdom. All these clubs will be the property of their own members: the function of the Society having been merely the rendering to the latter the help and guidance needed to enable them to acquire the ownership of their own clubs. Within the same period the same or a larger number of clubs may be expected to be organised by the upper and upper middle classes in connection with and under the auspices and influence of the Society. The operations of the national Societies should not extend beyond their own countries until the whole population of the country is supplied with clubs and brought within the reach of moral influence. When this amount of success has been attained, the Society may extend its operations and employ a portion of the funds at its disposal for the benefit of less fortunate and less civilised peoples in foreign countries.

The chief aim of the Society should, I think, be the cultivation of the principle of honour, which is the most powerful influence for good to which human nature is susceptible. It can operate in all classes of society and in all nationalities, and its ultimate effect is the moral equalisation of classes and peoples. The principle of honour is as capable of inculcation and of growth in the plebeian as in the patrician, in the civilised as well as the uncivilised community. The vendor of cabbages in the streets can, in the midst of poverty and sordid surroundings, be the possessor of honour to an equal extent as the wearer of a coronet. Apart from the natural gifts of physical strength or beauty, genius or affection, and such like, in no point can men of widely separated social station and of different nationalities be equalised, still retaining their social and national disparity, as in the common possession of honour. The aim of the Society should be the enlistment of the principle of honour in favour of morality. A second great quality to which special attention should be given is courtesy towards all, great or small, gentle or simple, black or white. It is an essential quality of the gentleman and gentlewoman. A third great aim of the Society should be the discouragement and reprobation of hypocrisy, or the divergence of practice from profession, in all its multitudinous forms. The extirpation of this vice will be a severe struggle. It has taken deep root in all civilised countries under the sway of ecclesiastical Christianity, and has been nourished and fostered by the practice and example of the clergy for eighteen centuries, from the rise of ecclesiastical Christianity in the second century to the present day. The professions of the clergy are to be found in the New Testament and in their own writings, and their practice and example in history. One of the greatest indictments against ecclesiastical Christianity or Credonism is that it has raised hypocrisy to a fine art and made it 'respectable.' The Reformation cleansed Credonism from a few doctrinal superstitions and superstitious practices, and the power of the laity succeeded in forcing morality to a very great extent upon the clergy, so that the grosser forms of immorality are no longer practised by them.[1] But the Reformation failed to suppress the insidious vice of hypocrisy. Let any who challenges this statement reflect upon the power and wealth lavished upon and accepted by the bishops of the Church of England for the last three centuries—the bishops who were the cream and flower of a great body of cultured clergy, and the chosen representatives of the highest and purest form of ecclesiastical Christianity; let him reflect upon the methods and means which they adopted or accepted for obtaining their elevation to their exalted stations, the uses and purposes to which they applied their power, wealth, and great talents, and honourably declare his opinion whether their history for the last three centuries is in accordance with their professions as declared in the New Testament and in their own writings.

The above remarks embody the reflections that passed through my mind while making my investigations into the origin of the Fourth Gospel. It appeared to me inevitable that ecclesiastical Christianity or Credonism, whose origin

[1] This remark applies only to the clergy of the various Churches whose lives are before the public: but it should not be held to apply to the clergy and *quasi*-clergy in monasteries and convents, which are removed from the public view and are subject only to ecclesiastical supervision. The revolutionary government of Italy in 1848 suppressed the monasteries: and the Pope, Pius IX., "is said to have declared that, though he was publicly bound to condemn the suppression of the monasteries, in his heart he could not but rejoice, as it was a blessing in disguise": a statement in which is to be found a strange confession of ecclesiastical hypocrisy and simple honesty. Cardinal Manning in 1887 confirmed the truth of the pope's views, and added that the success of the Revolution in Italy was in no small degree due to laxity of morals in the clergy, Seculars and Regulars (see *Life of Cardinal Manning*, by E. S. Purcell, 1896, vol. i. p. 387, footnote). It is with regret that I observe that the Anglican bishops, or some of them, are using their influence to establish these historically disreputable institutions in connection with the Church of England. About the middle of this century an Anglican clergyman set up an institution of this nature, which he called Agapemone; the proceedings of this community, as related by the popular writers of the time (Hepworth Dixon and others), may justly be described as bestial.

was based on roguery and knavery, cannot possibly survive the disclosures made in the last few years, and that are likely to be still further made in the coming years. The signs of its decadence are manifest. A few new religions have sprung up in the country this century, but, with the single exception of Mormonism, which, however, is a form of Credonism, none appear to have gained a secure footing. Believing that mankind while on earth are less in need of concrete religion than of morality, I have conceived the thought that it would be better for the happiness of the human family in the present world that a system of morality be substituted for concrete religion. It is my conclusion, arrived at from the study of the early Christian writers, that Jesus' design was not the introduction of a new religion, but the inculcation and practice of morality in all the relations of life. Not religious belief, but the practice of morality, in my judgment, is the means for attaining the kingdom of God which was passionately desired by Jesus.

INDEX.

Acta Pilati, 64, 192, 278.
Acts of the Apostles, 73.
Admission to moral society, 379.
Age of Jesus, 201, 297.
Agricultural Rates Act, 1896, 390.
Alexander, Archbishop, 113, 116, 118, 120, 250.
Alogi, 41.
Angels, 78, 340.
Anointing, 112, 267.
Antichrist, 115.
Apocryphal Gospels, 20.
Apollinaris, 258.
Apostles, stipendiary, 86, 100.
Apostolic constitutions, 242, 270.
Aristides, 19, 94, 203.
Arnold of Rugby, 249, 276.
Arnold, Matthew, 128, 196, 258.
Ascension of Jesus, 199, 280.
Athenagoras, 340.
Attendance at church, 355.
Auricular confession, 433.
Baptism, 176.
Barnabas, Epistle of, 203, 283.
Bazaars, 354.
Bede, 136.
Belief in God, 366.
Bethlehem, 169.
Bibles, sale of, 353.
Bishops, 81, 351, 452.
Brawling in church, 357.
Breach of promise, 441.
Bunyan, 40.
Caiaphas, 193.
Callistus, Pope, 275, 323.
Cana, miracle at, 145, 236.
Catalogue of early Christian writings, 16.
Cerinthus, 2, 41, 114, 119, 121, 125, 127, 129, 153, 333.
Charcot, Professor, 172.
Chrism, or ointment, 112.
Christ, 206.
Christianity, ecclesiastical, 99, 102, 315.
Chronicon Paschale, 258, 264.
Church of England, 422, 425.
„ Rome, 422.
Civil Courts, 446.
Clement of Alexandria, 80, 167, 237, 240, 251, 316.
Clement of Rome, 81.
Cleopatra, 148.
Clergy, 378, 398, 406, 408, 437.
Clerical dress, 124.
Clodd, 238.
Clubs, 370, 375, 449.
Cock crowing, Peter's denial, 193, 271.
Code of Morality, 371.
Colossians, Epistle to, 102.
Columbine incarnation, 26.
Companies Acts, 437.
Compulsory education, 395.
Concubinage, 419.
Contract, 442.
Corruptions, of Christianity, 68, 99.
„ Jewish, 70.
„ Gnostic, 104.
Courtesy, 451.
Credonism, 366.
Criticism, satirical, 312.
Crucifixion of Jesus, 71, 137, 265.
Crurifragium, 134, 261.
Cyprian, 308, 313.
Deaconesses, 324.
Deacons, 88, 102.
Death of Jesus, 202, 297.
Decadence of ecclesiastical Christianity, 349.
Deification of Jesus, 72.
Descent to hell of Jesus, 282.
Didache, 84.
Diognetus, Epistle to, 4.
Dionysius, 38, 120, 248.
Discourses of Jesus, 271.
Discrepancy between the Gospels, 257.
Divorce, 374.
Domitian, 303.
Dove of Cerinthus, 26, 49, 105, 249, 331.
Dress, clerical, 124.
Ebionites, 67.
Ecclesia, 86.
Education, 395.
Ellicott, Bishop, 188, 311.
Elohim, 174.
Eons, 347.
Ephesians, Epistle to, 102.
Ephesus, 244.
Eucharist, 137, 166, 237.
Eusebius, 49, 59, 68, 89, 132, 155, 240, 253, 266, 301, 311.
Evangelist, 22.
Faith cure, 172.
Father, declaration of the, 35.
Feet-washing, 138, 267.
Forgery, 47, 334.
Forgiveness of sins, 306.
Founders of ecclesiastical Christianity, 99, 102.
Gibson, Mrs, 25.
Gnostics, 234.
Godet, Professor, 153.
Gore, Rev. Charles, M.A., 288.
Gospel, 101.

INDEX

Gospel of James, 7, 25.
" Marcion, 66.
Gospels, ebionite, 67.
" sectarian, 62.
" synoptic, 66.
Guardians of the poor, 392.
Guinea-pigs, 354.
Harris, Rendel, 19, 52, 94.
Hebrews, Epistle to, 77, 204.
" Gospel of, 67.
Hegesippus, 68, 241, 301.
Heracleon, 238.
Hermas, Shepherd of, 18, 176.
Hippolytus, 43, 258, 323.
Honour, 451.
How, Bishop Walsham, 9, 164, 183, 184, 277, 311.
Hypocrisy, 451.
Ignatius, 17, 100, 199, 284.
Immortality of Jesus on earth, 70.
Incarnation, columbine, 26.
India, education in, 412.
Ireland, education in, 412.
Irenæus, 2, 11, 31, 42, 115, 132, 139, 201, 205, 230, 233, 237, 251, 253, 329, 334, 336.
James, Epistle of, 76.
" Gospel of, 25.
Japanese, 361, 444.
John, Apostle, 40, 244, 270.
" Baptist, 129, 162, 175, 238, 245.
" Epistle of, 37, 111, 248.
Josephus, 179.
Jowett, Professor, 184.
Judas, 138, 142, 268.
Judges, 434, 444.
Justices' 'justice,' 392.
Justin Martyr, 7, 28, 63, 135, 143, 157, 179, 230, 284, 340.
King, author of *The Gnostics*, 235.
Lactantius, 261, 287.
Lamb of God, 131, 247.
Lamb's wife, 124.
Law, 372.
" courts of, 434.
Laying on of hands, 88, 180.
Lazarus, 180.
Legislation, 389.
Lewis, Mrs, 25, 107, 144, 189, 194, 206, 242, 265, 266.
Liddon, Canon, 155, 235.
Lightfoot, Bishop, 42, 43, 46, 57, 85, 160, 186, 200, 208, 250, 251, 259, 330, 336.
Logos, 230.
Lourdes, 173.
Lucian, 53.
Mahomedanism, 415.
Marcion. Gospel of, 66, 98.
Mark, Gospel of, 30, 67.
Marriage, 372.
" in Cana, 145.

Martineau, Rev. Dr, 33, 44, 131, 196.
Matthew, Gospel of, 30, 67.
Medical men, 407.
Melito, 262.
Memoirs of the Apostles, 63, 100.
Messiah, 144, 206.
Miracles, 127, 145, 362.
Miraculous conception, 15, 23.
Mithraism, 177, 180.
Money lenders, 440.
Morality in Alexandria, 315.
" Carthage, 319.
" Rome, 323.
Moral system of Jesus, 68, 366.
Mormons, 72.
Muratorian fragment, 239.
Mysteries, 87, 237.
Naasseni, 235.
Nicodemus, Gospel of, 65, 192, 278.
Ophites, 235, 296.
Origen, 167, 238, 256, 260, 269, 277, 297, 307, 313.
Orphans, 53, 189.
Pagan Christians, 74.
Parables, 97, 105.
Paraclete, 105, 185, 250.
Parliament, 420.
Parthenogenesis, 288.
Paschal controversy, 132.
" Lamb, 131, 142.
Passive obedience, 435.
Passover, 131, 140, 256, 266.
Patripassians, 274.
Paul, Apostle, 71, 135, 142, 176, 201.
Payment of 'apostles,' 99.
Pedagogue of Clement, 316.
Peregrinus, 53.
Peschito, 124.
Peter of Alexandria, 264.
" Epistles of, 96.
Philip's interpellation, 272, 276.
Philo, 231.
Pilate, 191.
Pionius, 331.
Plagiarism, 334.
Pleroma, 233.
Pliny, 88.
Plummer, Rev. A., 118.
Polycarp, 47.
Polycrates, 133.
Polygamy, 417.
Popes, 325.
Prayer, 368.
Prodigal son, 98.
Prologue of Fourth Gospel, 3, 7, 207, 231.
Propaganda, 367.
Prophecy, 270, 281, 293, 300.
Protevangelium, 7, 25.
Prudentius, 333.
Public Schools Act, 394.
Punishments, 380.
Purification of the Temple, 154.

Quadratus, 285.
Rabelais, 326.
Railway travelling, 385.
Ramsay, Professor, 302.
Religion, 364, 367, 371.
Religious education, 397.
    ,,   indifference, 410.
Remission of sins, 307, 326.
Resurrection of Jesus, 70, 122, 197, 204.
Revelations, 122, 200, 244.
Revision committee of second century, 242.
Roberts, Lord, 365.
Roman Church, 432.
Salaries, disproportion of, 351.
Samaria, Woman of, 158.
Samaritan, Good, 98.
Schechter, Professor, 92.
Schools, elementary, 396.
Separation of Church and State, 358.
Sermons, sale of, 353.
Sexes, 380.
Shepherd of Hermas, 19, 178.
Simon Magus, 229.
Sins, forgiveness of, 306.
Sixth hour, 265.
Smith, Joseph, 72.
Socrates, historian, 113.
Sower, parable of, 97.
Standard of morality, 374.
Sunday, 376.
Suttee, 433.
Swift, Dean, 22, 175.
Synoptic Gospels, 66.
Tacitus, 171.
Tertullian, 12, 70, 188, 256, 267, 292, 307, 319, 341.
Theophilus, 3, 179, 232.
Titles, 430.
Torke, 57.
Trinity, 339, 341.
Unpaid service, 368, 381.
Ussher, Archbishop, 302.
Valentinus, 105, 188, 232, 234, 238, 296.
Vespasian, 171.
Victor, Pope, 275.
Virgin generation, 19, 125, 288.
Virginity, 18, 319.
Voluntary service, 368, 381.
Wake, Archbishop, 200.
Westcott, Bishop, 6, 9, 14, 37, 131, 138, 148, 151, 159, 160, 162, 163, 164, 169, 171, 181, 183, 184, 188, 192, 195, 239, 276, 285, 289, 309.
Wife, 416.
Woman, 148, 154, 279.
Writings, earliest Christian, 16.
Zephyrinus, Pope, 275, 323.

INDEX OF TEXTS.

Ch. i. 1-5, pp. 3, 207, 233, 251.
    2, p. 251.
    6-12, pp. 8, 252.
    10, pp. 9, 252.
    13-14, p. 11.
    15-34, p. 127.
    35-51, p. 144.
Ch. ii. 1-11, p. 145.
    12, pp. 154, 234.
    12-22, p. 253.
    13-17, pp. 154, 238.
    18-25, p. 156.
Ch. iii. 1-8, p. 156.
    9-15, pp. 158, 238.
    16-36, p. 158.
Ch. iv. 1-42, p. 158.
    43-46, p. 160.
    46-54, p. 161.
Ch. v. 1-18, p. 162.
    19-23, p. 162.
    24-47, p. 162.
Ch. vi. 1-3, p. 163.
    4-26, p. 163.
    27-50, p. 164.
    51-57, pp. 166, 237.
    58, p. 168.
    59-71, p. 168.
Ch. vii. 1-20, p. 168.
Ch. vii. 21-24, p. 169.
    25-52, p. 169.
Ch. viii. 1-11, p. 170.
    12-55, p. 170.
    56-59, p. 170.
    56-57, p. 298.
Ch. ix. 1-41, p. 170.
Ch. x. 1-16, p. 174.
    17-21, p. 174.
    22-29, p. 174.
    30-36, p. 174.
    37-42, p. 175.
Ch. xi. 1-46, p. 180.
    47-57, p. 183.
Ch. xii. 1-9, p. 131.
    10-19, p. 183.
    20-22, p. 183.
    23-43, p. 183.
    44-50, p. 184.
Ch. xiii. 1-30, pp. 138, 255.
    1-2, pp. 261, 264.
    18-20, p. 269.
    31-38, p. 185.
Ch. xiv. 1-14, pp. 185, 272, 275.
    15-18, pp. 185, 189.
    19-31, p. 189.
Ch. xv. 1-8, p. 189.
    9-27, p. 189.
Ch. xvi. 1-33, p. 190.
Ch. xvii. 1-25, p. 190.
Ch. xviii. 1-40, p. 192.
    28, pp. 261, 264.
Ch. xix. 1-24, p. 194.
    14, pp. 261, 264.
    25-27, pp. 195, 277.
    28-42, p. 196.
    31-33, pp. 261, 263.
    35, pp. 129, 246.
Ch. xx. 1-10, pp. 205, 279.
    11-31, p. 205.
    17, pp. 280, 305.
    21-23, pp. 306, 326.
    24-29, p. 327.
    31, p. 328.
Ch. xxi. pp. 207, 328.

PRINTED BY NEILL AND CO., LIMITED, EDINBURGH.

www.ingramcontent.com/pod-product-compliance
Lightning Source LLC
Chambersburg PA
CBHW022114300426
44117CB00007B/705